William Cornelius Reichel, Nicolaus Ludwig Zinzendorf

Memorials Of The Moravian Church

William Cornelius Reichel, Nicolaus Ludwig Zinzendorf

Memorials Of The Moravian Church

ISBN/EAN: 9783741117961

Manufactured in Europe, USA, Canada, Australia, Japa

Cover: Foto ©Lupo / pixelio.de

Manufactured and distributed by brebook publishing software (www.brebook.com)

William Cornelius Reichel, Nicolaus Ludwig Zinzendorf

Memorials Of The Moravian Church

THE

Moravian Book Association,

Instituted 1870,

FOR THE

ISSUING OF DOCUMENTS AND PAPERS

ILLUSTRATING THE

HISTORY OF THE MORAVIAN CHURCH.

MEMORIALS

OF THE

MORAVIAN CHURCH.

EDITED BY

WILLIAM C. REICHEL,

MEMBER OF THE MORAVIAN HISTORICAL SOCIETY, AND OF THE HISTORICAL SOCIETY OF PENNSYLVANIA.

VOLUME I

PRINTED FOR THE ASSOCIATION.

SOLD BY JOHN PENINGTON & SON.

PHILADELPHIA:

J. B. LIPPINCOTT & CO.

1870.

It is proposed by the Council to include in future volumes, among other papers of historical interest, Sketches of Nazareth and the adjacent settlements, by James Henry, and a complete Bibliotheca Moraviensis, by the Rev. Edmund de Schweinitz. At the same time it desires it to be understood that it is not answerable for any opinions or observations that may appear in the publications of the Association, the Editors of the several works being alone responsible for the same.

The edition of these Memorials being limited and the cost thereby enhanced, the Council finds it necessary to rigorously abstain from incurring all additional expense, such as that of presentation copies, of commission, of advertising, etc. And hence too it would hereby solicit the co-operation of all subscribers in furthering the interests of the Association, by extending its membership among their friends and acquaintances.

The present volume has unavoidably exceeded the limits proposed by the Council in its Circular.

THE

MORAVIAN BOOK ASSOCIATION.

Council.

JAMES HENRY,
REV. SYLVESTER WOLLE, } *Directors.*
REV. WILLIAM C. REICHEL,

RIGHT REV. HENRY A. SHULTZ,
REV. EDWARD H. REICHEL,
REV. LEWIS F. KAMPMAN,
REV. E. A. DE SCHWEINITZ,
REV. A. A. REINKE,
REV. EDWARD RONDTHALER,
DR. MAURICE C. JONES,
GERHARD WESSELS,
JAMES T. BORHEK,
GEORGE K. REED,
PROF. P. A. CREGAR,
E. A. VOGLER,
JACOB BLICKENSDERFER,
C. M. S. LESLIE,
NATHANIEL S. WOLLE.

REV. CHARLES B. SHULTZ, *Secretary.*

Treasurer and General Agent,

WILLIAM H. JORDAN.
Address No. 209 North Third Street, Philadelphia.

Remember the days of old, consider the years of many generations: ask thy father, and he will shew thee; thy elders, and they will tell thee.—*Deut.* xxxii. 7.

INTRODUCTION.

COMPARATIVELY little of the early history of the Moravian Church in this country has been given to the American public. A translation of Loskiel's Account of the Indian Mission,* Heckewelder's Narrative,† and Heckewelder's History of Indian Nations,‡ were the first means of calling attention to the character and extent of the mission among the Aborigines of this country, to prosecute which the Brethren were led to immigrate to the English Colonies of North America in the first half of the last century. Contributions to other departments of Moravian history, which followed after a long interval, were a Biography of the Missionary Heckewelder,§ a History of Nazareth Hall,‖ The Moravians in North Carolina,¶ a History of the

* *Geschichte der Mission der evangelischen Brüder unter den Indianern in Nordamerika*, durch Georg Heinrich Loskiel. Barby: 1789. Translated into English by Christian Ignatius Latrobe. London: 1794.

† *Narrative of the Missions of the United Brethren among the Delaware and Mohegan Indians*, by Rev. John Heckewelder, of Bethlehem, Pa. Philadelphia: 1820.

‡ *An Account of the History, Manners, and Customs of the Indian Nations who once inhabited Pennsylvania and the neighboring States*, by Rev. John Heckewelder, of Bethlehem, Pa. Philadelphia: 1818.

§ *Life of John Heckewelder*, by the Rev. Edward Rondthaler, of Nazareth, Pa. Philadelphia: 1847.

‖ *A Historical Sketch of Nazareth Hall, from* 1755 *to* 1855, by Rev. Levin T. Reichel. Philadelphia: 1855.

¶ *The Moravians in North Carolina, an Authentic History*, by Rev. Levin T. Reichel. Salem, N. C.: 1857.

Seminary for Young Ladies at Bethlehem,* Sketches of Moravian Life and Character,† The Moravians in New York and Connecticut,‡ and Nazareth Hall and its Reunions.§ The church periodicals also, "The United Brethren's Missionary Intelligencer," a quarterly, 1822–49; "The Moravian Miscellany," a monthly, 1850–55, succeeded by "The Moravian," a weekly, 1856, consecutively, —all conducted in English, and "Das Brüder Blatt," a monthly, 1854–1861, conducted in German (the latter especially during the editorship of Rev. Levin T. Reichel, who can justly be called the father of American Moravian History), have offered their readers numerous papers of interest, illustrating portions of this widely-extended field. The same can be said of "Die Biene," a weekly, 1846–1848; and of the "Transactions of the Moravian Historical Society."

A desire to further uncover and render available the mine of old-time lore which the Moravian Church possesses in her Archives, prompted some members of the Moravian Historical Society to associate themselves with others, lovers of her early history, for the purpose of issuing a series of memorials, treating of the varied activity

* *A History of the Rise, Progress, and Present Condition of the Bethlehem Female Seminary, with a Catalogue of its Pupils*, by William C. Reichel. Philadelphia: 1858.

† *Sketches of Moravian Life and Character, comprising a general View of the History, Life, Character, and Religious and Educational Institutions of the Unitas Fratrum*, by James Henry. Philadelphia: 1859.

‡ *A Memorial of the Dedication of Monuments, erected by the Moravian Historical Society, to mark the sites of early Missions in New York and Connecticut*, by William C. Reichel. Philadelphia: 1860.

§ *Historical Sketch of Nazareth Hall, from 1755 to 1869, with an Account of the Reunions of former Pupils*, by William C. Reichel. Philadelphia: 1869.

of the Moravian pioneers in this country, as missionaries, as evangelists, and as educators of youth, of their religious and social organization, of the life they led, and the spirit by which they were actuated, of their relation to each other as members of one body pervaded by a common purpose, and of the relation they sustained to those by whom they were surrounded.

Thus, it was thought, a service would be done to the cause of history generally, at the same time that these memorials (often documentary, and if not so, yet drawn from original sources) might tend to throw light upon or remove misapprehensions, entertained by members of the church as well as by others, in reference to important events and leading characters of the past.

The former presumption was based upon the fact, that as the Brethren labored in an extensive field, operating as evangelists or home-missionaries in nearly all the English Colonies along the Atlantic sea-board, and were required to render written reports of their journeys and daily experiences to the heads of the church at Bethlehem, the student of the Colonial History of this country would find much in such memorials that would bear upon his favorite department; the latter, upon a knowledge of the disposition common to mankind, to forget the past in the present, through indifference or designedly.

This volume of Memorials treats largely of the infancy of the Indian Mission; of the labors of apostolic men, such as Christian H. Rauch, J. Martin Mack, and Bernhard A. Grubé; principally, however, in that connection, of the part taken by Count Zinzendorf in promoting the movement that his followers had inaugurated, for the conversion to Christianity of one portion of a heathen race. While the first series of papers, entitled "Zinzendorf and the Indians," contains matters of history that are now published for the first time, recited in part by the Count, and in part by Martin Mack, their value is much enhanced by bringing the reader face to face, as it were, through the medium of his personal narratives, with the remarkable man of whom they so largely treat. Here he is heard to speak without reserve, giving utterance to his inmost feelings with the unaffected originality of expression that is the mark of genius; at times seemingly at a loss for language in which to convey the exuberance of thought that flows like an impetuous current through his soul, often in paradoxes, and apparently obscurely, always, however, with marked effect, and never in the fear of man, for the sake of popular applause, or actuated by the dubious policy of compromising truth and error. His views of the origin of the Indian race are highly interesting, and, to say the least, ingeniously made to harmonize with prophecies of the Old Testament Scriptures. Could they even be demonstrated to be altogether fanciful, there is so much of the charm of poetry thrown about them that the reader, we believe, would reluctantly admit their fallacy. Passing over the incidents of travel that are woven into his narratives of journeys to Shecomeco and to the Susquehanna, in the course of which he leads us through widely-distant and remote parts of the country, acquaints us with life among border men, among civilized Indians, and among savages, with the mode of travel prevalent at that day through the wilderness, whether along some "Warrior's Path," or some highway cut by the hands of adventurous men through forest and through swamp, beguiling the tediousness of the way by his observations on men and manners, on principles and doctrines in church and state, which are always truthful, though often expressed with a striking extravagance of quaint severity, of half-disguised humor, or of keen satire,—Martin Mack brings us to the journey's end among the perfidious Shawanese of Wyoming Valley. The missionary's recollection of what transpired here cannot fail to correct the erroneous accounts that have been reproduced on the subject of Zinzendorf's memorable sojourn at Wyoming until they have passed into history. Brief as it is, Mack's narrative is picturesque and full of character. The plan that the Count matured, on his return from the Indians, for the further prosecution of the mission among them, is neither more extended in its limits, nor more precise in its details, than were others he conceived for the execution of the church elsewhere. Most valuable for the historian, perhaps, in as far as it reveals the spirit of the man, and of the body which he directed, is the Count's Review of his experiences among the Indians. It is in fact an exposition of the principles by which the Brethren were governed, in their prosecution of the work of evangelizing the heathen, to which they believed themselves as a church to have been divinely called; principles which were drawn immediately from Christ's teachings, which sought his approval and his glory, rather than the approval of, and glory with, men; and to adherence to which we are compelled to ascribe the remarkable success that crowned their unpretentious efforts. The old translation of this paper is most happily done, Zinzendorf's presence and voice only being felt and heard throughout.

Following the first series is a Register of the Christian Indians who lie buried in the Old Moravian Grave-yard at Bethlehem, and Annals of Early Moravian Settlement in Georgia and Pennsylvania.

The Accounts of the Brethren at Bethlehem with the Commissioners of the Province, it was thought, might gratify the antiquary, so full are they of the details and commonplaces of life in a generation long since passed away. At the same time they illustrate the history of the Province in a critical period, and introduce the reader to Spangenberg, who directed the affairs of the Brethren in America for almost twenty years. To show that he was another representative of the spirit of his church, an unassuming Christian, and a very plain man, averse to the meretricious ornamentations of the simple Gospel of Christ, strong in faith, devoted to his heavenly Master, preaching by example as well as by word, of marked ability, although no genius, as was his fellow-worker abroad,—several of his letters relevant to the history they accompany have been presented to the reader.

The Christian Church, in all ages, has drawn from the beauties of Art to embellish her houses of worship, to adorn her ritual, to give shape to her religious conceptions, and to enable her to realize, by an appeal to the feelings through the senses, what she apprehends by faith. Painting, Music, and Poetry have thus, from time to time, been made to bring her right royal tribute, until her treasure-house is heaped with the choicest offerings of genius, as was the heathen shrine of old with ingots of pure gold, and with all rare and precious things. The Renewed Church of the Brethren also delighted to use Art as a handmaiden to Religion. There was a time when her chapels were hung with paintings depicting scenes in the life of the Redeemer, and when she always rose on the wings of devotion amid the harmony of sweet sounds. And to this day the experiences of the child of God in the life hidden in Christ, his confession to weakness, his renunciation of self and trust in the merits of a Saviour, his communion with the unseen object of his affections, his longing to go home and be forever with the Lord, and his apocalyptic views of glory, are portrayed in her German hymnology in the measures of a transcendingly beautiful poesy, than which none move the soul as divinely, save those to which the son of Jesse struck his inspired harp.

It was undeniably the spirit of the gifted Zinzendorf—which was a spirit glowing with ecstatic love and fervor, as glows the sunset sky with all warm colors of molten things —that in this way embellished the usages of his church, teaching her to apprehend the All-beautiful through the beautiful in Art, and leaving her a heritage of song not unmeet to be sung by the redeemed while yet in the body, just without the golden gate.

The figure facing the title-page of this volume is a relic of the Zinzendorfian period of the Brethren's Church. It is her seal,—an embodiment of the cardinal doctrine of her most holy faith, and symbolic both of the atonement made for the remission of sin by the sacrifice of the spotless Lamb of God, and of its acceptance by the Father, when Christ burst the bonds of death, and rose victorious from the grave.

On a shield sanguine a Paschal Lamb argent, passant, carrying a cross resurrection argent, from which is suspended a triumphal banner of the same. Motto: Vicit Agnus noster, Eum sequamur—"Our Lamb is victorious, let us follow him."

This device, in its full significance, is suggestive of Redemption from the dominion of sin in this world, through the sufferings and death of the Son of God, and of its completion in glory in the world to come. It blends the prophetic, the historic, and the apocalyptic, pointing to the Lamb without blemish, to the Paschal Lamb, to the Lamb of God that taketh away the sin of the world, to the Lamb slain from the foundation of the world, and to the Lamb that shall overcome, being Lord of lords and King of kings.

The following is a copy of a certificate which bears the impress in wax of the seal here reproduced. It is a simple pass, but nevertheless of historical interest, in as far as it produces evidence that this seal was appended by all servants of the church whenever they acted in her authority, that it was not used exclusively by bishops, and hence was not an episcopal seal:

[SEAL.] "BETHLEHEM IN THE FORKS OF DELAWARE,
"Aug. 22, 1746.

"These are to certify all it may concern, That the Bearer hereof James Burnside our Brother and Fellow-helper in the Gospel, goeth to Maryland to see some Friends there, with our full Consent and hearty Wishes that he may be attended with many Blessings.

"In Testimony whereof we have hereunto affixed the Seal of the Church, the Day and Year aforesaid.

"NATHANAEL SEIDEL, E."*

Carried away by their adoration of Him who made the Great Atonement by going like a lamb to the slaughter, the Brethren of the first half of the last century never spake or sang of Christ otherwise than the Lamb, styled their church a Congregation of the Lamb, called themselves followers of the precious Lamb, and embellished with its device their publications, their church service, and even the tokens of affection wrought in lowly art which they were wont to exchange on festal occasions, or to offer to each other on the dawn of each succeeding year of their earthly pilgrimage. Of this there is an evidence existing even at the present day; for, after the lapse of one hundred and twenty-four years, there still hovers over the venerable house of prayer at Bethlehem, in which Zinzendorf first, and after him Spangenberg preached or sang ceaselessly of the Lamb of God that taketh away the sin of the world, —the Paschal Lamb passant, with the banner of victory suspended from the Cross of the Resurrection.

---

* Nathaniel Seidel, born 1718, was at this time in Deacon's orders. On the 7th of February, 1746, during the sessions of a Synod convened at Bethlehem, he had been elected, by sixty-one of ninety-seven votes cast, head of the Brethren who preached the gospel as itinerants, and was styled, in the language of the Church prevalent at that day, *Elder of the Pilgrims*. In 1748 he was ordained a Presbyter, and in 1758 was consecrated a Bishop.

CONTENTS.

COUNT ZINZENDORF

AND

THE INDIANS.

1742.

COUNT ZINZENDORF

AND

THE INDIANS.

In the preparation of the following papers, the editor has consulted—

1. Church Diaries, Church Records, Journals and Narratives of missionaries, Autobiographies and Memoirs, and Letters preserved in manuscript in the Moravian Archives at Bethlehem, Pa.

2. The following Moravian publications, viz.:

Geschichte der Mission der Evangelischen Brüder unter den Indianern in Nordamerika, durch Georg Heinrich Loskiel. Barby, 1789.

Leben des Herrn Nicolaus Ludwig, Grafen und Herrn von Zinzendorf und Pottendorf, von August Gottlieb Spangenberg. Barby, 1772.

Leben August Gottlieb Spangenbergs, Bischofs der Evangelischen Brüderkirche, von Jeremias Risler. Barby, 1794.

Nachrichten aus der Brüder-Gemeine. Gnadau, 1819–1869.

Das Brüder-Blatt, redigirt von Levin T. Reichel. 1854–1857.

Büdingische Sammlung, einiger in die Kirchen-Historie einschlagender sonderlich neuerer Schrifften. Büdingen, 1744–1745.

Memoirs of James Hutton, by Daniel Benham. London, 1856.

The Moravians in North Carolina, by Rev. Levin T. Reichel. Salem, N. C., 1857.

Die Biene, ein Volksblatt, redigirt von Dr. A. L. Huebener. Bethlehem, 1846–1848.

The Moravians in New York and Connecticut. A memorial of the dedication of monuments erected by the Moravian Historical Society, to mark the sites of the ancient missionary stations in those States. New York, 1860.

And also—

3. Minutes of the Provincial Council of Pennsylvania. Published by the State, 1852.

Pennsylvania Archives, selected and arranged by Samuel Hazard. Philadelphia, 1853.

Otzinachsen, a History of the West Branch Valley of the Susquehanna, by J. F. Meginness. 1857.

A History of the Minnisink Region in Orange County, New York, by Charles E. Stickney. 1867.

The Delaware Water-Gap, by L. W. Brodhead. Philadelphia, 1867.

History of the Lehigh Valley, by M. S. Henry. Easton, 1860.

Journal of Conrad Weisser to Onondaga, August and September of 1750. Manuscript in possession of Pennsylvania Historical Society, Philadelphia.

Narrative of a Journey made in February, March, and April of 1737, by Conrad Weisser, to Onondaga. Collections of the Historical Society of Pennsylvania. May, 1851.

Nachrichten von den vereinigten Deutschen Evangelisch-Lutherischen Gemeinen in Nord-America, absonderlich in Pensylvanien. Halle, 1745–1787.

Historical Account of Bouquet's Expedition against the Ohio Indians. Cincinnati, 1868.

Documentary History of New York, by J. O'Callaghan. Albany, 1850.

Draft of sundry Tracts of Land surveyed to divers Purchasers in ye Forks of Delaware River, in Bucks County. Drawn 1740, by Benjamin Eastburn, Surveyor-General.

Map of the improved part of the Province of Pennsylvania, humbly dedicated to the Hon. Thomas Penn and Richard Penn, Esqs., true and absolute Proprietaries and Governors of the Province of Pennsylvania, and Counties of New Castle, Kent, and Sussex, on Delaware, by Nicholas Scull. Published according to Act of Parliament, January 1, 1759.

The History of Northampton, Lehigh, Monroe, Carbon, and Schuylkill Counties, by I. Daniel Rupp. Harrisburg, 1845.

History of the Counties of Berks and Lebanon, by I. Daniel Rupp. 1844.

History of Lancaster County, by I. Daniel Rupp. 1845.

Memoirs of Rev. David Brainerd, Missionary to the Indians, chiefly taken from his own Diary, by Rev. Jonathan Edwards. New Haven, 1822.

Historical Collections of New Jersey. Newark, 1844.

Select Works of William Penn. London, 1771.

History of Wyoming, by Charles Miner. Philadelphia, 1845.

Annals of Luzerne County, by Stewart Pearce. Phila., 1866.

In elucidating the narratives herein produced, the editor has resorted to conjecture only in the matter of determining routes, when such were imperfectly indicated; which conjecture, however, was ventured cautiously, and never except in the light of relevant information drawn from reliable sources. The first narrative is based upon Loskiel's account, in his History of the Indian Mission.

These papers treat of a remarkable man and of a remarkable people,—of a man who, early in life, renounced the prospects of worldly distinction, of honors and of fame, so as to remove every impediment in the way of devoting the powers of his gifted soul to the promotion of Christ's kingdom. His personal endeavors in this object among the despised and degraded aborigines of our country, although viewed by many at the time as the fantastic vagaries of an enthusiast, exemplified his chivalric love of the Saviour, for whom he boldly entered the lists, ever approving himself a true red-cross knight.

It was for this man to take part in one of the historic movements set on foot in behalf of ameliorating the condition of a portion of that race whose origin is shrouded in mystery, over whom a destroying angel broods, who once lived where we now live, but who are gone,—save a remembrance of them only in the names of their favorite rivers and streams, and valleys and hills, that fall upon the ear like the echo of a sound that is past.

Count Zinzendorf landed at New York on the 2d of December, 1741. On the 10th of that month he reached Philadelphia,* in which city he designed to fix his abode

* Here he at once became an object of general interest, and excited much remark, as a man of rank, of fortune, and of education, and also as the recognized head of the Moravian movement lately initiated in the Province. In both characters, he was brought into contact with or was courted by prominent men of the day. How he and his mission were viewed by contemporaries of this class may partly be inferred from the following notices, some of the few that have been preserved. James Logan, in a letter to Governor Clarke, of New York, dated March 30, 1742, writes: "I must not omit observing

for the first three months of the year he purposed spending in Pennsylvania. Having visited the Brethren's settlement

---

that last fall there came over a German Count of the title of Zinzendorf, of a good estate as well as family and education. He speaks Latin and French, is aged I suppose between forty and fifty years, wears his own hair, and is in all other respects very plain as making the propagation of the Gospel his whole purpose and business. In this view he or some of his people have purchased those 5000 acres which one Seward, a companion of Whitefield, had not long since bought, about 50 miles north from hence, near Delaware River, to erect on it, as they gave out, a college or school for the instruction of Negroes, or some such other whimsical business; but the purchaser dying very soon after his return to England, his wise executors immediately turned it into money again, and now another order of *religieux*, and, in my judgment, a much better sort of people, is in possession of it. They are so much for universal charity that without binding themselves to any form, they join with all persuasions that profess their being inwardly guided by the Spirit of Christ,—Papists or Protestants, as far as I can learn, without distinction; for though they utterly dislike the fopperies of the Romish service,—the adoration of saints, images, etc.,—yet, if the heart be right, they dispense with all the rest as the exteriors in worship of a more indifferent nature; and hence, in a conversation I had last week with the Count, he spoke of Cardinal Noailles, Archbishop of Paris, as his most particular and intimate friend."

December 15, 1741.—"Count Zinzendorf arrived here ye beginning of this week, and will probably cause large quantities of land to be taken up by ye Moravians in this Province. He does not propose to stay longer than ye winter, his intention by this voyage being only to view ye country, cause some houses to be built, and some lands to be taken up for ye use of his Moravian Brethren, and to try what effect his preaching will have."—*Richard Peters to Thomas Penn.*

July 9, 1742.—"I find you will do much better with Mr. Spangenberg in London than I can do with ye Count or ye Moravians here. The land is really poor land, and best to be bought by those who have not seen it, though on account of its conveniency ye Moravians must buy it. Y^e^ Count says ye design of ye Brethren is to have a space of land of two miles in breadth and eight in length, which is the distance

in the Forks of Delaware, and named it Bethlehem (December 24), he made a circuit of the German neighborhoods which lay to the southwest, as far as Conestoga, and returned to Germantown on the 30th of December. On the following day he appeared for the first time in an American pulpit, preaching to a large audience in the German Reformed Church of that place.

The interval between this date and the 20th of June was perhaps the period of his most varied activity during his sojourn in Pennsylvania. Few men could have accomplished in that time what he did. Besides conducting the deliberations of seven religious convocations, or synods, in which the most antagonistic elements were represented, he preached the Gospel statedly in the Reformed Church at Germantown, and for Lutherans of Philadelphia in their place of worship on Arch Street, traveled through the rural districts of Bucks and Philadelphia, supplying destitute and isolated neighborhoods with the means of grace and the means of education, organized churches, wrote multitudinous papers and essays, some theological, others controversial and apologetical, and carried on a large correspond-

---

between Bethlehem and Nazareth, in order to have a continuation from one place to the other; and on this space of two miles by eight, they propose to build small villages for ye Brethren to live in, the same in number, and to have the same names as are found on the maps of the Holy Land."—*Richard Peters to Thomas Penn.*

November 21, 1742.—"Conrad Weisser is with me now, and desires me to acquaint the Proprietaries that ye Count Zinzendorf and the heads of ye Moravians will come under the strongest engagements to them, that in case ye Moravians may be permitted to have ye preference in the next Indian purchase of a large body of land together, they will transport above ten thousand people and settle them there, and give the Proprietaries such a price for their land as shall be generally put on lands in that place."—*Richard Peters to Thomas Penn.*

ence with leading Brethren in England and on the Continent. In the interval between March 16 and June 20 he resided in Germantown, surrounded, as he had been at Philadelphia, by a corps of assistants, chief among whom were Bishop Nitschmann, Andrew Eschenbach, Gottlob Büttner, Jno. C. Pyrlaeus, J. Wm. Zander, Anton Seyffert, Johanna S. Molther, and Anna Nitschmann.

On the 20th of June he again repaired to Bethlehem, and having organized the Brethren there into a congregation, completed arrangements for his contemplated visit to Shecomeco, and for his tour of exploration into the Indian country.

It is with these movements in Zinzendorf's career in North America that the following papers are concerned.

ZINZENDORF'S OBSERVATIONS

CONCERNING THE SAVAGES IN CANADA.—1742.

(Copy of an Old Translation preserved in the Archives at Bethlehem.)

THE Savages in Canada* are thought to be partly mixed Scythians, and partly Jews of the 10 lost Tribes,† wc^{h} thro' ye great Tartarian wilderness wandered hither by

* Zinzendorf repeatedly uses this name, in the general sense in which it was applied by Europeans of his day, to designate the Northern British Colonies in North America. The name *Florida* he extends to the Southern Colonies.

† Zinzendorf's views of the origin of the Indians accorded with those propounded by Eliot, and held by William Penn.

"For their original, I am ready to believe them of the Jewish race; I mean of the stock of the *Ten Tribes*, and that for the following reasons: First, they were to go to a 'land not *planted* or *known*,' which, to be sure, Asia and Africa were, if not Europe; and He that intended that extraordinary judgment upon them might make the passage not uneasy to them, as it is not impossible in itself, from the eastermost parts of Asia, to the westermost of America. In the next place, I find them of like countenance, and their children of so lively resemblance, that a man would think himself in Duke's-place or Berry-street, in London, when he seeth them. But this is not all: they agree in *Rites;* they reckon by *Moons;* they offer their *First Fruits;* they have a kind of *Feast of Tabernacles;* they are said to lay their *Altar* upon *Twelve Stones;* their *Mourning a Year, Customs of Women*, with many things that do not now occur."—*Wm. Penn in a Letter to a Friend, dated, Phila., the 16th of the 6th month, called August*, 1683.

way of hunting, and so they came farther and farther into y[e] country.

The reason why they make this conjecture is—

1. Because they are not black as they of Florida, Mexico, etc., but they are white, and have only that yellow colour prophecy'd in Deuteron[y].*

2. They have Jewish customs.

3. They call their enemies† and strangers *Assaroni*, for a remembrance of y[e] Assyrians, by whom their fathers were turned out.

4. *Achsa, onas*, and innumerable other words are pure Ebrew, or at least so far as y[e] English, Swedish, Dutch, Norway and Danish tongue are German.

5. Notwithstanding they have many wifes,‡ their families are yet so small, that y[e] 5 Nations are altogether hardly so many,§ as there are sometimes in a large village in our

---

* Deut. xxviii. 22. "The Lord shall smite thee *with mildew*," Luther translates, "Der Herr wird dich schlagen *mit Gelbsucht*."

The Hebrew is בירקון, *with yellowness, with jaundice*.

The Septuagint renders the word τῃ ὠχρᾳ, *with ochrous pallor, with an ochrous tint*.

The Vulgate, rubigine—*with rust color*.

† Quære—The *Mobilian* or Southern Indians, the *Catawbas*, the *Cherokees*, the *Creeks*, etc.?

‡ "Plurality of wives is not in vogue here, except among the chiefs, who take three or four to themselves."—*Description of New Netherland*, 1671.

§ Wentworth Greenhalgh, in his "*Observations made on a Journey from Albany to y[e] Indians westward* in 1677," gives the following enumeration:

"The *Maquaes* pass in all for about 300 fighting men. The *Onondagos* are said to be about 350 fighting men. The *Senecques* are counted to be in all about 1000 fighting men. The *Onyades* have

country; wch agreeth a great deal better with Deuteronʸ: than with yᵉ nature of yᵉ barbarish Nations, who commonly multiply themselves in many thousands far beyond yᵉ Europeans. But they have been foretold so.* Therefore one believes that some 100 years ago, five or six men or women lost themselves hither, each of whom by and by became a Nation, who, because of yᵉ curse resting on them, consumed themselves so, that none of them surpassed yᵉ number of 2000 Persons,—yea, some of them are a few hundred.

And these Nations are five. The French call them *Irokois;* but they call themselves *Aquanuskion*, or yᵉ *Covenant People.*

A. 1. The *Maquas*, whose language is yᵉ nearest to yᵉ Ebrew is yᵉ chiefest of their Nations according to dignity; yet in Reuben's† way, that is despised because of their Levity and paid off with yᵉ Title. Yet their Language goes throughout.

2. The *Onondagos* are yᵉ chief Nation in Reality; yᵉ Judah‡ amongst their Brethren.

3. The *Senekas* are yᵉ most in number.

These three Nations are called *yᵉ Fathers.*

a. Many of yᵉ first are English Presbyterians.§

---

about 200 fighting men. The *Caiougos* pass for about 300 fighting men."

"The Six Nations of Indians including the River and Schaaghcoke Indians, are about fifteen hundred fighting men."—*Governor Clarke, of New York, to the Commissioners of Indian Affairs*, February, 1737.

Sir Wm. Johnson, in 1763, estimates the fighting men of the Six Nation Confederacy and their tributaries to have been 1950.

* Deut. xxviii. 62. "*And ye shall be left few in number, whereas ye were as the stars of heaven for multitude.*"

† Genesis, xlix. 3, 4. ‡ Genesis, xlix. 8–12.

§ Quære—Does the Count use *Presbyterian* in the ordinary acceptation of the term? "The conversion and civilization of the American In-

b. The second sort remains Heathens, and reason in a philosophical manner of ye nature of ye gods with Cicero.

c. The last are superstitious Cross and Rosecranz bearers.*

4. The *Oneidas*, and

5. *Cayugers* are their *Children.* They must respect them, and have also Children's right.

B. The *Gibeonites*, or water-bearers, are People gathered on y[e] Rivers as y[e] Gypsies, and a good part of y[m] are Europeans.

1. *Canistokas.*†

---

dians engaged the attention of Europeans at an early date. The christianizing of the Iroquois especially, became the object of the Jesuits of Canada as far back as 1642; and a few years afterwards Father Isaac Jogues laid down his life on the Mohawk River, for the Gospel. The Dutch, who colonized those parts, did not give the subject much consideration. In 1712, Rev. Samuel Andrews was sent as a missionary to the Mohawks by the Society for Propagating the Gospel, and a church was built at the mouth of Scohary Creek; but he soon abandoned the place, and was the last as well as the first that resided among them. The Society afterwards allowed a small stipend to the clergyman at Albany, to act as missionary to the Mohawks."—*Memoir of the Rev. John Stuart, D.D., the last Missionary to the Mohawks.*

"The Mohocks, who have long lived within our settlements, though greatly reduced in number, are still the acknowledged Head of the Iroquois Alliance. They have less intercourse with the Indians and more with us than formerly—besides which they are at present *members of the Church of England:* most of them read, and several write very well."—*Sir Wm. Johnson to Arthur Lee, Esq. Johnson Hall, February* 28, 1771.

* The Jesuit Fathers, Julien Garnier (1668–1683), Jacques Fremin (1668), Pierre Rafeix (1679), Jean Purron (1673–1679), Jacques De Heu (1709), were the first missionaries to the Senecas.

† In 1701, Wm. Penn treated with the *Susquehanna Minquays*, or *Conestoga Indians*, living on Conestoga and Pequea.

"The Conestogas were formerly a part of the Five Nations or Mingoes, and speak the same language to this day. They actually pay

2. *Mahikans,** of whom our congregation consists (vide I. Cor. chap. i.).

3. *Hurons or Delaware Indians.*

These must call ye other *Uncles,* and are called *Cousins.*

C. The *Floridans*† are *Confederates,* and

The *Tuscaroras*‡ are called *Brothers.*

D. The *Captives* are kept well, and become in time Cousins.

Concerning *ye Enemies,* it comes in my mind whether they (except ye Europeans) are not Scythians, Idumeans, Arabians, Gypsies, etc., with whom they continually quarrel, and cannot bear y^m^ amongst y^m^.

---

tribute to the Five Nations, and either from natural affection or fear, are ever under their influence and power."—*Minutes of Provincial Council, October,* 1722.

* The Mohicans were members of the great Algonquin family, and inhabited the country now embraced in Southwestern New England, and that portion of New York east of the Hudson. "Higher up the *Manhattans* or *Great River,* lie the *Makwaes* and the *Mohicans,* who are constantly at war with each other."—*Description of New Netherland,* 1671.

They were gradually driven eastward across the hill country into the valley of the Housatonic, by their implacable enemies.

† Shawanese.

‡ At the settlement of North Carolina, the Tuscaroras had their seats on the upper waters of the Neuse and Tar Rivers, and in 1708 still mustered 1200 warriors. A collision with the whites a few years later, which resulted in their defeat, broke their spirits, and was the cause of their suing for admission into the Iroquois Confederacy. The alliance was formally concluded in 1722, although the Tuscaroras had emigrated to the North as early as 1712.

ZINZENDORF AMONG THE DELAWARES.

JULY 24—AUGUST 2, 1742.

AT 6 P.M. of the 24th of July, Zinzendorf set out on his visitation of the half-civilized Delawares still living in the Forks,* and of such of that nation who, as he had learned, were residing in the first main valley north of the Blue Mountain. Thither there had been a migration from New Jersey,—from Crosswicks† and Cranberry, from the Raritan and the Atlantic coast,—not ten years previous.

This is to be inferred from remarks made by the Brethren, in connection with their records of Indian baptisms; and the fact that many of the Indians whom Zinzendorf met there spoke English, goes to prove that they had at one time lived in a white neighborhood. Evidently aware of this, he had provided himself with an interpreter in the person of Bro. J. William Zander,‡ who spoke English, a

---

* The name given at that time to the lands lying within the confluence of the Delaware and the Lehigh, running back indefinitely, even as far as the Blue Mountain. The Indian name for the latter river was *Lechau-weki* ("the fork of a road"), abbreviated by the Germans into Lecha, and corrupted by the English into Lehigh. As an Indian thoroughfare crossed the Island below Bethlehem, and *forked off* into different paths, running northward, the name of "Forks" may for this reason have been given to the region which they intersected.

† Corruption of Crossweeksung (*separation*).

‡ John William Zander, born in Quedlingburg, came to America in October of 1741. July, 1742, married Johanna Magdalene, daughter

language with which the Count himself was not conversant.

He was accompanied as far as Nazareth (ten miles north of Bethlehem) by David and Judith Bruce,* Peter and Elizabeth Böhler,† Abraham and Judith Meinung,‡ Fred-

---

of Peter Müller, of Germantown. Before the close of the year, was dispatched to Berbice as missionary to the Indians and negroes.

* David Bruce, from Edinburgh, came with Count Zinzendorf to America, in the autumn of 1741. July 10, 1742, married Judith, oldest daughter of John Stephen Benezet, merchant, of Philadelphia. Was appointed elder of the English congregation, settled temporarily at Nazareth. Labored in the ministry in destitute English neighborhoods in the then County of Bucks. In January, 1749, was dispatched to the Indian Mission at Wechquadnach (Indian Pond), in Northeast Center, Duchess County, New York. Here he deceased July 9, of that year.

† Peter Böhler, born December 31, 1712, at Frankfort-on-the-Main. From April, 1731, to Sept. 1737, a student of Divinity, at the University of Jena. While here, an intimacy sprang up between him and the Brethren, which resulted in his joining their communion. September, 1737, was appointed to South Carolina to missionate among the negroes on the plantations between Purysburg and Savannah, and to be pastor of the Moravian colonists settled in and near the latter place. Preparatory to setting out for America, he was ordained. On the abandonment of the colony in Georgia, Böhler led the Brethren to Pennsylvania. This was in April of 1740. Here he was with them on the Whitefield tract to the close of the year. Sailed for Europe, January 29, 1741. Returned to America in June of 1742, with the first colony of Brethren sent to Pennsylvania. Appointed pastor of the English congregation at Nazareth, and on its transfer to Philadelphia, went thither. In September, accompanied Zinzendorf to the Susquehanna, as far as Otstonwackin. After the Count's return to Europe, Böhler was acting-superintendent of the Brethren's church in America until Span-

---

‡ Abraham and Judith Meinung came from Europe with Zinzendorf. They were sent to St. Thomas in 1747. Here Bro. Meinung deceased. His widow returned to Bethlehem in July of 1751.

eric Martin,* and John Hagen,† beside his escort proper, which consisted of Anton Seyffert,‡ Andrew Eschenbach,§ Jacob Lischy,|| Henry Müller,¶ William and Johanna Zan-

---

genberg's arrival in November of 1744. Sailed for Europe in April of 1745. Between this date and May of 1753, Böhler labored in the congregations in both England and Germany,—having, in the interval, been consecrated a bishop. In September, 1753, returned to America again to administer the affairs of his church, and again sailed for Europe in September of 1755. His last sojourn in America was between December, 1756, and May, 1764. On his return to Europe, took a seat in the Directory; in 1766, visited England and Ireland; in 1767, was in Holland, and in 1774, in England. Deceased in London, April 27, 1775.

* Frederic Martin, missionary among the negroes on St. Thomas, at this time on a visit at Bethlehem. Deceased February, 1750, on Santa Cruz.

† John Hagen, from Brandenburg, was, in April of 1740, sent to Georgia to missionate among the Cherokees of the low country. (See his letter, Part vii. No. 15, *Büdingen Sammlung.*) Came to Bethlehem in February of 1742, whither he was accompanied by Abraham Bühninger (Bininger), from Purysburg, Beaufort County, South Carolina. Labored as a missionary among the Delawares, the Susquehanna tribes, and the Mohicans of New York. Deceased, while at Shamokin, September 16, 1747.

Abraham Bühninger, born at Bulach, Canton Zurich, in 1720, was the ancestor of the well-known *Bininger* family of New York. Deceased in Washington County, New York, March, 1811.

‡ Anton Seyffert, from "German-Bohemia," was a member of the first colony of Brethren sent to Georgia in the spring of 1735, in view of establishing a mission among the Creeks. Accompanied Böhler and others to Pennsylvania in 1740. During his stay in America, filled the office of Elder. Returned to Europe in April of 1745.

§ Andrew Eschenbach was sent to Pennsylvania in the autumn of 1740, to missionate among the destitute German immigrants scattered throughout the four counties of the Province.

|| Jacob Lischy, from Mühlhausen, Switzerland, was a member of the

---

¶ Henry Müller, book-printer.

der, Peter Müller,* and an Indian, by way of messenger and interpreter. His daughter, the Countess Benigna,† was also of the company. The first named brethren and sisters were on the way to Nazareth, in order to complete arrangements for the reception of the English colonists who had arrived on the "Catharine" in June, and who had just been organized into a congregation. There were but two dwellings on the Nazareth tract at that time; he log-houses which the Brethren employed there by Whitefield in the erection of a school had thrown up in the summer and fall of 1740. Here the travelers halted a day.

On the morning of the 26th the cavalcade set out. Making a detour a few miles to the northeast, they crossed the Lehietan,‡ and came to Moses Tatemy's reserve (near Stockertown, in Forks Township). Tatemy was a Delaware from New Jersey, professed Christianity, and was farming in a small way on a grant of 300 acres given him by the Proprietaries' agents, in consideration of services he had rendered as interpreter and messenger to the Indians. He received them well, was communicative, and, in course of conversation, gave an account of the mode of sacrifice

---

first colony of Brethren sent to Pennsylvania. September 17th, 1742, married Mary, second daughter of John Stephen Benezet, merchant, of Philadelphia. Labored in the ministry. In 1747, withdrew from the Brethren. Deceased in 1781, on his farm, near York, on the Codorus, and lies buried not far from "Wolff's Church."

* Peter Müller, a boy, brother-in-law of J. W. Zander.

† Benigna, H. J., oldest daughter of the Count,—at this time in the seventeenth year of her age. Returned with her father to Europe in January of 1743.

‡ Now the Bushkill. In maps of that day, also called Tatemy's Creek and Lefevre's Creek. The latter name was given the stream for John Lefevre, who resided near Messinger's tavern-stand, six miles above Easton. Lefevre was a French Huguenot. His ancestors had immigrated to New York about 1689.

practiced by his heathen brethren, which afforded Zander an opportunity of speaking to him of the great sacrifice of the Lamb of God, made for the remission of sins.

Following the Indian path that led past Tatemy's house north into the Minnisinks, or upper valley of the Delaware, they came to the village of Clistowackin, five miles above, on Martin's Creek, near the three churches, in Lower Mount Bethel. David Brainerd,* it is said, preached here

---

* David Brainerd labored among the Indians in the Forks of Delaware at intervals between *May* 13, 1744, and *February* 24, 1746. On the first-mentioned day he "reached a settlement of Irish and Dutch people, *about* 12 *miles above the Forks of Delaware.*" (Quære, *Huntersville*, or *Hunter's Settlement*, along *Martin's Creek*, in Lower Mt. Bethel, settled by one wing of the Scotch-Irish, who came into this northern part of Bucks County between 1728 and 1730?) Near here was an Indian village called by the Delawares, *Sakhauwotung*, to whose inhabitants he preached, and among whom he resided. "The number of Indians in this place is but small; most of those that formerly belonged here are dispersed, and removed to places farther back in the country. There are not more than 10 houses hereabouts that continue to be inhabited. When I first began to preach here, the number of my hearers was very small, often not exceeding 20 or 25 persons; but toward the latter part of the summer their number increased, so that I have frequently had 40 persons, or more, at once. I usually preached in the King's house."—*Brainerd to Rev. Ebenezer Pemberton, Forks of Delaware, November* 5, 1744.

"*July* 24. *Rode about* 17 *miles westward, over a hideous mountain*, to a number of Indians; got together about thirty, preached to them in the evening, and lodged with them." In the letter quoted above, he gives the distance 30 *miles westward*, and calls the place over the hideous mountain *Kauksesauchung*. (Quære, *Poch-ko-poch-kung*, *Pocopoco*, old Captain Harris's town, on the creek of that name?) In December of 1744, Brainerd built himself a hut at *Sakhauwotung*. Here, on Sunday, July 21, 1745, he baptized *Moses Fonda Tatemy*, who had been acting interpreter for him since his arrival among the Fork Indians. February 23, 1746, he preached for the last time at the scene

in 1744. In the lodge of an Indian medicine-man lay his grandchild sick unto death. The Count prayed in behalf of the sufferer, commending him to the keeping of his Creator and Redeemer, and Zander spoke to the Indian of God's purposes in Christ for the salvation of all men from sin and eternal death. His words were interpreted by the latter to the villagers who had assembled about the lodge.

Toward evening they reached a second village, inhabited chiefly by Delawares. Having been overtaken by a shower, they gladly accepted the captain's invitation to enter his hut, dry their clothes, and pass the night with him.

On the morning of the 27th, joined by a German trader, Remsberger by name, they rode on, and crossed the Blue

---

of his missionary labors in Pennsylvania, discoursing on the words of John, vi. 35–37.

"Brainerd had a station at what is now known as '*Allen's Ferry*,' 7 miles below the Gap, on the Delaware. The Indian town there was called *Sakhauwotung* ('*the mouth of a creek where one resides*'). There was another Indian town, called *Clistowackin* (*fine land*), where Brainerd built a cottage, and lived for a time. It was situated near the residence of Mr. Baker, 15 miles south of the Gap."—*Brodhead's Delaware Water-Gap.*

In May of 1747, Bishop Cammerhoff wrote to Count Zinzendorf as follows: "It appears as if the Lord designed to bring Mr. David Brainerd's Indians into connexion with us. They reside not far from Raritan, on this side of Brunswick (*Cranberry*). A week ago, some five visited us, and attended meetings. Almost all of our Pachgatgoch Indians were awakened by his preaching." (This was during Brainerd's residence at *Kaunaumeek*, twenty miles from Stockbridge, and fifteen from Kinderhook, between April of 1743 and April of 1744.)

David Brainerd deceased at Northampton, October 9, 1747. He was succeeded by his brother John, who visited Bethlehem in October of 1749, in company with Rev. Mr. Lawrence, the clergyman of the Irish settlement in East Allen. He was at Bethlehem a second time, in 1751.

Mountain.* They were now in the Indian country, and what was then justly the Indian's country, although white settlers were trespassing within its precincts. Only a few weeks before, heads and deputies of the Six Nations (whose dominion reached from Onondaga as far as the waters of the lower Susquehanna), met in conference with the Governor, had insisted that the dividing line between white and Indian be the Kittochtinny, or Endless Mountain, forever. Keeping on to the northwest some ten miles, they struck the eastern terminus of the valley of the Pocopoco,† or Big Creek (Long Valley),‡ down which they turned, and came to a village on the bank of the stream. This had been the home of a well-known Delaware chief, old Captain Harris, father of Teedyuscung, King of the Delawares during their alienation from the English; and here Nicholas Scull and Benjamin Eastburn, Surveyors, passed the night on the completion of the one and a half day's walk, made in September of 1737, to settle the extent of a tract of land bought by William Penn, which tract has passed into history as the "walking-purchase."§

The Brethren pitched their tent near the lodge of a

---

* Probably at Tat's Gap, two and a half miles west of the Delaware Water-Gap. So named for Tatemy.

† Corrupted from the Indian Poch-co-poch-co. Drains Long Valley, and empties into the Lehigh at Parryville.

‡ Near Brodheadsville.

§ The *walking-purchase.* The name given to a certain purchase of lands, situate in part in the Forks of Delaware, deeded by the Indians to William Penn, August 28, 1686, the line of which was run in September of 1737, by a one and a half day's walk (performed in pursuance of the conditions of said deed), begun at a place near Wrightstown, in the County of Bucks.—*See Nicholas Scull's Deposition of the Walk*, vol. vii. p. 399, Prov. Records. Also, *Charles Thomson's Enquiry into the Causes of the Alienation of the Delawares and Shawanese.*

medicine-man. Zander was again spokesman in the interview that followed. Here, also, they passed the night, and this was the extreme northern point of their journey.

On the morning of the 28th the cavalcade once more set out. Crossing Chestnut Hill Mountain, they came down into the narrow valley of the Aquanshicola,* to a Delaware town, called Meniolagomeka.†

They were about resuming their journey for the last time, intending to reach Bethlehem the same night, when the Count met with a remarkable experience. He had a presentiment that his presence was required at Conrad Weisser's, in Tulpehocken. He felt himself drawn thither by an irresistible power; "and in strong faith," he says, "I obeyed the call, although knowing neither why nor wherefore."

Retaining Zander, Lischy, and the Indian, as escort, he dispatched the rest of the company to Bethlehem, where they arrived in the evening.

Zinzendorf's route, after fording the Lehigh at the Gap (for he probably passed down the valley of the Aquanshicola), lay through the counties of Lehigh and Berks, in a

---

* The *Aquanshicola* rises a little east of "Ross Common" Tavern, thence runs some eighteen miles southwest, draining the first narrow valley north of the Blue Mountain, and emptying into the Lehigh at the Gap. The old "fire-line" road skirts its upper bank for a mile from its mouth, and then doubling toward the Lehigh, passes the "Healing Waters,"—a chalybeate spring, on the farm of the late Stephen Snyder, now in possession of the Lehigh and Susquehanna R. R. Co. This spring was visited as early as 1746 by the Brethren, and its waters bottled by them for the use of invalids in Philadelphia. It is marked on Scull's map of 1759.

† Meniolagomeka—written also by the Brethren, *Meniwolagomekah* and *Mellilolagomegok*—Delaware, signifying "*a tract of fertile land surrounded by barrens.*"

southwesterly direction. Passing through *Allemängel,** and the valley of the Ontalaunee, or Maiden Creek, he forded

* *Allemängel* ("destitution"), a significant name given by the early German settlers to the present townships of Lynn, in Lehigh, and Albany, in Berks County, which lie adjoining at the foot of the Blue Mountain. Both are drained by the Ontalaunee ("*the maiden*"). The soil, which is a light gravel and slate, and ill adapted to agriculture, barely remunerated the pioneers in that obscure corner of the Province for their labor in tilling it. In 1741, Albany contained only thirty-seven taxables. A correspondent of the "Biene," in a narrative of a pedestrian tour through Lynn, in the summer of 1738, describes the church or school-house which the Brethren had built in Allemängel, "as an old-time, weather-boarded log-house, known throughout the neighborhood as '*the Old White Church.*'" It stood in Albany, near the line of Lehigh County. In 1843 it was removed. The aversion manifested, or perhaps the inability expressed by the settlers of Allemängel to support a schoolmaster (as we infer from Zinzendorf's allusion in the narrative of his journey through this barren region), was gradually removed, and in February of 1747 the Brethren opened a school there. December 14th, 1751, Nathaniel Seidel dedicated a newly-erected school-house ("*the Old White Church*"), on which occasion sixty persons partook of a love-feast, and seventeen, of the Sacrament. In January of 1755, Abraham Reincke officiated at the first interment made in the grave-yard adjoining the house. Thus Allemängel became the seat of a small congregation in connection with, and ministered to by the Brethren, until the outbreak of Indian barbarities in October of 1755.

John Holder and George Biebighausen and their families, in December of 1769, removed from Allemängel to the lands on the Mahoning, which had lain idle and deserted since November of 1755. Here they were joined by Samuel Warner, Sr., Edmund Edmonds and others, from *Sichem*, in "the Oblong," Duchess County, New York, and organized into an English congregation, which was at first supplied from Bethlehem. Joseph Neisser was stationed at "*Gnadenhütten, on the Mahoning*," in 1776. In 1778, George Schmidt was the incumbent. Caspar Freytag was the last minister settled there.

After the above-named families left Allemängel, "*the Old White Church*," or school-house, was sold to the Lutherans. They erected a new place of worship on its site in 1843, called the "*Friedens-Kirche.*"

the Schuylkill, entered the borders of Tulpehocken on the 2d of August,* and on the following day repaired to Conrad Weisser's house in Heidelberg.

Here it was that he met with heads and deputies of the Six Nations, on their return from a memorable conference with Governor Thomas, at which an important subject for final settlement had been the persistent stay of the Delawares, within the Forks, and south of the Blue Mountain. With these the Count ratified a covenant of friendship in behalf of the Brethren as their representative, stipulating for permission for the latter to pass to and from, and sojourn within the domains of the great Iroquois Confederation, not as strangers, but as friends. The meeting was conducted with all the etiquette and magniloquence of Indian diplomacy, and finally a string of wampum† was

---

* G. Büttner's private diary states that Zinzendorf, in company with Zander and Lischy, arrived in Tulpehocken on the 2d of August, and that they repaired to Weisser's house on the 3d. The descriptive poem, appended to this paper, was written on the 1st of August, in *Siki-hille-hocken* (quære, the land lying west of the Schuylkill, as far as Tulpehocken Creek?), and dispatched to Bethlehem probably by the Indian messenger.

† This string of wampum was carefully preserved for the use of the Brethren in their subsequent dealings with the Six Nations. On his return to Europe, the Count handed it over to Spangenberg, who gave the following

RECEIPT,

written in Lamb's Inn (Broad Oaks), County of Essex, England, March 10, 1743.

This is to certify that Bro. Ludwig has entrusted to me the token of a covenant ratified between him and the Five Nations, or Iroquois (which kind of token the Indians call fathom, or belt of wampum), consisting of 186 beads,—given him by said Iroquois on the 3d day of August, 1742, on his return from the Indian country;—this, I say, is to certify that he has entrusted it personally, and in the presence of

handed to the Count by the savages, to impress him with the sincerity of their decision, and for preservation as a perpetual token of the amicable relations just established. In this transaction Zinzendorf found a solution of the mysterious necessity which had impelled him to turn to Tulpehocken; and he recognized a special Providence as having guided him thither, and there opened a door for entrance among a people which, of all others, could be made most instrumental in the spread of the gospel among the various tribes of North American Indians.

This was at the time the most important result of the exploratory tour among the Delawares. Much of what it promised was never realized; and yet, although the Brethren were unsuccessful in their attempts to missionate among the Iroquois, they could never have effected as much as they did among the Delawares and Mohicans had they failed to secure the good-will and approval of the powerful coalition on which the latter were in a state of unqualified dependence.

The acquaintance made with the Delawares in the valleys of the Pocopoco and Aquanshicola was from that time unremittingly cultivated, and the Brethren Seyffert and Nathaniel Seidel* intrusted with the new field. When,

---

sundry eye-witnesses, to my safekeeping and for judicious use; which I desire hereby to testify by my own name in writing, with the promise not to give it into other hands, unless otherwise ordered.

AUGUSTUS G. SPANGENBERG,

m.p.p.

* Nathaniel G. Seidel, born 1718, at Lauban, in Lusatia. Deceased May 17, 1782, at Bethlehem. Came to Pennsylvania in June of 1742. After the abrogation of the "*Economy*," became proprietor of the estates held by the Brethren in this country. While abroad, between 1750 and 1760, was consecrated a bishop.

in the spring of 1746, a mission settlement was commenced at Gnadenhütten, on the Mahoning,* the ties of

---

* Gnadenhütten (Huts of Grace) was commenced in the spring of 1746, on a tract of 197 acres, near the mouth of Mahoning Creek (Carbon County), west of the Lehigh, as a temporary home for the Christian Mohicans who had come to Bethlehem from Shecomeco. It was designed from the first to locate them permanently on the Susquehanna; the project was, however, postponed from time to time, and thus the settlement on the Mahoning grew, and became the seat of a most flourishing mission. Here Martin Mack labored from April, 1746, to November, 1755, and here his wife, Jeannette, deceased December 15, 1749. She lies buried in the grave-yard on the hill, with some forty of her Indian brethren and sisters. Successive parcels of land were added to the original tract, on both sides of the Lehigh, until, in 1754, there were 1382 acres belonging to the establishment. In 1747, a grist- and saw-mill, erected on the Mahoning, and a blacksmith-shop, gave evidence of the march of improvement in this village of Christian Indians. The farm-buildings lay at the foot of the hill, near the creek: on its first ascent were the huts of the Indians, arranged in a half-moon; behind these an orchard, and on the summit, the grave-yard. The latter was laid out in August, 1746. November 14, 1749, the mission-house and chapel were solemnly dedicated by Bishop Cammerhoff. There were accessions from Pachgatgoch and Wechquadnach in 1747 and 1748, and from Meniolagomeka in 1754. In May of that year, the seat of the mission was transferred to the lands on the east side of the Lehigh. In December the mission numbered 137 Mohicans and Delawares, besides 86 converts residing at Wyoming, Nescopeck, and elsewhere in Indian villages along the Susquehanna.

But this child of magnificent promise was doomed to sudden destruction; for on the night of the 24th November, 1755, the "Family" of Brethren residing in the farm-house on the Mahoning was surprised by a party of Shawanese warriors, ten of their number shot, or tomahawked, or burned, and one carried into miserable captivity, which death soon terminated. The Indians at New Gnadenhütten and their surviving missionaries fled to Bethlehem. That place was sacked on New-Year's Day of 1756, Fort Allen, built by Franklin, on its site,

intercourse were drawn more closely; the missionary Bernhard A. Grubé* was stationed at Meniolagomeka,† in 1752,

before the close of March,—and thus a calamity befell the mission, from the disastrous effects of which it never fully recovered.

In October of 1751, Nicholas Garrison, Jr., took sketches of Gnadenhütten and vicinity, which were forwarded to Europe.

* Bernhard Adam Grubé, born 1715, near Erfurth, and educated at Jena, came to Pennsylvania on the Irene, in June of 1746. At first he was employed in the schools at Bethlehem. In January of 1752 he was stationed at Meniolagomeka. While here, he tells us, his awkwardness at handling an axe almost cost him a limb, and confined him

† Meniolagomeka. This village lay in "Smith's Valley," eight miles west of the Wind Gap, on the north bank of the Aquanshicola, at the intersection of the old Wilkesbarre Road, which crosses the mountain at Smith's Gap—in Eldred Township, Monroe County. The grave-yard was one-eighth of a mile south of Mr. Edward Snyder's limestone quarries. Jno. Smith, deceased about ten years ago, stated that his father, one of the early settlers in that neighborhood, had pointed out to him the sites of both village and grave-yard.

In October of 1743, A. Seyffert, D. Nitschmann, and N. Seidel, visited both here and on the Pocopoco—Seyffert and Hagen in January of 1744. In June of that year, Seyffert, P. Böhler, and Henry Antes. In February, 1748, Rauch visited at Meniolagomeka. Bishop Jno. M. de Watteville, on his visitation to the Brethren in America in the last-mentioned year, passed through Meniolagomeka to the Pocopoco. April 25, 1749, George Rex, the captain of the village, while on a visit to Bethlehem, was baptized by Bishop Cammerhoff, and received the name of Augustus. In 1750, Secretary Richard Peters urged his claim to the lands on the Aquanshicola, on which the village lay, and desired the Brethren to have the Indians removed. It was this that occasioned the exodus from Meniolagomeka to Gnadenhütten, on the Mahoning, in June of 1754.

Abraham Bühninger was the last missionary in the Indian village on the Aquanshicola.

The following draft shows the huts and population of the village in December of 1753.

THE DELAWARE VILLAGE OF MENIOLAGOMEKA, ON THE AQUANSHICOLA, DECEMBER, 1753.

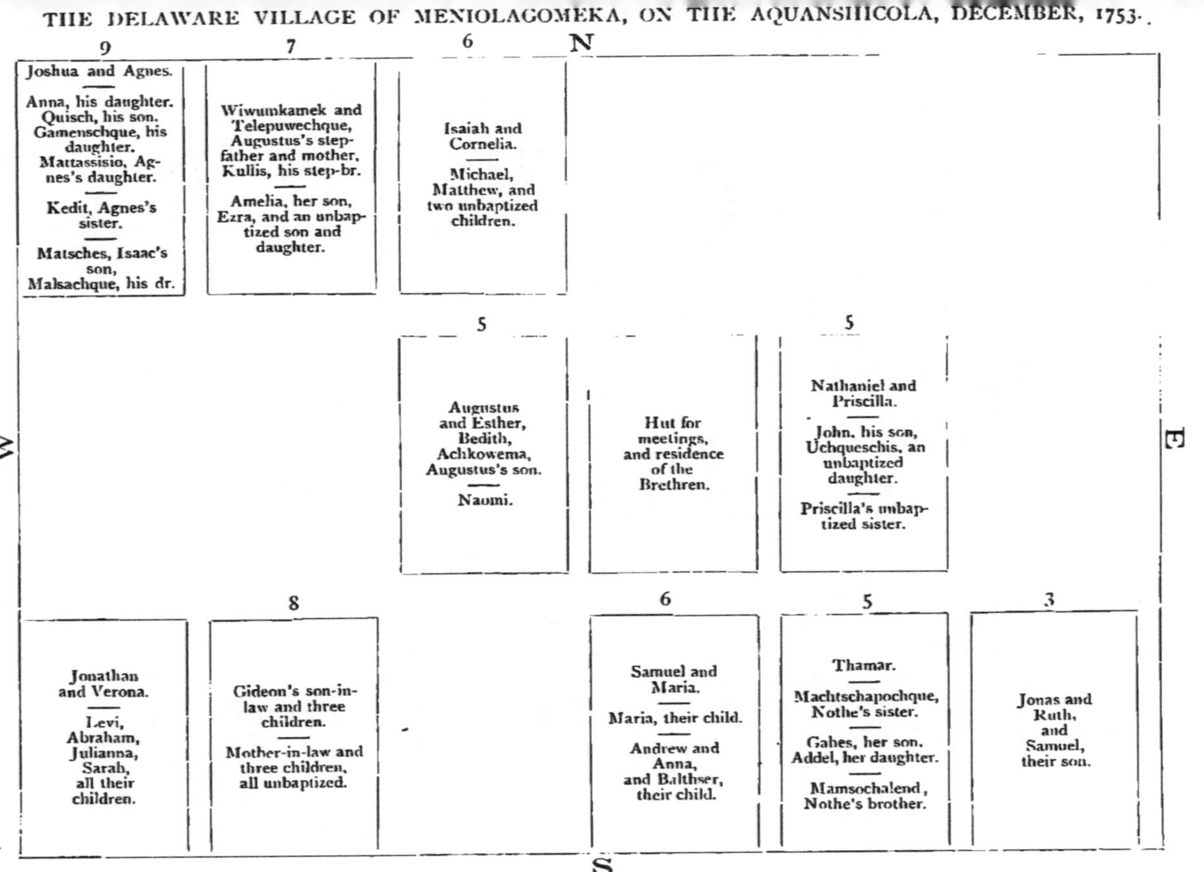

and two years later the villagers, numbering fifty-one all told, removed to Gnadenhütten, and were incorporated

---

for weeks in a cold hut, where he lay on a board, with a wooden bowl for a pillow. He, in the mean time, studied the Delaware, and daily held meetings for the Indians. In the summer of the year he visited Shamokin and Wyoming, and in the Shawanese town at the latter place baptized a Mohican woman, whom Zinzendorf had met there in October of 1742. He was fifteen months at Shamokin. "Here," he says, "we had hard times, and lived amid dangers. Our smithy became the resort of the savages passing through this central town, and on one occasion thirty warriors took possession of the house, and for eight days made it the scene of their drunken revels."

In October, 1753, Grubé was dispatched to North Carolina, to plant a colony of eleven young men on the tract of 100,000 acres purchased by the Brethren of the Earl of Granville, in what was then Rowan County. In the spring of the next year he returned to Bethlehem. Here, in 1755, he married Elizabeth Busse, and was appointed to Gnadenhütten, whence he barely escaped with his life in the memorable night of the 24th of November. In 1758 he was dispatched to Pachgatgoch (Kent), in Connecticut. In October of 1760 he removed to Wequetanc, on Head's Creek, Monroe County, where a part of the Christian Indians had been located in the spring of the year. On the outbreak of the Pontiac war, in October of 1763, this station was abandoned, and Grubé withdrew with his forty-four Indians to Nazareth and Bethlehem. From the latter place, where he was joined by seventy-seven Christian Indians from Nain, the faithful missionary accompanied his charge to the barracks at Philadelphia, and thence to Province Island, whither government was necessitated to remove them for safety. During the trying experiences made in the interval between November of 1763 and March, 1765, at Philadelphia,—in the unsuccessful attempt to effect an escape from popular fury, into New York,—and on the return to Bethlehem, Grubé approved himself true to duty, and brave in the face of dangers, as he had done at Wequetanc on the 11th of October, 1763.

His missionary career was now at an end, for, as he tells us, "in April of 1765 I took a sad and touching farewell of my dear Indians, as they set out for Wihilusing, on the Susquehanna." Soon after this he was stationed at Litiz, Lancaster County. In 1780 he was com-

with the congregation of Christian Indians at that place. No mention of Captain Harris's village on the Pocopoco is made by the Brethren subsequent to 1748.*

---

missioned to visit Schönbrunn, Gnadenhütten, and Salem, mission stations on the Muskingum. After his return, he labored at Gnadenthal, near Nazareth, and was for a year pastor of the congregation at Philadelphia. His last appointments were at Hope, on Paulin's Kill, in Warren County, New Jersey, and at Emaus, in Lehigh County, Pennsylvania. The evening of his long life was spent at Bethlehem, and on his ninety-first anniversary, the hale old man, with staff in hand, walked on a lovely June day ten miles to Nazareth, there once more to talk over with his friends the incidents of his life among the Indians. He deceased at Bethlehem, March 20, 1808.

* It is questionable whether Zinzendorf and his companions penetrated the Pine Swamp, on the great plateau of the Broad Mountain. The time was too short to allow of such an undertaking. Furthermore, it is stated in the Bethlehem diary that Nicholas Garrison, Jr., in May of 1749, "*went to the Pocopoco to take sketches of the places which Zinzendorf had visited seven years previous.*"

In 1760 the Brethren bought lands on Head's (Höth's) Creek, one of the affluents of the Pocopoco, and thither transferred their Indian converts from Bethlehem. This settlement was called Wequetanc. It lay on the flats on the north side of Wire Creek, about a quarter of a mile north of the State Road, where the present road to Effort leaves said State Road. This may have been the site of old Captain Harris's village.

A POEM

COMPOSED BY COUNT ZINZENDORF, AUGUST 1, 1742,

In Sikihillehocken, on the west bank of the Schuylkill, Philadelphia County.

1.

Hier schrieb ich einen Brief,
Als alles um mich schlief,
In der finstern Wüsten
Sickihillehoken,
Wo wenig Vöglein nisten;
Wird ich doch kaum inn'
Dasz die *Schuylkill* rinn
Ueber Nachbar *Green.*

2.

Herr Jesu, wach'st Du nicht
In deinem stillen Licht,
Rührt sich niemand neben
Dem himmlischen Gesicht
Des Lamms, im ew'gen Leben?
Fragt die muntern Vier
Ob sich etwas rühr?
Euch? Wenn ruht denn ihr?

3.

Gewisz in *Penn's*-Gestrüpp,
Selbst in *Allemängelship*
Fragt kein armer Bauer
Der seines Leibs Gerípp'
So hinbringt schwer und sauer,
Mehr nach einem Herr'n
Der die Kinder lern,
Als ich auch hätt' gern.

4.

Ihr auserwählte Vier!
Kommt her und saget mir
Wie ichs immer mache,
Dasz ich mein Amt recht führ
Und bleib auf meiner Sache,
Bis sie sich nach dem Plan
Der Kreuzcaravan,
Heiszt *in Gott Gethan.*

5.

Doch ich verirre mich;
Welch Muster suche ich,
Was vor ein Exempel?
Als ganz alleine Dich,
Du lebendiger Tempel
Aller Gottesfüll,
Der in seiner Still
Macht so viel er will.

6.

Die Hauptentschuldigung
Ist vor Dir nicht genung,

Die ich machen müsste,
Warum ich mit der Zeit
Nicht auszukommen wüsste.
Flehn war deine Freud',
In der Einsamkeit
Und Versunkenheit.

7.

Das Beten blieb nie aus:
Allein wenn Feld und Haus
Dir nicht Raum vergönnte
Vor der Geschäfte Braus,
So lang die Sonne brennte,
Hat Dirs deine Wacht
In der lieben Nacht
Immer eingebracht.

8.

Ach! das erworb'ne Recht
Fürs heilige Geschlecht,
Das Dich Blut gekostet,
Verleihe deinem Knecht
(Dem oft sein Werkzeug rostet,
Weil er's nicht so braucht
Wie es vor Dich taugt)
Arbeit, dasz es raucht.

9.

Nun, ich verlasse mich
Auf dein Verdienst und Dich,
Auf dein Blut das heisze,
Das Blut vom Seitenstich,

Das helffe mir zum Fleisze:
Denn auch aller Muth,
Dasz man's seine thut,
Kömt von deinem Blut.

10.

Inzwischen opfr' ich Dir
Ein Theil der Nachtzeit hier,
In dem offnen Zelte
Am *Indischen Revier.*
O! dasz es vor Dir gelte!
Doch vors Streiterthor
Hat das Beterchor
Alle Nacht dein Ohr.

11.

In Harmonie mit dem
Der itzt in *Bethlehem*
Priesteramtes pfleget,
Seyn dir die Zehen Stämm'
Zuerst ans Herz geleget.
Ach manch armes Schaaf
Fühlt der Gelbsuchtstraf,
Die sein Volk betraff!

12.

In *Tulpehocken* brennt's
Nun rund um alle *Fence:*
Denn die Nationen
Gehn durch dieselbe Grenz'
Zurück hin, wo sie wohnen—
Bringen meinen Pfad

Mit dem Zeugenrad
Bald in ihre Stadt.

13.

Das wird als denn gescheh'n
Wenn *Stissik* erst beseh'n,
Und vor diese Horden
Mit sanftem Lobgetön
Dem Lamm gedanket worden.
Abrah'm, *Israel*,
Isa'c, *Hannes'* Seel
Bürgt die Wundenhöhl.

14.

Wenn geht der Segen an?—
Dort überm Ocean
Ist uns eine Schule
Der Heiden aufgethan,
Wo auf dem Lehrerstuhle,
Gott der Heil'ge Geist,
Manchen unterweisst,
Der ins Wilde reist.

15.

O mein Herr Jesu Christ,
Der Du so willig bist
An dem Creuz gestorben,
Und dasz ein *Herrnhut* ist,
Dem *Bethl'em* hast erworben;
In dem Streiterthor
Sey gelobt davor
Von dem Priesterchor.

16.

Das Haus *Marienborn*
Des mit dem spitzen Dorn
So zerdroschnen Hauptes,
Das hat so manches Korn
Gesäet, und beglaubt es:
Segne seine Saat!
Es ist in der That
Dein Novitiat.

17.

Vohr zehen Jahren war
Es mit der Zeugenschaar
So, dass itzo *hundert*
Vor *zehen* stehen dar.
Ich wäre sehr verwundert,
Ja, es wär 'mir Weh,
Wenn ich nun nicht eh'
Tausend Zeugen säh'!

18.

Des Lammes nächster Freund,
Der's Lamm in allem meint,
Und nichts anders predigt,
Und wenn ein Herze weint,
Es in dem Lamm erledigt,
Das Jehovah heisst,
Sey davor gepreist,
Herr Gott, heil'ger Geist!

ZINZENDORF'S

JOURNEY TO THE MOHICAN TOWN OF SHECOMECO*—AUGUST 10—AUGUST 31, 1742.

On the 11th of August, 1742, Count Zinzendorf, his daughter, and Anton Seyffert, left Nazareth for Shecomeco, by what might be called the "overland route," leading almost due northeast one hundred and twenty-five miles to Kingston, on the Hudson.

At that time there was no connection by road between Lower Smithfield, in Monroe County, the Forks of Delaware, and the comparatively populous part of the Province south of the Lehigh. The great highway from Philadelphia to the Forks terminated at Nathaniel Irish's stone-quarry, near Iron Hill, Saucon Township. All above this was new country. The Blue Mountain was passable only with difficulty at three depressions or gaps in that part of its barrier-like extent which Zinzendorf and his companions would cross in their course to the Delaware, at the Wind Gap, at Fox Gap, and at Tat's Gap, respectively eleven, five, and two and a half miles west of where that river escapes from the Kittatinny. An old Indian trail leading into the Minnisinks led over the mountain through the latter. Crossing at the Wind Gap (even as late as 1750) was a difficult undertaking,—although the presence of an inn near there at that time would indicate the fact of its having become a thoroughfare.

* Twenty miles southeast of Rhinebeck, New York.

In August of the year just named, the Rev. Henry M. Muhlenberg accompanied his father-in-law, Conrad Weisser, to Sopus, and in his journal writes as follows: "Aug. 3, we rode on five miles above Nazareth, and put up for the night at a tavern. Aug. 9. Early in the morning we were in our saddles, climbed the first Blue Mountain, and were compelled in its ascent to lead our horses several miles over rocks and stones." It is not improbable, then, that the Count and his fellow-travelers followed the Indian path that led through Tat's Gap. This ride of thirty miles to Depew's Ford, at the Delaware, was unquestionably the most fatiguing part of the journey as far as Rhinebeck; for, after crossing that river into the Jersey Minnisinks, they struck into one of the oldest roads in the country, so far inland, and no natural avenue of trade and intercourse. This was the "old mine-road," constructd, it is said, at a very early day by Dutch adventurers from Sopus, who, following the first main valley* north of the Shawangunk, or "White Hills," and its continuation in that of the Mackhackemack branch of the Delaware, penetrated the Minnisinks proper east of that river. Here they discovered copper, worked a mine,† and built a road for the transportation of the ore to their settlements on the Hudson.

It was by means of communication thus opened, that the Dutch now seated themselves along the whole extent of this beautiful valley, even to its most southerly limit,—most numerously, however, on the Jersey shore of the Delaware.

When Nicholas Scull, surveyor, for the first time visited the Minnisinks in 1739, he was surprised to find unmistakable indications of very early settlement,—even on the Penn-

* The *Mamakating Valley*.

† The mine was opened about three miles northwest from Nicholas Depew's house, in Walpack Township, Sussex County (now Warren), New Jersey.

sylvania side of the river. He lodged with Mr. Samuel Depew, and from him learned the history of the mine-road, along which the latter had been accustomed for years to take his cider and grain to Kingston to market. The names of Van Etten, Van Aucken, Van Inwegen, Van Campen, and Cortrecht, still prevailing in the valley of the upper Delaware, perpetuate the memory of the Dutch that came down the mine-road, and opened them farms and built them homesteads in the historic land of the Monsey, or Wolf tribe, of the Lenni-Lenape.*

NARRATIVE OF A JOURNEY TO SHECOMECO, IN AUGUST OF 1742.

(*Translated from a German MS. in the Archives at Bethlehem.*)

Communicated to the Brethren in Europe in a letter written by Zinzendorf, on his way to Wyoming, dated

SHAMOKIN, THE FEAST OF ANGELS (MICHAELMAS),
Saturday, Sept. 29, 1742.

SERVANTS OF THE PRECIOUS LAMB,—

I will proceed to communicate to you as much more† as I can of my second journey, and something of the one in which I am now engaged. I keep no diary, and have no gift for narrative, and these are the reasons why I have

---

* John Adams, while attending Congress, during its session at Philadelphia, as late as 1800, passed down the "mine-road" as the most eligible route from Boston to that city. He was accustomed to lodge at Squire Van Campen's, in the Jersey Minnisinks.—*Information from Mr. Albert G. Brodhead, of Bethlehem.*

† He had given a partial account of the journey to Shecomeco in a former letter.

failed to keep the dear Brethren at Bethlehem informed of my movements. You are indebted solely to this day of rest* and leisure for the following outpourings of my heart in reference to persons and things, which I would otherwise not have committed to paper. As I remarked before, I have no faculty to relate, being inclined to forget and to repeat. I am also without my Secretary.† You will, therefore, excuse imperfections, and allow the Brethren Spangenberg‡ and Herman to select what they think proper for communication. Blessed are those who can read church intelligence aright!

Aug. 10. We set out from Bethlehem.§

Aug. 11. Crossed the Blue Mountain,|| en route for

---

* It was *Saturday*, and, as is well known, the Brethren of the last century observed that day as a day of rest. It was done agreeably to a proposition made by Zinzendorf at Bethlehem, on the 23d of June, 1742, in which he expressed himself, in reference to Saturday, as follows: "The observance of this day having been enjoined on men by divine command, prior to the giving of the law, is obligatory upon us. Let us, therefore, spend it in quiet and in communion with the Saviour. The Jews, it is true, observe the day; but not only as Jews,—also as members of the human family."

† John Jacob Müller, the Count's amanuensis during his stay in America, by profession a portrait painter, from Nuremberg, united with the Brethren at Herrnhut in 1740. Remained in the Count's family until 1760. In that year he was ordained, and settled at Nisky. Deceased there in 1781.

‡ Spangenberg spent the greater part of the year 1742 in London and Yorkshire. Quære—John Gothofred Herman?—*See Benham's Memoirs of James Hutton*, p. 239.

§ Bethlehem Diarist states that Zinzendorf's traveling companions were Anton Seyffert, Benigna von Zinzendorf, and Anna Nitschmann. The latter appears to have gone to New York, and thence up the river as far as Sopus.—*See Narrative, farther on.*

|| Quære—At the Wind Gap? There were, however, two other passes over the mountain.

Sopus.* The road tried our horses severely. We were, however, in a tranquil frame of mind. Anton Seyffert† and Benigna‡ were the principal persons in the company.

---

* *Sopus.* "Zopus is a place upon Hudson's River, 80 miles distant from New Yorke; consists of 5 small towns, whose inhabitants manage husbandry, & have not above 3,000 acres of manureable land, all the rest being hills and mountains, not possible to be cultivated."—*Governor and Council of the Province to William of Orange*, 1791. *Documentary History of New York*, vol. i. p. 407.

"About 18 German miles up the N. River, half-way between the Manhattans and Renselaer, or Beverwyck, lies a place called by the Dutch, Esopus or Sypous; by the Indians, *Atkarkarton.* It is an exceedingly beautiful place. There some Dutch inhabitants have settled themselves, and prosper especially well. They hold Sunday meetings, and then one among them reads something out for a postille."—*See Letter to the Classis of Amsterdam, d.* 15 *August*, 1657. Ibid.

Sopus was rich in horses. Here the Dutch quality of New York, according to Diedrich Knickerbocker, bought their switch-tails; and hither, says the Bethlehem Diarist, Matthias Seybold was dispatched, in August of 1742, to purchase four working horses for the Bethlehem Family.

† Anton Seyffert was one of the nine colonists whom Spangenberg led to Georgia in the spring of 1735, where the Brethren proposed establishing themselves with the view of missionating among the Creeks and Cherokees. On the abandonment of the project, he accompanied Böhler and others to Pennsylvania in the spring of 1740, assisted at the building of the Whitefield house, and at the settlement of the Allen tract (Bethlehem). During his stay in America, he was the Elder of the congregation. He returned to Europe in April of 1745.

‡ Benigna Henrietta Justina von Zinzendorf, oldest daughter of the Count, accompanied her father on many of his journeyings during his stay in Pennsylvania. Was born at Berthelsdorf, December 28th, 1725. In the spring of 1742 she was engaged in a school which the Brethren had opened in a house rented of Mr. J. Ashmead, in Germantown, for the Count and his corps of assistants. (See a letter of hers to the congregation in Europe, Büdingen Sammlung, Part xiii. No. 19.)

In the evening we reached the bank of the Delaware, and came to Mr. De Pui's,* who is a large landholder, and wealthy. While at his house, he had some Indians arrested for robbing his orchard.

Aug. 12 (*Sunday*). His son escorted us to the church,†

In 1746, she married John M. de Watteville. In 1784, she accompanied her husband on a visitation to the Brethren's settlements in the United States. Deceased at Herrnhut May 11th, 1789.

* Samuel De Pui (Depew) was settled on the west bank of the Delaware, three miles above the Water-Gap, prior to 1730. He was one of the Walloons who came to New York about 1697. Rev. H. M. Muhlenberg, who lodged at his house in 1750, states he had been Justice of the Peace, was a man of prominence in Smithfield, and at that time advanced in life. The river is fordable at the head of Depew's Island, a little above the house. The old homestead is still in the Depew family. Nicholas, one of Samuel's sons, is well known in provincial history between 1750 and 1770.

Bro. John Brandmüller, who was commissioned in February of 1747 to visit the Walloons in the townships of Sopus and New Paltz, west of the Hudson, reported on his return, "that they conducted their worship partly in French, had a lector, and used the Psalms; that a Dutch-Reformed Dominic preached to them occasionally; that they had intermarried with the Dutch, were industrious and well to do, and had immigrated to New York fifty years ago."

† There were five churches in this neighborhood. On the Pennsylvania side of the river, on Depui's land, stood the *Smithfield*, or old *Shawnee* church, removed about 1854. On the New Jersey side, about eleven miles north of Depui's, in the Walpack bend of the Delaware, the *Walpack* church, removed in 1815. Seven miles above this stood the *Shapenac*, an octagon, removed prior to 1818. In its church-yard lie the remains of General Harrison's mother-in-law. Twelve miles farther on was the *Minnisink* church; and eight miles above this, in the forks of the Delaware and Neversink, the *Mackhackemac*, removed about the time Port Jervis was settled,—some forty years ago. The last-named four churches were on the line of the old mine-road. The distance between Depui's and Port Jervis is thirty-eight miles. Zinzendorf visited either the Walpac or the Shapenac church,—probably

and, in course of conversation, put a number of indifferent and idle questions on religious subjects. My inability to answer him gratified rather than chagrined me, and was, I thought, altogether an advantage on my side.

We dismounted at the church, and were compelled to listen to two sermons, which wearied us.

In the morning the heat had been overpowering. In order to avoid being drawn into religious controversy, I went into the woods and read Josephus. The Dominie came to me and annoyed me with questions and remarks. Although my curt manner provoked him, it served to bring him to reflection, and he sought to propitiate me afterwards by riding with us for several hours.* He is the well-known Caspar,† from Zurich, a well-meaning man,

---

the former. After service, the company rode on perhaps as far as *Minnisink*, nineteen miles beyond, and halted there for the night. This would allow some thirty-six miles for the next day's journey, which, we are told, brought them half way through the valley west of the Shawangunk,—the distance between Port Jervis and Kingston being upward of fifty-four miles.—*Information obtained from Mr. Albert G. Brodhead, of Bethlehem.*

The Brethren preached and kept a school in the upper valley of the Delaware, on the Jersey shore, in 1746 and 1747. In the former year, Joseph Shaw was settled at *Walpack*. Here his wife deceased. He also preached at the Minnisink church, and on one occasion, in April of 1747, had a promiscuous audience of Swedes, English, Scotch, Irish, Welsh, Germans, Walloons, Shawanese, Mohawks, Delawares, and Catawbas.

* Quære—After service, at the Walpack church?

† "In 1742, Jno. Caspar Freymuth returned from Holland, whither he had been sent to study for the ministry, and took charge of the 4 churches in the Minnisinks."—Stickney's Hist. of the Minnisink Region of Orange Co., 1867. In a "*Naam-register der Predicanten der Reformde Kerk*" for 1744, Johannes Casparus Fryenmoet, is enrolled in charge of the churches in Menissink, Machhakomach, Walpek, and Smitsfield.—*Documentary History of New York.*

I must confess,—one of the so-called "Convictionists," without much conviction, however, and yet efficient for good in his denomination.

Aug. 13. As we rode along, we were joined by a man who complained of the burden of his sins, and who inquired of me what to do to be saved. From his remarks, during the conversation, I failed to discover any solid ground, in his religious experience, on which to erect an abiding superstructure.

On passing a house, a female stepped out, spoke to us, and, after the interchange of a few words, asked us to dismount, adding that her son, she knew, would be pleased to converse with us. We were unable to gratify her wish, as we had purposed passing the Minnisinks, and through half of the wilderness beyond, and there was a journey of *thirty* miles before us. When we reached the house that stands in the heart of it, night had already set in, and it was dark as pitch.

Aug. 14. Set out early in the morning; rode through the remainder of the wilderness, and reached Mombach and Marbletown.* We were much annoyed by ill-natured questions that were put to us, at a house at which we dismounted. Rode on through Hurley† to Sopus.‡ Here we

* Passed the night, perhaps at the "Jagd-house," half way between Port Jervis and Kingston, or at Emanuel Pascal's.

† In 1784, "Dirck Romein was pastor of Marbletown and *Mombach*." Marbletown, six miles west of Kingston, on the old mine-road, was the birthplace of Daniel Brodhead, who deceased at Bethlehem, in 1755, and of Rachel (née Bogart), widow of Isaac Martens Ysselstein, who was settled on a farm south of the Lehigh, when the Brethren came into the Forks of Delaware, in 1740.

‡ Hurley was a township of Ulster County as early as 1728. The present village of that name is a post-town, four miles west of Rondout. Conrad Weisser, in his Journal to Onondaga, in August of 1750, gives the following stations and distances:

met Sr Anna* and Christian Fröhlich† and his wife. I dispatched Christian to the Delawares,‡ to be with them at their festival, and retained Mary.

In the afternoon, we resumed our journey, crossed the North River, and halted for the night. The people here regarded us as saints.

Aug. 15. At noon we reached Bro. Jacob Maul's,§ in Rhinebeck. Having rested, we set out for Shecomeco, and, after riding through an almost impenetrable swamp, came to our journey's end at 1 o'clock in the morning of the 16th.‖

Aug. 17. Came to Nazareth.		
" 18. To Niklas Depuy, in Smithfield, on Delaware,	39	miles.
" 19. " Henry Cortrecht, at Menissing,	25	"
" 20. " Emanuel Pascal, "*the Spaniard,*"	35	"
" 21. " King's-town (Sopus),	44	"

* Anna Nitschmann.—*See her Memoir elsewhere in these papers.*

† Christian Fröhlich, from Felsburg, in Hesse, came to Pennsylvania in 1741, and joined the Brethren on the Whitefield tract. Missionated among the Delawares in Capt. John's village. (See his letter, Part viii. No. 11, Büdingen Sammlung.) July, 1742, married Mary Esther Robins. Went to Europe, and returned in 1744. Again among the Delawares, and also at Pachgatgoch. 1750–1752, on St. Thomas. On his recall, remained in New York, and for upwards of twenty years managed the sugar-refinery of P. V. B. Livingston. Deceased at Bethlehem, April 5th, 1776. A confectioner by trade, in which capacity he was some time in the Zinzendorf family.

‡ The Delawares in Capt. John's village, on the Nazareth tract. Quære—Which of the five great feasts annually observed by that nation?

§ One of the Palatines, who had immigrated to New York in 1710, under the auspices of Queen Anne.

‖ The site of the Indian village was about two miles south of the village of Pine Plains (Duchess County, New York), near "*the Bethel,*" in the valley of the Shecomeco, a small stream, which, rising near "*Federal Square,*" runs in a northerly direction, and falls into *Roelif Jansen's Kill*, in Columbia County.

On the 5th of October, 1859, the Moravian Historical Society erected

Bro. Rauch lodged us in his hut for the night, and on the 17th we occupied the house that had been built for us. I was delighted with it; it was a perfect palace of bark, and furnished with a table and writing materials for my special convenience. My seat was on the ground. Here we lodged eight days, and, although it rained almost continuously, and we underwent numerous internal conflicts, our dear Indians had clear sky overhead, and rejoiced us each day anew. They are Mohicans, a confessedly worthless tribe of Indians.

The Maquas, who belong to the Six Nations of the Iroquois, are their neighbors, and the acknowledged head of that great Confederacy, although their passion for strong drink, by making them hopelessly indolent, has rendered them unworthy of the distinction. They are one division of the Indians with whom I ratified a covenant at Tulpehocken,* whither I had turned at the close of my journey into the Indian country, drawn by an irresistible power, which I followed in strong faith, although I knew neither why nor wherefore.

The Mohicans, although naturally fierce and vindictive, and given to excessive drinking, are tender-hearted, and susceptible of good impressions. When our pale-faced Bro. Rauch first came among them, they regarded him as a fool, and threatened his life. But after his recital of the Saviour's sufferings had made a powerful impression upon the most abandoned of their number (an impression which allowed him peace neither day nor night, until he experienced the preciousness of grace), the work of the Lord proceeded, and others were moved.

All the machinations of his mother-in-law, who sought to

---

a granite block over Büttner's grave, on the farm of Mr. Edward Hunting.

* August 3, 1742.

perplex him, were unsuccessful, although they proved effectual in causing his wife and daughter to vacillate. This brand snatched from the fire, is no longer Tschoop,* but *John*, and is an esteemed teacher among his people. Abraham, Isaac, and Jacob, who, you recollect, were baptized at Oley,† were appointed to offices in the mission—Abraham elder, Jacob exhorter, and Isaac sexton.

The four are in all respects incomparable Indians, and men of God. When met in conference on affairs of the mission, they deliberated in a manner which astonished us. I confess that at times I felt pity for these poor people, whose imperfect language is inadequate for the expression of their new experiences, and of their views and wishes, as assistants in the Saviour's work. Our language is divine in comparison with theirs, and yet how unsatisfactorily can we give utterance to the emotions and aspirations of our hearts!

The result of our deliberations while at Shecomeco, was the adoption of the following resolutions, viz.:

1. To mark out a new plan of operations for Bro. Rauch.‡

2. To preach the gospel to the whites of the neighborhood, and gather a congregation from them.

3. To organize our Mohicans§ into a congregation.

---

* *Wasamapah*, alias *Tschoop*, baptized by the missionary, Christian Henry Rauch, at Shecomeco, April 16, 1742. Deceased at Bethlehem, August 27, 1746.

† In Mr. John de Turck's barn, February 22, 1742, by Christian H. Rauch.

‡ Quære—His exploration of the Mohawk country, and visit to Canajoharie, or his recall to Bethlehem?

§ This was done on the 22d of August, after the missionary Rauch had baptized the Indians *Kaubus*, *Kermelok*, *Harris*, and the wives of *Abraham*, *Isaac*, and *Harris*, who, in baptism, were called respectively

4. To contract a marriage between Jeannette Rau* and Bro. Mack, to which union we have her father's consent.

5. To visit Conrad Weisser.†

6. To employ Benigna and Jeanette in the Indian mission.

7. To baptize twelve Indians.

8. To appoint native assistants in the infant congregation here.

9. To take with us on our return to Bethlehem, Gabriel,‡

Timothy, *Jonas*, *Thomas*, *Sarah*, *Rebecca*, and *Esther*. These ten constituted the first congregation of Christian Indians, in charge of the Brethren.

* Daughter of John Rau, a Palatine farmer in the neighborhood, at whose house Bro. Rauch had been entertained on his arrival among the Mohicans in 1740. He deceased in July of 1768, and was buried at the English meeting-house in "The Oblong," by Bro. Francis Böhler, at that time stationed at Sichem.

† John Conrad Weisser (father of the interpreter) immigrated to New York in 1710, and along with his countrymen from the Palatinate, was first settled on Livingstone Manor. Thence he removed to the Mohawk country. In 1743, he was again residing on the east side of the Hudson, within half a day's journey of Shecomeco, as appears from the following entry in Büttner's diary,—"May 4th, 1743, visited old C. W. and returned in the evening." In 1746, soon after his removal to Tulpehocken, he deceased at his son's house. Weisser, while in the Mohawk country, was one of the leaders of his countrymen in resisting the encroachments of large Dutch landholders in Albany, who eventually necessitated the Palatines to vacate their farms, and migrate elsewhere. Some of these, following the course of the Susquehanna southward, and passing up the Swatara and Tulpehocken Creeks, settled along those streams in 1723..

‡ *Gabriel*, alias *Wanab*, and *Nanhan*, alias *Tassawachamen*, Mohican catechumens, were baptized at Bethlehem on the 15th September following, the first by Zinzendorf, the second by the missionary Büttner, receiving in baptism the names of David and Joshua, respectively. This was the first baptism of Indians at Bethlehem, and performed in the chapel, on the upper floor of the "Gemein-house," next the Moravian

Nanhan, and Abraham's son. Techtanoah, John's daughter, will not accompany us, as she is entertaining an offer of marriage.

10. To explore Albany* and New England.

11. To confer with Abraham, Isaac, Jacob, and John, on our method of laboring among the heathen, and on its object, which is not the indiscriminate acquisition of large numbers, but the admission into the congregation of souls that have been renewed to life in Christ.

12. To commend the awakened Indians here to the blessing of the Lamb, and to inform them of the course we design to pursue in their case.

13. To consider the propriety of admitting a son and a second daughter of John Rau into our communion, and of appointing them to labor among the class of Indians just named.

14. To take a public farewell.

I shall never forget my stay here, and when we parted, it was with sadness and regret, though with mutual assurances of the tenderest love.

---

church. The two accompanied the Count as far as Shamokin on his second journey to the Indian country.

* *Albany.* The County of Albany at that time embraced all of New York State north of Ulster, and eastward as far as Vermont. The heart of this extensive tract was the Valley of the Mohawk, or the Mohawk country. Here Rauch and Pyrlaeus visited the Indians in 1743. Rauch was at Schoharie and Canajoharie. Pyrlaeus, in order to perfect himself in the Mohawk (which he had been studying at Conrad Weisser's), resided for some time with Rev. Henry Barclay, near Fort Hunter, and next at Canajoharie.

To the Indians here, Mr. Barclay had been appointed Catechist in 1735. He deceased 1764, while Rector of Trinity Church, New York. The Brethren never effected a settlement in the Mohawk country, although their missionaries visited their towns or castles as late as 1750.

On the *24th of August* we set out on our return home, crossed Stissing Mountain, penetrated the wilderness beyond, and reached Rhinebeck. Here we found Maul's family down with dysentery. Jeannette was taken sick, and was an invalid to the end of the journey.

Aug. 25. Crossed the North River. Sopus being the Sodom of New York, we resolved to pass through, and not spend Sunday within its borders. This prolonged our journey into the night, and we barely succeeded in finding lodgings on the other side of Hurley.

Aug. 26 (*Sunday*). I spent the whole day out of doors, and although I kept by myself in the woods, I nevertheless got into difficulty. It was beyond my control to escape what the people here were determined to inflict upon me. For in the evening, as Benigna and myself were writing by candlelight in our lodgings, a Justice of the Peace came into the room, and forbade us in the King's name. He then left in a storm of rage. Next morning at 5 o'clock (we were scarcely out of bed) a Constable sent by him arrested me, Benigna, and Anton, and led us back to Hurley. Here we were examined by the Justice in public; and without a proper hearing were convicted, and fined 18*s*. for Sabbath-breaking. He then dismissed us, with manifest regret that it was not in his power to impose a severer punishment. I really believe it would have afforded the people extreme pleasure to have seen us bound as scoffers of God and the King, and taken down to New York. One of our Indians, on being asked whether he wished to look on at the examination, rejoined, saying, "Why should I look on at such a malicious proceeding?" This answer vexed the bystanders.

Aug. 27. Reached Minnisink.

Aug. 28. Came to the Delaware, across which we swam our horses. Anna, as usual, took the lead.

Aug. 29. Jeannette was seriously indisposed, and scarcely able to bear up. We, however, pushed our way through the wilderness, crossed the Blue Mountain, and after nightfall reached Nazareth. Here we designed leaving Jeannette with the English* Brethren and Sisters. She, however, accompanied us, on the 31st, to Bethlehem.

DEPOSITION—*Büdingische Sammlung,* Part xv. No. 18.

"On the 26th of August, 1742, about 9 o'clock A.M. we, the undersigned, and three Mohican converts, sat down near a thicket, a short distance on the other side of Hurley. Soon after, our Brother von Thürnstein came to us out of the woods, and asked us whether we intended traveling farther. We told him we thought of doing so. Hereupon, he earnestly advised us to lay over, reminding us that it was Sunday, that the Presbyterians took offence at Sunday-travel, and that on this account he had thought proper to make a halt. From regard to him, we did as he bade us. He remained the greater part of the day in the woods (as was his custom), although it rained incessantly, and about candlelight returned to the house where we were lodging. Seeing his daughter Benigna seated at a table, he handed her a poem on the Indians he had composed a few days ago, and asked her to copy it. She being unable to do it at once, he engaged in conversation, and spoke with much feeling of God's gracious dealings with the Economy at Halle, in the welfare of which institution he always took a lively interest.

"In the midst of the discourse, a messenger entered the

* The English Brethren, Powels, Hussey, Turner, Yarrel, Rice, etc. who had come on the Catharine in June, were organized into a congregation, and settled at Nazareth. David Bruce was their Elder. This organization was temporary.

room, and inquired whether any one of the company present had known the late Isaac Ysselstein, of the Forks of Delaware. As Dominie von Thürnstein had had little acquaintance with him, and as he was always averse to engaging in any conversation with people on Sunday, he referred the inquirer to Dom. A. Seyffert. Dom. von Thürnstein now handed the poem to his daughter to copy, and at the same time began to write in his memorandum.

"Although he expressly requested that no one should disturb him that day, several persons nevertheless entered the room and sat down. It was always left for him to conduct the religious discussions which usually followed the arrival of obtrusive visitors; but on the present occasion he confined himself to his writing, appearing disinclined to speak in the presence of the Indians, who all understood Low Dutch. Accordingly, he took no part in the conversation (there being some five or six of us, enough to answer all questions) until he was addressed personally. He had just finished his memoranda, and the Countess had completed the copying, when one of the visitors, who appeared to be the leader, remarked to him that he, the Dominie, seemed to be very industrious. 'Not at all,' said the latter, adding, at the same time, that he was merely noting down a few thoughts. To this the man rejoined, saying that it was Sunday. Hereupon, Dom. von Thürnstein, wishing to avoid useless controversy, observed that probably they differed in their religious views, but that, according to his belief, such writing as he had been engaged in was not unlawful on Sunday. 'The King,' said the other, 'has ordered that Sunday be strictly kept in every particular, even in the face of the religious liberty which prevails in the land.'

"This remark, as well as the speaker's statement that he was a Justice of the Peace, and had spoken in the King's name, induced the Dom. to address a letter to the Governor in New York, in which he related what had happened.

"He took this step with the presumption, that in case the Justice were acting illegally in the premises, it would bring him to reflection; in case, however, his course was lawful, the Governor's indorsement of it would screen himself and his followers from slanderous reports. As often as this letter was presented to the Justice for delivery, he persistently returned it with coarse invective; and early next morning, as we were about to resume our journey, a Constable, sent by him, came to the house, and arrested, with his tipstaff, first, the Countess Benigna, and next, Dom. A. Seyffert. Dom. von Thürnstein accompanied them without compulsion, and hence the officer need not have touched him with his staff, and made a formal arrest. What else transpired, these deponents say not.

"We learned subsequently that the three were fined for Sabbath-breaking, despite their protestations of innocence; that the Justice had alleged the Dominie's incivility to him on the previous night as the cause of the arrest, and that he had returned the letter written to the Governor for the last time, in a passion and with threats.

"The bystanders on asking our Indians, after the arrest, whether they wished to be present at the examination, the latter replied, that they took neither interest nor pleasure in such a malicious proceeding.

"Above deposition, although not made before a magistrate, we, the undersigned, eye-witnesses of the occurrences therein stated, affirm to be strictly true.

N. N. and N. N."

ZINZENDORF'S NARRATIVE

OF A JOURNEY FROM BETHLEHEM TO SHAMOKIN, IN SEPTEMBER OF 1742.

Dated SHAMOKIN,
September 29, 1742.

CONRAD WEISSER* finally concluded to be my guide to the Shawanese country.

---

* Conrad Weisser, for more than twenty years acting interpreter to the Province of Pennsylvania, was born in 1696, in Wurtemberg. In 1710 he accompanied his parents to America, with a colony of Palatines, who immigrated to New York under the auspices of Queen Anne, and who were settled in a body on Livingston Manor, in Columbia County, for the production of naval stores. In 1713 the Weisser and 150 other families removed to Scoharie, in the Mohawk country, where young Conrad was schooled in the language which enabled him later in life to render invaluable services to the Proprietaries' governors of Pennsylvania. In 1729 he followed his countrymen to the Swatara and Tulpehocken, whither numbers of them had removed a few years before, and here he began a farm in Heidelberg Township, Berks County. His fluency in Mohawk recommended him to the notice of the Proprietaries' agents, and by special request of deputies of the Six Nations, met in conference with Governor Patrick Gordon, at Philadelphia, in 1732, he was by him appointed Interpreter for that Confederation. From this time his career was identified with the history of the Province in all its relations with the Indians. In 1734 he was appointed a Justice of the Peace, and in the old French War commissioned Colonel of all forces raised west of the Susquehanna. A few years before his death he removed to Reading, and while on a visit to his farm in Heidelberg, in July of 1760, deceased, and was

I now proceed in the first place to state my object in undertaking the present journey, and will then relate some of its incidents.

---

buried in the family grave-yard near Womelsdorf. The following inscription, copied from his tombstone, is the only memorial that has, as yet, been erected to perpetuate the remembrance of Pennsylvania's efficient Interpreter to the Indians:

Dieses ist die
Ruhe Staette des
Weyl. Ehren geachteten M. Conrad Weisser.
Derselbige ist geboren 1696, *den* 2 *November,*
in Astaedt in Amt Herrenberg, im
Wuertemberger Lande, und gestorben
1760, *den* 13 *Julius, ist*
alt worden 63 *Jahr,*
8 *Monate,* 13 *Tage.*

Weisser's connection with the Brethren dates from the time of Spangenberg's sojourn among the Schwenkfelders of Towamensing Township, Montgomery County, in 1736. In that year, the two met for the first time; and the information the interpreter gave him of the degraded condition of the Indians, led Spangenberg to present their case to the Brethren abroad, as one deserving special consideration. The result of this appeal was Christian Henry Rauch's commission. Zinzendorf, soon after his arrival in Pennsylvania, repaired to Tulpehocken to profit from Weisser's knowledge and experience, and to enlist his co-operation in the movement he proposed to inaugurate among the Indians. In 1743 he visited Shecomeco. In 1745 he accompanied Bishop Spangenberg to Onondaga. Although disinclined to unite with the Brethren, not sympathizing with them in all their views and projects, he was a warm friend of their mission, and a contributor to the Society organized at Bethlehem in 1745 for its maintenance. We annex the following letter written to one of its Trustees, dated

HEIDELBERG, February 15, 1746.

"DEAR BRO. BROWNFIELD,—

"It is long since I received yours of December, with the enclosed account of the Society for the furtherance of the gospel. I am obliged

Hitherto I have felt no freedom to operate directly upon the Iroquois in their seats,* as I have been unable to discern any promising indications or signs of grace among them, excepting in the case of a few individuals. Their intercourse with the French and English has not been for good. In

---

to you for the trouble therein taken in sending me a copy. I have been very little at home since the receipt thereof. You will therefore be pleased to excuse my delay in writing you an answer, which I will do by this opportunity.

"I desire you will let the Committee know that according to the Eleventh Article in the plan of the Society, I will contribute thereunto (I mean toward the furtherance of the gospel among the Indians of North America), and deliver or send my contribution accordingly.

"By your letter I understand that the Society is likewise to be employed for the service of the white people in general; for which service I have nothing to contribute nor to say. For it may be properly said of them what Paul says in *Rom.* x. 18. The method made use of in preaching the gospel in our days to the white people has only divided them more into parties and sects without any reformation, in my judgment. Every party has given sufficient proof that it seeks its own, and not the interest of Christ Jesus. However, as to the poor Indians, it may be properly said of them what Paul says in the recited chapter, verses 14–17, and therefore I assure you, that nothing shall be wanting that lies in my power to promote the good design of the Society among these poor heathens. May the great God be pleased to send true laborers among them by whom their souls may be brought to Christ Jesus, to whom be worship and glory for evermore.

"I salute you very heartily, and am desirous to be and remain your well-known

"True friend and Brother,

"CONRAD WEISSER."

* The Mohawks, originally restricted to the valley of the river that bears their name, extended their seats in virtue of conquest, from Lake Champlain to the sources of the Delaware and Susquehanna Rivers. The Oneidas, Onondagas, Cayugas, and Senecas, respectively, lived west of them, and south of Lake Ontario. The Tuscaroras had no country of their own.

addition to the vices of civilized life they have thus acquired, I find they have adopted erroneous views of religion. I must therefore be extremely prudent, in order to succeed in effecting any good among them. They will be apt to infer from my speech, and from my connection with these two nations, that I am one of the same sort of people,—which I am not. The Dutch in Japan are *afraid*, and I among the Indians am *ashamed*, to pass for a European Christian.

With these considerations, I told the Iroquois distinctly in my first interview with them,* that I had a different method from those who came to instruct them in religion, and begged them to have patience with me, in case I failed at once to preach long sermons. I remarked furthermore that I was specially and intimately acquainted with the Great Spirit, and asked them finally to permit me and the Brethren simply to sojourn in their towns, as friends, and without suspicion, until such time as we should have mutually learned each other's peculiarities. I defined my position and my object in this manner, so as to avoid being regarded by them as a Don Quixote† in religion; and also so as not to bind myself by any positive engagement.

The six confederate tribes of the Iroquois,—the Maquas, Onondagas, and Senecas (these are called *Fathers*, and some of them are at times cannibals),‡ and the Cayugas,

---

* at Conrad Weisser's house, August 3, 1742.

† It is a singular coincidence in the use of terms, that James Logan, in a letter to a friend, expresses himself in these words: "He (the Count) has lately been visiting the Iroquois. In short, he appears a mere knight-errant in religion, and scarce less than Don Quixote was in chivalry."

‡ "It happened this year (1625) that the *Mohicans* being at war with the *Maquas* (Mohawks), requested to be assisted by the commander of Fort Orange and six others. Commander Knickebeck went up with

Oneidas, and Tuscaroras (who are called *Children*), are to all outward appearance admirable hypocrites, and on account of their indomitable pride, as remote from Jesus as the heavens are distant from the earth. Therefore I concluded to operate upon them indirectly, and not to visit their castles or towns, but rather to go to,

1. *Shamokin*,* which is 80 miles from Tulpehocken, and

---

them a mile from the fort, and met the Maquas, who peppered them so bravely with a discharge of arrows, that they were forced to fly, leaving many slain, among whom were the commander and three of his men. Among the latter was Tymen Bouwensz, whom they devoured, after having well-cooked him."—*From Wassenaer's Historie van Europa*. Amsterdam, 1621–1632.

"In the beginning of July, 1676, those Indians who were known by the name of *Mauguawogs*, or Mohawks, *i.e. man-eaters*, fell on Philip of Pokanoket, and killed forty of his men."

* Shamokin, situated a short distance below the Forks of the Susquehanna on its north branch, was, in consequence of its commanding position, the most important Indian town in the Province of Pennsylvania. The Six Nations held this as a strategic point at an early day, and made it the seat of a Viceroy, who ruled for them the tributary tribes that dwelt along the waters of the "Winding River." It is mentioned by name in the Colonial Records, first in 1728. Here the Iroquois warriors, on their return from predatory expeditions against the Cherokees and Catawbas, would make a halt and hold carousals for the last time before reaching Onondaga. Conrad Weisser visited the town in March of 1737. Martin Mack and his wife were the first missionaries sent hither by the Brethren. Mack, in his autobiography, notices his stay here thus: "In Sept. of 1745, my wife and I were sent to Shamokin, *the very seat of the Prince of darkness*. During the four months we resided there, we were in constant danger, and there was scarcely a night but we were compelled to leave our hut, and hide in the woods, from fear of the drunken savages."

David Brainerd visited Shamokin in the same year, reaching there on the 13th of September, and in his journal writes: "The town lies partly on the east and the west shores of the river, and partly on the island. It contains upwards of 50 houses, and 300 inhabitants. The

the residence of the King* of the Delawares, and of the Oneida† viceroy. The latter virtually maintains the bal-

Indians of this place are accounted the most drunken, mischievous, and ruffian-like fellows of any in these parts; and *Satan seems to have his seat in this town* in an eminent manner. About one-half are Delawares, the others Senecas and Tutelars."

In the summer of 1747, the Brethren, at the chief Shikellimy's request, built a smithy at Shamokin, and on the 18th of August, Anton Schmid, from Bethlehem, was formally introduced by Christian H. Rauch to the Indians met in council as the blacksmith of the village. They called him *Rachustoni*. September 16, John Hagen deceased here, and was buried in the turnip-patch near the mission-house. Mack, Post, Pyrlaeus, Zeisberger, and other Brethren labored here until the abandonment of the station in October of 1755. In 1756, Fort Augusta was built, one mile above Shamokin. Sunbury, the county town of Northumberland, occupies the site of the old Indian village.

* *Allummapees*, or *Sassoonan*, was King of the Delawares as early as 1718, and in that year headed the deputation of Indian chieftains at Philadelphia who signed an absolute release to the Proprietaries *for the lands situate between Delaware and Susquehanna, from Duck Creek to the mountains on this side Lechay*, which lands had been granted by their ancestors to William Penn.

In 1728 he had removed "from on Delaware to Shamokin."

"The Delaware Indians last year (1746) intended a visit to Philadelphia, but were prevented by Allummapees' sickness, who is still alive, but not able to stir. They will come down this year, some time after harvest. Allummapees has no successor of his relations, and *he will hear of none so long as he is alive*, and none of the Indians care to meddle in the affair. Shikellimy advises that the government should name Allummapees' successor, and set him up by their authority, that at this critical time there might be a man to apply to, since Allummapees has lost his senses, and is uncapable of doing anything."—*C. Weisser's Report to Anthony Palmer, June*, 1747.

While David Brainerd was instructing the Delawares at *Sakhauwotung*, in the Forks of that river, in the truths of Christianity (between

† *Shikellimy*, father of Logan. (*See later.*)

ance of power between the different tribes of Indians, and between the Indians and the whites, in North America, acting agent for the Iroquois Confederacy in all affairs of state and war.

2. *Otstonwakin*,* where Madame Montour, an Indianized French woman from Quebec, resides; and—

May of 1744 and February of 1746), he visited Shamokin annually. In September of 1745, he writes from that town: "Visited the Delaware King (Allummapees) who was supposed to be at the point of death when I was here in May last. Discoursed with him and others about Christianity. He appeared kindly disposed, and willing to be instructed."

In 1747, Allummapees, together with Shikellimy, took part in the treaty with the Brethren concerning the erection of a smithy at their town. In the fall of that year he deceased. "Allummapees is dead," writes Weisser to Peters, in October of 1747. "*Lapappiton* is allowed to be the fittest to succeed him, but he declines. He is afraid he will be envied, and consequently bewitched by some of the Indians."

"Allummapees would have resigned his crown before now, but as he had the keeping of the public treasure (that is to say of the Counsel Bagg), consisting of Belts of Wampum, for which he buys Liquor, and has been drunk for this 2 or 3 years almost constantly, it is thought he won't die, so long as there is one single wampum left in the bagg. Lapappiton is the most fittest person to be his successor. He is an honest, true-hearted man, and has very good natural sense; he is also a sober man, between 40 or 50 years of age, and well esteemed among his country people and others."—*C. Weisser to R. Peters*, July 20, 1747.

Teedyuscung was made King of the Delawares, west of the mountains, in the spring of 1756.

* *Otstonwakin*, or "French Town." Written also *Olstuago, Otsuchage*, and *Otstuacky*, by Weisser, who visited the town for the first time in February of 1737. "It is so called" (he writes in his journal), "from 'a high rock' which lies opposite. We quartered ourselves with Madame Montour, a French woman by birth, of good family, but now in mode of life a complete Indian." The village lay on both sides of

3. *Skehandowana*,* 100 miles from Otstonwakin, the seat of the nation of the Shawanese, who are confederates of the

---

the mouth of the Loyal Lock (the *Olstuago*), which coming down from the northeast here empties into the West Branch. Weisser's last visit to Otstonwakin was in June of 1755. The village was at that time almost deserted. It is not noted down on Scull's Map of 1759. *Montoursville*, in Lycoming County, occupies its site, and perpetuates the name of Madame Montour.

* Skehandowana. One of the names of Wyoming Valley. The first allusion to this Indian Eldorado, which lay in the heart of an almost limitless territory that the Iroquois had made their own by conquest in pre-historic times, is on record in the minutes of a conference held by Governor Gordon with Indians from the Susquehanna, at the great meeting-house in Philadelphia, in June of 1728. On this occasion, the Delaware King (Allummapees) stated "that the Minnisinks lived in the Forks of Susquehanna, above *Meehayomy*." Again, *September* 2, 1732. *Metaguantagechty*, the speaker added, "that having now ended all they have to say, they must request to be helped on their journey homewards (to Onondaga) with horses, from Tulpehocken to *Meehayomy*."

According to Heckewelder, Wyoming is a corruption of *M'cheuwami*, a Delaware word signifying *large plains*.

It almost appears as if Wyoming (written also *Wyomen*, *Wyomink*, *Wyomik*) were the English approximation to the Indian *Meehayomy*. The word *M'cheuwami* does not occur in the records of transactions between the Governor of Pennsylvania and the Indians. Conrad Weisser uses the name *Skehandowana* in a narrative of a journey to Onondaga, undertaken in February of 1737. On his return from the great capital he writes, under date of *April* 26, 1737: "We reached *Skehandowana*, where a number of Indians live,—*Shawanos* and *Mahickanders*. Found there two traders from New York, and three men from the Maqua country, who were hunting land; their names are Ludwig Rasselman, Martin Dillenbach, and Piet de Niger. *Here there is a large body of land, the like of which is not to be found on the river*." Writing to Governor Morris, in December of 1755, Weisser reports that the Indians with whom he had conferred at John Harris's Ferry, had told him that the French were influencing the Delawares living at Nescopec, half-way from Shamokin to *Schandowana*, or *Wy-*

Iroquois, and a people wholly ignorant of and averse to Christians and Christianity. Here there are also villages

---

omick. In a speech made by deputies of the Six Nations at a meeting with Sir William Johnson, in July of the above-mentioned year, the speaker said, "the land which reaches down from Oswego to *Schahandowana*, we beg may not be settled by Christians."

There were Indian towns at different times on both sides of the river. The Shawanese, with whom Zinzendorf desired to treat, had their cabins on the flats west of the Susquehanna,—now the site of Plymouth, or Shawnee. Near the northern limit of the valley, on the same side of the river, was a village inhabited principally by Mohicans. In 1751, some Nanticokes, outliers of the tribe, which had migrated from Maryland, and settled at the mouth of the Juniata in 1742, were residing in the lower part of the valley, on the eastern shore. The Six Nations continued to guard this favorite spot with jealous care until its evacuation, in 1756, by the mixture of Indians who were residing there with their consent. Up to this time they reiterated their request, and stated their determination "that these lands should not be settled, but reserved for a place of retreat to such as in this time of war and confusion between the French and English might be obliged to leave their habitations; and that there was no part of their lands that lay so convenient as Wyomink for a number to live together." And in December of 1754, their viceroy, John Petty Shikellimy, complained to Governor Morris, "that some foreigners and strangers who live on the other side of New York, and have nothing to do in these parts, are coming like flocks of birds to disturb us in our possession of them."

In February of 1756, an Indian scout reported to government that there were three towns in the valley,—one inhabited by Delawares, another by Shawanese, and a third by Six Nation Indians, Chikasaws and Mohicans. At this time it was Teedyuscung's head-quarters. Three months afterwards, he and his Indians left for Diahoga.

Pursuant to a request made by the Delaware King at a treaty held at Easton (July 25—August 7, 1757), that government would assist him and his people in making a settlement in Wyoming, instructing them how to build houses, etc. (Prov. Records, vii. 678), Governor Denny appointed John Hughes, Edward Shippen, James Galbraith, and Charles Beaty, Commissioners "to construct a fort there, and build

inhabited exclusively by Mohicans, besides a mixed population of Indians.

At the first place I designed making a short stay; at the second I proposed sojourning eight days; and at the third about three weeks; my object being to see and learn the condition of the Indians there, and to try what could be done for the Saviour, without exposing myself rashly to dangers.

The Six Nations of the Iroquois are admirable warriors in their way,—faithful as friends, but implacable as foes; and yet even in the latter relation they act honorably. If, for instance, the ambassador of a hostile tribe which has violated national law, appear before the great Council at Onondaga, he pays the penalty of his presumption by suffering summary death. If, however, he first apply to the Senecas, —who control all matters of war,—they either furnish him with an escort to the capital, or else reprimand him as follows: "Your people have been guilty of an unpardonable offence in murdering our ambassador. We could retaliate by taking your life, but this would be base. Begone, therefore, to your country. There we will meet you, and chastise you."

These Indians perpetuate the memory of their heroes in heroic poems, which are so accurately handed down orally,

---

as many houses as shall be necessary for the present residence, security, and protection of the Indians from their enemies."

In the spring of 1758, "Teedyuscung's town" was finished. It stood a little below the site of Wilkesbarre. Scull's Map of 1759 notes it *Wioming*. This was the last Indian settlement in the historic Valley of the Five Nations. Here Teedyuscung was burnt in his lodge on the night of the 19th of April, 1763, and hence the Indians fled in October of the same year, after having struck the last blow for the possession of the "Great Plains," when, on the 15th of the month, they fell upon the whites, who a year before had come from Connecticut, and built and planted upon their "perpetual reserve."

that it is impossible for any one to boast of feats which he has not performed. The Black Prince* of Onondaga is a terrible savage. On one occasion he broke into the stockaded castle of the enemy, scalped the inhabitants, and escaped unhurt. While on a visit to Colonel Nicolls, one of the colonel's servants poured water on him. With a thrust of his knife, the enraged Indian stabbed the man in the stomach, so that he fell dead at his feet. Straightway he informed Nicolls of what had occurred. "This act," said the latter, "would be regarded a capital offence in Europe?" "With us," retorted the Prince, "trifling with a warrior, is regarded a capital offence, and hence I slew your man. If death is decreed me, here I am; do with me, according to your laws." The Prince is still living.

My dear Caxhayton† is still a member of the great Council at Onondaga. I will give you an instance of the equitable manner in which this body of legislators administers justice. It was through them that the difficulties which Captain John‡ had raised about our right to the Nazareth tract, were satisfactorily adjusted. We had offered to buy his claim. This Governor Thomas forbade us to do, as something had transpired, which in that case would implicate government. John and other Indians who like him were squatters, having leagued together, informed the Proprietaries that they would not abandon their settlements, that they would defend themselves in case an attempt were made to eject them, adding that the Six Nations were pledged to sustain them. Some time after this

---

* Quære—The *Black Briar*, mentioned by Conrad Weisser as a Sachem at Onondaga in 1745?

† A private counsellor of Cannassatego, Sachem of the Onondagas.

‡ Captain John, a Delaware, son of old Captain Harris, of Pocopoco, and half-brother of Teedyuscung.

(it was in June), Sachems of the Onondagas, Senecas, and Tuscaroras came to Philadelphia. There were no Maquas present. In treaties relative to the sale of lands they seldom take part, as they have long since bartered away for rum their interest in the estates of the Confederacy. The deputies brought complaint against the government of Maryland for the remissness of the whites in that colony in paying for lands taken by them from the Indians.* This induced Gov. Thomas† to write to Annapolis;‡ whence, in consequence of his representation, an ambassador, empowered by that government to render satisfaction, was sent to Shamokin. The Governor next brought before the consideration of the Sachems the case of Captain John and

---

* "We have further to observe," continued Canassatego, "with respect to the lands lying on the west side of the Susquehanna, that though brother Onas has paid us for what his people possess, yet some parts of that country have been taken up by persons whose place of residence is to the south of this Province, from whom we have never received any consideration. You will inform the person whose people are seated on our lands, that that country belongs to us in right of conquest. We have bought it with our blood, and taken it from our enemies in fair war; and we expect, as owners of that land, to receive such a consideration for it as the land is worth. We desire you will press him to send us a positive answer. Let him say yes or no; if he says yes, we will treat with him; if no, we are able to do ourselves justice, and we will do it by going to take payment on ourselves."—*Minutes of Provincial Council, July* 7, 1742.

† George Thomas, "Lieutenant-Governor of the Province of Pennsylvania and of the Counties of New Castle, Kent, and Sussex, on Delaware," for the Proprietaries, John and Thomas Penn, from June, 1738, to June, 1747, in which year he returned to England.

‡ "It was the opinion of the Board that the Governor write to Gov. Ogle, of Maryland, without delay, to inform him of the Indians' complaint and threats, and to request a satisfactory answer, and that his letter be sent by a special messenger at the public expense."—*Minutes of Provincial Council, July* 8, 1742.

others. After having examined the drafts and deeds of purchase, and having satisfied themselves that the lands in dispute had been justly bought, they summoned the Delawares to appear and answer for their intrusion. The latter alleged in defense that the English had deceived them, that they had cheated them out of their lands, and were treating them like dogs, adding, that they would retaliate. Hereupon the Iroquois, addressing the Delawares, said:—"Cousins, you are a contentious people. The lands have been justly bought of us by the English. You have no right to them, and we order you to leave. Brother *Onas** allotted seats to you on the other side of the Blue Mountain. But even there some of you have given us trouble. You are all children, devoid of understanding, and unable to govern yourselves. Therefore we now order you to come up to Shamokin, where you will be under our immediate oversight." The Delawares, hereupon, asked time for consideration; and a few weeks ago an ambassador from them arrived here and brought the following reply: "Uncles, you spoke the truth when you said that we were children, devoid of understanding, and unable to govern ourselves. We confess that we do not know what to do, and what not to do, and that we need fathers and guardians to watch over and counsel us. We thank you for your reproof, and next spring we will come here and occupy the lands you promised to give us."

Friday, September 21, 1742. We met in conference at Bethlehem, in the course of which Brother Anton† installed

* *Onas.*—"Onas, signifying a *quill*, in the language of the Five Nations, is the name they give the Governors of Pennsylvania, since it was first settled by William Penn."—*Minutes of Provincial Council, September* 10, 1722.

† Anton Seyffert.

Huber* into the office of Vice-elder. We concluded Benigna had better not accompany us, as the journey was likely to be fatiguing and dangerous. After having taken affectionate leave of her, of Anton, and of Rosina,† we set out, and took the road to Tulpehocken,‡ keeping between Long Swamp§ and the Oley Hills.|| We rode on until late at night. Before we reached our place of destination it grew dark as pitch, and riding became very difficult. I

---

* John Michael Huber, from the Tyrol, came to Pennsylvania with the first colony of Brethren in June of 1742. Lost at sea in a hurricane on the passage to St. Thomas, in October of 1747, along with the missionaries Joseph and Mary Shaw.

† Rosina, wife of Bishop David Nitschmann, came to America with Zinzendorf in December of 1741. She was appointed Eldress of the Bethlehem congregation in June of 1742.

‡ *Tulpehocken* originally comprised the lands lying along the creek of that name, now in the counties of Berks and Lebanon. It is here used to designate Heidelberg Township, in which Conrad Weisser resided.

§ *Long Swamp*, now a township in the southeastern part of Berks County. It is noted on Scull's map of 1759.

|| The Oley Hills are a continuation of the South Mountain, and terminate at Reading. *Oley* (Swedish ?), also called *Malothon*, *Moletten*, *Molatton* (now a township of Berks County, west of the *Manatawny*), was settled by the Swedes prior to 1700. About 1712 the *De Turcks*, the *Bertolets*, the *De Levans*, the *De Langs*, and other French Huguenots from Esopus, took up farms in Oley. With these, and also with John and Henry Leimbach and other families, the Brethren became acquainted through Eschenbach. As Oley was within his circuit, Zinzendorf, on his first tour through the German settlements southwest of Bethlehem, preached there, in Mr. John Bertolet's house, on second Christmas, 1741.

In 1745 a school for boys and girls was opened by the Brethren on the farm of John Leimbach. In 1750 a building for that purpose was erected by them, and dedicated, in December of the year, by Gottlieb Pezold. In July of 1751 the school was discontinued. The house is said to be still standing. Several of the Leimbachs removed to Moravian settlements in North Carolina in 1765.

was struck on the cheek and on the left eye by the limb of a tree, and several of the Sisters fell from their horses. No one, however, was seriously injured. At last we entered the borders of Oley, and reached Brother Bürstler's* house. As the family were in bed and asleep, we awakened them by singing "*Herr Zebaoth*,"† whereupon they recognized their visitors, and gave us a hearty reception.

Sept. 22. Came as far as Henry Leimbach's.‡ Here we laid over, as I was expecting the Elder,§ and as it was Saturday. I retired into my private apartment to attend to

---

* Jacob Bürstler, a Palatine. In 1747 he had 102 acres of land on the Lehigh Mountain patented him by the three Penns. This he sold to the Brethren in 1749. Still residing in Oley in 1755, in the spring of which year his wife came to Bethlehem to instruct the girls of "The Family" in the manufacture of straw hats.

† "Herr Zebaoth!
Du wahrer Gott der Kreatur!
Gott, Schöpfer der Natur!
Gott, der die ganze Welt erhält!
Und was verdarb
Mit Blut erwarb
Und heiliget,—
Sey von uns angebet!

"So wahr Du lebst,
Und dich erhebst auf Cherubim,
Und blendst die Seraphim,
Und der Jehova bist und Christ;—
So bleibt dein Blut
Das höchste Gut
Der Sünderschaar;—
Du bist uns alles gar!"

"*Hymnus der Gemeine zu Bethlehem, mit der See-Gemeine vollendet*," June 13, 1742.

‡ Henry Leimbach accompanied the Count and his companions as far as Olstonwakin.

§ Anton Seyffert.

correspondence and to official business, although I was indisposed, as I had been since leaving Bethlehem. We fitted Sr. Molther* out for Europe, confirmed Pyrlaeus's† appointment to Philadelphia,‡ and Büttner's§ to Shecomeco. I had a long and edifying conversation with Antes,|| who had come specially to see me, about our work in general.

---

* Johanna Sophia Molther, wife of Philip H. Molther, who at this time was laboring in England with Spangenberg. She had come to America with Anna Nitschmann in December of 1740, to aid Andrew Eschenbach in the cause of home missions among the destitute German immigrants. Deceased at Herrnhut in 1800.

† John Christopher Pyrlaeus.

‡ As minister of the gospel among the Lutherans.

§ Büttner left Bethlehem for his new field on the 4th October, 1742.

|| *Henry Antes*, wheelwright and farmer in "Falkner's Swamp," now Frederic Township, Montgomery County, became acquainted with the Brethren through Spangenberg, while the latter was residing at Christopher Wiegner's, in Skippack, between 1736 and 1739. Until his decease in 1755, Mr. Antes maintained friendly relations with the Brethren, and for five years (1745–1750) resided with his family at Bethlehem. Here he was intrusted with the secular affairs of the settlement, superintending the erection of buildings and mills both at that place, on the Nazareth tract, and at the Mahoning Station. His farm and house were in the mean time rented by the Brethren, and the latter used as a school for boys. So great was the confidence they reposed in him, that they had the deeds to their first purchases of lands drawn up in his name, they being prevented, as foreigners, from having any legal title to them. In 1752 he accompanied Bishop Spangenberg on a tour of exploration into the wilds of North Carolina. He deceased on his farm on the 20th of July, 1755. A number of official Brethren from Bethlehem attended his funeral, and Spangenberg, in the course of the services, bore public testimony to the Christian worth of the pious layman of Frederic Township. His children were educated at the schools of the Brethren. Margaret, a daughter, accompanied Zinzendorf to Europe in January of 1743, and was married to Benjamin Latrobe at Herrnhut in April of 1756. John, a son, united with the Brethren at Bethlehem in 1752, and entered the service of his adopted

Sept. 23. Antes preached with unction. After service we set out for Tulpehocken. On the way we concluded that Böhler should accompany us. The Indian Joshua resolved to go with us also. As we were riding along we met Weisser, accompanied by an English Justice of the Peace and an Anabaptist preacher. The latter plied me with curious questions, which I declined answering. I came to the conclusion that the Baptists are the Inquisitors of Christianity. Conrad pointed out a remarkable spring,* the largest in this section of country, covering an acre of ground, and fifteen feet deep. It drives a mill at its very outlet.

In Tulpehocken I had a slight contest with Satan about the sacraments. A fierce fight was imminent, but a few hours removed the occasion of offence. I changed my plan in reference to Meurer,† and felt dispirited. His hearers

---

church. Pursuant to a call to Cairo, he started for London in the spring of 1769. Here he embarked for Alexandria. At Cairo he met the missionaries Hocker and Danke, awaiting a favorable season for an entrance into Upper Egypt, where they designed to missionate among the Copts. The intelligence which the traveler Bruce brought to them, on his return from Abyssinia in 1773, of the implacable animosity of the Copts against all Christians, discouraged them from making any attempt in that field. In 1781, John Antes was recalled to Europe. He deceased at Bristol, England, December 11, 1811.

* *Sinking Spring*, five miles southwest of Reading.

† John Philip Meurer, from Alsace, came to Pennsylvania in June of 1742. Succeeded G. Büttner in the ministry among one party of Lutherans, who had requested Zinzendorf on his first visit to Tulpehocken, in February of 1742, to supply them with a pastor. In 1745 left, and labored in the gospel successively in Donegal, Lebanon, along the Swatara, in York, Oley, Salzburg, and Lynn. Deceased at Bethlehem in April, 1760. The log-church at which the Brethren at first preached in Tulpehocken had been built about 1730, and was four miles from Weisser's house. In 1744 they erected a place of worship on Tobias Böckel's farm, which was consecrated in April of 1745 by

presume to rank him equal with, and even superior to Büttner or Eschenbach.* I conferred on him temporary powers as minister of the gospel by giving him a written certificate to that effect, and this satisfied them. I feel convinced that he will discharge his new functions with acceptance and blessing.

The plan I had proposed for the journey was somewhat disconcerted by two circumstances which transpired while I was here. In the first place, a message was brought to Conrad, in reference to his embassy to Shamokin in the interests of the government of Maryland, by which we learned that Governor Thomas endeavored by all the means in his power to dissuade him from accompanying me. The Governor even went so far as to urge him to weigh the insignificance of my journey with the importance of the services he could render him as his partisan in the disagreement existing between him and the Assembly. The expressions made use of by the Governor were highly unbecoming a person in his position. Conrad, however, after some hesitation, resolved to accompany me. A second source of

---

Spangenberg, and the log-church reverted to the Lutherans. This was the *Heidelberg* church. Ellert Coortsen was the last incumbent. He left in 1795.

* Andrew Eschenbach, from Naumburg, was sent to Pennsylvania by the Brethren to continue the work that Spangenberg had initiated among the Germans, as well as to second Whitefield in his great religious movement among a population that his preaching failed to reach. Eschenbach arrived at Philadelphia in October of 1740. Setting out from here, he preached the gospel at Germantown, in Skippack, Fredericktown, Oley, Conestoga, Tulpehocken, Heidelberg, and along Mill Creek, preparing the way for Moravian settlements in most of these neighborhoods. He was, therefore, the pioneer in the work of home-missions, to which the Brethren devoted themselves with surprising energy between 1742 and 1750. In 1747, Eschenbach withdrew from their communion. Deceased on his farm, in Oley, in 1763.

annoyance was the intelligence I had received of the Neuberts'* arrival from England, of their inopportune stay at Philadelphia, and of the sensation they had caused at Bethlehem by having brought with them an adopted child.

Dated—In tent on the bank of the Otschtonwaky (Loyal Sock), en route for the Shawanese and other Indians of Skehandowana, Oct. 3, 1742.

Sept. 24. Set out from Weisser's,† and in the evening came to a log-house at the foot of the Kittatinny,‡ or Blue Mountain. Just before we reached the end of the day's journey, and not far from our contemplated stopping-place, a man met us, and in a very friendly way offered us a bottle of wine. Weisser remarked that as he was aged he perhaps wished to do one more good act in his life. I, however, ascertained, before we left the house at which we lodged, that he had a petty suit-at-law pending, and as Weisser was a Justice of the Peace, he evidently wished to conciliate him.§

---

* Daniel and Hannah Neubert.

† Near Womelsdorf.

‡ Written also *Kechkachtany*, *Kittochtinny*, Delaware, signifying *endless hills*.

§ The route taken by the travelers from Weisser's to Shamokin, was probably the same that the interpreter had followed on his memorable journey to Onondaga, in February of 1739, by which Spangenberg had traveled thither in 1745, and which is traced on an old map of Pennsylvania, drawn by the Brethren to show the various neighborhoods and points in the Province where they labored. In 1742 this route still lay within the Counties of Lancaster and Philadelphia, bearing away from Heidelberg, or Tulpehocken, about forty miles to the northwest. The passage of the "first Blue Mountain" was effected at the Great Swatara Gap in Lebanon County, called *Tolheo* by the Indians, corrupted into "*The Hole*." Here *Bethel* was commenced a few years later, and here in 1754 there was erected a block-house, gar-

Sept. 25. The weather was very unpleasant. We crossed an exceedingly high mountain,* which was almost impass-

risoned by Captain Busse's Company of the Pennsylvania Battalion, commanded by Lieut.-Col. Weisser. From this point the road led through an Alpine region of country over the successive ridges that run parallel to the Kittatinny, over *Second, Third, Peters's, Berry's,* and *Mahantango* Mountains, in Dauphin, and over *Line* and *Mahanoy* Mountains, in Northumberland. The *Wicomsco, Mahantango, Mahanoy,* and *Shamokin* Creeks were the largest streams that lay in the way. Weisser has the following record in his journal: "*Feb.* 28, 1737.—We remained at *Tolheo* on account of bad weather, and to procure some necessaries for the journey. *March* 1, we set out from *Tolheo*, which is the last place in the inhabited part of Pennsylvania, and the same day we reached the top of the *Kiditanny* Mountain. The snow was about a foot deep. The 2d and 3d, we found nothing but ice under the new-fallen snow on the north side of the mountain, which caused dangerous falls to ourselves and horses. The 4th, we reached *Shamokin.*"

The map of Pennsylvania alluded to above, notes the places at which the Count and his fellow-travelers halted on the journey, in the following order: *Ludwig's Fountain* (south of Swatara Gap), *The Hole, Erdmuth's Spring, Ludwig's Rest, Anna's Valley, Benigna's Creek, The Double Eagle, Jacob's Heights, Fürstenberg, Königsberg,* and *Shamokin.* Most of these names were probably given by the Count for present and absent friends.

Spangenberg's journal is more explicit in the enumeration of the stations. He writes as follows: "*May* 31, 1745.—Set out from Tulpehocken, crossed the *Great Swatara*, and climbed the steep and rocky *Thürnstein.* On its summit drank of *Erdmuth's Spring*, descended the mountain, and nooned at *Ludwig's Rest.* Next came to *Anna's Valley*, and encamped on *Benigna's Creek* (quære—the *Mahantango?*), near '*The Double Eagle.*' *June* 1st.—Crossed *Leimbach's Creek* (quære—the *Mahanoy?*), ascended *Jacob's Heights*, and at noon struck the Susquehanna, fifteen miles south of *Shamokin.* Now passed through *Joseph's Valley.* Having rested at *Marienborn*, we climbed the steep *Spangenberg*, crossed *Eve's Creek* (the Shamokin), and arrived at Shamokin."

* Quære—*Third Mountain?* Zinzendorf was also Count and Lord

able on account of rocks and sharp stones. As the ridge had no name, and as it lay in the route usually traveled by Weisser and by the Six Nations, he named it *Thürnstein.* The forest here was of high growth, composed chiefly of the tallest hemlocks, and we were about entering upon a very wild region of country. We fixed our first encampment on the journey at the foot of the mountain, and passed the night comfortably in the spacious tent with which we were provided.

Sept. 26. We passed a memorial stone that had been set up by an Iroquois brave. On it was a delineation of his person so accurately executed as even to represent the lines cut in upon his face. Besides, he had affixed strokes of red, black, and white paint, respectively indicating the different fights in which he had been engaged; the red strokes by their number denoting his victories, the black his defeats, and the white the drawn battles in which he had contended. At Conrad Weisser's Creek we had passed a stone with a similar painting, from the character of which we discerned that the hero who had erected it belonged to the Wolf tribe or division of Indians, for they are divided into three, called the *Wolf*, the *Bear*, and the *Turtle.* Not far from the same place we saw also the tomb of a hero. On this day we met with fewer difficulties on the road, but had to encamp for the night in a savage wilderness, and David grew fretful.

Sept. 28. The word of Scripture which had been allotted us as a subject for meditation contained a promise of en-

---

of Pottendorf, and Lord of the Baronies of Freydeck, Schöneck, and *Thürnstein.* The latter was the name he retained when, soon after his arrival in Pennsylvania, he renounced his rank so as to screen the name of Zinzendorf from the opprobrium he feared would be cast upon it by the assaults of his detractors.—See *Büdingische Sammlung*, Part xv. No. 17.

courågement. I remarked that we would see this promise fulfilled before night, as the Lord designed to encourage us by permitting us to meet Shikellimy.* "That is im-

---

* Shikellimy, alias *Swatane*, an Oneida chief of the *Oquacho*, or Wolf tribe of Indians, was in 1728 acting representative of the Five Nations in business affairs with the Proprietary government. About 1745 he was appointed their vicegerent, and in this capacity administered their tributaries within the Province, with Shamokin for his seat. It was because of the large influence he came in this way to wield that the English always courted his favor, and this they ever retained. Scarce a treaty (and these were of frequent occurrence between 1728 and 1748, respecting the purchase of lands) but Shikellimy was present, and by his moderate counsels aided in an amicable solution of the intricate questions with which these conferences were concerned. The acquaintance which Zinzendorf made with him was carefully followed up by the Brethren, and ripened into a friendship which ceased only with the death of the noble old chief. In the summer of 1745 he was Spangenberg's escort to Onondaga. During a stay of three weeks at Bethlehem, prior to setting out on the journey, he formally adopted several of the leading Brethren into the Indian race by naming them for distinguished chiefs, an act which conferred privileges as well as honor upon the recipients. Spangenberg received the name *T'gir-hitontie*, "a row of trees," on the way to Onondaga. It was at Shikellimy's request that the Brethren built a smithy at Shamokin in 1747, which then became the central point of their operations along the Susquehanna. Marx Kieffer, the resolute blacksmith, kept to his anvil here until late in October of 1755, and was the last white man to leave the doomed region, in which the sudden appearance of French Indians, painted for war, betokened the approach of the storm that was soon to sweep the defenseless borders of the Province.

"On the 6th of October, 1747, I set out for Shamokin, by the way of Paxtang, because the weather was bad. I arrived at Shamokin on the 9th, about noon. I was surprised to see Shikellimy in such a miserable condition as ever my eyes beheld; he was hardly able to stretch out his hand to bid me welcome; in the same condition was his wife, his three sons not quite so bad; also one of his daughters, and two or three of his grandchildren, all had the fever; there were three buried out of the family a few days before, viz.,—Cajadies, Shi-

possible," said Conrad. "Shikellimy can, under no circumstances, return to Shamokin within six weeks." This he said, as the Sachem had undertaken a journey to Onondaga in the interests of Maryland, and not a week had elapsed since he had parted with him at Tulpehocken.

We traveled on, and soon struck the lovely Susquehanna. Riding along its bank, we came to the boundary of Shamokin, a precipitous hill, such as I scarce ever saw. I was reminded by it of Wenzel Neisser's experience in Italy. Anna,* who is the most courageous of our number, and a

---

kellimy's son-in-law, that had been married to his daughter above fifteen years, and reckoned the best hunter among all the Indians; also his oldest son's wife, and his grandchild. Next morning, I administered the medicines to Shikellimy and one of his sons, under the direction of Doctor Graeme, which had a very good effect upon both. Shikellimy was able to walk about with me with a stick in his hand before I left Shamokin, which was on the 12th, in the afternoon."—*C. Weiser to Provincial Council.*

Shikellimy died at Shamokin, December 17, 1748, in the presence of a daughter, and of the missionary, David Zeisberger, who had attended him in his illness. Several days after his decease, his second son, Logan, returned home from a far-off journey, to weep over the lifeless body of the parent he so much esteemed. The Brethren, Zeisberger and Henry Fry, made him a coffin, and the Indians, having painted the corpse in gay colors, and decked it with the choicest ornaments, carried the remains of their honored chieftain to the burial-place of his fathers on the banks of the "Winding River."

Shikellimy was succeeded in the vicegerency by his oldest son, *Tachnachdoarus*, "a spreading oak," alias *John Shikellimy*. His second son was *James Logan*, named for Secretary Logan, of Germantown. Logan was lame. *John Petty* was the youngest of the three brothers, and bore the name of an Indian-trader.

* Anna Nitschmann, born 1715, at Kunewalde, in Moravia, was the daughter of David Nitschmann, Sr., a Moravian confessor, and a fugitive from Roman Catholic persecution. Fled to Herrnhut with her parents in 1725. While here, she became the subject of deep religious impressions, was admitted into communion with the Brethren, and,

heroine, led in the descent. I took the train of her riding-habit in my hand to steady me in the saddle, Conrad held to the skirt of my overcoat, and Böhler to Conrad's. In this way we mutually supported each other, and the Saviour assisted us in descending the hill in safety. Toward evening we reached Shamokin, where Conrad, to his surprise, met Shikellimy, by whom he was welcomed to the town.

While the tent was being pitched, I took a stroll. An Indian whom I chanced to meet presented me with a melon,

---

before having attained her fifteenth year, filled the responsible office of Eldress of the congregation. In 1736 she left Herrnhut, and with others accompanied Count Zinzendorf into banishment to the Castle of Ronneburg, near Frankfort-on-the-Main. The next year she spent in England. In 1740 she sailed for Pennsylvania, in company with her father, Christian Fröhlich, David Nitschmann, *Episc.*, and Johanna S. Molther. Here she and Molther traveled through the rural districts, laboring in spiritual things among the females and children of the different and distant neighborhoods which constituted Eschenbach's circuit. So as not to be a burden to the hard-working people among whom she missionated, she assisted them in the labors of the house and of the farm; for Anna Nitschmann was the daughter of a peasant, and had often watched her father's sheep in the pastures of Kunewalde. On Zinzendorf's arrival in Pennsylvania, she repaired to Philadelphia, and thence to Germantown, where, in company with his daughter Benigna, she was employed in the Brethren's school for children. "In 1742," she writes in her autobiography, "we were three times among the Indians. The last journey was into the heart of their country, where we sojourned forty-nine days, encamping under the open heavens in a savage wilderness, amid wild beasts and venomous snakes." She returned to England with Zinzendorf. The interval of her life between 1743 and 1756 was passed in England and on the Continent. In June of 1757, not long after the decease of Countess Erdmuth, she became Zinzendorf's consort, and on the 21st of May, 1760, followed the man at whose side she had labored many years in the cause of Christ's kingdom, into the eternal world. Several of her sacred lyrics are in the authorized collection of German hymns in use in the Brethren's Church, and are incomparably beautiful.

in return for which I gave him my fur cap. I also met Shikellimy. The Viceroy took my hand in his, pressed it repeatedly, and then turned to Weisser, "*to steal my mission,*" as the Indians say; in other words, to sound him as to what proposals I intended to make. The latter reiterated what he had already told him, saying that I was a servant of the living God; that as such I wrought in a different way from others of that class who had called upon him, and that I taught mercy and grace, and not works or moral duties, as a ground of pardon or justification. Shikellimy hereupon expressed his pleasure at the arrival of such a messenger among his people, and then took Conrad into his lodge.

On returning to the tent from my stroll, I found Jeannette engaged in conversation with a Mohican woman. They conversed in Indian. I was surprised at meeting a Mohican at Shamokin, and more so on learning that the woman was the sister of Nannachdausch, who had built my hut at Shecomeco, and who had been my provider while there. This was a trifling coincidence; but *Shikellimy's presence I interpreted as a special divine token.* I need not say it was opportune, for Joshua was indisposed, and David was disheartened on account of the fatigues of the journey, and we needed encouragement.

The train of circumstances which had resulted in Shikellimy's unexpected and early return to Shamokin, was this. While on the way to Onondaga he had met Caxhayton, the Indian with whom I became acquainted at Philadelphia. Shikellimy deputed him to convey the dispatches with which he had been intrusted to the Iroquois, notifying the latter that the bearer had been duly authorized. Thus he was at liberty to return; and at the same time he brought word to Weisser from the Shawanese King at Skehandowana, that he wished to see him once more before he died.

On the previous evening, while reprimanding David, I had almost stepped into a pitfall, when, although I had been severe in my remarks, he kindly pointed out the danger.

Sept. 29. Shikellimy came into my tent. Seating myself between him and Conrad, I requested an audience. It having been granted, I proceeded to explain the object of my visit, stating that already in early childhood I had been favored with an intimate acquaintance with God, with his being and with his attributes, and that I had come hither in order to reveal this knowledge to the Indians. Where, or in what tribe I would begin to teach, I had not yet determined; it being my custom, I continued, to instruct only such as God himself had already addressed, and who felt the need of some one to interpret to them the meaning of the words He had spoken. In reply, he said that he approved of my object, and expressed a willingness at the same time to aid me in its accomplishment.

I next observed that his own case was an illustration in point, and went on to relate my experience. "My early return home and your arrival here simultaneously," responded the Sachem, "are an extraordinary coincidence. I believe it was preordained." Hereupon, perceiving that he had no shirt, I handed him one, begging him to accept it as a token of my childlike intercourse with him, and not as a gift. "I thank you," he replied, as he took it.

I will now proceed to describe Shikellimy more fully As the Iroquois Sachems were about setting out for home, after my interview with them in Tulpehocken, I took occasion to study their peculiarities. One of them in particular arrested my attention. I was irresistibly drawn toward him, and I longed to tell him of the Saviour. "He is my choice," I remarked to Conrad (presuming the man to be Canassatego, of whom he had just spoken to me in the highest terms).

"He is the Onondaga Sachem, I presume?" "No," replied Conrad, "he is Shikellimy, the Oneida." These words, I confess, disconcerted me, as it was altogether improbable that we would visit the Oneida country. On learning, however, that Shikellimy resided at Shamokin (which town we intended to visit on the way to the Shawanese), I was reassured, and I also regarded our final determination not to journey to the Mohawks as significantly providential.

On the road hither, I spoke much of Shikellimy, and of the hopes I entertained of enlisting him in my service. Weisser persisted in assuring me that, in consequence of his prior engagements, the Sachem would be absent, and hence it was presumption in me to reckon on his co-operation. He spoke so positively, that I was almost inclined to believe that Satan was bent upon foiling me.

"As you appear to be fascinated by this Indian," said Conrad, "I will relate you an incident, which will serve to illustrate his character. While on a journey to Onondaga, whither I had been sent to negotiate a peace between the Iroquois and the Cherokees,* and while passing through a

* "The Hon. James Logan, the President, acquainted the Board, that not long after receiving, on the 20th of Dec'r last (1736), the letter from the Governor of Virginia on the subject of negotiating a peace between the Indians of the Six Nations and the Southern Indians,—the Cherokees and Catawbas,—he, the President, had an opportunity of seeing Conrad Weisser in this place, and judging him, from the experience this government has had of his honesty and fidelity, to be the most proper person to carry to the Six Nations the message proposed in that letter, he, the President, engaged Weisser to undertake the business, and gave him proper instructions to that end; that being returned, he, in his own words and handwriting, had given a very distinct and satisfactory account of the errand he was sent on, in a paper, which being laid before the Board and read,—the answer of the Six Nations is, in substance, that they were ready and willing to treat and conclude a peace with their enemies, the Southern Indians, and proposed Albany for the place of meeting, where they desired their Brother Onas might

savage wilderness, I was one day so completely exhausted that I left my companions, and sat down by a tree, resolved to die. Starvation stared me in the face, and death by freezing was preferable to death by hunger. They hallooed and shot signal-guns, but I remained quiet.

"Shikellimy was the first one to discover me. Coming before me, he stood in deep thought, and in silence, and after some time asked me why I was there. 'I am here to die,' I replied. 'Ah! brother,' said he, 'only lately you entreated us not to despond, and will you now give way to despair?' Not in the least shaken in my resolution by this appeal, I replied by saying, 'My good Shikellimy, as death is inevitable, I will die where I am, and nothing shall prevail upon me to leave this spot.' 'Ah! brother,' resumed the Sachem, 'you told me that we were prone to forget God in bright days, and to remember him in dark days. These are dark days. Let us then not forget God; and who knows but what He is even now near, and about to come to our succor? Rise, brother! and we will journey on.' I felt ashamed at this rebuke administered by a poor heathen, rose, and dragged myself away.

"Two days after this occurrence we reached Onondaga."*

---

be present, and that they had agreed to a cessation of arms for one year."—*Minutes of Provincial Council, May* 12, 1737.

* "In the year 1737 I was sent the first time to Onondaga, at the desire of the governor of Virginia. I departed in the latter end of February very unexpectedly for a journey of 500 English miles, through a wilderness where there was neither road nor path, and at such a time of the year when animals could not meet with food. There were with me a Dutchman and three Indians.

"On the 9th of April I found myself extremely weak, through the fatigues of so long a journey with cold and hunger which I had suffered. There having fallen a fresh snow about twenty inches deep, and we being yet three days' journey from Onondaga in a frightful wilderness, my spirit failed, my body trembled and shook, and I

Such was Shikellimy, the Sachem who had arrested my attention in Tulpehocken, and with whom I had been brought into contact by the Providence of the Lamb.

Meanwhile the Lord was trying our faith; for David, who was disheartened on account of the length and fatigues of the journey, declared his inability to proceed farther, and Joshua fell sick. David's conduct displeased me. Perceiving that he was growing irritable, I advised him, by all means, to turn back in time. He said he would. And yet he remained sullen. I accordingly took him to task, and although I did this severely, I found that I effected nothing as long as I failed to convict him of the true cause of his conduct. The moment I did this, however, he manifested contrition, grew cheerful, kissed my hand, and became perfectly docile.

I desire to impress the Brethren with the necessity of exercising patience and wisdom in their intercourse with the Indians, and of abstaining from conjecture when adducing the reasons of things, which reasons the latter already know, as they fail to discriminate between emotions

---

thought I should fall down and die. I stepped aside, and sat down under a tree, expecting there to die. My companions soon missed me. The Indians came back and found me sitting there. They remained awhile silent; at last the old Indian said, 'My dear companion, thou hast hitherto encouraged us; wilt thou now quite give up? Remember that evil days are better than good days, for when we suffer much we do not sin; *sin will be driven out of us by suffering*, and God cannot extend his mercy to the former; but contrary-wise, when it goeth evil with us, God has compassion on us.' These words made me ashamed. I rose up and traveled as well as I could."—*Conrad Weisser to a Friend*, 1746.

These words of Shikellimy, reported by Spangenberg to Christian David, in a letter from Towamensing, dated November 19, 1737, moved several of the young Brethren at Marienborn, among whom was *Christian H. Rauch*, to consecrate themselves to the work of missions among the North American Indians.

of the mind, and incentives to action, that are opposite in their character. Excepting when they look full into the wounds of the Lamb, their expression of countenance is dark and sombre. The indigestible Indian corn that constitutes their principal diet tends to thicken their blood and to stupefy their mental faculties. I would furthermore observe that writers who represent the Indians as a more highly favored race than the whites, are too hasty in their conclusions. Perhaps the representation is made with design; at all events it is incorrect. To ascribe their custom of going naked, or at least with outer wrappings only, to a stoical indifference on their part to comfort, is altogether erroneous; it is a necessity imposed on them by beggarly poverty. The only point of difference between the Gipsy and the Indian lies in the fact, that the latter refrains from stealing from motives of fear rather than from motives of honesty; this I think is demonstrated by the eagerness with which he accepts shirts, horse-cloths, and whatever else may serve to protect his person. The Indians are averse to wearing breeches, or garments that interfere with the free use of their limbs. They also dispense with caps. The consequent exposure of the lower limbs and of the head induces disease, subjects them to fevers and to chronic headaches, afflicts them with boils, and weakens their constitutions generally. Although they are aware of this, they refuse to change their mode of dress, and live up to the truth of the adage, "*video meliora*," etc., just as we do.

Persons born in America do not, usually, live as long as the natives of other countries. A woman of forty here is old. The Indians are disposed to overestimate their age, and it is not an uncommon thing to learn from one or another that he is a hundred years old, while his neighbors assert positively that he is not much above fifty. Yet there are such as attain a high age, but their condition is truly deplorable; witness Captain John's father,* who was left to starve to death.

The Iroquois have peculiar institutions and customs. "*A tiger at home, a hare abroad,*" and "*A lion abroad, a lamb at home,*" are some of their maxims. Their mode of life is directly opposed to the spirit of Christianity, as they spend all their time in the chase or in war. The great distance† to which they carry the latter is an evidence that deep-seated revenge, and not self-defence, impels them to engage in it. Onondaga is the seat of their Parliament, or Council of Sachems or old men. They have no kings, in our acceptation of the term; but they are governed by Sachems, Judges, or old men. The word king conveys to their minds an erroneous idea of a king's authority and power, as they invariably associate with it the idea of a usurper, such as occasionally wields their Parliament at his pleasure, in virtue of his prowess, which no one is willing to contest. And yet, when speaking of the King of England, at treaties and conferences, they always style him *Sachem;* whence, I infer, that the two terms are probably synonymous in their minds. The Delawares have a hereditary monarch who is called King by the English, and the Shawanese style their chief *King;* but whether the latter is hereditary, I am unable to say. The Delawares are subjects, the Shawanese confederates, of the Six Nations. The form of government among the latter resembles that of the Romans during the time of the Consulate. In war, however, they differ from that people, in not converting conquered territory into provinces.

---

* Old Captain Harris of Pocopoco.

† "The 5 Indian Nations are the most warlike people in America @ are a bulwark between us @ the French @ all other Indians. *They goe as far as the South Sea, the North West passage @ Florida to warr.*"—*Gov. Dongan's Report to the Committee on Trade of the Province of New York, Feb.* 1687.

The Indians are proverbially revengeful, and, like the Israelites, transmit resentment to succeeding generations. Such is their repugnance to labor, that rather than engage in it they cheerfully undergo severe privation. An Indian that is given to work, you may rely upon it, is either a child of God, or else one that has been infected with the spirit of avarice, the root of all evil, by contact with the whites. It prompts him, however, merely to provide a sufficiency of clothing and of rum; the acquisition of wealth he never entertains. Our Mohicans at Shecomeco go decently clad, are cleanly in their habits and in their huts, and have forbidden rum to be brought to their village.

His continued indisposition had compelled us to leave Joshua at Shamokin, in care of Mack and his wife. The Lord so ordered.

> "Wer weisz was sie da säen,
> Dasz Er zu seiner Zeit kann gehen mäh'n!"

On *Saturday, the 28th*, we wished to pray the Litany, but the merry-making of the Indians disconcerted us. I accordingly dispatched Conrad to Sachem Shikellimy to inform him that we were about to speak to our God. This had the desired effect, and immediately on the former's return, the beating of drums ceased, and the voices of the Indians were hushed. Obedience among this people is yielded only when it is positively demanded, as they are without laws to enforce it. The Indian's national history is inscribed on his memory, and I am inclined to believe nevertheless that it is almost as reliable as our own.

Sept. 30. Set out on our journey. The Sachem pointed out the ford over the Susquehanna. This river is here much broader than the Delaware, the water beautifully transparent, and were it not for smooth rocks in its bed, it would be easily fordable. In crossing, we had therefore to pull up our horses, and keep a tight rein. The high banks of American rivers render their passage on horseback extremely difficult.

To the left of the path, after crossing the river, a large cave in a rocky hill in the wilderness was shown us. From it the surrounding country and the West Branch of the Susquehanna are called *Otzinachson*,* i.e. the "*Demon's Den*;" for here the evil spirits, say the Indians, have their seats and hold their revels.

We had ridden past scarcely two miles, when the pack-horse which carried our provisions suddenly grew restive, made a spring, broke the rope by which he was attached to Henry Leimbach's animal, and galloped headlong in the direction of the cave. This did not disconcert us otherwise than to bring us to a halt. Conrad dismounted, went in search of the horse, and found him a mile back, caught in the bushes by the rope.

The country through which we were now riding, although a wilderness, showed indications of extreme fertility. As soon as we left the path we trod on swampy ground, over which traveling on horseback was altogether impracticable. We halted half an hour while Conrad rode along the river bank in search of a ford. The foliage of the forest at this season of the year, blending all conceivable shades of green, red, and yellow, was truly gorgeous, and lent a richness to the landscape that would have charmed an artist. At times we wound through a continuous growth of diminutive oaks, reaching no higher than our horses' girths, in a perfect sea of scarlet, purple, and gold, bounded along the horizon by the gigantic evergreens of the forest.

During the journey thus far I have not seen any snakes, although the banks of the Susquehanna are said to be the resort of a species which lies on the tops of the low bushes

* Written variously, *Chenasky*, *Zinachson*, *Quinachson*, *Oxenaxa*.

in wait to spring upon the passing traveler. The country generally abounds in reptiles, bears, and other wild animals.

We camped out twice on the journey. During the second night there was a sudden and heavy fall of rain, and all our horses excepting one strayed away. As we were not far from Otstonwakin, Conrad rode to the village. He soon returned in company with Andrew,* Madame Montour's oldest son. Just then our horses came in.

Andrew's cast of countenance is decidedly European, and had not his face been encircled with a broad band of

---

* Andrew Montour, alias *Sattelihu*, was for a number of years in the employ of the Proprietaries as assistant interpreter in their negotiations with the Indians of the interior. He usually accompanied Weisser on his missions to their country, and when negotiating with Delawares, interpreted for the former, who was ignorant of the Delaware. As both spoke Mohawk, they were prepared to confer with all the Indian tribes with which the English had dealings. At the time of the Count's visit Andrew was residing on an island in the Susquehanna above Shamokin. Hence he accompanied Spangenberg to Onondaga in June of 1745. In 1748 he entered the service of the Province, and soon after requested permission to settle near the whites. "Andrew has pitched upon a place in the Proprietary's manor, at *Canataqueany*, and expects government to build him a house there, and furnish his family with necessaries. He seems to be very hard to please." (*Weisser to Richard Peters.*) In April of 1752, Governor Hamilton furnished him with a commission under the Lesser Seal, "to go and reside in Cumberland County, over the Blue Hills, on unpurchased lands, to prevent others from settling there or from trading with the Indians." In 1755 he was still residing on his grant, ten miles northwest of Carlisle, between the Conedogwinet and the mountain, and was Captain of a company of Indians in the English service. Rose to be a Major. Andrew acted as interpreter for the governor of Virginia at several important treaties. The French, in 1753, set a price of £100 upon his head. In May of 1761 he was his Majesty's Interpreter to the United Nations. He is said to have led the party of warriors who, in 1780, surprised and took captive the Gilbert family, near Lehighton.

paint, applied with bear's fat, I would certainly have taken him for one. He wore a brown broadcloth coat, a scarlet damasken lappel-waistcoat, breeches, over which his shirt hung, a black Cordovan neckerchief, decked with silver bugles, shoes and stockings, and a hat. His ears were hung with pendants of brass and other wires plaited together like the handle of a basket. He was very cordial, but on addressing him in French, he, to my surprise, replied in English.

When a short distance from the village, Andrew left us and rode ahead to notify the inhabitants of our approach. As soon as they saw us, they discharged their firearms by way of salute, and repeated this mode of welcome on our arriving at the huts. Here we dismounted and repaired to Madame Montour's* quarters. Her husband, who had

* Madame Montour, one of the characters in the history of English intercourse with the various tribes of Indians, settled along the Susquehanna or moving over that great thoroughfare of Indian travel, was a French Canadian. In early life she married Roland Montour, a Seneca brave, and on his death, *Carandowana*, alias *Robert Hunter*, chief of the Oneidas, with whom she was living on the Chenasky, probably at Otstonwakin, as early as 1727. In that year she acted as interpreter to the Province at a Conference held in Philadelphia, between Governor Gordon and Sachems of the Five Nations. Again in October of 1728. "It was afterwards considered by the Board what present might be proper to be made to Mistress Montour and her husband, Carandowana; and it was agreed that Five Pounds in Bills of Credit, should be given to Mistress Montour and her husband."—*Minutes of Provincial Council, October* 11, 1728.

In September of 1734, while attending a treaty in that city, the Proprietaries, John and Thomas Pęnn, condoled with her publicly at the loss of her husband, who had been killed since their last meeting in war with the Catawabas. "We had a great esteem," they said to the Indians present, "for our good friend your chief, Carandowana, and were much grieved to hear of his death, but as you and we have long since covered his dead body, we shall say nothing more of that subject." At

been a chief, had been killed in battle with the Catawbas. When the old woman saw us she wept. In course of conversation, while giving her a general account of the Brethren and their circumstances, I mentioned that one of our towns was named Bethlehem. Hereupon she interrupted me and said: "The place in France where Jesus and the holy family lived was also named Bethlehem." I was surprised at the woman's ignorance, considering she had been born and brought up a Christian. At the same time I thought I had evidence of the truth of the charge brought against the French missionaries, who are said to make it a point to teach the Indians that Jesus had been a Frenchman, and that the English had been his crucifiers. Without attempting to rectify her misapprehension, I in a few words stated our views, replying to her inquiries with sincerity of purpose, without, however, entering into an explanation, as I had purposed remaining retired for a few days. She was very confidential to Anna, and told her, among other things, that she was weary of Indian life.

---

this time Madame Montour was already advanced in years; for a Minute of the Council, October 15, 1734, after censuring her for duplicity at the late treaty, states that "her old age only protects her from being punished for such falsehoods." In June of 1745 she was still residing at Otstonwakin, and Spangenberg, on his way to Onondaga, in company with David Zeisberger, made a detour at Shamokin, specially to visit the old Indian Queen. Mack and Grubé, in the narrative of a journey made among the Indians on the West Branch in June of 1753, make no mention of her as there, although Mack pointed out to his comrade the spot where the Disciple and his companions had pitched their tent. By Roland Montour she had four sons, *Andrew*, *Henry*, *Robert*, and *Lewis*. French Margaret was her niece. Even after her marriage with Hunter she retained the name of Montour.

Montoursville, commenced in 1769, at the mouth of the Loyal Sock, stands on the site of Otstonwakin or French Town, and perpetuates the name of Madame Montour and her half-breed son, Andrew.

A knowledge of my rank is unquestionably prejudicial to our successful labors among both heathens and Christians. As soon as people discover who I am they view me from a worldly stand-point. My enemies also delight in publishing to the world that I am a nobleman, and hence I endeavor as much as possible to conceal or at least not to allow the fact to excite remark.

The Indians erect either a stone or a mound in honor of their deceased heroes. This custom is decidedly Israelitish.

Early in the morning of the *3d of October* we heard a a woman wailing at the grave of her husband. Andrew asked the loan of my horse to bring in the bear and deer he had shot, as his had strayed into the woods. He certainly intends to feast us.

There is a promiscuous Indian population in this village.

Madame Montour brought two children to me and asked me to baptize them, alleging the custom of the Canadian Fathers as an excuse for her request. I refused, telling her that whenever a Brother settled here we would take the matter into consideration, as we were in the habit of baptizing only such persons as we thought we would have frequent opportunity of reminding of the significance of the rite. At the same time I spoke to her of that spiritual baptism which the heart, even of the unbaptized, may, without any effort or premeditation on his part, experience. She left me displeased.

Now, my dear Brethren, I must dispatch Conrad to Shamokin, as the Brethren there and Shikellimy are expecting him. The latter has been assigned us as guide to the wild Shawanese. Andrew, who is a proficient in various Indian languages, will probably also accompany us.

.Remember Johanan,* Anna, Martin, Jeannette, Joshua,

* The name given the Count by the Indians.

and David, who are followers of the Lamb, and your fellow-members of His congregation.

P. S. We will probably resume our journey about the 9th inst. At times we have observed signs of grace in Andrew. Anna has experienced the same in the case of Madame Montour's granddaughter.* Andrew has concluded to give his hunting companions the slip, and to forego the great annual hunt which the Indians are accustomed to prolong into the month of February, and to accompany us to Skehandowana.

---

* Quære—Mary Magdalene, alias *Peggy*, who interpreted at a treaty held at Lancaster, in February of 1760? In youth she had been baptized by a Catholic priest in Philadelphia. In 1790 she joined the Indian congregation at Salem, on the Pequotting. Her last husband was a white man named Hands, and on marrying him she was called Sally Hands. After his decease she resided among the whites at the mouth of the Thames, in Canada, maintained by her son, a merchant in Montreal. As late as 1816 she visited the Brethren's Indian settlement at New Fairfield. At that time she was far advanced in years, and yet well remembered the Count's sojourn at Otstonwakin in 1742. She also spoke of Anton Schmid, Daniel Kliest, and Marx Kieffer, the Shamokin blacksmiths. She deceased soon after her visit at New Fairfield.

J. MARTIN MACK'S RECOLLECTIONS*

OF A JOURNEY FROM OTSTONWAKIN TO WYOMING, IN THE WILDS OF SKEHANDOWANA, IN COMPANY WITH COUNT ZINZENDORF AND ANNA NITSCHMANN, AND OF HIS SOJOURN IN THE LATTER PLACE IN OCTOBER OF 1742.

(*Translated from a German MS. in the Archives at Bethlehem.*)

As I recollect, you accompanied the sainted Disciple† as far as Otstonwakin, and then returned to Shamokin. From

* These Recollections were written at the request of Peter Böhler, after Mack had set out for the West Indies in May of 1762 (in which year they met for the last time at Bethlehem), and probably after Böhler's return to Europe in 1764. Upward of twenty years had therefore elapsed since the occurrence of the events and their recital.

John Martin Mack, for many years a missionary among the Indians, was born April 13th, 1715, at Leysingen, in Wurtemberg. In 1734 went to Herrnhut. In 1735 came to Georgia, and there entered into full communion with the Brethren. Left for Pennsylvania in April of 1740, assisted at the building of the Whitefield school, and was one of the founders of Bethlehem. In March of 1742 was appointed Rauch's assistant at Shecomeco. September 14th, married Jeannette, daughter of John Rau, of "The Oblong." While among the Indians at Pachgatgoch in 1743, Mack and the Brethren Pyrlaeus and Shaw were

† Zinzendorf deceased at Berthelsdorf, near Herrnhut, May 9, 1760. He was called "*the Disciple*" as early as 1747, and although he bore other titles significant of offices he had filled in the church, this appellation was the favorite one associated with his name and memory after he had passed away.

here my sainted Jeannette and myself, with Shikellimy as guide, and a grandchild of his, set out for Otstonwakin on the next day, arriving there late at night.*

---

taken in arrest to Old Milford, Connecticut, examined before a magistrate, and forbidden to preach the gospel within the precincts of the Established Church. Hence returned to Shecomeco, and was there until the close of 1744, and the abandonment of the mission, in consequence of acts passed against the Moravians by the Assembly of New York.

In 1745 was appointed "*Heiden Aeltester.*" Visited the Indians at Shamokin. In April, 1746, he commenced the settlement at Gnadenhütten, on the Mahoning, the field of his labors, until the autumn of 1755. During this interval he visited the Indian villages on the West Branch of the Susquehanna annually, and in 1752 accompanied David Zeisberger to Onondaga. His wife deceased at Gnadenhütten, December 15, 1749. Her knowledge of the Mohawk (the current medium of communication between many of the members of the Algonquin family of Indians), which she had acquired in the home of her girlhood, and of the Delaware, rendered her an efficient assistant in the mission.

In 1753 Mack married Anna Rebstock. In the autumn of 1757 he commenced Nain, near Bethlehem, for the relief of the Christian Indians sojourning there. "Here," he states in his autobiography, "I made my most trying experiences as a missionary, enduring not only temporal privations, but harassed also by constant anxiety for the spiritual welfare of my charge. I commenced the work with misgivings, as the project of settling the Indians so far down in the Province was viewed with displeasure by whites and savages." Having again labored at Pachgatgoch, Mack, in 1761, was assigned the superintendence of the missions in the Danish West Indies. Thither he went in the following year. While on a visit to Bethlehem in 1770, he was consecrated a Bishop. Deceased on Santa Cruz, January 9, 1784.

A portrait of Martin Mack is in the Archives at Bethlehem. His daughter, Theodora, born December 28, 1758, deceased at Bethlehem February 16, 1851.

* Zinzendorf and his traveling companions, Böhler, Mack, and wife, Anna Nitschmann, Leimbach, Weisser, and David and Joshua, had reached Shamokin in the evening of September 28. On the 30th they set out out for Otstonwakin, leaving Mack and his wife at the former

The Disciple and Anna were rejoiced to see us. We remained there several days, and on two occasions held meetings, which were attended by Andrew Montour and his grandmother (?), and some of the Indians. The services were conducted in French, which language the former understood.

Leaving Otstonwakin,* our way lay through the forest, over rocks and frightful mountains, and across streams swollen by the recent heavy rains. This was a fatiguing and dangerous journey, and on several occasions we imperiled our lives in fording the creeks, which ran with impetuous current. On the fifth day, at last, we reached Wyoming, and pitched our tent not far from the Shawanese town. The Disciple's reception by the savages was unfriendly, although from the first their visits were frequent. Painted with red and black, each with a large knife in his hand, they came in crowds about the tent, again and again. He lost no time, therefore, in informing the Shawanese chief,† through Andrew Montour, of the object of his

---

town in charge of Joshua. Böhler, Leimbach, Weisser, and David returned to Shamokin October 4, en route for their homes, and next day, Mack and wife, escorted by Shikellimy, set out to join the Count. Provincial business called Weisser to Tulpehocken; on leaving the latter, however, he promised to rejoin him at Wyoming within a specified time. Böhler and the Mohicans reached Bethlehem October 11.

* The travelers probably followed the "*Warrior's Path from the Great Island*" (Lock Haven), which skirted the northern bank of the West Branch as far as Otstonwakin, some forty miles, and thence led due east through the present counties of Lycoming, Sullivan, Columbia, and Luzerne, about seventy miles to the Shawanese village (Plymouth), on the Wyoming Flats, west of the Susquehanna. Through the fastnesses of this primeval forest, never before traversed by white men save adventurous traders like James Le Tort and Pierre Bizaillon, Andrew Montour guided these first Evangelists to the heathen dwellers on the plains of Skehandowana.

† Quære—*Weh-Wehlaky*, one of the Sachems whom the Count had met at Weisser's?

mission. This the wily savage affected to regard as a mystery, and replied that such matters concerned the white man, and not the Indian.

Our stock of provisions was by this time almost exhausted, and yet the Disciple shared with the Indians what little was left. The very clothes on his own back were not spared. One shirt-button after another was given away, until all were gone, and likewise his shoe-buckles, so that we were obliged to fasten his under-clothes and tie his shoes with strings made of bast. For ten days we lived on boiled beans, of which we partook sparingly three times a day, as the supply was scanty.

The suspicious manner which the Shawanese* manifested

---

* The Shawanese were a tribe of Southern Indians, who, prior to 1700, had been expelled from their seats by the Spaniards of Florida, and migrated northward. In 1698 sixty families of them, the first to come into the Province, settled at Conestoga with the knowledge of Col. Markham and with the consent of the Conestogas, the former holding the latter responsible for the good behavior of their Southern brethren. Hence they moved up the river, and built a town at Pextang. Others followed and seated themselves on the Delaware near Durham, or pursuing the course of that river into its upper valley, planted in the Minnisinks. In April of 1701 William Penn "ratified relations of friendship with the King of the Conestogas and with the King of *the Shawanese inhabiting at the head of Potomac.*" The Proprietaries' agents always sought to propitiate the good-will of these strangers. In 1728 some of the tribe, fearing the resentment of the Six Nations for an injury done by them to the Conestogas, removed to the Ohio, and put themselves under the protection of the French. Hereupon government called upon the Six Nations to aid in their recall, and in their recovery to the English interest. This attempt was only partially successful; and although conferences were held with them at various times between 1732 and 1739, and Thomas Penn in September of the first year offered them ample seats near Pextang, west of the Susquehanna, they hesitated to return to their allegiance, and even sought to entice the Delawares to follow them to the French. It was Allummapees

at our first arrival remained unchanged, and at times their deportment was such as to lead us to infer that it would be their greatest delight to make way with us. Notwithstanding this the Disciple remained in the town, and made repeated efforts to have the object of his visit brought before the consideration of the chiefs. They, however, evaded every approach, and in their disappointment at not receiving large presents gave unmistakable evidence of displeasure, so that we felt that the sooner we left the better it would be for us.

One day Jeannette, on returning to the town from visiting the Indians, informed the Disciple that she had met with a Mohican woman in the upper town, who, to her unspeakable joy, had spoken to her of the Saviour. This intelligence deeply affected him. He rose up and bade us go with him in search of her, and in the interview that followed he magnified the love of Jesus to her in terms of most persuasive tenderness. This woman now became our provider, furnishing us with beans and corn-bread, until we could procure other supplies. Hymns Nos. 1853 and 1854 in Supplement XI. of the Hymn-book, contain allusions to her; and the Disciple's prayer in her behalf, ex-

---

who prevented the defection of his countrymen at that time. In July of 1739 the same Penn treated with deputies of "*the Shawanese scattered far abroad from 'the Great Island' to the Allegheny*," and a covenant was formally ratified with them, the conditions of which it was hoped would bind them firmly and lastingly to the interests of the English and the Province of Pennsylvania. But this was not the case; for, with few exceptions, these swarthy rovers harbored distrust of the English, and became their implacable enemies. Weisser found Shawanese in Wyoming in the spring of 1737. Hither it is said they were invited at some earlier day by the Six Nations, who were confident that they could place no custodians more reliable than the ferocious Shawanese in charge of that lovely valley among the hills, which they designed to keep for themselves and their children forever.

pressed in the 18th stanza of the former, has been heard and answered.* On another occasion, on informing him that I had seen *Chikasi*,† he asked me to find him and bring him into his presence. To him also he extolled the Saviour's love.

One day, having convened the Indians in the upper town, he laid before them his object in coming to Wyoming, and expressed the desire to send people among them that would tell them words spoken by their Creator. Most of these were Mohicans, and not as obdurately perverse as the Shawanese. Although they signified no decided opposition, they stated their inability to entertain any proposals without the consent of the latter, according to whose decision they were compelled to shape their own. Should these assent, they said they would not object, but be satisfied. My Jeannette acted as interpreter of what passed during this meeting.

In reference to the removal of our tent to another locality, to which there is allusion in the words of the hymn, "*Der dritte ein verborgner Schatz, wo Blaseschlangen nisteln*," I have the following in mind to relate. The tent was pitched on an eminence. One fine sunny day, as the Disciple sat on the ground within, looking over his

---

* At her urgent request she was baptized by the missionary Bernhard A. Grubé, July 28, 1754, while he was on a visit to the Indians at Wyoming, receiving the Christian name of *Mary*. The rite was administered in the Shawanese Chief Paxanosa's wigwam, and was the first baptism performed by the Brethren in Wyoming Valley.

† A Catawba, who had been brought prisoner to Wyoming by the Iroquois on their return from an annual maraud. In August of 1749, *Chikasi* visited Bethlehem on his way with other Indians from Wyoming to Philadelphia. Mack and Grubé met him in September of 1753 in a small village of Shawanese on the Susquehanna, below the *Occohpocheny* (Monsey Creek). These Shawanese had lately left Wyoming.

papers that lay scattered around him, and as the rest of us were outside, I observed two blowers* basking at the edge of the tent. Fearing that they might crawl in I moved toward them, intending to dispatch them. They were, however, too quick for me, slipped into the tent, and gliding over the Disciple's thigh, disappeared among his papers. On examination we ascertained that he had been seated near the mouth of their den. Subsequently the Indians informed me that our tent was pitched on the site of an old burying-ground in which hundreds of Indians lay buried. They also told us that there was a deposit of silver ore in the hill, and that we were charged by the Shawanese with having come for silver and for nothing else. This statement proved to be a fiction invented by the wily savages in order to afford them some grounds for an altercation with us, and to bring us into general disrepute; for we subsequently learned that the height on which our tent had been pitched was not the locality of the precious ore.†

From our first encampment (see *Hymn* 1853, *stanza* 2) I once rode out with the Disciple and Anna. There was a creek in our way, in a swampy piece of ground. Anna and myself led in crossing, and with difficulty succeeded in ascending the farther bank, which was steep and muddy. But the Disciple was less fortunate, for in attempting to land, his horse plunged, broke the girth, and his rider

---

* *Blower*, or *swelling adder*, a small, hissing snake, said to be venomous. The Bethlehem Diarist states that in the harvest of 1744 the harvesters were much annoyed by blowers, *Blaseschlangen*, which they would take in their hands with the rakings in binding sheaves. The blower is a small, ash-gray snake. When provoked, its neck swells to several inches in extent.

† It is believed that the Iroquois invented this figment so as to have a pretext for harboring the Shawanese, and in the hope of deterring intruders by involving Wyoming in a mystery.

rolled off backwards into the water, and the saddle upon him. It required much effort on my part to extricate him, and when I at last had succeeded, he kissed me and said, "*Du armer Bruder! Ich plage dich doch was rechtes!*" (*My poor Brother! I am an endless source of trouble!*) Being without change, we were necessitated to dry our clothes at the fire and then brush off the mud. Adventures of this kind befell us more than once.

At length the Brethren, David Nitschmann, Anton Seyffert, and Jacob Kohn,* whom we had long been expecting, arrived.

On the following day we moved higher up the Susquehanna, and here was the extreme limit of our journey. The words of the hymn, "*Der viert' ein unwegsame Spitz, Der Susquehannah Quellen,*" allude to this encampment. The Disciple, I have no doubt, was led to go to this point, in order to have an opportunity of reading his letters from Europe undisturbed, and to be farther away from the Indians. Here Conrad Weisser joined us on his return. He manifested decided impatience at our prolonged stay, told us that the Shawanese were plotting mischief, and that our lives were not secure. We now returned to our second encampment, where the Disciple formally laid his proposi-

---

* These Brethren had set out from Bethlehem on the 15th of October. From Shamokin they probably followed the Indian path to Wyoming, which kept along the upper bank of the Northeast Branch, to the Shawanese town. Kohn had recently arrived from Europe, and had brought letters for the Count.

"Ich habe Dero Schreiben in der Wüsten Skehandowana in Canada, unter einem barbarischen Volcke aus Florida die Shavanos genannt,—welchen von den Spaniern in diese Gegend vertrieben sind und worunter ich Herzen suchte die einen Heiland brauchen, wohl empfangen."—*Zinzendorf to Court-Chaplain Bartholomäi, Oley, Nov.* 7, 1742. *Büdingische Sammlung*, Part xiii. No. 36, b.

tions before the Shawanese chief. The latter, however, turned a deaf ear to our approaches, and grew vehement. "*Der König liebete uns zwar; Alleine kam's zur Sache, Wo uns zum Trost so bange war, So that er wie der Drache.*" Upon this the Disciple produced the string of wampum that the Sachems of the Six Nations had given him at Tulpehocken, but even its authoritative presence failed to move the savages in their determination or to mollify their murderous intentions. We were completely foiled, and saw that our mission was a failure. This might have been owing to misstatements made by our interpreter* to the Shawanese, who, as we subsequently learned, had not been fully in our interests.

From this time we had no rest. By day and by night the vagabond savages swarmed around our tent. The Disciple warned us continually to be on our guard, and forbade us even to accept supplies from them, as they were to be trusted under no circumstances.

We now made preparations for our return home, and divided into two companies. Jeannette, David Nitschmann, Andrew, and myself, set out for Bethlehem by way of the Great Swamp† and Dansbury.‡ The Disciple and the others took the path to Shamokin.§

---

* Quære—Andrew Montour?

† The *Pine Swamp*, or *Shades of Death*, extending northward on the plateau of the Broad Mountain, in Monroe and Carbon Counties—called the *Great Swamp* on Scull's map of 1770.

This division reached Bethlehem on the 1st of November. Montour remained there until the 13th.

‡ Dansbury (Stroudsburg), a settlement commenced in Smithfield by Daniel Brodhead about 1735, near the junction of Anolomink and

§ The Count and his companions, after a tedious journey, in which they suffered from the hardships and privations incident to travel on

While thus in daily danger of his life on the Shawnee Flats of Wyoming Valley, Zinzendorf was engaged in the

McMichael's Creeks, Monroe County. Mr. Brodhead was born at Marbletown, Ulster County, New York, in 1693, and was a grandson of Daniel Brodhead, a captain of grenadiers, who had come to New York with Colonel Richard Nicolls in 1664. He became acquainted with the Brethren soon after their settlement in the Forks of Delaware, on his way to his relative, Isaac Ysselstein. At his house they often lodged as they traveled to or returned from their mission stations in New York and Connecticut, and at Dansbury they preached between 1743 and 1749. In June of 1755, Mr. Brodhead came to Bethlehem for surgical treatment at the hands of Dr. Jno. M. Otto. He lodged with James Burnside, and deceased in his house in July of that year. His remains were interred at Bethlehem.

horseback and exposure in the cold rains and bleak winds of approaching winter, reached Oley on the 7th, and Bethlehem on the 8th of November.

With this memorable journey Zinzendorf's endeavors, by personal visitation and appeal, to further the interests of the Brethren's mission among the Indians, ceased. Although he had failed to interest the Shawanese in the reception of Christianity, he had by this hazardous exploration opened a way for his Brethren into the heart of the Indian country; and from this time they carried the gospel to the mixed population of Indians scattered along both branches of the Susquehanna, at *Shamokin*, *Otstonwakin*, *Quenischachschaky* (Linden), *Long Island* (Jersey Shore), *Great Island*, *Nescopec*, *Wyoming*, and *Diahoga*. Among the Shawanese they never effected much. The first convert was *Schitemoque*, who in baptism received the name of Anna Charity. Elizabeth, *the wife of the old chief Paxanosa*, was baptized at Bethlehem in February of 1755. Twice in the interval between Zinzendorf's visit to Wyoming and the autumn of 1755 the Shawanese from there addressed themselves to the Brethren at Bethlehem. In July of 1752 they came apparently with a desire to establish relations of friendship, and expressed a readiness to receive the gospel. In March of 1753 they came in the interests of the Six Nations to ask permission of the Brethren for the Christian Indians residing at Gnadenhütten to remove to Wyoming. On his visit to Europe, in the summer of that

preparation of Supplements XI. and XII. to the Collection of Hymns at that time in use among the Brethren.

---

year, Spangenberg reported these overtures to the Count, whose distrust of the perfidious savages among whom his life had been in jeopardy almost overcame the broad spirit of good-will and peace to all men that shone so resplendently from out the great heart of the beloved Disciple. Spangenberg has recorded the following memoranda:

1.

"*Chelsea, June* 16, 1753. The Disciple is displeased with our late dealings with the Shawanese. He stated that the Lord had intimated to him to let them alone, and added that it was disrespectful toward him, the representative of the Brethren, and distrustful of both, for the Six Nations to send a message by proxy; that the circumstance was suspicious, and might lead to complications with government; and finally, that the Shawanese were a perfidious race and desired no knowledge of God and the Saviour."

2.

"*Chelsea, June* 29, 1753. The Disciple told me last evening, to my great joy, that on examining his notes and memoranda (which he is in the habit of consulting after the manner of the old prophets, who, according to Peter, 'search what, or what manner of time the Spirit of Christ which is in them did signify'), he had ascertained how we were to act with regard to the Shawanese. As to those of the tribe who were residing at Skehandowana at the time of his sojourn there, he stated that the Saviour had told him it would be useless for us to attempt to effect anything with them, as they were treacherous and cruel and totally averse to the reception of Christianity. As to the rest of the tribe, he stated that from an intimation the Saviour had given him at the time of his stay in Wyoming, he was inclined to believe that they would become an admirable people on their conversion, and that our efforts in their behalf would not be in vain. Furthermore, he observed, that the promise the Saviour had made him to effect the removal of the Shawanese, among whom his life had been in danger, was going into fulfilment; that the lot he had cast and which had warned him of the Shawanese did not apply to that part of the tribe with which we had lately been negotiating; and finally, that the Saviour had also made this decision."

They are prefaced with a few words addressed to the Congregations, beginning thus: "*Ich bin hier in der Wüsten, und lauer auf Wilde wie sie auf die wilden Thiere,*" and subscribed, "*Aus dem Zelte vor Wayomik, in der grossen Ebene Skehandowàna, in Canada, am* 15. *Oct.* 1742.

Euer unwürdiger

Johanan."

From this collection the following hymns are taken. Both were written by the Count to commemorate his experience among the Indians, and the first is alluded to by Martin Mack in his Recollections.

WAYOMIK IM NOV.

1742.

Wir dachten an die Hirtentreu
Des Jesuah Jehovah,
In der betrübten Wüsteney
Mit Namen *Skehandowa*.

Des Zeltes erster Ruheplatz
Das waren Dorn und Disteln,
Der dritte ein verborg'ner Schatz,
Wo Blaseschlangen nisteln.

Der viert' ein unwegsame Spitz
Der *Susquehanna* Quellen,
Der and're und der fünfte Sitz,
Das waren gleiche Stellen.

Da sassen wir das erste Mal
Acht Tage, zu erfahren
Was unser's Lammes Hochzeitsaal
Zum Theil mag offenbaren.

Ein unaussprechlich edles Glück
  Für uns're eigne Seelen—
Allein, in einem andern Stück,
  Ein unbeschreiblich Quälen.

Das Glücke war an dieser Stell
  Sein Herze tief zu finden,
Zum Theil die Kräfte von der Höll
  Durchs Lammes Blut zu binden.

Allein der Schmerz, der Seelenschmerz,
  Den wir in diesen Landen
Um so manch, Indianer Herz
  Im innern ausgestanden,

Die blut'ge Thränenmäsz'ge Noth,
  Die uns das Herz gebrochen
Bei ihren unerkannten Tod,
  Wird schwerlich ausgesprochen.

Ein Volk, im *Irokaner* Rath
  Zum Untergang bestimmet,
Dieweil doch nichts als Uebelthat
  Im wilden Herzen glimmet;

Das war daneben Tag vor Tag
  Um uns herum vagiren,
So dasz man kühnlich sagen mag,
  Wir war'n bey wilden Thieren.

Und was der Herr in seinem Wort
  Von uns'rer Leute stillen
In Wäldern schlafen sagte dort,
  Das wust er zu erfüllen.

Allein das mörderische Herz
  Der wilden *Schawanosen*,
Verdrosz so wohl der Zeugenschmerz,
  Als all' ihr Liebekosen.

Der König liebete uns zwar;
  Alleine kam's zur Sache,
Wo uns um Trost so bange war,
  So that er wie der Drache.

Doch kam ein Paar ums gute Herz
  In eine rechte Klemme,
Sie fühlten einen wahren Schmerz
  Nach einer Seelenschwemme.

Die erste Brüder, die einmal
  An diese Gegend streiffen,
Die solten sie zur Gnadenwahl
  In's Blut des Lammes täuffen.

Die Gnade, die uns hie und da
  So Seelen zugewiesen,
Wie sie Philipp' und Simon sah,
  Sey gleichwohl hoch gepriesen.

Doch lindert uns kein *Hurons* Herz,
  Die Kirch voll *Mahikaner*,
Noch einzler *Chikasi* den Schmerz
  Um diese *Floridaner*.

Und bis der erste *Schawanos*
  Sich gläubt zu'n ew'gen Hügeln;
So wollen wir das Gnadenloosz
  Von diesem Gang versiegeln;

Und alle Spur vom Zeugenglück
So wohl in *Otstonwakin*,
Als in der Fläche *Wayomik*
Und endlich in *Shomakin*.

Kein ewig's Zähr und Thränelein,
O Vater! soll inzwischen'
Aus deinem Thränenpüschelein,
Wo Du's gezählt, entwischen.

Gedenke nicht an unsern Schweisz,
Gedenk' an Jesu Narben,
Der diesen Lohn fur seinen Fleisz
Nicht lange mehr kann darben.

Supplement XI. No. 1853.

WYOMIK IM NOV.
1742.

Dort in der Fläche *Wajomik*
Auf einem wüsten Ackerstück,
Da Blaseschlangen nisteten
Und ihre Bälge brüsteten,—

Auf einem Silbererznen Grund,
Wo's Leibes Leben miszlich stund,
Da dachten wir;—Wir sähen gern,
Das würde eine Stadt des Herrn.

Darüber wurden eins, zwey, drey,
Und denken itzt noch einerley,
Und kriegen ihr noch mehr dazu;
Nun fehlt nichts mehr, als das ER'S thu'.

Supplement XII. No. 1902.

ZINZENDORF'S ACCOUNT

OF HIS EXPERIENCE AMONG THE INDIANS.

Communicated at a general Meeting of "the Society* for the Furtherance of the Gospel," assembled at the Brethren's Chapel in Fetter Lane, London, March 7, 1743.†

(*A MS. in the Archives at Bethlehem.*)

It is not necessary, my Brethren, to relate the matters which happened among the Christians; for we have Documents enough, and those publickly printed, to illustrate them. But what relates to the Heathen cannot be brought under any Heads of Documenta, seeing they are unable to make any. Therefore that is, according to my Judgment, the only Matter which remains to be related.

'Tis also my Intention to be as brief as I can in relating what has been my Plan in the whole Affair of the Heathen, and how far Matters were carried on during my being there,

---

* This association, composed of Brethren and of friends of their missions, was organized by Spangenberg in London, May 8, 1741. Dr. Doddridge, Rev. Benjamin Ingham, and John Bray were members.—*Benham's Life of Hutton.*

† Zinzendorf sailed from New York, January 20, and reached Dover Feb. 28, 1743. Hence he repaired to Yorkshire, and next to London. During his stay there, between March 11 and 24, he preached to and held meetings for the Congregation in their Chapel in Fetter Lane, *James Hutton acting as his Interpreter.—Ibid.*

See *Büdingische Sammlung*, Part xvi. No. 53, for a discourse he delivered before the Society, March 24, 1743.

since it is what we believe in general, that the Time of the Heathen is not yet come. For it is believed in our Church that the Conversion of the Jews, and of all Israel must needs go before, ere the proper Conversion of the Heathen can go forward. And we look upon all what has been done hitherto, even by ourselves, among the Heathen, *as first Fruits only;* so that one must likewise go about the Conversion of the Heathen with great Care and Circumspection.

Therefore we directly oppose the Conversion of the Heathen Nations to the Profession of the Christian Religion; and likewise the Methods hitherto made Use of in the Conversion of both Jews and Heathens. For if Christian Princes and Divines should go so far as to convert the Heathen Nations to their Customs and Ways in our Days, they would thereby do the greatest Piece of Service to the Devil. Therefore I do not in the least believe that the Devil would oppose any one in such an Undertakeing, but wo'd rather help them as much as he co'd.

And I believe concerning those quick and wonderful Conversions of whole Nations, where all Sorts of People, good and bad are made Christians, 'tis much the same whether one calls it the Work of the Lord or the Work of the Devil.

This one finds verified to this very Day in those Nations which are well known unto us, and which have been called *Converted* these several 100 Years; the Wends, the Lettlanders, the Estlanders,* for instance; great Numbers of which even to this very Day Worship Images; that it is impossible to evade it by putting the common Gloss upon this Matter and saying it is only a Relic of Heathenism.

The Idea which we have of the Samaritans is much more evident, who worshipped the true God and false one at the

* Letts and Esthonians.

same Time for this Reason, that the Worshippers of the true God might not give them any Disturbance.

For certainly so long as our Saviour gets no better Footing in Christendom, we are neither constrain'd by Necessity, Duty nor Love, nor by any Inclination, to convert whole Nations of the Heathen.

Therefore it is most plain to us that the Conversion of the Heathen must be of the same Kind as the Conversion among those that are already called Christians. And that all the Souls among the Heathen whom we shall admit to Baptism, must be awakened to eternal Life by the Lord Jesus and his Spirit in like Manner as a Person in Christendom who would be Converted must first be awaken'd. And therefore have we, in the Conversion of the Heathen, entirely rejected the Method of Teaching them such Matters as they can keep in their Head, and learn by Rote, to say after one. And a Heathen by our Way of Preaching or Instructing in heavenly Things, shall not be able so much as to talk when he has not the Matter in his Heart.

Therefore it is impossible that we can convert the Heathen by thousands; yea, 'tis even a Wonder to ourselves when we convert them by twentys or thirtys. And I often tremble to this Hour when I see and must believe (and 'tis not possible to do otherwise) that out of a 1000 awakened in St. Thomas* within these 6 years, 300 are become United

---

* A mission among the slaves on this island was the first in which the Renewed Church of the Brethren engaged. In Dec. of 1732, Leonhard Dober and David Nitschmann (subsequently a bishop) commenced the work on the Danish West India Company's plantation near the town of St. Thomas. The first station was named New Herrnhut. Zinzendorf visited the missionaries in January of 1739. *Andrew*, *Gratia*, and *Oley Carmel*, three converts, are introduced in the painting of the "First Fruits from the Heathen," that Zinzendorf had executed about 1750.

Brethren and Sisters. For the whole Nation together is but about 3000. And that the 10th Part of a Nation sho'd be wholly our Saviour's is a Thing never heard of before. Undoubtedly ev'ry one of us wou'd think it a great Matter when the 10th Part of Great Brittain should consist of true Children of God, Brethren of the Lamb.

And one must also say in general, that the Conversion of the Nations, both Negroes and Savages, hath been carried on further than we ourselves believ'd it wou'd.

There is a real little Church settled among the savage Nations in Greenland* and another among the Hottentots;† concerning wch. Parts of the World Christendom for several hundred Years past, have thought it impossible for them ever to be converted. Indeed not one Instance co'd be produced for they have been the only People among the Heathen, who have been so honest as to declare, that they wo'd not believe tho' it shou'd be told them.

But one may observe that the Mistake of all the Preachers that have been among these People consists in this, that they would convince them that there was a God; and have thereby made the poor Creatures either crafty or stupid. Had their teachers but once rightly read the Bible they wou'd have seen what Paul says in the first of the Romans, that there is no Heathen in all the World to whom it is not evident that there is a God. For he allows

---

* Matthew and Christian Stach, and Christian David, commenced to missionate among the Greenlanders on the coast, near the Danish trading-post of Godhaab, in May of 1733. *Samuel Kajarnak*, his wife and two children were baptized there, March 30, 1739. The first station was named New Herrnhut. *Kajarnak* appears in the "First Fruits."

† George Schmidt was sent to the Hottentots of the Cape of Good Hope in the summer of 1737. *Kibbodo*, who in baptism received the name of Jonas, is one of the eighteen converts in the painting of the "First Fruits."

of no Atheists but what there are in Christendom; who as a particular distinguishing Punishment for not seeking the Lord Jesus, are given over to a reprobate Mind.

The Punishment of the Heathen is that they must needs commit Sin; that of the Christians who wou'd not have the Lord Jesus is that they become Atheists. And when Christ shall also be preached unto the Heathen, and they likewise will not receive him, then will Atheists arise among them also as well as among us. Thence it is that one finds Atheists among all such Heathens where the Christian Missionaries have labored in vain. Here indeed one finds Atheists because here an Occasion is giv'n for it. As for Instance, when they are told that the Son of God has died for them, and that this is a weighty Matter, and they afterwards observe the Manner of Life these People who told them do lead, they presently begin to think it is impossible that these men believe this, it must needs be a Contrivance or a pretty Fable.

We have hitherto made it our Business among the heathen and indian Nations that our Brethren might not labor in vain, first of all to inquire concerning the People, whether or no, and by what Means the Preaching is already corrupted, and if they have already receiv'd false Christianity; and what part of 'em still adhere to mere Heathenism.

There is a wonderful mixture of these in Canada, which makes the Conversion of these Heathen very difficult. The principal Heathens in Canada are allied Nations, who give themselves the particular title of (*Aquanusmiani*) Covenant People; the French call them Iroquois, and the English the 5 Nations. But there are properly 6 of them, they having added the Tuscaroras to their Number. These Nations govern the whole District of Canada; the rest being either in subjection to them or else continually at War with them.

These Nations are divided into Fathers, or Children, or Brethren, or Members of the Covenant, and such as do not belong to one of these three Classes they call *Cousins*, which signifies as much as Subjects; and these former are again by them called *Uncles*.

The 3 first Nations which are called *Fathers*, are the Maquas, the Onondagoes, the Senekas. The Maquas are most part of them Christians so called, having been converted by the English Missionaries; and have lost all their Credit with the others, because they have guzzl'd away all their Land to the Christians. And with this Nation we have not hitherto so much as spoken, since we fear nothing so much as when such Sort of People do endeavour to belong to us. And we have esteemed it a very great Grace of our Saviour, that, altho' these are as it were the next Neighbours of the Heathen to our Congregations,* yet we have had no Manner of Fellowship with them.

The 3[d] Nation are the Senekas who have been converted by the French Missionaries some time ago, when they had to do with them; and of these I have observ'd that their Christian Knowledge is nothing more than this, that they believe that our dear Saviour was born at Bethlehem in France, and that the English have crucified him. Upon which Account they are very much offended with the English; and one sees them make Crosses and such like Ceremonies. This is all I could find among them; and when any of them comes to Philadelphia, they go to the Popish Chapel† to Mass.

The 2[d] Nation, and which properly governs the rest is

---

* At Shecomeco, and its dependencies, *Wechquadnach* and *Pachgatgoch*.

† Quære—The chapel on the northeast corner of Walnut and Front Streets, mentioned in *Watson's Annals?*

the Nation of the Onondagoes. Those are Philosophers and such as among us are called Deists. They are brave honest People who keep their word; and their general weakness is that they delight in Heroick Deeds; and this will be the main Difficulty in the way of their Conversion, to make them forget these their heroick Notions; for they have the Principles of the old Romans, that they look upon every one as a miserable Creature, scarce worth a Thought, who will not submit himself to them. Their Government is very equitable and fatherlike, but whoever will not stoop to them they are ready to root out that Nation from among the Indians. On the other Hand, they carry themselves very civil and orderly towards the Europeans (as may be seen from the Compacts between them) and altho' they in general hate the Europeans in their Hearts, and call them Assaroni or Assyrians (which is the same as Enemies) yet they have a particular Respect for several private Persons. Nevertheless 'tis as much as an Indian life is worth, who belongs to their Nation, if he is discover'd to have a good Reputation among the Europeans. And Alommabi,* the King of the Delawares stabb'd his presumptive Successor because that in Philadelphia he was looked upon as an Oracle.

The Two other Nations which are stiled *Children*, are the Cajugas and Oneydoes who regulate themselves after these Two Nations and also are Philosophers like them; and when at any time they have general Proposals made them about Christianity, they give for Answer that they will follow the Onondagoes, and what they shall do in that Case, these likewise will do the same.

As concerning this Nation, Things so fell out that one

* Some time in 1731, Allummapees killed his nephew, *Sam Shakatawlin* (who occasionally acted as interpreter at Philadelphia), in a drunken brawl at Shamokin.

of their Kings came to Philadelphia as Ambassadour,* going before the grand Embassy of the 5 Nations, which came last Year with Commissions to Philadelphia. This Prince was recommended to me and lodged 14 Days in my House† with his Wife & Children. At that Time I did

* Caxhayton, counselor of Canassatego, Sachem of the Onondagas, came to Philadelphia in February of 1742 to announce the intention of the Six Nations to meet the Governor in conference there in the course of the following summer. The "grand embassy" arrived in that city on the 30th of June. It consisted of thirteen Onondagas, nineteen Cayugas, fourteen Oneidas, three Senecas, twenty-one Tuscaroras, five Shawanese, eight Conestogas, six Delawares from Shamokin and four from the Forks. The principal personage was Canassatego. Eleven other chiefs attended. "The Board directs that £5 be given to Caxhayton on acct. of the Province for his services as messenger."—*Minutes of Provincial Council, July* 12, 1742.

† A short time before the Count's arrival at New York, Christian Frölich, who was then conducting Capt. Wallace's sugar-refinery in Philadelphia, had rented a house of three stories on *Second Street near the northeast corner of Race*, for the Count and his household. Here he entertained Caxhayton. Governor Thomas wrote to Conrad Weisser, under date of February 26, 1742, in reference to the Count's hospitality,—"Although I have a very high opinion of Count Zinzendorf's integrity and religious zeal, and consequently esteem him much, I was not altogether willing that the messenger and his family should be at his home, lest his manner of treating them should not prove agreeable and they should think we failed in courtesy to save expense, and so make a report to our prejudice when they return to their countrymen. I should be very well pleased that the Count could make them good Christians; but I would not have the business of the Province depend upon his success with them nor run the risk of their being disobliged by being put into the hands of agents, who, out of good-will, would restrain them from what they think there is no crime in making a moderate use of—drunkenness,—a very bad thing, and I discourage it in Indians and others as much as I can, but should they become Christians if they are no better than Christians in common, they will be as drunk as some of them are apt to be at present, be greater thieves, cheats, &c. than the most of Indians are. The knowledge of God and Christ

not know of what Benefit this wou'd be to me. But being on my first journey among the Indians by an Indian River,* I met the grand Embassage on their return. I came into an House where all the Kings of these Nations were assembled together.† Kackshajim was among them, with his Wife and little Child, who all 3 had been in my House at Philadelphia. The Child ran to me and fell about my Neck in the Presence of all the Indians, which made them look one upon another, and enquire among themselves how that came about. At the same Time Brother Zander came also into the Room. The Indian Prince was very glad to see his Zander again, who had been his Provider and Messinger thro'out Pennsylvania, and immediately ran and kissed him; so that the whole was an astonishing Scene to their People.

Then I spoke to all them present (and there was none wanting but the King of the Tuscaroras who was at that Time got drunk) and asked them if I might have a Conference with them? They answer'd yes, and sat themselves down; and they were presented with a Piece of red Cloth as a Token that we had something of Importance to relate to them: which they receiv'd. Then I spoke thus

---

ought to make men better; but how it happens I cannot tell, yet so it is, the common sort of people among Christians are worse than the Indians who are left to the law of nature, *i.e.* to their own natural reason to guide them. If these people are any way dissatisfied, you will excuse me and put it upon their own consent or choice, as you tell me it was."

* The Schuylkill, "*hidden channel*," so named by the Dutch who settled on Delaware Bay. The Indians called the river *Ganschowe-hanne*, "*der rauschende Strom.*"

† Present at Weisser's house were the sachems *Canassatego* and *Caxhayton*, Onondagas, *Saristaque* and *Shikellimy*, Oneidas, *Kakaradascy* and *Sahughsoewa*, Cayugas, and *Weh-welaky*, a Shawanese. The Mohawks and Senecas were not represented. *Sawantka*, the Tuscarora chief, remarks Zinzendorf, "*war ausser Stand zu erscheinen.*"

to them by an Interpreter: "That seeing Kackshajim was already personally acquainted with me, and wou'd give them an Account of me, I wou'd therefore take this Opportunity to inform them what was properly my Business in this Country, and wherefore I travell'd so about. That I believed many of my B^{rn} wou'd come into their Districts; that our way of proceeding wou'd appear very strange to them, seeing we wear no Parson's Habits nor preach'd publickly, but only convers'd with the Souls; that indeed we were such a Sort of People who as earnestly attend the Conversion of Souls as any Body. But we had quite a different Method which I wou'd now beforehand explain to them. For it might so fall out, that one of us might happen to be a whole Year among them, and not so much as speak with any of them; which might perhaps give Occasion of Suspicion. We are a People who believe that before we tell the People something of our God, our God himself must first have spoken to their Hearts. And we would speak with none concerning our God, but with Hearts which sigh and long to know him. And moreover I desir'd nothing further of them than this, that they would give a Token whereby to know our B^{rn}, so that we might avoid Suspicion on both Sides. And that our Brethren when they should see good to depart from a Nation might be at Liberty to do so without giving any Reason for it: and might also be at Liberty to speak together concerning what may be of Use to any Soul here or there. That they wou'd also give their People Freedom to act freely with us concerning their Hearts, for we wou'd at no Time meddle with Matters of State or Trade among them; for we had nothing at all to do with such things; and as for Necessary Things we wou'd take Care to provide ourselves with them."

Whereupon they withdrew and held a Consultation of an

Hour long, & then returned again, and the chief of them, the King of the Onandagoes spoke to me after this Manner.

"Brother, thou art come hither; we have known nothing of thee, nor thou of us; and thou art also come quite unexpectedly by us, as we by thee. The chief Spirit must have some hand in this. We hear that thou art come over Two Seas and over the great Sea, and that thou hast something to declare from the Great Spirit and no worldly thing. We wou'd only let thee know that thou and thy Brethren when they come, shall allways be welcome to us; and tell us then what you have to say when you come. And as a Proof that thou and thy Brethren shall be welcome to us, we give thee this Fathom of Wampon."*

Here the Matter rested; nor had we any Thing more to make out with these Nations, but only that we might be able to dwell among them without being suspected by them. That was the general outward Affair, and which I thus Transacted with the government itself so that no Suspicion could arise. And seeing I had this Adventure towards the end of my first Journey among the River Indians, I will also say something of the Journey itself.

These River Indians† are a People allmost quite Spoil'd by the Christians with Drunkenness, Thievery and Whoredom, &c. Yet they have this Advantage, that they know little or nothing of the Christian Religion. For the Christians have other sort of business with them, and upon that

---

* It was a string of 186 *white beads*, subsequently often produced by Bishops Spangenberg and Cammerhoff in conferences with the Indians. Quære—Was this relic taken to Europe on the division of the Archives at Bethlehem in 1766, and on the transfer to Herrnhut of many of its records, made in pursuance of a resolution of the General Synod of 1764?

† The Delawares. The name was also applied to the Mohicans.

Account forget to mention their Religion to them; wherefore when one speaks to them, 'tis something new to them, which strikes and leaves an Impression behind upon their Hearts.

This I took particular Notice of at the 3^d^ Synod* in Pennsylvania, whereat there were three of our Indians which now are Elders and Deacons of the Congregation in Shecomeko, and were Baptiz'd in the Synod; at wch time there came some of the River Indians out of Curiosity to see of what Nation they were. Our Indians felt a great Stirring in their Hearts on Acco^t^ of these People, and begun a preaching to them from Noon till towards Midnight. For there was one of our Indians who understood the Delaware Language.

These People express'd so much Admiration and listen'd some Hours with so much Attention, that any one that knew them (for they were known to be some of the worst sort of their People) could not but be astonished at it.

Thro'out my whole Journey where I have spoken to any of the Indians by Bro^r^ Zander, and with all the River Indians, I have found a particular Quietness, Attention and Friendliness.

We never went from them but they intreated us that we wo'd return to them again: and they have a particular word

* The third of seven religious convocations convened between January 13 and June 12, 1742, at Germantown, Falkner's Swamp, Oley, and Philadelphia. Three of the seven met at Germantown. Zinzendorf and Henry Antes led the attempt made in these meetings to harmonize the differences which distracted the various religious elements in Pennsylvania, and to unite all sects and denominations on the ground of Evangelical Christianity. The *third* Synod met at Mr. Jno. de Turk's, in Oley, February 20, 1742. The baptism of the Indian converts took place on the 22d. A large concourse of spectators having collected to witness the act, it was found necessary to repair to the barn for the administration of the rite.

which I have often heard the old King of the Delaware* Indians at Shamokin make use of, that when they hear any thing that affects them they cry *kahelle! kahelle! ay! is it so?*

We soon found it proper to go on gently with our Visitation of these Indians, since we have not to fear that they will soon be Converted by the Christians. We have given it in charge to Bro^r Anton and Seidel,† now and then to make a particular visit to *Sickehillehocken*, and observe if there is a Soul here or there who require that something may speedily be done for them. What chiefly gives us hopes concerning these River Indians is that they are very diligent in coming to Bethlehem, and are exceedingly pleas'd with their coming to see our Love feasts,‡ and with Quietness and Respect take Notice of what we do. So that we believe the Church will bring these Heathens to our Saviour without speaking a Word. They have already given us their Children to take care of for whole Days and Weeks together;§ which is looked upon among the Indians as the greatest Thing they can do, for they have a Wonderfull Affection for their Children.

Indeed the white People have done us that Kindness as to tell them, that we wo'd make Slaves of all the Children which they left with us; tho' they have never regarded it, but came and told us what the white People had said to

---

* Allummapees, or Sasoonan, a Delaware word signifying "*one who is well wrapped up.*"

† Nathaniel Seidel.

‡ "*July* 10, 1742. Thirteen Delawares visited us. As several companies have been here within the month we have concluded to send a Brother among them to acquire their language."—*Bethlehem Diarist.*

§ "Capt. John, who lives near by, has entrusted his son, an intelligent boy of eleven, to my care. He has been with me during the winter, and has become quite attached to me."—*Chr. Frölich to Leonhard Dober, Nazareth, March* 21, 1741.

them. The Heathen continually wonder at this that the Christians are so much against us and speak all manner of Evil of us; for they have warned them against us as Hereticks even at the same time when the Heathen do not know what Heresy means.

This was my first Journey.

My 2[d] was to Checomeko, which lies beyond the North River, between New England, New York and Albania. Just on the Borders of these three Provinces dwell our Heathen; they are the Nation of the Mahikans, a desperate and furious People.

Among these Mahikans our Sav[r] has given us a Whole Congregation within the space of Two Years; our Bro[r] Rauch has been the Instrument in this Work, who spent the greatest part of the first Year among them, in manifest Danger of his Life, for they are the most savage People among all the Indians; who not only have been excessive Drunkards, but have been exceedingly given to Fighting and Murder. And this is one Thing which has made the Neighbours thereabouts such as are our Opposers, be Astonish'd,* to see People upon whose Accot. they have been afraid to remain in their Houses now become like Lambs, and they have told me myself that they were

* Conrad Weisser, who visited Shecomeco in May of 1743, expressed himself in terms of unqualified astonishment at the change wrought in this ferocious people through the instrumentality of the Brethren. In a letter to Büttner (who was at New York during the interpreter's visit), dated *Heidelberg, June*, 1743, he writes,—"The evidences of Divine Grace I observed in your Indians, their unaffected piety and their simple faith in Christ and his atonement impressed me deeply. As I saw their old men seated on rude benches and on the ground listening with decorous gravity and rapt attention to the words of Post, I fancied I saw before me a congregation of primitive Christians. John, who is truly a child of God, interpreted with demonstration of the spirit and of power."

highly obliged to us for having Converted them, since before they had not been secure even in their own Houses. And *John* who is now the chief Teacher of the Indians was the worst of all. He was exceeding Drunk when Bro[r] Rauch first began to speak something good to Him, and did not remember a Word that Rauch had said to him save this one word *Blood* which he so often had heard repeated. *Blood*, *Blood* that continualy was coming again into his mind; and he wanted much to ask the Man what that meant, *Blood!* for he had looked so friendly even while he was talking about *Blood*. *Blood!* thought he, what must that be? and he even dreamed about it what manner of Man must that be who looks so pleased and yet speaks allways about Blood? And once he came in haste to Bro[r] Rauch, and sitting down by him, he earnestly desired him to tell him why he allways spoke of Blood with such a Motion and Joy of Heart. Then Rauch told him that he might easily conceive why it was so with him, for he was telling the People that their Creator had Died and shed his Blood for them, and he also belong'd to these People; and it had been shed for him likewise. He then asked him if this was true? and what must one do to get a Share therein? Rauch answered, Nothing but believe and with one's Heart hang upon the Man, conversing with him so long in the Mind till one experienc'd what he did. Then he told him but he was so much inclin'd to Drunkenness. Rauch replied, the reason of that was his not having as yet that Blood in his Heart; and that he should first get that, and then his Drunkenness would soon fall away. From this time the Heathen constantly attended and begg'd with sighs that God would make this Thing so to him as it was to Rauch. And from that Time he had no Leasure to get drunk any more; for he wo'd not let this Thing go out of his mind. And his Wife and Mother who had been Excessively grieved at his getting Drunk so much, were now much more Displeas'd that he wo'd have nothing more to do with drinking, but was now wholly taken up with such Things as they could not Comprehend. This made him wonder how it came to pass that his People were become such Enemies to him upon his altering his former course of Life. And the Christians were also no less angry with him. He asked Rauch about this Thing, who took that opportunity to tell him plainly, That all men were such by Nature, and that it was a very great Grace when God took a person from the Bulk of Mankind, and made him quite another Man ; and therefore People Envied such a One because they were Convinced of the Matter in their Hearts, and yet would not themselves be Converted. Now could the Heathen understand why the Heathen persecuted Rauch ; and all his Doubts were removed from him.

To this Company whilst they were as yet very few in Numbers, I with some of my Brethren took a Journey, and tarried wlth them Eight Days.* These 8 Days we spent intirely in Conference with the first Indians, how our Sav[r] would have his work carried on among the Heathen. They would fain have the Gospel preached among their People, and our Brethren were allmost of their Opinion, but I opposed it. At last we all agreed so to Manage the whole affair, as to make a Bundle of living ones wherein none should be taken but such as should never be able to come out again. Upon this Footing has it hitherto proceeded, and that with such a Blessing that indeed they have been obliged to Baptize 14† at one time and certainly we can-

---

* Arrived at Shecomeco August 16, and set out for Bethlehem August 24.

† The "Great Baptism" here alluded to, was performed at Shecomeco on the 23d of December, 1742. Among the Indians baptized on that

not deny but that our Sav[r] does more at once upon the Heathens then he is generally wont to do upon Souls. For Instance they have such Severe Morals, which spring up in them intirely of themselves (for they have no outward Instruction on those Matters) and according to these they Manage their outward Affairs with the greatest Exactness in all Respects. The Heathen have a surprizing Love for Hunting and they are not only Lovers of the Thing but it is also intirely their Livelihood. Our dear Br. Jonathan, who at the time of my being there was one of the most Eager Hunters among them, is since that time Converted to our Sav[r] and Baptiz'd.* This Man had once with a great deal of Pains for several Days, at last kill'd a Dear with a Bullet and brought it home, when a so called Christian, an English Man came to him and told him Sorrowing that he had Shot at a Dear some days before but it had run away from him; upon which the Indian said to him, then the Dear is yours for I have found some Shot in him, and I had no Shot with me, and Straightway he gave him the Dear. The Christian could not Comprehend that a Savage should give him a Dear to which he had no manner of right, seeing the other had caught it and had it now in his possession. The Heathen told him he should let him have that Satisfaction, and that he thanked God that he had found the proper Person for the Dear; and that he wo'd have nothing to do with what did not belong to him, whereupon the Man said, "Surely you are a Christian." "No," replied Jonathan, "I am none as yet, tho' I am upon the point of becoming one." "But," says the English Man,

occasion by Büttner and Mack was Nicodemus, Elder of the Indian congregation at Bethlehem in 1746.

* Jonathan, a Mohican, baptized by Büttner at Shecomeco, October 21, 1742, a few days after the missionary and his wife reached the station.

"where will you get another Dear?" "Our Sav^{r}," answered he, "will surely give me another; and besides that Hunting has been allways my Chief Enemy; and when he will have it so that I shall have a Dear, he will send me one, and when he sees it is not good for me yet still I am Contented."

The next Day he got two Dears which he brought to the Brethren and said, "How good is the Dear Sav^{r}! Yesterday I gave away one Dear and to Day he gives me two in return, but it will not be so allways. I will be content tho' the next Time I get none."

Now this Church injoys unspeakable Blessings. What we have now had an Acc^{t} of in Büttner's Letter is but the least part of them, for we have received some other Letters from thence since his which are full of Wonders.

I will speak briefly of my 3^{d} Journey and therewith Conclude. This fell out in Autumn, in the Months of October and November and took up 49 Days,* during which time I and my Company could do nothing else but dwell in Desarts of all Sorts.

I visited several Nations but with no Success except in Three places which be an 100 Miles distant from each other. The nearest Place I went to by Checomeko is called Ostonwaxin. Here I met with French Indians, who yet are under the protection of the English. I found no Freedom to speak among them but I spoke to our Sav^{r} earnestly for them in their presence, and they understood me in their Language, and were affected with it. And the Chief person among them† is become so hearty, that he Conducted me some 100 Miles thro'out my whole Journey, as far as Bethlehem where he continued with us 8 or 10 Days and at length departed—with a Heart very much Affected and Convinced. There will be a Brother and a

---

* September 21 to November 8.

† Andrew Montour.

Sister be sent to reside among them which they have earnestly desired.*

The other Tour was as far as the great Desarts of Skehantowanno, where no Christians either come or dare to come, Which tract of Land I hear they will not sell to the Christians.

For which reason they have used that Policy not to receive one among them who belong to the Six Nations; but do let the Floridas an exceeding savage people come and settle there; among these I remained 20 Days, and one may easily imagine how difficult it was. Yet we travelled so long till we found 2 Souls for our Sav^r^. One of them was a *Schikasi* from Florida who was Prisoner there, and the other was an old Mahikan Woman, a relation to the King of the Schawanos, who more properly belonged to Chekomeko, where our Congregation is but knew nothing of the Conversion there. To those Hagen and his Wife† are now going.

As I return'd from thence I came back to *Schomako* where the Indians have their Rendevous, and it is in some measure like the Hague in Holland. Here I renewed my compact with them and gave them to understand what our future Conduct wo'd be among them, and that the Pilgrim Congregation‡ wch would intirely disperse itself among them wo'd come and dwell there a Couple of Years.

This place is at least 80 Miles distant from the nighest

---

* David Bruce and his wife were sent to *Otstonwakin*, and sojourned there a few weeks in 1743. His wife was conversant with French.

† John Hagen, September 19, 1742, married Margaret, daughter of David Dismann, of Providence Township, Montgomery County, Pennsylvania.

‡ Those of the Brethren who were employed as missionaries, or as ministers of the gospel, and as such led an itinerant life, constituted the "Pilgrim congregation," and were called "Pilgrims."

Settlement of the Christians, but Three Hundred Miles from Onandago, and 'tis not to be supposed that the Christians should come thither, for the very sending thither is allmost quite Impossible on account of the Surprizing Mountains w[ch] are impassable to any but our Sav[r]'s Children.

This was the Conclusion of my Labour among the Indians.

From thence I return'd in some Days to Bethlehem and there began my general Land preaching after which I took my leave of Pennsylvania on the $\frac{1}{12}$ of January this present Year.*

The Brethren who are to go among the Heathen are allready appointed, and 20 of them by this Time know the places designed for them and when they are all come together there will be 40 of them, which will be Enough among the Heathen for some Time; for we intend allways to take as many Chief Labourers, as may be out of their own Nations that our Saviour may get Souls among them.

---

* On his return from the Indian country in November of 1742, Zinzendorf matured a plan of operations for the Brethren at Bethlehem. It included the preaching of the Gospel in the four counties of the Province, the care of the congregations gathered in Oley, Germantown, Philadelphia, Tulpehocken, and Fredericktown, and the establishment of schools in the townships. On the 2d of December he set out on a circuit of the German settlements in Macungy, Oley, Tulpehocken, Heidelberg, and Conestoga. He returned to Bethlehem on the 12th, and, excepting a week's absence at Philadelphia (December 14–20), remained there until the last of the year. On that day he bade adieu to the "*House on the Lehigh*," the "*House of Bread*," on which reposed the hopes he cherished for the extension of Christ's kingdom among whites and Indians.

Having for the last time conferred with his colaborers in the Gospel of other denominations in Philadelphia, on the 9th of January, 1743, on the 12th of the month he set out for New York, and from that port took ship for Europe.

I carefully forbear saying any thing more at present of my Journeys among the Heathen, tho' I and my dear Companions shall continually keep them in mind with constant satisfaction.

Sung the 2[d] and 3[d] Verse of the Hymn,*

"Most worthy Spirit, Guide of Jesus' Train."

---

* No. XXXIII. in a "Collection of Hymns never before published." London: Printed for James Hutton at the Bible and Sun, in Little Wild Street, near Lincoln's Inn Fields, 1742.

DIVISION OF THE FIELD

AND PLAN OF OPERATIONS

To be pursued by the Brethren, in the Mission among the North American Indians, with comments, made by Count Zinzendorf on his return from the Indian country, in November of 1742.

(*Translated* from a German Autograph in the Archives at Bethlehem.*)

I. BETHLEHEM.—On which depends

1. The direction of the work in all its details.
2. The stated visitation of the River Indians.
3. The appointment to and support of missionaries at the following places in the order named (*in accordance with information obtained from the interpreter at Tulpehocken?*) viz.: *a*, on the North River.
   b, in the neighborhood of Bethlehem in huts.†
   c, at Shamokin, near Spangenberg Hill.
   d, * * * * * *

---

* The translator found difficulty in deciphering portions of this MS. The Count wrote a running hand, which is often almost illegible.

† The hope or intention here expressed of beginning an Indian settlement at or near Bethlehem was partially realized in the temporary stay of the Mohicans there in 1746. It was fulfilled when *Nain* was built in the summer of 1758, on *the upper Benezet tract.*

e, at Gnadenstadt (*City of Grace*) on the great flats of Skehandowana.*

II. OTSTONWAKIN.—The center of operations among the French half-breeds, who are to be reached through Andrew Montour, alias *Sattelihu*, and the rendezvous of missionaries appointed to labor

1. Among the Tuscaroras,
2. On "the Long Island,"
3. At Ohio,† and
4. Among the Senecas.

III. CHEKOMEKO.—The seat of our congregation of Christian Indians, whence colonists will be sent to Skehandowana, whenever its increase will render a transfer elsewhere necessary.

IV. WAYOMIK.—Although occupied by savages who guard the silver mines, yet the seat of a small congregation of believers composed of the captive *Chikasi*, and an aged Mohican and her daughter. These three will entertain and provide for missionaries on their way thence, to

1. The Mohawks,
2. The Oneidas,
3. The Onondagas, and

---

* This town was never built. When Spangenberg was at Wyoming, in the autumn of 1746, he expressed a hope that in time it would become the seat of a mission and of a congregation of Christian Indians. In 1757 he proposed to Teedyuscung to purchase of him that part of the valley in which the Shawanese had resided in 1742, for a settlement of the Christian Indians then at Bethlehem. The king did not entertain the proposal.

† Chr. Frederic Post missionated among the Indians on the Ohio in 1760.

4. The Cayugas,

among whom we already have acquaintances.

Two Sachems of the last named nation were present when I received the string of wampum.

V. New England.—Albany is to be the center of operations in this field. As the Mohicans are the dominant tribe, and as their language is the prevalent dialect, a colony will be sent from Checomeco thither, to form the nucleus of a congregation.

1. Apostles among the Indians.—Rauch* and Mack.
2. Elder among the Indians.—Antonius.†
3. Superintendents of the Mission.—The General Elder of the congregations in America and his wife.‡
4. Evangelists.—Büttner,§ Tschoop, *et alii.*
5. Secretaries.—Pyrlaeus‖ and George Neisser.

---

* Christian Henry Rauch.

† Quære—Anton Seyffert?

‡ Spangenberg was General Elder from his arrival in America in the autumn of 1744 to the abolition of that office in November of 1748. Until his return to Europe in July of 1762, he continued to superintend the Brethren's work in all its departments.

§ Gottlob Büttner, from Silesia, born January 9, 1717. Deceased at Shecomeco (where he had labored since Oct. of 1742) March 6, 1745.

‖ Jno. Christopher Pyrlaeus, the Mohawk scholar, was born at Pausa, Voigtland, in 1713. Studied for the ministry at the University of Leipsic between 1733 and 1738. Here became attached to the Brethren, visited Herrnhut, and accepted an appointment as missionary. Sailed from London in company with Büttner and Zander, and reached Bethlehem October 19, 1740. Ordained to the ministry during the sessions of the Synod convened in Oley. July 10, 1742, married Susan, youngest daughter of Jno. Stephen Bénezet, and soon after repaired to Philadelphia to assist Zinzendorf in the ministry. Pursuant to the Count's instructions, Pyrlaeus and his wife repaired to Tulpehocken in Jan-

6. Agents.—Conrad Weisser, King Shikellimy, Andrew Montour, Isaac, and Caxhayton in Onondaga.

---

uary of 1743, and for three months engaged in the study of the Mohawk, under Weisser's direction, in whose house they lodged, and whose children they in turn schooled. In June they set out for the Mohawk country. Having visited Shecomeco, they traveled west, through Albany and Schenectady, and reached the Mohawk castle of Canajoharie on the 17th of July. "Here," he writes in his autobiography, "we lodged in the cabin of a poor German opposite the Indian town, suffering many privations and often in danger of our lives. My wife, who had left a home of plenty, was but ill able to contend with the hardships that fell to her lot, and yet she bore up bravely. In order to perfect myself in the Mohawk, I spent much of my time among the Indians. In August I was summoned to Shecomeco to confer with some of the Brethren from Bethlehem, and, after an absence of eleven days, returned to Canajoharie, accompanied by Anton Seyffert. Together, we now visited the other Mohawk castles, and resolved to go to Onondaga. On arriving at the last white settlement on our way thither, we met a Sachem of the Six Nations, who, on learning our purpose, opposed its execution, first by using dissuasion and then by threatening violence. Thus foiled, we returned to Canajoharie, and soon afterwards set out for Bethlehem. This was the latter part of September." The Brethren having failed to procure a Mohawk Indian from Freehold to instruct in that language such of their number as were set apart for the mission, Pyrlaeus undertook this, and on the 4th of February, 1744, opened his *Indian School.* Abraham Bühninger, Joseph Möller, Michael Schnall, John J. Bull, alias *Shebosh,* David Zeisberger, the well-known missionary, and John and Margaret Hagen, were his pupils. In September of 1745, his first translations of hymns into Mohican appeared. This was the beginning of a collection for the use of the mission. While at Gnadenhütten, on the Mahoning, between 1747 and 1749, he prosecuted the study of the Mohican, and gave Mohawk lessons to David Bruce, Henry Frey, Daniel Oesterlein, and others. From January of 1749 to September of 1750, when the Institute was closed, he was engaged at the school for boys in Fredericktown. This was his last appointment in America. In November of 1751, he sailed for

The language for general use in the mission,—the *Mohawk.*

England, where he labored until 1770. He next went to Germany. His wife died at Herrnhut May 28, 1779. He deceased there May 28, 1785.

Pyrlaeus' contributions to the department of American philology, to which he applied himself with laborious devotion, and for the study of which his high scholarship well qualified him, were the following:

1. *A Collection of Words and Phrases in the Iroquois or Onondaga Language explained into German.* 4to. 140 pp.

2. *Affixa Nominum et Verborum Linguæ Macquaicæ.* 4to. 25 pp. With this are bound several Iroquois Vocabularies and Collections of Phrases, together making 178 pp.

3. *Adjectiva, Nomina et Pronomina Linguæ Macquaicæ, cum nonnullis de Verbis, Adverbiis, ac Præpositionibus ejusdem Linguæ.* 4to. 86 pp.

Mrs. Henry B. Luckenbach, of Bethlehem, is a great-granddaughter of the missionary.

CHRISTIAN INDIANS

BURIED AT BETHLEHEM, PA.

NAMES AND PERSONAL NOTICES

OF CHRISTIAN INDIANS WHO LIE BURIED AT BETHLEHEM, PENNSYLVANIA.

(Compiled from Authentic Records.)

WHO are these Indians, and what brought them here to die? are questions often asked by those who read the epitaphs of the dead that lie buried in the old Moravian grave-yard at Bethlehem.

Most of them were converts from heathenism. Some came here as to a city of refuge, because they had been driven by white men from their ancestral seats, and others came because they confided only in the Brethren at a time when their race was an object of almost universal abhorrence.

The persecution of the Moravians in New York by Acts* of Assembly in 1744 resulted in the abandonment of the Shecomeco Mission, which event was followed by an influx of Mohicans to Bethlehem. These were transferred in 1746 to Gnadenhütten, on the Mahoning. Here the Mission received accessions from the Delawares. After the memorable massacre in the night of the 24th of November, 1755, upward of seventy Christian Mohicans and Delawares fled to Bethlehem, and remained there, or at Nain, until 1761, in which year the last Indian interment was made in the Bethlehem grave-yard.

---

* These Acts are published in *O'Callaghan's Documentary History of New York.*

Fifty-eight converts were buried there in the interval between 1746 and 1761,—representatives of all the tribes and stations among and at which the Brethren then labored as messengers of the Gospel. And now, although a full century has passed since the remains of the Delaware maiden, Theodora, were carried to their long home, these dead of another race in the white man's cemetery still tell of a time when Bethlehem was the central seat of a Mission, of which there is no trace but the hillocks that cover the mouldering bones of her Indian converts.

---

1. John, a Mohican of Shecomeco, baptized by the missionary J. Martin Mack, at Bethlehem, July 13, and deceased July 15, 1746. Infant son of Joseph and Mary. No. 40.*

2. Anna, infant daughter of Zaccheus and Magdalene, Mohicans of Shecomeco; born at Bethlehem, July 17th, baptized by J. Martin Mack, on the same day, and deceased July 18, 1746. No. 42.

3. Magdalene, alias *Aguttáguos*, a Mohican, baptized by J. Martin Mack at Shecomeco, December 23, 1742. Deceased July 20, 1746. Mother of Anna. No. 43.

4. Joseph, alias *Nan'nachdausch*, a Mohican, baptized by J. Martin Mack at Shecomeco, December 23, 1742. Deceased July 21, 1746. Husband of Mary. No. 44.

5. Benjamin,† alias *Schabat*, a Wampanoag of Pachgatgoch, baptized by Bro. Peter Böhler at Shecomeco, August 18, 1743. Deceased July 28, 1746. No. 46.

---

* The figure appended to each notice indicates the number of the interment.

† The first Indian that resided at Bethlehem. An inmate of the Single Brethren's House.

6. Peter,* alias *Nachsábamit*, a Mohican of Wechquadnach, baptized by J. Martin Mack at Shecomeco, January 6, 1743. Deceased July 28, 1746. No. 47.

7. *Wesakau*,† a Wampanoag of Pachgatgoch. Deceased July 28, 1746. No. 48.

8. Isaac,‡ alias *Otabawánemen*, a Wampanoag of She-

---

* The husband of Christiana. After Peter's decease she was married to John Joseph Bull, whom the Indians called *Shebosh*, "running water." Both were assistants in the Mission for many years, and followed the fortunes of the Moravian Indians, north and west, in their exodus from the settled portions of Pennsylvania in 1765. Christiana deceased in the autumn of 1787.

† Was not baptized.

‡ One of three Indians baptized at the close of a Synod held at Mr. Jno. de Turcks. The rite of baptism was on this occasion administered for the first time to Indians by the Brethren. The three candidates were *Schabash*, *Otabawanemen*, and *Mashak*. They had been brought from Shecomeco by their missionary, who, after having received ordination at the hands of Bishop Nitschmann, baptized them, naming them respectively Abraham, Isaac, and Jacob. All of them became assistants in the mission among their people. Abraham deceased in Wyoming in December of 1762, and Jacob was buried in "Potters' Field" (Washington Square), Philadelphia, in February of 1764. Zinzendorf had dispatched Büttner to Shecomeco for Rauch and the catechumens. While at Philadelphia, on their return home, they waited on James Logan (February 3), who alludes to the interview in these words in a letter to Governor Clarke, of New York: "Some weeks ago two Moravians called on me, by the Count's direction, with three of ye Mohican Indians in their company. One of the latter speaking good English served for an interpreter. All three were proselytes, exceeding grave but with free and no ill countenances. Though the young Germans drank one glass of wine apiece with us, the others would taste nothing but water. I hope if these two Germans, or either of them should settle in your Province, ye traders and others of ye people will treat them courteously; since I think we may all be assured they have no views whatever (as ye Romish Priests and other Emissaries have) that can be inconsistent with the British interests. So much I thought it might be requisite to say of them."

comeco, baptized by the missionary Christian Henry Rauch, in Oley, Berks County, February 22, 1742. Deceased August 2, 1746. Husband of Rebecca. No. 52.

9. Samuel, a Delaware, baptized by Brother John Brandmüller at Bethlehem, August 9, 1746, and deceased the same day. Infant son of Beata. No. 54.

10. Gabriel, a Mohican, baptized by the missionary Gottlob Büttner, at Shecomeco, May 21, 1744. Deceased August 13, 1746, aged 3 years. Son of Joshua. No. 55.

11. Elisabeth, a Mohican, baptized by Bro. John Brandmüller at Bethlehem, August 12, and deceased August 14, 1746. Infant daughter of Peter and Christiana. No. 56.

12. Thomas,* alias *Pechtawáppeed*, alias *Harris*, a Sopus Indian, baptized by Christian H. Rauch at Shecomeco, August 22, 1742. Deceased August 15, 1746. Husband of Esther. No. 57.

13. Zipporah, alias *Wawóttackem*, a Hogeland† Indian, baptized by Bishop David Nitschmann at Shecomeco, August 18, 1743. Deceased August 23, 1746. Wife of Nathaniel. No. 59.

14. Thomas,‡ a Mohican of Shecomeco. Deceased August 26, 1746, aged 10 years. Son of Jephthah. No. 60.

---

* A Mohican of Sopus, or a "*Lowlander*." Thomas, and Esther his wife, left Shecomeco for Bethlehem in August of 1743, and were appointed steward and stewardess of Indians residing or visiting there. Both were highly esteemed by their people and instrumental in the conversion of *Gehntachquishigunt* and *Olelemináu*, the first converts from the Delawares, who were baptized at Bethlehem April 26, 1745, by Rauch and Mack, receiving the names of Gottlieb and Mary, respectively. Thomas is introduced in the painting of the "First Fruits," the original of which is at Herrnhut, one copy at Zeyst, in Holland, and a second at Bethlehem.

† Hogeland, or Hoogland, Dutch for Highlands, a name applied to the Highlands of New York. The Indians called them *Wequehachke*, the hill-country.

‡ Was not baptized.

15. John,* alias *Wasámapah*, alias *Tschope*, a Mohican, baptized by Chrn. H. Rauch, at Shecomeco, April 16, 1742. Deceased August 27, 1746. No. 62.

16. Salome,† a Wampanoag, baptized by Gottlob Büttner, at Shecomeco, December 23, 1742. Deceased September 16, 1746. Wife of Joshua. No. 65.

---

* John, alias *Wasamapah*, alias *Tschoop* (Job), was one of the company of drunken Indians whom Rauch met on the streets of New York, a few days after his arrival from Europe, in July of 1740. Invited by these strangers to their village on the Shecomeco, the missionary went thither and preached the Gospel. Its power was soon demonstrated in the conviction of Tschoop, who expressed a desire to become, by baptism, a member of the Christian Church. Indisposition preventing him from accompanying three other candidates to Oley, the administration of the rite, in his case, was postponed. John left Shecomeco for Bethlehem in August of 1745. Here he acted as interpreter in the service held for the Indians on Sunday afternoon in the Brethren's chapel. He also gave instruction in Mohican to a number of brethren and sisters who were designed for missionaries. On the organization of the refugees from Shecomeco into a Christian congregation, at *Friedenshütten* (the Huts of Peace), on the 24th of July, 1746, John was appointed their teacher. Soon after, small-pox broke out at the Indian quarters. To this malady he fell a victim, after a painful illness of seven days, during which he gave evidence of the mighty work of grace which the Spirit of God had wrought in his heart. In the presence of his weeping countrymen, who had been summoned to his bedside, and amid the prayers of Spangenberg and Rauch, the spirit of the patient sufferer was released from its tenement of clay. This was on the 27th of August. In the afternoon of Sunday, the 28th, a funeral sermon was delivered by Rauch, and the remains were then conveyed to the grave-yard amid the strains of solemn music. As the body was being lowered into the earth, Nicodemus, the Elder, knelt by the grave and offered prayer. The concurrent testimony of those who knew John shows that he was not unworthy of the name of the beloved disciple which he bore, and that this evangelist among his people was a marvelous instance of the transforming power of divine grace.

† Stewardess at *Friedenshütten*.

17. Gottlob, a Mohican, baptized by Chr. H. Rauch, at Bethlehem, September 9, and deceased September 23, 1746. Infant son of Joshua and Salome. No. 66.

18. Nathaniel, a Mohican, baptized by the missionary John Christopher Pyrlaeus, at Bethlehem, December 17, and deceased December 18, 1746. Infant son of Nathaniel and Zipporah. No. 73.

19. Beata, a Delaware, baptized by Bishop John C. Frederic Cammerhoff, at Bethlehem, March 22, 1747, and deceased the same day, aged 18 months. Daughter of Beata, and brother of Samuel (9). No. 74.

20. Lucas, alias *Quawátschonit* (*he takes a child by the hand and leads it*), a Wampanoag of Pachgatgoch, baptized by J. Martin Mack, at Shecomeco, March 27, 1743. Deceased October 3, 1747. Father of Rachel Post. No. 77.

21. Theodora, alias *Atechtanoàh* (*soon ripe*), a Wampanoag of Pachgatgoch, baptized by J. Martin Mack, at Bethlehem, October 5, 1747, and deceased the same day, aged 80 years. Grandmother of Rachel Post. No. 78.

22. Rachel Post, a Wampanoag, baptized by Gottlob Büttner, at Pachgatgoch, February 13, 1743. Deceased December 26, 1747. Daughter of Lucas (20) and Priscilla, alias *Amanariochque*.

Rachel received her first religious impressions under David Brainerd's preaching, at Kaunameek.* September 8, 1743, she was married to the missionary, Christian Frederic Post, at Shecomeco. She bore him two children —a son, Ludwig John, born at Bethlehem, September 24, 1744, baptized by Brother Paul D. Pryzelius, and deceased there May 13, 1745; and a daugher, Mary, born at Bethlehem, April 10, 1746, baptized by Brother Abraham Meinung, and deceased there December 26, 1747. Their

* Twenty miles west of Stockbridge, Mass.

numbers are 23 and 82. A still-born child was buried with Rachel. No. 83.

23. Salome,* a Monsey, baptized by J. Martin Mack, at Gnadenhütten, April 9, 1747. Deceased May 18, 1748. Infant daughter of Benjamin and Zipporah. No. 102.

24. Thomas,† a Mohican, baptized by J. Martin Mack, at Gnadenhütten, November 17, 1746. Deceased July 7, 1748. Infant son of Thomas Pechtawappeed and Esther. No. 106.

25. Daniel, a Delaware, baptized by Bishop John M. de Watteville, at Bethlehem, March 5, and deceased April 19, 1749. An adult brother of Salome, a Delaware. No. 121.

26. Lydia,‡ a Delaware. Deceased May 4, 1749, aged 2 years. Daughter of Henry and Dorothea. No. 122.

27. Anna, a Delaware, baptized by Bishop de Watteville, at Bethlehem, February 16, and deceased June 20, 1749. Infant daughter of Henry and Dorothea. No. 123.

28. Anna Salome, a Delaware, baptized by Brother Samuel Krause, at Bethlehem, October 9, 1749, and deceased the same day,§ aged 3 years. Daughter of Salome. No. 127.

29. Theodora,|| a Delaware, baptized by Brother Gottlieb Pezold, at Bethlehem, October 23, and deceased November 24, 1749. No 129.

---

* An inmate of the Institute for Children, at Bethlehem.

† Also an inmate of the Institute.

‡ Was not baptized. Her parents were from New Jersey. Both had been baptized at Bethlehem in January of 1749. Henry was born *when corn needed hoeing the first time*, in 1727, in an Indian village on the Delaware, a few miles east of Hunter's settlement, or Huntersville, in Lower Mount Bethel. Dorothea was born at Good Luck, on the Jersey coast, and thence removed to Cranberry.

§ At Friedenshütten.

|| Came to Bethlehem, from her home on the Schuylkill, north of the Blue Mountain. She was very aged, and totally blind.

30. Rachel,* a Delaware, baptized by Bishop Cammerhoff, near Bethlehem, January 10, and deceased January 15, 1750. No. 130.

31. Anna Mary, alias *Taübchen* (*Little Dove*), a Mohican, baptized by Brother Abraham Reincke, at Nazareth, January 1, 1747. Deceased January 23, 1750, aged 12 years. Daughter of Nathaniel and Zipporah (13). No. 131.

32. Jonas, a Mohican of Wechquadnach, baptized by Bishop Cammerhoff, at Bethlehem, August 28, and deceased August 29, 1750, aged 9 years. Son of Jonas.† No. 144.

33. Martin,‡ alias *Mahab*, a Wampanoag, of Shecomeco, baptized by J. Martin Mack, at Bethlehem, January 23, 1749. Deceased October 26, 1750, aged 6 years. Son of Philip and Lydia. No. 146.

34. Salome,§ alias *Jankoch*, a Hogeland Indian of Shecomeco, baptized by Bishop Cammerhoff, at Bethlehem, May 4, 1748. Deceased April 18, 1751. Foster-daughter of Nicodemus. No. 154.

35. Zipporah,|| alias *Wechnawashque*, a Mohican, of Shecomeco, baptized by Bishop Cammerhoff, at Bethlehem, August 4, 1748. Deceased May 9, 1751, aged 18 years. Daughter of Nathaniel and Zipporah (13). No. 156.

---

* A widow, and sister of Old *Nutimus*, the Delaware king of *Nescopec*. Baptized in an Indian encampment on the Manakasy, a mile northwest of Bethlehem.

† Came to Bethlehem from Shecomeco, in May of 1746. Was nurse at Friedenshütten.

‡ Born at Shecomeco, *in the time of wheat harvest*, in 1744. In 1747 was entered at the school in Frederictown. Thence transferred to the Institute at Bethlehem.

§ Born in December of 1733, in *Wequchachke*, the Highlands. An inmate of the Single Sisters' House.

|| An inmate of the Single Sisters' House.

36. Benigna Christiana, a Mohican of Shecomeco, baptized by Bishop Cammerhoff, at Nazareth,* November 23, 1748. Deceased June 4, 1751, aged eight years. Daughter of Peter (6) and Christiana. No. 158.

37. Agnes Post, a Delaware of the *Unami*, or Turtle tribe, from New Jersey, baptized by Bishop Cammerhoff at Bethlehem, March 5, 1749. Deceased July 8, 1751, aged 22 years.†

Agnes's father and grandfather were Six Nation Indians. She had attended Brainerd's preaching at *Crossweeksung*, near Bordentown. In September of 1749 was married to Christian Frederic Post, at Bethlehem. She bore him a son, Christian Frederic, who was baptized by Bishop Cammerhoff, November 1, 1755, and who deceased January 11, 1751 (No. 151). Agnes's sister, Juliana, was the wife of *Amos*, King Teedyuscung's oldest son. No. 160.

38. Caritas,‡ a Delaware of Meniolagomeka, baptized by Bishop Cammerhoff at Bethlehem, May 6, 1749. Deceased January 30, 1752, aged 8 years. Daughter of Daniel and Ruth. No. 165.

39. Gottlieb, a Wampanoag, baptized by J. Martin Mack at Gnadenhütten, September 7, 1750. Deceased January 5, 1753, aged 2 years. Son of John Peter (46) and Esther. No. 177.

40. Anna Maria, alias *Nannachpelema*, a Delaware of Gnadenhütten, baptized by Bishop Matthias G. Hehl, at Bethlehem, February 27, 1752. Deceased October 28, 1753. Wife of Tobias, alias *Laochalent*, alias *Tom Evans*. No. 181.

---

* At the time in the Institute for Children in the Whitefield House.

† Died of consumption at Friedenshütten, where she and her husband were superintendents.

‡ An inmate of the Institute for Children, at Bethlehem.

41. Anna Caritas,* alias *Schitemoque*, a Shawanese from *Skehandowana* (Wyoming), baptized by Bishop de Watteville, in Frederictown, Montgomery County, November 21, 1748. Deceased December 31, 1755. No. 196.

42. Isaac,† a Wampanoag of Shecomeco, baptized by Bishop Cammerhoff, at Bethlehem, January 17, 1749. Deceased February 18, 1756, aged 18 years. A son of Isaac *Otabawanemen* (8) and Rebecca. No. 203.

43. Anna, a Delaware, baptized by J. Martin Mack, at Meniolagomeka, May 2, 1753. Deceased at Bethlehem, April 23, 1756, aged 3 years. Daughter of Joshua and Agnes. No. 204.

44. Simeon,‡ a Delaware from New Jersey, baptized by the missionary Bernhard Adam Grubé, at Bethlehem, January 6, and deceased October 17, 1756, aged 70 years. No. 209.

45. Samuel, alias *Achgónoma*, a Delaware of Meniolagomeka, baptized by the missionary John Jacob Schmick, at

---

* Born in North Carolina, near the Wachovia tract. Thither her mother, a Shawanese, had been brought by some Mohawk warriors on their return north from a maraud. Immediately after giving birth to her child she died, and *Schitemoque* was left to the care of a sister, who reared her on the pulp of the calabash. Migrated with others of her people to Wyoming, whence she came to Bethlehem, a widow, in 1747. She was the first convert from the Shawanese.

† Born in Shecomeco, *when corn was ripe*, in 1738. Came to Bethlehem in 1746. Was entered at the school in Frederictown. Thence transferred to a school for boys, opened in 1747, south of the Lehigh, near the "Crown," and from there into the Single Brethren's House.

‡ Stepfather of Augustus, alias *George Rex*. Born at Egg Harbor, on the Jersey coast. A medicine-man, in high repute among his people. Thence he removed north of the Blue Mountain, and became acquainted with the Brethren at Meniolagomeka. In 1754 settled in Gnadenhütten, east of the Lehigh. Fled to Bethlehem after the massacre on the Mahoning. He was totally blind.

Bethlehem, January 5, and deceased January 11, 1757, aged 14 years. Son of Augustus, alias *George Rex*, Captain of Meniolagomeka, and Elder of the Christian Indians at Bethlehem between November of 1755 and October of 1758. No. 212.

46. John Peter,* alias *Peter Robert*, a Wampanoag of Pachgatgoch, baptized by Bishop Cammerhoff at Bethlehem, November, 1748. Deceased April 1, 1757. No. 215.

47. Christiana, a Mohican, baptized by J. Martin Mack, at Gnadenhütten, October 18, 1755. Deceased April 1, 1757. Infant daughter of John Peter (46) and Esther. No. 216.

48. Samuel, a Delaware, baptized by Bishop Böhler, at Bethlehem, December 11, and deceased December 14, 1757. Infant son of Aquila† and Maria, of Gnadenhütten. No. 224.

49. Sophia, a Delaware, baptized by J. Martin Mack, at Bethlehem, January 6, and deceased January 7, 1758. Infant daughter of Paul and Magdalene. No. 225.

50. Michael,‡ alias *Hendrick*, a Monsey, baptized by Gottlob Büttner, at Shecomeco, December 23, 1742. De-

---

* Came to Gnadenhütten in the autumn of 1746. May, 1749, married Esther, the relict of Thomas *Pechtowapped*, then at Gnadenhütten. In 1752 removed to Bethlehem, and was appointed steward at the new Indian quarters opened on the Manakasy, west of the grist-mill.

† Half-brother of Augustus, alias *George Rex*.

‡ In early life Michael had been a noted brave in his tribe, and once in an engagement had kept his post resolutely, although the tree at which he stood had been struck by twenty bullets. After his baptism he was true to his profession, and he died the death of the righteous. As he lay a corpse, the serenity of his countenance contrasted markedly with the barbaric devices with which his face had been scarified in the days when deeds of blood were the delight of "the Crown of the Indian Mission."

ceased July 24, 1758, a widower, aged 70 years, called "*The Crown of the Indian Mission.*" No. 233.

51. Eve, a Hogeland Indian, baptized by Bro. Anton Seyffert, at Shecomeco, August 18, 1743. Deceased at Nain, November 18, 1758.* No. 241.

52. Hannah, a Monsey, baptized by J. Martin Mack, at Nain, November 12, and deceased there December 24, 1758. No. 244.

53. Eleonora, a Mohican, baptized by J. Martin Mack, at Nain, November 12, 1758, and deceased there February 25, 1759. Infant daughter of Daniel and Elisabeth. No. 247.

54. Henry, a Mohican, baptized by J. Martin Mack, at Nain, February 26, and deceased February 27, 1759. Infant son of Abel and Philippina. No. 248.

55. Joseph, a Mohican, baptized by Bishop Spangenberg, at Bethlehem, August 25, 1758. Deceased at Nain, March 10, 1759. No. 250.

56. Theodora, alias *Aktees*, a Delaware of Gnadenhütten, baptized by Bernhard A. Grubé, at Bethlehem, February 22, 1756.† Deceased January 17, 1761, aged 19 years. Daughter of *Sam Evans*, and niece of *Teedyuscung*, King of the Delawares. No. 291.

---

* In April of 1759 the Brethren Spangenberg and Böhler selected the site for a grave-yard at Nain. The first interment there was that of the Delaware, Nicodemus, alias *Joe Evans*, in January of 1760.

† After her baptism, Theodora was admitted into the Single Sisters' House. There she deceased.

ANNALS OF EARLY

MORAVIAN SETTLEMENT

IN

GEORGIA AND PENNSYLVANIA.

THESE are the simple annals of lowly ones of the earth who crossed the seas as ambassadors of a King.

To many they may appear dead things, and dry as the bones that the seer of old saw in the Valley of Vision, or prove only a passionless picture of still life. But as we look we observe the figures moving; and beautiful upon the wooded mountains and in the green valleys of a new world, in crowded mart, and among the cottages of the poor, are the feet of these Evangelists as they pass in quick succession like the forms of some shifting panoramic scene. And we should not be surprised to meet with grotesque shapes too, in this rare old picture of religious life a hundred years ago in the wilds of Pennsylvania,—forms of cowled monk and hooded nun by the side of Moravian peasant and scholar and unmitered Bishop and untitled Count. For hither thousands had come from an old world, bringing with them the remembrance of ancient things, which sprang up anew into life or were recast in fantastic moulds in the seclusion and solitude of their woodland homes.

And simple as these annals are, we should not forget that they are the annals of those lowly ones of the earth, who, with others of like spirit, reared a fabric of Missions, whose pillars are planted in the four quarters of the earth, and under whose dome are gathered together worshipers of the true God out of many nations and kindreds and tribes and tongues.

ANNALS OF EARLY MORAVIAN SETTLEMENT

IN GEORGIA AND PENNSYLVANIA

Recording the movements of the Brethren, and events of interest that occurred in the interval between September of 1734 and July of 1742.

(*Extracted chiefly from George Neisser's Compilation, a MS. in the Archives at Bethlehem.*)

1734.

September 22. George Böhnisch, Christopher Baus, and Christopher Wiegner arrived at Philadelphia on the "St. Andrew,"* Captain Stedman.

1735.

March 22. Spangenberg, Anton Seyffert, John Töltschig, Gottfried Haberecht, Gotthard Demuth, Peter Rosa, Michael and George Haberland, Frederic Riedel, and George Waschke arrived off Savannah, on the "Two Brothers," Captain Thompson.†

---

* This vessel brought the Schwenkfelders, whom Zinzendorf had received at Berthelsdorf, on their banishment from Silesia. Böhnisch accompanied them to Pennsylvania, at their request, and during his stay among them resided at Wiegner's. He returned to Europe in 1737. See "*Erläuterung für Herrn Caspar Schwenckfeld*" (*Breslau*, 1771), for a narrative of the voyage.

† Riedel, from Schlen, Moravia, deceased at Savannah in September of 1735. His widow married Peter Rosa.

Waschke, from Kunewalde, Moravia, left Georgia for Pennsylvania

July. John Francis Regnier* arrived in Savannah.

---

in February of 1737. Settled in Germantown. His wife deceased at the "Falls of Schuylkill" in 1766, and was buried in "Levering's Graveyard." In 1779 he was still living at Germantown, totally blind. Some of his descendants moved to Baltimore.

Haberecht, from Peila, Silesia, left Georgia in April of 1737. Settled in Germantown. Entered the convent of the Seventh-day Baptists at *Ephrata*, on the Cocalico. Resumed connection with the Brethren in 1742. Returned to Europe with Zinzendorf. Missionated among the Christian slaves in Algiers?

Demuth, from Radelsdorf, Bohemia, left Georgia in June of 1737. Settled in Germantown. Deceased there in December of 1744. His widow married David Tanneberger, of Bethlehem, and deceased in 1774. John Christopher, a son, born in 1738, deceased at Lancaster in 1818.

G. Haberland, from Schönau, Moravia, deceased at Savannah in 1737.

Töltschig, from Zauchtenthal, Moravia, sailed for Europe in the spring of 1738.

Rosa, from Bohemia, left for Pennsylvania in November of 1739, with his wife and infant daughter, Maria. Settled in Germantown. Deceased there in March of 1740. His widow married John M. Huber, of Bethlehem, and deceased there 1798. A portrait of her is in the "Archives."

M. Haberland, from Schönau, sailed for Europe in February of 1740.

* Regnier immigrated from Switzerland to Pennsylvania in 1728. Joined the Seventh-day Baptists, on the Cocalico. Thence went to Georgia. In 1738 sailed for Europe, attached himself to the Brethren at Herrnhaag, and was sent by them to Surinam. (See his *Report of November*, 1740, *Büdingische Sammlung*, Part viii. No. 3.) In 1743 returned to Pennsylvania. Of him the chronicler of Ephrata writes: "Endlich hat er, mit blosem Haupt und Füszen, eine Reise von 600 Meilen zu Fusz durch die grosse Wüste gethan nach Georgien, und sich daselbst zu den Mährischen Brüdern gesellet. Endlich hat er in auswärtigen Landen sein unruhiges Leben geendet. Gott seye ihm gnädig am Tag des Urtheils!" Regnier was the author of a defamatory pamphlet aimed at the Brethren.

1736.

February 16. David Nitschmann, *Episc.*, Christian Adolph von Hermsdorf, Henry Rascher, Andrew and Anna Dober, David and Rosina Zeisberger, David and John Tanneberger, David Jag, Augustine and George Neisser, John Michael Meyer, Rosina Haberecht, John Martin Mack, Matthias Seybold, Jacob Frank, Judith Töltschig, Gottlieb and Regina Demuth, Catharine Riedel, Anna Waschke, Juliana Jäschke, John Böhner, and Matthias Böhnisch arrived off Savannah on the "Simonds," Captain Cornish.*

---

* Frank, from Wirtemberg, deceased at Savannah in March of 1736.

Rascher, from Upper Lusatia, Rosina Haberecht, from Silesia, and Matthias Böhnisch, from Kunewalde, deceased at Savannah in the same year.

Andrew and Anna Dober, from Mönchsroth, Franck, and von Hermsdorf, from Upper Lusatia, returned to Europe in 1737.

Juliana Jäschke, from Moravia, married George Waschke, and left for Pennsylvania with him and his mother, Anna Waschke, in February of 1737. The latter deceased at "the Bethel," near Germantown, at an advanced age.

David and John Tanneberger, from Zauchtenthal, left for Pennsylvania in June of 1737. Settled in Germantown. Removed to Bethlehem in 1742. David deceased there in 1760. John, his son, deceased in Philadelphia in 1778.

Demuth, from Radelsdorf, left for Pennsylvania in June of 1737. Settled in Matetsche. Removed to Bethlehem in 1742. Deceased at Schöneck, Pa., in 1776.

Regina Demuth left with her husband, Gotthard, in June of 1737.

David Jag, from Zauchtenthal, and Michael Meyer, from Silesia, left for Pennsylvania in 1737. Jag settled in Goshenhoppen, and Meyer in Macungy.

Augustine Neisser, from Sehlen, left for Pennsylvania in September of 1737. Settled in Germantown. A cutler and clock-maker. In 1770

April. Early in the month Spangenberg arrived at New York, and proceeded to enter upon his labors among the Schwenkfelders, who were settled along the Skippack, in Worcester and Towamensing Townships, Philadelphia County. He made his home here at the house of Christopher Wiegner.* David Nitschmann followed him from Georgia.†

---

married Catharine Reisinger. Had three sons, George Henry, born in 1771, Augustine, born in 1774, and Jacob, born in 1777.

Seybold, from Wirtemberg, left for Pennsylvania in November of 1739. Lived among the Schwenkfelders, and worked for Wiegner until Böhler's arrival, in April of 1740. Returned to Europe, and deceased in 1787.

Judith Töltschig, from Schönau, returned to Europe with her brother, Michael Haberland, in February of 1740.

General Oglethorpe and John and Charles Wesley were on board the Simonds.

* The "Wiegner Farm" lies two miles south of Kulpsville, and about eight southwest of the Hatfield Station, on the North Pennsylvania Railroad, in Montgomery County. It is now in possession of Mr. George Anders. The farm-house is no longer standing. It was interesting as having been the home of the first Moravians in Pennsylvania, and also as the head-quarters of *The Associated Brethren of Skippack*," who met there for the worship of God and for religious edification. Among these old worthies were Henry Frey, John Kooken, George Merkel, Christian Weber, John Bonn, Jacob Wenzen, Jost Schmidt, William Bossen, and Jost Becker, of Skippack; Henry Antes, William Frey, George Stiefel, Henry Holstein, and Andrew Frey, of Frederic Township; Matthias Gmelen and Abraham Wagner, of Matetsche; John Bertolet, Francis Ritter, and William Pott, of Oley; John Bechtel, John Adam Gruber, Blasuis Mackinet, and George Benzel, of Germantown. Edmund B. Bensell, the meritorious artist, is his only descendant resident in Germantown.

† His brief sojourn in Pennsylvania, in the spring of 1736, was spent by Bishop Nitschmann in ascertaining the religious condition of its German population. With this object, he traveled through the rural districts, and was thus brought into contact with representatives

June. David Nitschmann sailed from New York on his return to Europe.

August. Toward the close of the month Spangenberg sailed for St. Thomas, as he had been deputed by Nitschmann to hold a visitation.

November. Spangenberg returned from St. Thomas.

1737.

February. In this month George Neisser arrived at Wiegner's. He had been dispatched by the Brethren in Georgia to report their distress to Spangenberg, and to urge him to repair to London and lay their grievances before the "Trustees for the Colony of Georgia."

May. Spangenberg sailed for Georgia to counsel with the Brethren.

---

of the numerous sects who were distracting the Christianity that had been transplanted into the wilds of this part of the new world. Accompanied by Spangenberg, he visited the Seventh-day Baptists also. "Um dieselbe Zeit," writes the chronicler of Ephrata, "sind die ersten Mährischen Brüder in Pensilvanien angekommen, nehmlich Spangenberg und Nitschmann, welche drei einsame Brüder alsbald in Schippach bei einer Familie, Wiegner genannt, besuchten. Bald bei dem ersten Anblick bemerkte man zu beyden Theilen einen magnetischen Anzug der Geister; denn man war zu beyden Seiten noch in der ersten Liebe. Darum nahmen sie sich auch vor mit gedachten Einsamen zu reisen und im Lager einen Besuch abzustatten, welcher auch sehr gesegnet ist ausgeführt worden. Bey dem Abreisen gaben ihnen die Brüder ein Stück Wegs das Geleit, schlossen einen Kreis und nachdeme sie Gott durch ein Lied gelobet hatten, herzten sie einander unter Empfehlung der Gnade Gottes."—*Chronicon Ephratense, enthaltend den Lebenslauf des ehrwürdigen Vaters in Christo, Friedsam Gottrecht weyland Stiffters und Vorstehers des geistlichen Ordens der Einsame in Ephrata in der Grafschaft Lancaster in Pensilvanien. Zusammengezogen von Brüder Lamech und Agrippa. Ephrata,* 1786.

August. David Zeisberger, Jr., and John Michael Schober arrived in Georgia.*

September. Spangenberg returned to Pennsylvania.

1738.

October 15. Peter Böhler and George Schulius† arrived at Savannah. Böhler had been appointed minister to the Brethren in that town, and was also commissioned, with Schulius, to missionate among the negroes on the plantations between Savannah and Charleston.

1739.

August. In this month Spangenberg closed his labors among the Schwenkfelders and sailed for Europe.

1740.

April. On the 13th of the month Peter Böhler, Anton Seyffert, Martin Mack, John Böhner, David and Rosina Zeisberger, David Zeisberger, Jr., Hannah Hummel,‡ and Benjamin Sommers and James —— (indentured boys), sailed from Savannah on "the Savannah," Whitefield's sloop, for Philadelphia. They landed on the 25th.

May. On the 3d, Whitefield "agreed with William Al-

---

* Young Zeisberger, subsequently and for forty years of his life a missionary to the Indians, was from Zauchtenthal. Schober was from Hoffmansdorf, Moravia. Both were mere boys, whom the spirit of adventure had brought unbidden to the new world. Samuel L. Shober, an eminent merchant of Philadelphia, was one of his descendants.

† From Moravia. Deceased at Purysburg, Beaufort County, S. C., August 4, 1739.

‡ From Purysburg.

len, of Philadelphia, for 5,000 acres of land in the Forks of Delaware, for £2,200."

On the 5th he proposed to Peter Böhler, at Wiegner's,* to engage the Brethren who had accompanied him from Georgia, to do the carpentering at a house he designed to erect on his land for a school for negroes.

Böhler and Seyffert, with Henry Antes of Falckner Swamp† as their guide, set out to view the tract, and camped on it in the night of the 7th.

On the 10th the Brethren, with the approval of the lot, accepted Whitefield's proposal.

On the 18th John Hagen, missionary to the Cherokees, reached Savannah.

On the 27th the Brethren set out from Germantown for Whitefield's tract, which he named Nazareth.

---

* "*Thursday, May* 5. Preached at Skippack, sixteen miles from Montgomery, where the Dutch people live. It was seemingly a very wilderness part of the country; but there were not less, I believe, than 2000 hearers. Rode twelve miles, and preached in the evening to about 3000 people at a Dutchman's plantation, who seemed to have drank deeply into the consolations of the Holy Spirit. We spent the evening in a most agreeable manner. I never saw more simplicity; surely that house was a *Bethel.*"—*Whitefield's Journal, London,* 1761.

"It was surprising to see such a multitude of people gathered together in such a wilderness country, 30 miles distant from Philadelphia. Our brother was exceedingly carried out in his sermon to press poor sinners to come to Christ by faith, and claim all their privileges, namely, not only righteousness and peace, but joy in the Holy Ghost; and after he had done, our dear friend, Peter Böhler, preached in Dutch to those who could not understand our brother in English."—*Journal of a Voyage from Savannah to Philadelphia, by Wm. Seward, Gent. London,* 1740.

† Frederic Township, Montgomery Co. So named for Daniel Falckner, who settled there about 1700. In 1702 he published his "*Curieuse Nachricht von Pensilvanien.*" *Frankfurth und Leipzig.*

On the 30th they arrived there and assembled for worship under "Böhler's Oak."

June. Toward the close of the month, the first house at Nazareth was completed and occupied.

July 21. Christian H. Rauch, the Apostle to the Indians, arrived at New York.

August 29. He reached Shecomeco and commenced his labors among the Mohicans.

October. Andrew Eschenbach* arrived at Philadelphia.

November. Early in the month the second house at Nazareth was completed and occupied.

Toward the close of the month Böhler repaired to Philadelphia to report progress to Whitefield. Since they had last met the latter had conceived a dislike of the Brethren based on difference of opinion respecting doctrine. Failing to bring Böhler over to his views at this interview, he became irritated, and in the heat of controversy discharged the Brethren from his employ. He closed the conference, which had been conducted in Latin, with the words, "*Sic jubeo; stet voluntas pro ratione.*"†

December. On the 15th of the month David Nitschmann, *Episc.*,‡ David Nitschmann, Sr.,§ Christian Fröhlich, Jo-

* From Naumburg.

† Whitefield was in Philadelphia between the 19th and the 29th of the month. See his *Journal.*

‡ David Nitschmann, born 1696 in Zauchtenthal, immigrated to Herrnhut in 1724. In March of 1735 was consecrated a Bishop (the first of the Renewed Church of the Brethren) by Bishop Ernst Jablonsky, of Berlin, with the approval of his associate, Bishop Christian

§ Uncle of the Bishop. Born 1676 in Zauchtenthal, a descendant of the old Moravian and Bohemian Brethren. In October of 1750 he was naturalized at the Supreme Court in Philadelphia, and was thus qualified to hold the Brethren's estates in this country. All purchases

hanna S. Molther, and Anna Nitschmann, arrived at Philadelphia and repaired to Nazareth.

Böhler left on the 27th for New York, thence to set sail for Europe, pursuant to his recall. He was accompanied there by David Nitschmann, *Episc.* They spent the 31st of the month, which was Böhler's twenty-ninth birthday, at Christopher Wiegner's.

1741.

January 29. Böhler embarked for Bristol.

February 4. David Nitschmann, *Episc.*, reached Nazareth on his return from New York. The Brethren now concluded to purchase a tract of land lying at the confluence of the Lehigh and Manakasy, which had been offered to Böhler by Nathaniel Irish,* of Saucon, an agent for

---

Sitkovius, of Lissa, Poland. In 1740 was dispatched to America to establish a Brethren's settlement in the Northern English Colonies. In virtue of this commission he founded Bethlehem. Much of his life was spent in travel, as the visitation of the missions and the discharge of episcopal functions in that field of the Church constituted his sphere of labor. In his long service he is said to have made fifty voyages. Subsequent to 1761 he resided at Bethlehem. Here he deceased Oct. 8, 1772. To his end he was a strenuous advocate of the simple ways and mode of life that had prevailed among the old Moravian and Bohemian Brethren.

---

of lands and all contracts were now made by him for the Brethren. He deceased April 14, 1758, in the 82d year of his age. There is a portrait of him in the "Archives." He is popularly known as the founder of Bethlehem.

* According to Eastburn's map of 1740, Nathaniel Irish was in that year settled on 306 acres, at the mouth of "Saucong Creek." Here he built a mill, and hither Böhler was wont to come to await the grinding of grist for his Brethren at Nazareth, as it was the nearest market for bread. Irish's house stood on the site of Mr. Wm. Shimer's residence, in Shimersville. It was removed in 1816. The ruins of the

William Allen,* for the sale of lands in this part of Bucks County.

February 9. David Nitschmann, *Episc.*, came to Frederictown† to consult with Antes about the projected settlement.

March. In the beginning of the month the Brethren at Nazareth received a visit from a company of Seventh-day Baptists from Ephrata,‡ who expressed admiration at the

---

mill are yet to be seen on the premises of Mr. Jno. Knecht, of that place. It was demolished in 1812, and a part of the stone worked up into the mill at present owned by Mr. Knecht. About a mile southwest of Shimersville, near Mr. Isaac Pearson's farm-house, in the forks of the Hellertown road, was Irish's stone-quarry, which, in 1740, was the terminus of the high road from Philadelphia into the northern part of Bucks.

* A large dealer in lands purchased of the Proprietaries. This tract was a part of 5000 acres he had bought of Joseph Turner in 1736. In 1741 was Recorder of the City of Philadelphia. Chief Justice of Pennsylvania before the Revolution, and died 1780, a refugee Loyalist in London.

† George Neisser was at this time working in wood for Mr. Antes, who was a millwright by trade.

‡ Followers of John Conrad Beissel. In 1719 Peter Becker immigrated to Pennsylvania with a company of Schwarzenau Baptists. In 1720, Conrad Beissel, one of this sect, followed and settled in Germantown. Hence he removed, in 1721, with Jacob Stuntz and George Stiefel, to Conestoga, and built a house on Mill Creek, a stream that heads near Adamstown, and eight miles below falls into the Conestoga, forming the dividing line between East Cocalico and Brecknock Townships, in Lancaster County. He was now fully possessed of the idea to found a sect. His asceticism, however, deprived him of his followers. Of Stiefel, the Chronicle of Ephrata states: "*Er hat sein Leben in Bethlehem geendet. Gott gebe ihm Barmherzigkeit am Tage des Gerichts!*" Beissel now built at Swedes' Spring. In 1724 he was joined by Michael Wohlfarth, and in the same year baptized in the Pequea. In 1729 his followers seceded from the Baptists, and as Beissel had enjoined upon them the observance of the Seventh day,

industry and contentment of the former in their indigent circumstances. The first house* built on the Allen tract.

---

and they practiced adult baptism, they were named accordingly. In 1732 he settled at Ephrata, eighteen miles from Lancaster, on the Cocalico. Here there were large houses built for the society, first *Kedar*, for the Sisters, and then *Zion*, for the Brethren, the latter having lived as eremites in huts until the completion of the monastery in 1738. These old-time buildings still haunt the green meadow on the Cocalico like the specters of strange things that belonged to another age. Beissel's followers were rigid ascetics, abstaining from many of the common enjoyments and comforts of life, and resembling in dress also some of the monastic orders of the old world. The men were tonsured, wore a tunic that reached to the feet, and an outer garment, furnished with apron and Capuchin cowl, and a veil that hung low down over the shoulders. A girdle controlled this flowing attire. The females were similarly habited. Both cultivated music, in which art Beissel was a proficient. Many of the Sisters were engaged in illuminating manuscripts or in embroidering. At an early day the society had a printing-press. Beissel deceased July 6, 1768, aged seventy-seven years. His followers are extinct, if *old Barbara* no longer lives.

* The following extracts throw light on the time when and on the circumstances under which the settlement on the "Allen Tract" was made:

"After a passage of nine weeks from Portsmouth," writes David Nitschmann, Sr., in his *Autobiography*, "we landed at Philadelphia, and joined the Brethren who had preceded us to America at Nazareth. There we passed the winter, and in the spring of 1741 we went out into the forest and began to build Bethlehem." His *biographer* adds, "It was in the spring of 1741 that our deceased Bro., Father Nitschmann, David Nitschmann, *Episc.*, Anton Seyffert, Martin Mack, Mathias Seybold, David and Anna Zeisberger, and David Zeisberger, Jr., began the settlement on the 'Allen Tract.' The weather was severe, and they often stood leg-deep in the snow while felling timber."

Mack writes in his *Autobiography*, "In the spring of 1741 I assisted in locating the settlement in the 'Allen Tract,' and in felling the first tree." It is not improbable, and the inference is deducible from remarks that occur in Neisser's compilation, that the Brethren began to fell trees on the Bethlehem tract immediately on Bishop

March 12. David Zeisberger, Sr., came to Frederictown to consult with Antes about the settlement.

April 2. The purchase of the tract of 500 acres, which had been offered by Nathaniel Irish, was concluded at Philadelphia between William Allen and Henry Antes, for the Brethren.

April 4. Anna Nitschmann and Sr. Molther came to Frederictown.

April 9. (*Good Friday, O. S.*) Eschenbach came to celebrate Easter with our friends.

April 11. The three set out for Oley.

May 15. Eschenbach returned and had a conversation with George Neisser, respecting the latter's settling in the Forks of Delaware.

May 20. Eschenbach set out for Wiegner's.

May 27. Antes left for the Forks to assist the Brethren. He went by way of Wiegner's to celebrate Whitsuntide there.

June 25. David Nitschmann, *Episc.*, arrived.

June 27. He set out for the Forks, accompanied by George Neisser. They reached them in the evening.

The Brethren had by this time removed from Nazareth, and were living together as a family in a small house they had built hurriedly in the spring. It was now time to proceed to the erection of a more commodious dwelling.

Nitschmann's return from New York in February. It was then that they finally dismissed projects they had entertained of purchasing elsewhere in the Forks, or in Skippack, Oley, Conestoga, or on the Susquehanna, and they certainly lost no time in removing from the Whitefield tract, on which their stay had been prolonged only by permission of Mr. Irish. The first house was removed in 1823. It stood on Rubel's Alley, in the rear of the "Eagle Hotel," was built of hewn logs, was of one story, and had a peaked gable and far-projecting roof. Its dimensions were forty by twenty feet.

June 28. They accordingly commenced squaring the timber that had been felled in the course of the winter.

The following were the members of the household at this date. Nitschmann, *Episc.*, Seyffert, Nitschmann, Sr., Mack, Seybold, Böhner, G. Neisser, David and Anna Zeisberger, David Zeisberger, Jr., Fröhlich, Hannah Hummel, Sommers,* and James ———. Eschenbach, Anna Nitschmann, and Sr. Molther were occasional visitors.

July 2. Rauch arrived from Shecomeco.

July 8. The Brethren celebrated Lord's Supper.

July 9. Rauch preached from *I. Peter*, i. 18, 19. In the afternoon Augustine Neisser came from Germantown to visit us.

July 10. Eschenbach and Rauch set out for Wiegner's.

July 12. Anna Nitschmann,† accompanied by David Zeisberger, Sr., set out to visit at Ephrata.

July 15. Gotthard Demuth and David Tanneberger came on a visit from Germantown.

July 17. They left for home.

July 18. Eschenbach and Rauch returned from their visit to our friends in Skippack, Germantown, and Philadelphia.

July 21. Anna Nitschmann and Zeisberger, Sr., returned from Ephrata. They had visited John Zimmermann in Conestoga Swamp. He is the head of a sect that holds its principal meeting at the time of new moon, and hence he and his followers are called "NEW MOONERS."

---

* In August of 1745, Benjamin Sommers was indentured to Joseph Graff, blacksmith, in Goshenhoppen.

† "Eine ihrer vornehmen ledigen Schwestern hat sich drei Tage im Schwesternhaus aufgehalten."—*Chronicon Ephratense.*

July 22. The Brethren in the Forks held "*Gemeintag.*"*

Aug. 1. Eschenbach, Sr. Molther, and George Stiefel arrived.

Aug. 5. Stiefel returned to Frederictown. The Brethren celebrated Lord's Supper.

Aug. 9. Rauch and Nitschmann, *Episc.*, set out for Shecomeco.

Aug. 13. Anna Nitschmann, Sr. Molther, and Zeisberger, Sr., went to Skippack.

Aug. 18. They returned with letters from Hagen.

Aug. 19. We built a foot-bridge across the Manakasy, and then held "*Gemeintag.*"

Aug. 22. Our friends Abraham Dubois, from the Great Swamp, and Henry Holstein and Andrew Frey, from Falckner Swamp, or Frederictown, paid us a visit. They were deeply impressed, and expressed themselves much edified by the simplicity of Sr. Anna Zeisberger.

Aug. 23. They left for home.

Aug. 25. Antes, Wiegner, and Adam Schaus,† and William Pott,‡ from Oley, arrived.

Aug. 26. Schaus, Holstein, and Pott left.

Aug. 28. Wiegner left. We had been enabled to pro-

---

* "*Congregation or Church-day.*" A day set apart for prayer and intercession for the welfare of the church, of her congregations, and of her missions in all parts of the world.

† Secretary for the Synod that met in Falckner Swamp. Removed to Bethlehem. Miller at the old mill built there in 1743. The present name of the family is Shouse.

‡ "William Pott immigrated to Pennsylvania with the Schwenkfelders in the autumn of 1734. Settled first in Germantown and then in Oley, Berks Co. John, a son, was one of the pioneers of Schuylkill County; in 1806 settled north of Sharp Mountain, and erected Greenwood Forge. Pottsville is named for him."—*Rupp's History of Schuylkill County.*

vide bountifully for our late visitors, having taken a number of rock-fish in the Lehigh.

Sept. 2. We celebrated Lord's Supper.

Sept. 10. David Nitschmann, *Episc.*, returned from his visit to New York and Shecomeco.

Sept. 13. He set out for Skippack. On the road he met Gottfried Haberecht who had joined the Baptists at Ephrata.* Haberecht appeared depressed, and was desirous of seeing the Brethren.

Sept. 15. Nitschmann, *Episc.*, returned in company with John Stephen Benezet.† From them we learned of the purchase of the "Whitefield Tract."‡ They also brought letters from Europe.

---

* "Eine Zeitlang hernach hat sich einer Nahmens *Haberecht* der von den Mährischen Brüdern abstammte bei dem Vorsteher um die Taufe angemeldet, welcher ihm auch hat darinnen willfahret. Darauf ist er in das Convent Zion eingezogen, aber dabey hat er sich viele Versuchungen zugezogen. Als aber Anna Nitschmannin einen Besuch im Lager abstattete, hat sie ihn wieder an ihre Gemeinschaft übergebracht, und da verstund man erst warum der Vorsteher ihn auf den Glauben seiner Gemeinschaft getaufft hat. Er ist mit ihnen wieder nach Deutschland gereist, und hat hernach ihren Arbeitern in Algier gedienet, von da ist er wieder nach Pensilvanien gereist, und hat sein Leben in ihrer Anstalt geendat. *Gott gebe ihm eine selige Auferstehung!"—Chronicon Ephratense.*

† John Stephen Benezet, born in Abbeville, France, in 1683, was of a wealthy and noble Huguenot family which fled to Holland and thence to England in 1715, after the Revocation of the Edict of Nantes. In London the family became attached to the Friends. Immigrated to Pennsylvania in 1731. On his arrival in Philadelphia, Count Zinzendorf was the guest of Mr. Benezet, who resided on Second Street.

Between the latter and the Brethren there long existed friendly relations. Three of Mr. Benezet's daughters were married to Moravians at Bethlehem, who have numerous descendants resident there.

‡ Purchased a few months previous of Whitefield, in England, by Spangenberg.

Sept. 16. Held Prayer-day. Benezet joined us. We felt the presence of the Lord in our midst most sensibly. The letters from Europe were communicated at our meeting.

Sept. 17. Benezet set out for home by way of the Great Swamp.

Sept. 22. Eschenbach arrived from Tulpehocken and Skippack.

Sept. 19–27. In this interval we dug the cellar of the large house.

Sept. 24. Gotthard Demuth, who had been working for us during the summer, returned from a visit to his family in Matetsche and resumed work.

Sept. 26. Gottfried Haberecht and Augustine Neisser arrived. The former had met with ill treatment at Ephrata and came here for refuge.

Sept. 28. *Thursday.* The "Daily Words"* were *Ezekiel*, xliii. 7. Early in the morning we proceeded to lay the first stone for the foundation of the large house. David Nitschmann, *Episc.*, and Andrew Eschenbach opened the ceremonies with fervent prayer. A tin box containing an inscription and the names of the spectators written on parchment, was cemented into the stone, which we laid in the southeast corner.†

---

* A collection of texts of Scripture, arranged so as to afford a subject of meditation for each day of the year. It was entitled "*Täglichen Loosungen, welcher sich die Verbundenen Brüder in allen Welttheilen aufs Jahr* 1742 *bedienen, und die Gemeinschaft des Geistes dadurch unterhalten.*"

† The dimensions of this house were forty-five by thirty feet. It was of two stories, built of hewn logs and chinked with clay and straw. Originally the angles of its peaked roof were truncated at the gables, as may be seen in an old drawing of it, called "*Das Haus an der Lecha.*" Two apartments on the second floor at the west end were hurriedly completed for Count Zinzendorf, in December of 1741. The building was occupied in the summer of 1742. An addition

September 29. Augustine Neisser returned to Germantown. Gottfried Haberecht remained in the Forks.

October 10. Michael Schaefer, from Tulpehocken, came to visit us.

October 12. As Gottfried Haberecht had withdrawn from the Baptists, at Ephrata, and had concluded to remain in the Forks, David Nitschmann, *Episc.*, wrote them respecting his decision, and dispatched John Böhner to Ephrata with a letter.

October 17. Anna Nitschmann and Sr. Molther returned from their protracted visit in Skippack. Christian Weber,* carpenter, came with them.

October 21. Christopher Baus, a member of "Wiegner's Economy," in Skippack, came to visit us.

October 22. John Stephen Benezet, an estimable man, and a warm friend of ours, arrived, and brought with him Captain Wallace, of Philadelphia. The latter proposed to engage Christian Fröhlich to superintend his sugar-refinery. The Brethren took the proposal into consideration.

October 25. Baus returned home.

October 26. The Brethren Gottlieb Büttner, John C. Pyrlaeus, and J. William Zander arrived from the Congregation in Europe, to our great joy.

October 28. We celebrated Lord's Supper.

November 14. Eschenbach and Fröhlich set out for Philadelphia, the latter in response to the proposal made on the 22d ult.

---

to the east end, built soon after, lengthened the front to ninety-three feet. The house has long been known as the "*Gemein Haus*," and was in part the residence of ministers and missionaries of the church for many years. It stands on the northeast corner of Church Street and Cedar Alley.

* Married a daughter of John Bechtel, of Germantown. Descendants are residing in Bethlehem.

November 17. Anna Nitschmann and Sr. Molther went to Germantown.

November 18. They went to Philadelphia.

December. On the 2d of the month Count Zinzendorf landed at New York. Having remained several days with our friends in that city, he set out for Philadelphia on the 6th and arrived there on the 10th inst.* David Nitschmann, *Episc.*, arrived there from the Forks on the same day.

The following Brethren and Sisters came with the Count from Europe:

Benigna, his daughter,
Rosina Nitschmann, wife of David Nitschmann, *Episc.*,
John Jacob Müller, the Count's amanuensis,
Abraham and Judith Meinung, and
David Bruce.

John Henry Müller,† printer, was a fellow-passenger.

December 13. Eschenbach reached Philadelphia.

December 17. Countess Benigna, in company with Sr. Molther, left Philadelphia to visit her acquaintances from Herrnhut residing in Germantown.

---

* Previous to the Count's arrival, Christian Fröhlich had rented a house of three stories, on Second, near the northeast corner of Race Street, for him and his company.

† John Henry Müller (Miller) was born in Rheden, in Waldeck, in 1702. In boyhood he removed with his parents to Basel, and there was apprenticed to a printer. Worked at his trade as journeyman in Zurich, Leipsic, Altona, London, and Amsterdam. While in America the first time he worked in Franklin's printing-office. Returned to Europe in 1742, and there married. Managed a printing-office for the Brethren, to whom he became attached, in Marienborn, near Frankfort-on-the-Main. Returned to America in 1751, and established himself in business. Again went abroad, and returned to Philadelphia in 1760 with new press and type. In 1780 he sold out and removed to Bethlehem. Deceased March, 1782.

December 18. In the evening of this day the Count and his company arrived at Germantown.*

December 19. They set out for Wiegner's.

December 20. They left Wiegner's and rode as far as Henry Antes'.

December 21. In the evening they arrived in the Forks.

December 24. (*Sunday.*) We celebrated Lord's Supper and held the Festival of Christmas-eve. The Brethren's settlement in the Forks received the name of Bethlehem on this day.†

December 25. The Count and his company set out for Oley and Conestoga. In Oley he preached at the house of Jean Bertolet,‡ from *Acts*, xvi. 14.

---

* Here he lodged with John Bechtel, a Palatine from Franckenthal, and a man much esteemed by his countrymen of the Reformed Church. His daughter Margaret, who in 1742 married the missionary Büttner, relates, in her autobiography, that the Count, on his arrival in Philadelphia, had requested her father, by letter, to meet him there without delay. Fearful of incurring the displeasure of such of his friends as had been prejudiced against the Count, Mr. Bechtel hesitated to comply with the request. "I urged him to go," she continues. "I gave him no rest, and as my verbal persuasions were of no avail, I ran to the pasture, caught his riding horse, and brought it, bridled and saddled, to the door. This appeal father could not resist, and from regard to me he rode to town to see the remarkable man, who impressed me deeply when I saw him next day at our house, and indelibly so, when, not two weeks afterwards, I heard him, for the first time, proclaim the words of eternal life."

† "The Count arrived in the Forks a few days before Christmas. While celebrating the vigils of Christmas-eve in the first house, and as we were closing the services (it was already past nine o'clock), the Count led the way into the stable that adjoined our dwelling and commenced singing the hymn that opens with the words, '*Nicht Jerusalem, sondern Bethlehem, aus dir kommet was mir frommet,*' and from this touching incident the settlement received the name of Bethlehem." —*Martin Mack's Autobiography.*

‡ Jean Bertolet, a French Huguenot, from Chastedeaux, immigrated

December 26. Henry Antes issued a call* for a Synod, or Religious Conference, irrespective of denominationalism, to convene at Germantown on the 12th of January next.

December 30. The Count and his company reached Germantown.

December 31. (*Sunday.*) He preached to a large audience in the German Reformed Church, from the words, "*And without controversy, great is the mystery of godliness.*" *I. Tim.* iii. 16.†

1742.

January 5. (*Friday, Christmas-day, O. S.*) The Count preached in the German Reformed Church in German-

---

to Pennsylvania in 1726, and settled in Oley. "Als ich in Philadelphia zwei Wochen gewesen berufte mich der Heiland in den Busch zu arbeiten, nachdem ich mich lange nach Arbeit geschnt hatte. Der Ort (nehmlich die Gegend) hiesz Oley. Als ich dahin kam logirte ich bey einem Mann namens *Jean Bertolet*, dessen seine Frau, welche auch eine dergleichen alte Heilige war, machte der Heiland durch seine blutige Gnade doch bald zur Sündern, und nahm sie darauf zu sich in seine obere Gemein."—*Countess Benigna to the Congregation abroad.*

* *Büdingische Sammlung*, Part xii. No. 1.

† This was his first appearance in an American pulpit. The church in which he preached had been built in 1733, and stood opposite the market-house, on the main street. The Reformed Congregation that worshiped here having not yet been supplied with an ordained minister by the mother-church, Mr. John Bechtel had been chosen to act as lector and exhorter.

All of Zinzendorf's discourses held in this country were written down from his lips by his amanuensis. His public discourses were published abroad with the title *Reden von dem Herrn der unsere Seligkeit ist, und über die Materie von seiner Marter in Nord-America gehalten.* Büdn., 1744. 2 vols. Another edition has the title *Eine Sammlung öffentlicher Reden, 1742 in Canada gehalten.* 2 Thle. Büdn., 1744. This collection has been republished, and is one of great interest to the theological student.

town, from the words, "*Justified in the Spirit.*" *I. Tim.* iii. 16.

January 7. (*Sunday.*) He preached from the words, "*Seen of Angels.*" *I. Tim.* iii. 16.

Immediately after his arrival he prepared for publication a small selection of hymns, old and new: it was entitled *Hirtenlieder von Bethlehem, enthaltend eine kleine Sammlung evangelischer Lieder.*

January 8. George Neisser took this selection to Christopher Sauer's* printing-office in Germantown.

January 12. In response to Henry Antes' call, a Synod met in Theobald Enten's house in Germantown.†

January 14. (*Sunday.*) Bro. Ludwig‡ preached in the German Reformed Church in that place from the words, "*Preached unto the Gentiles.*" *I. Tim.* iii. 16.

January 16. Bro. Ludwig went to Skippack.

January 17. (*Epiphany, O. S.*) He preached at Wieg-

---

* "Christoph Sauer was the first printer in the country to print the German Bible. It passed through three editions following in 1743, 1762, and 1776. The sheets of the greater part of the last edition in Sauer's possession were confiscated in the Revolution, and used in the manufacture of cartridges."—*History of the Moravian Church in Philadelphia, by Abraham Ritter.* Philadelphia, 1857.

† This house still stands on the west side of Germantown Avenue, near the corner of Queen Street. It is of stone, of two stories, with a quaint penthouse overhanging the door and windows of the lower floor. The heavy sash, set with small lights, and the solidity of the inside wood-work, show that it was built at an early day. Mr. Enten was a clockmaker. His descendants, calling themselves *Ent*, are now living in Germantown.

‡ The Count, on his arrival in America, thought proper to substitute the title of Thürnstein for that of Zinzendorf. His signature was simply Thürnstein. Being not averse to the plain mode of address in vogue among the Friends, he was spoken to and of by many as Friend Ludwig, or simply Ludwig, and hence his Brethren called him Bro. Ludwig.

ner's from the Gospel appointed for the day, and afterward returned to Philadelphia.

January 21. (*Sunday.*) In the forenoon Bro. Ludwig preached for the first time to the Lutherans in their place of worship,* from the words, "*For why will ye die?*" *Ezek.* xxx. 11.

In the afternoon he preached at Germantown in the Reformed Church, from the words, "*Believed on in the world.*" *I. Tim.* iii. 16.

January 22. Bro. Ludwig set out for Falckner Swamp to attend the sessions of the Synod that had been appointed for the 25th of the month. Rode as far as Skippack.

January 24. At Martin Kulp's house he had an interview with heads of the Mennonites,† and discussed with them their doctrine and practice. In the evening he arrived at Henry Antes', in Falckner Swamp.

January 25. The Synod met for the second time, and in George Hübner's house.

January 27. Bro. Ludwig returned to Germantown.

January 28. (*Sunday.*) In the morning he preached from *John*, ii. 1–11.

In the afternoon he preached in the Reformed Church in Germantown, from the words, "*Received up into glory.*" *I. Tim.* iii. 16.

Soon after his arrival at Philadelphia he had instituted meetings for worship in his house (*Haus-Versammlung*), which were free for all. At these he or the Brethren Pyr-

---

* A barn that had been fitted up with a pulpit and with seats, on Arch above Fifth Street. It had been rented for worship by the German Reformed and Lutherans jointly.

† Followers of Menno Simonis, who began to immigrate to Pennsylvania in 1683, settling in and about Germantown. In 1709 others followed from the Palatinate and settled in Pequea Valley, Lancaster County. They are Baptists.

laeus, Seyffert, Eschenbach, or Büttner, usually delivered an address.

February 4. (*Sunday.*) Bro. Ludwig preached in "Bachelor's Hall,"* near Philadelphia, from *Matt.* viii. 1–13, with marked effect.

In the afternoon he preached in the Reformed Church in Germantown, from *Matt.* xxii. 11–14.

February 18. (*Sunday.*) In the forenoon Bro. Ludwig preached from *Matt.* xiii. 24–30.

In the afternoon he preached in Germantown. After the service he and his company set out for Oley, and rode as far as Farmer's mill,† in White Marsh.

John Hagen arrived at Philadelphia, by way of the Eastern Shore, from Georgia.

February 19. Hagen set out for Oley in company with George Neisser.

---

* Bachelor's Hall was a building near the present Kensington market-house, to which resorted the gay youth of the day for social recreation.

Its fate is shown by the following extract from the MS. diary of Christopher Marshall, under date of April 4, 1775: "Cloudy, windy weather, with rain. This morning a fire begun at nine o'clock, at Bachelor's Hall, which soon consumed that building."

† In October of 1704, "Edward ffarmer, of White Marsh, was appointed a Justice of y[e] County Court of Philadelphia." In May of 1712, Governor Gookin "rode out to Edward ffarmer's house to meet the Delaware Indians according to appointment, before they set out on their journey to the Five Nations." On this occasion "they laid before him the collection they had made of their tribute to offer to the Mingoes, namely, thirty-two belts of wampum of various figures, and a long Indian pipe called the calamet, with a stone head, a wooden or cane shaft and feathers fixt to it like wings. This pipe, they said, on making their submission to the Five Nations who had subdued them, would introduce them as friends and subjects, and they would be well received as such."—*Minutes of Provincial Council.*

February 20. Bro. Ludwig and his company reached Oley.

February 21 and 22. The Synod met and sat for the third time, and in John de Turck's* house. On the second day Andrew Eschenbach, Christian H. Rauch, Gottlob Büttner, and John Christopher Pyrlaeus were ordained to the ministry by David Nitschmann, *Episc.*, Bro. Ludwig, *Episc. emerito*, and Anton Seyffert. Three Indians from Shecomeco were baptized into the death of Jesus by Bro. Rauch, and Bro. Hagen was solemnly set apart as a missionary. It was here resolved to abandon the attempt to colonize in Georgia.

Bro. Ludwig set out the same day for Tulpehocken.

While in Tulpehocken he preached to the Lutheran adherents of the late Caspar Leutbecker,† in the old log-church. On the same day he had an interview with Onesimus, Father of Zion in Ephrata.‡

He returned to Oley, and thence set out for Germantown by way of New Hanover, Frederic, and Skippack. In New Hanover he preached, and also at Henry Holstein's.

March 2. He arrived at Germantown.

March 5. The "*Hirtenlieder von Bethlehem*" came from Sauer's press;—a duodecimo of 95 pp., containing 369 hymns.

March 6. Fifty copies were sent to Philadelphia and fifty to Frederic, for distribution in the townships.

March 11. (*Sunday Esto Mihi.*) Bro. Ludwig preached in Philadelphia, from the Gospel for the day.

---

* A son of Isaac de Turck, a French Huguenot, or Walloon, who had immigrated to New York in the reign of Queen Anne, and settled in Sopus. Thence the family removed to Oley, in 1712.

† See "*Nachrichten von den Evangelisch Lutherischen Gemeinen in Nord-America,*" vol. i. p. 250.

‡ See "*Acts of the Synod of* 1742," page 50, for the substance of this interview.

In the afternoon he preached from *I. Cor.* xiii. 1–13.

At this time he began to revise the Eleventh Supplement to the Collection of German Hymns, adapting its contents for general use.* He also compiled a Catechism entitled "*Kurzer Catechismus für etliche Gemeinen aus der reformirten Religion.*"†

March 15. Bro. Ludwig's household ("*Die Pilger Familie*") held love-feast.

March 16. Eschenbach and Rosina Nitschmann arrived at Philadelphia from Oley, and David Nitschmann, *Episc.*, arrived there from Bethlehem.

On this day Bro. Ludwig and his household removed to Germantown, and occupied a house rented of Mr. Ashmead,‡ near the German Reformed Church. Social worship held here in the evening was conducted in the English language.

March 18. (*Sunday.*) In the forenoon Bro. Ludwig preached in Philadelphia from *Matt.* iv. 1–11. In the afternoon he preached in Germantown from *I. Cor.* ix. 18.

March 19. The rite of baptism was administered by Bro. Ludwig, in Germantown, to Hermann Bonn and to Anna Mary, his sister, of Skippack, aged respectively twenty-two and twenty-eight. A large number of spectators were present, and the occasion was deeply impressive.

March 20. The Deputies to the Synod arrived in Germantown.

March 21. The Synod met for the fourth time, and in Mr. Ashmead's house.

March 25. (*Sunday.*) Bro. Ludwig organized a congre-

---

* This revision was completed in Wyoming Valley in October.

† Printed in English type, in Franklin's office. *Duodecimo.* 42 pp. Sauer had refused to print it.

‡ Near the Market-house, and almost opposite the German Reformed Church. The house is still standing.

gation in Germantown, and preached in the Reformed Church, from *Ps.* lxix. 21.

March 26. Eschenbach, Benigna, and Abraham and Judith Meinung went to Oley. David Nitschmann, *Episc.*, and Haberecht set out for Bethlehem.

March 29. Bro. Ludwig set out for Oley, by way of Skippack, where he preached in the Mennonite meeting-house.

March 30. He organized a congregation in Falckner Swamp.

March 31. He organized a congregation in Oley, and preached.

April 1. (*Sunday.*) He preached on the Manatawny to an audience of Lutherans and Reformed, from the words, "*Christ is all and in all.*"

April 3. Bro. Ludwig returned to Germantown.

April 6. He went to Philadelphia.

April 7. He wrote a letter to Conrad Beissel in Ephrata.*

April 8. (*Sunday.*) In the forenoon he preached in Philadelphia, from *John*, vi. 1–14.

In the afternoon he preached in Germantown, from *Ps.* cxxi. 3.

April 12. Bro. Ludwig united Matthias Seybold, of Bethlehem, and Anna Mary Bonn, of Skippack, in wed-

---

* *Büdingische Sammlung*, Part xv. No. 15. On his last rural circuit, made toward the close of the year, the Count called at Ephrata. The Prior informed Beissel of the arrival of the distinguished visitor. "*Der seye ihm kein Wunder*," answered Beissel; "*wenn er ihm aber ein Wunder seye, müsse er zu ihm kommen.*" A few weeks previous Beissel had written him a letter (*Büdingische Sammlung*, Part xiii. No. 17), in which he subscribes himself, *Friedsam Fr. sonsten genannt Conrad Beissel, dermalen ein Fremdling und Pilgrim auf dieser Welt.*

lock, in the German Reformed Church. After the ceremony, there was a wedding-feast in Bro. Ludwig's house.

April 17. As none but parents who were Brethren or persons attached to the Brethren had responded to a circular that had been issued on the 1st inst., relative to opening a school in Germantown, it was resolved to commence one on the model of the Brethren's schools in Europe.

April 18. The Synod met for the fifth time, and in the Reformed Church in Germantown.

April 20. George and Maria Elizabeth Weber and Gottlieb Israel, missionaries, arrived from St. Thomas.

April 21. George Neisser set out for Tulpehocken, to preach on the coming Sunday, in Büttner's absence.

April 22. (*Palm Sunday.*) In the forenoon Bro. Ludwig preached in Philadelphia, from *Matt.* xxi. 1–9.

In the afternoon he held catechisation.

April 23. David Nitschmann, *Episc.*, took leave of the Brethren and set out for New York, thence to sail for St. Thomas.

April 26. Büttner returned to Tulpehocken.

April 29. (*Easter Sunday.*) Bro. Ludwig preached in Germantown, from *John*, xx. 24, *et seq.*

We held love-feast in his house.

May 4. The proposed school was opened in Bro. Ludwig's house with twenty-five girls. The Brethren Seyffert, Zander, and George Neisser, and the Sisters Benigna, Magdalene Müller, and Anna Dismann, were employed in the Institution.*

May 16. The Synod met for the sixth time, and in Lorenz Schweitzer's house in Germantown.

---

* "Nun hat mich das Lamm auf einen Posten geführet. Ich habe eine Kinderanstalt von 25 Mägdchen und da habe ich mich willig dazu aufgeopfert."—*Countess Benigna to the Congregation abroad.*

May 20. (*Sunday.*) In the forenoon Bro. Ludwig preached in Philadelphia, from *John*, xvi. 16–23.

May 23. David Nitschmann, Sr., who had for several weeks been a member of Bro. Ludwig's household, returned to Bethlehem. He was accompanied thither by Rosina Nitschmann and David Bruce.

May 24. Rauch and Mohican John arrived in Germantown from Shecomeco.

May 26. Bro. Ludwig made a formal renunciation of his rank and title as Count of Zinzendorf, before Governor Thomas, members of the Provincial Council, and clergymen and gentlemen of Philadelphia, in the Governor's house.*

---

* This act on the part of the Count excited much remark and speculation at the time. Logan writes: "About this time he framed an instrument of resignation of all his honors and dignities to some relative. This was done in Latin. He desired me to put it into English, but as I could not, he had it printed as it was, and invited Governor Thomas and all who understood Latin to meet him. Several met, when he read off the instrument, having given each of them a printed copy; but after all he withdrew his papers and himself too, saying, on reflection, he must first advise with some of his friends in Germany."

The meeting was in the Governor's house, and the following persons were present:

Doctor Thomas Graeme, one of the Provincial Judges.

William Allen, Recorder of the city.

Tench Francis, Attorney-General.

James Hamilton, a Justice of the Peace, and Prothonotary of the Court of Common Pleas. Governor between Nov. 1748 and Oct. 1754.

Thomas Lawrence, one of the Governor's Council, and a Justice of the Peace.

Doctor Patrick Bard, the Governor's Secretary.

William Peters, Esq.

James Read, Esq.

Rev. Mr. Eneas Ross, Minister of Christ Church, Philadelphia.

Rev Jno. C. Pyrlaeus.

Mr. Benezet, merchant.

Mr. Jo. Sober, merchant.

May 27. (*Sunday.*) He preached in Philadelphia, from *John*, xvi. 5–15.

May 30. Intelligence came of the arrival at New London of a colony* of Brethren from Europe. On this day Bro. Ludwig received a call from the Lutherans of Philadelphia to the pastorate of their congregation.†

June 3. (*Sunday.*) Bro. Ludwig preached in the German Reformed Church, from *Jeremiah*, li. 9.

June 6. Peter Böhler, who had arrived with the colony, or "sea-congregation," came to Philadelphia.

June 7. (*Ascension-day.*) The colony of Brethren arrived in Philadelphia.

June 8. They were qualified in the Court-house.‡

Mr. Graydon, merchant.

Mr. Samuel McCall, merchant.

Mr. Charles Willing, merchant.

Benjamin Franklin, Postmaster.

Mr. Charles Brockden, Deputy Master of the Rolls of the Province, and Recorder of Deeds for the City and County of Philadelphia.

A desire to be disencumbered from the form and circumstance that necessarily attended rank, and which might prove embarrassing in his ministry, was a consideration that moved him to take this step.

* This colony having been organized into a congregation for the passage across the Atlantic, on the eve of its departure from London, in February, is known in Moravian chronicles as the "*Sea-Congregation*," the *first* of two colonies similarly fitted out. There were fifty-six on the "Catharine," Captain Gladman.

† *Büdingische Sammlung*, Part xii. No. 4, *a*.

‡ "The great influx of Germans, without leave from the crown, into the Province in the first half of the year 1727, arrested the attention of Governor Gordon and his Council, as a matter deserving of legislation. They reasoned that the security of the Province might be endangered by such numbers of strangers daily pouring in, who, being ignorant of both language and laws, and settling in a body together, were forming a people distinct from his Majesty's subjects. Hence it was resolved that they be required, in the first place, to take the oath of allegiance,

June 12. The Synod met for the seventh time, and in the house of Mr. Edward Evans, in Philadelphia.

June 17. (*Whitsunday.*) Bro. Ludwig preached for the last time in the Reformed Church in Germantown. The members of the "sea-congregation" proceeded as far as that place on their way to Bethlehem; held love-feast with their Brethren, in Theobald Enten's house, and lodged there for the night.

June 18. George Piesch, who had led the colony, set sail for Europe.

The major part of the colonists set out for Bethlehem with George Neisser and J. William Zander. As the day was warm, and long confinement on shipboard had almost incapacitated them from travel on foot, it was long after nightfall when they reached Peter Bonn's, in Skippack. Here they were hospitably entertained. They lodged at his house and at John Kooken's.

June 19. Early in the morning the travelers proceeded on their journey, and toward evening arrived at Henry Antes' house. Here they lodged.

Bro. Ludwig, John Brandmüller, and Anna Nitschmann left Germantown* in the afternoon for Bethlehem.

June 20. Pyrlaeus, with some of the Sisters, set out in a wagon from Germantown for Bethlehem.

---

or some equivalent to it, to his Majesty, and promise fidelity to the Proprietor and obedience to the established Constitution."—*Minutes Provincial Council, Sept.* 22, 1727.

* During his stay in Germantown the Count was a frequent visitor at the house of Mr. John Wister, grandfather of the late John and Charles J. Wister. There are still in the old homestead of the family, which was built in 1741, a walnut stand and chairs, left by the Count as mementoes to his host. In April of 1752, Mr. John Wister entered a daughter in the Single Sisters' House at Bethlehem. With Caspar, a brother (Caspar Wüster), the Brethren at an early day dealt for glassware and drugs. One branch of the family has adopted the name *Wistar*.

The other colonists proceeded this day as far as Joseph Müller's house, in the Great Swamp, and lodged there.

Henry Antes had provided a wagon to convey the females of the company from his house to Bethlehem.

June 21. (*Thursday.*) The different divisions of the colony,* and Bro. Ludwig and his companions, arrived at Bethlehem at noon. The "Daily Words" were, "*This is the day which the Lord hath made; we will rejoice and be glad in it.*" *Ps.* cxviii. 24.

---

* The following are the names of those who came on the "Catharine:"

Peter and Elisabeth Böhler,	Joseph Müller,
Adolph Meyer,	John George Endter,
John Brandmüller,	Matthew Witke,
Paul D. and Regina D. Prycelius,	John Philip Meurer,
Joachim and Ann Cath. Sensemann,	John Christoph[r] Heyne,
George and Elisabeth Harten,	Reinhard Ronner,
David and Ann C. Bishoff,	George Wiesner,
Michael and Hannah Micksch,	Michael Huber,
John and Marg[t] B. Brucker,	Jacob Lischy,
David and Mar. Elis[h] Wahnert,	George Kaske,
Michael and Rosina Tanneberger,	George Schneider,
Henry and Rosina Almers,	C. Frederic Post,
Thomas and Ann Yarrel,	Leonhard Schnell,
John and Elisabeth Turner,	Christian Werner,
Owen and Elisabeth Rice,	John G. Heydecker,
Samuel and Martha Powel,	John Okely,
Joseph and Martha Powel,	William Okely,
Robert and Martha Hussey,	Joseph Shaw,
Nathaniel Seidel,	Hector Gambold,
Gottlieb Pezold,	Andrew, a negro.

ACCOUNT

OF THE

UNITED BRETHREN

AT BETHLEHEM

WITH THE

COMMISSIONERS OF THE PROVINCE OF PENNSYLVANIA

DURING THE INDIAN WAR OF 1755, '56, AND '57.

ACCOUNT

OF THE

UNITED BRETHREN AT BETHLEHEM

WITH THE

COMMISSIONERS OF THE PROVINCE OF PENNSYLVANIA,

During the Indian War of 1755, '56, *and* '57.

WHEN, in 1755, Pennsylvania became the theater of the prolonged contest in which the French and English were engaging for territorial aggrandizement in the New World, her defenseless borders along the entire extent of the easterly outliers of the great Appalachian chain of mountains were, for the first time, scourged with the barbarities of Indian warfare.

Braddock met with disaster on the 9th of July. This was the signal for the uprising of the Delawares, whose affections had been alienated from the English ever since they saw them in league with the hated Iroquois, for the iniquitous purpose of dispossessing them of their hereditary seats.* Allured by the representations of French emissaries, in which the prospect of recovering their national independence and the homes of their forefathers was flatteringly

* See chapter i. of *An Account of the History, Manners, and Customs of the Indian Nations who once inhabited Pennsylvania and the Neighboring States.* By Rev. John Heckewelder, of Bethlehem. Philadelphia, 1818.

held out, and emboldened by the success of the French arms, the Delawares of the East met the Delawares of the West in council on the Alleghany, and prepared for war. But first they rehearsed their wrongs, dwelling on the loss of the lands on the Tulpehocken and on the Conedogwinet; but chiefly, and amid bitter denunciations, on the fraud of 1737,* perpetrated, as they maintained, to confirm the deedless purchase of all that tract of country which extended from the Tohickon and the Hills of Lechauweki northward and westward as far as the great plains of Skehandowana, or Wyoming. Wherever the white man was settled within this disputed territory, there they resolved to strike him as best they could with the most approved weapons and appliances of their savage warfare. And that the blow might be effectually dealt, each warrior-chief was charged to scalp, kill, and burn within the precincts of his birthright, and all simultaneously, from the frontiers down into the heart of the settlements, until the English should sue for peace and promise redress.

In these hostile preparations, and in strengthening their arms with alliances, the summer and early months of autumn passed away. October came, and no sooner had the first biting frost reddened the maple and hardened the yellow corn in the husk, than French Indians, and chiefly Delawares and Shawanese painted black for war, in bands

---

* See the relations of Thomas Furniss and Joseph Knowles "concerning the walk made between the Proprietors of Pennsylvania and the Delaware Indians, by James Yates and Edward Marshall," in *An Enquiry into the Causes of the Alienation of the Delaware and Shawanese Indians from the British Interest.* Written by Charles Thomson, the American patriot, who in 1774 was elected Secretary to Congress, whom John Adams styled the "*Sam Adams of Philadelphia, the life of the cause of liberty*," and whose last literary labor was a translation of the Septuagint, which was published, in 4 vols., in 1808.

of two or four abreast, moved eastward with murderous intent. The line of the Blue Mountain, from the Delaware to the Susquehanna, became the scene of the carnival which the exasperated savages held with torch and tomahawk during the latter part of the winter of 1755. The defenseless settlers were taken as in a snare. They were harassed by an unseen foe by day and by night. Some were shot down at the plow, some were butchered at the fireside; men, women, and children were promiscuously tomahawked or scalped, or hurried away into distant captivity, for torture or for coveted ransom. There was literally a pillar of fire by night and a pillar of cloud by day going up along the horizon, marking the progress of the relentless invaders, as they dealt out death, and pillage, and conflagration, and drove before them, in midwinter's flight, hundreds of homeless wanderers, who scarce knew where to turn for safety or for succor in the swift destruction that was come upon them.

On the 16th of October the savages fell upon the whites on John Penn's Creek, four miles south of Shamokin, in Snyder County. Here they killed or took captive twenty-five persons; and it was only the twenty-third of the month when all the settlements along the Susquehanna between Shamokin and Hunter's Mill, for a distance of fifty miles, were hopelessly deserted. Early in November the Great and the Little Cove, west of the Conecocheague, and the Canalaways, in Franklin County, were attacked, the inhabitants either put to death or taken prisoners, and the settlements totally destroyed. This was the field of operations that had been assigned to the French Indians, and to the Delawares from the Ohio under Shingas.*

---

* Brother of *Tamaque*, called King Beaver by the whites, many years head chief of the Western Delawares. During the Indian war

On the 16th of November the savages for the first time crossed the great river which it had vainly been hoped would prove a barrier to their incursions. Falling upon the rich farms along the Swatara and the Tulpehocken,* they fired the harvested grain and fodder in barns and in barracks, destroyed large numbers of cattle and horses, and murdered thirteen persons. It was now apparent that a second division of the enemy was on the war-path; and when, in the evening of the 24th of the month, the Moravian house on the Mahoning† was surprised and ten of its inmates were scalped, or shot, or tomahawked, or burned to death, the prelude only had been performed to the tragedy which the savages were resolved to enact within the precincts of the by them detested walking-purchase. Along its northern line, which had been fraudulently surveyed so as to embrace a goodly portion of the Minnisinks or Upper Valley of the Delaware, was laid the first scene of this resentful Indian warfare. It was here that Teedyuscung with his Eastern Delawares (and chief among these the implacable Monseys), mindful of the indignities that had been heaped upon him and his kinsmen of the Forks by the imperious Canassatego, at the Treaty of 1742, wreaked his

---

Shingas had the reputation of being the greatest warrior among his people, and such a terror was he become to the frontier settlements of Pennsylvania that Government set a price of £200 on his head or scalp. See *Heckewelder's Names of Chieftains and Eminent Men of the Lenni Lenape*, published in the Proceedings of the Historical Society of Pennsylvania, September, 1847, and also page 264 of his *History of Indian Nations*.

* Corrupted from *Tulpewihácki*, Delaware, signifying *a land abounding in turtles*.

† Corrupted from *Mahonhánne*, Delaware, signifying *a stream flowing near a lick*, a tributary of the Lehigh, heading on the northern declivity of Tamaqua Mountain, in Schuylkill County, and emptying into that river below Lehighton.

long-cherished resentment on the whites who had planted in Long Valley, or who were trespassing within the Minnisinks west of the Delaware. And thus, within a short month, fifty farms, with their houses, were plundered and burned, and upward of one hundred persons were killed on the frontiers of Northampton, on both sides of the Kittatinny, or "endless hills." "All our border country," writes a chronicler of the day, "extending from the Potomac to the Delaware, not less than one hundred and fifty miles in length and between twenty and thirty in breadth, has been entirely deserted, its houses reduced to ashes, and the cattle, horses, grain, and other possessions of the inhabitants either destroyed, burned, or carried off by the Indians; while such of the poor planters who, with their wives, children, and servants, escaped from the enemy, have been obliged, in this inclement season of the year, to abandon their habitations almost naked and to throw themselves upon the charity of those who dwell in the interior of the Province."

A combination of causes served to render this time of general distress peculiarly trying to the Brethren. Their mission among the aborigines, owing to the enlightening influence it exerted upon a people who had long been the easy subjects of design and of fraud, was unpopular with that class of the whites who were interested in their degradation. These were now loud in denouncing the Brethren, in publishing them to the world as an association in league with the savages, in the interests of the French, and as deserving of being treated as a common enemy. Thus a strong feeling was roused against them, and twice did their exasperated fellow-Christians conspire to exterminate them in their settlements root and branch. Meanwhile their situation in the northern part of the Province exposed them to sudden attack from the hostile

Indians, by whom they plainly saw that they had been singled out as objects of an especial hate. And for this reason. They had refused to use compulsion, when messenger after messenger had come down from the Susquehanna with sinister invitations to the unwilling Delawares and Mohicans of Gnadenhütten, to come up to them and plant in Wyoming. And when Teedyuscung, in April of 1754, had used his persuasive arts so effectually with the members of the congregation as to draw away seventy of his fellow-converts (among whom was Abraham Shabash, the first of the patriarchs), their silent rebuke of his breach of faith, and their reluctance to allow their sheep to go among wolves, roused the hatred of the chieftain and his consorts who were preparing for war. "Are they not our brethren, and is it not best that they return to their own people? For who can love them more than we their brethren?" was their insidious plea. Meanwhile they and the others reasoned among themselves as follows: "If these Moravian Indians continue at Gnadenhütten, they may thwart us in our plans when the time has come for us to take up the hatchet; they may become informers, or they may be employed as scouts and runners; and even if they hold themselves neutral, their proximity to the settlements will embarrass our movements." Foiled in effecting this coveted removal, the hostile chieftain spoke angrily of the Brethren, and the evil report was spread throughout the Indian country that the pale-faced preachers at Bethlehem were craftily holding red men in bondage. And thus was engendered in the hearts of the Indians who had been alienated from the English, that bitter animosity against their benefactors which paralyzed the latter in their labor of love, while it cost them a heavy loss and precious lives.

In this way the Brethren were between two fires, and in an apparently hopeless dilemma. It needed indeed a

Divine interposition to extricate them from the twofold peril in which they were involved, and to set them in a safe place where all men could see and confess to their innocence. And this interposition came at an early day. It came, it is true, in blood, but the Brethren received it as a dispensation of mercy, for their faith in the righteousness of the Lord's dealings was strong.

Locked in among high hills on the west bank of the Lehigh, a few miles north of where the river escapes from the embraces of the Blue Mountain, is a sequestered valley. It was always a lonely spot, and still remains such, although now so near one of the great thoroughfares of traffic and seats of mighty labor, swarming with strong workingmen, and dim and lurid with the smoke and the fires of glowing furnaces. The valley of the Mahoning is a silent little world of wild mountain and of barren hills, shelving down into a narrow expanse of lowland through which the Mahoning winds its wizard stream. In this amphitheater the Lord was pleased to vindicate the Brethren. He did this on the 24th of November, and as follows.

There were fifteen persons in the dwelling-house on that fatal night. It was in the gloaming, and they were about finishing their evening meal when the angry barking of the dogs in the farm-yard apprised them of the approach of strangers. Joachim Sensemann being reminded that the meeting-house (it stood not more than fifty yards higher up on the hill) was not locked for the night, hastened thither to secure it. This precaution saved him; for no sooner was he in the hall and in the act of striking a light, than he heard the report of fire-arms. It startled him; only momentarily, however, as he recollected that a scouting party of Scotch-Irish had ridden past a few hours before, and he concluded that they were discharging their pieces on their return home. He finished his errand, and was on his way down the hill, when he met George Partsch, who, breathless, informed him in broken speech of the presence of hostile Indians below. "Twelve Shawanese painted for war," he said, pointing behind him, adding at the same time that the dwelling was beleaguered, that the Brethren and Sisters were at the mercy of the savages, and that he had escaped by leaping out of a window at the first surprise with a bullet whistling past his head. A brief reconnoissance of the position showed them the folly of any attempt to render assistance, and they accordingly resolved to cross the river without delay and to give the alarm to the inhabitants of Gnadenhütten East.

Meanwhile the following had transpired at the doomed house. The barking of the dogs had been indeed portentous; for soon after there were voices and then footsteps heard without. Martin Nitschmann opened the door to see whose they were, was shot, and fell a corpse. Two bullets at the same moment grazed Joseph Sturgis, and as the door remained open the savages poured a random volley into the room, killing or wounding John Gattermeyer, Martin Presser, and John Lesley. Of them nothing more is known. Hereupon the others (there were nine) retreated precipitately into the adjoining apartment, and from there up the stairway into the attic, closely pursued by the Indians. It was in this retreat and on the steps that Susanna Nitschmann was disabled by a ball, and, reeling backward, fell into the hands of the enemy. Her loud and piteous cries for help were soon hushed; for if we are to credit the relations of Isaac Nutimus, of Joachim and of Teedyuscung, she was gagged and handed over to an attendant by her captor to grace his triumph on his return to Diahoga. The eight who had succeeded in reaching the attic, barricaded the trap-door with bedsteads and with what other furniture was at hand, the strong arms of George Schweigert, a teamster, rendering the barrier proof against the attempt of the murderous assailants to force it with their hatchets and the butts of their guns. Failing to reach those for whose blood they thirsted, the Indians now charged their pieces and fired volley after volley, some into the floor, and some from without into the roof, in the hopes of killing or of bringing to terms the objects of their fiendish ferocity. Foiled in this also, the exasperated Shawanese applied the torch. The cruelly-hunted men and women above were soon sensible of the new danger by which they were beset, and saw that they must either perish by fire or fall into the hands of demons. There were three helpless women in that doomed company, and they were long the most composed. Anna Sensemann was last seen seated upon a bed with folded hands and upturned eyes, and ever and anon she said, "My Saviour, I thought that this would be my end!" The second was a mother with an infant in her arms. Wrapping the child in her apron, she hugged it closely to her bosom and sat in silence; for the flood of feeling and affection for her offspring that poured through her heart in that perilous time deprived her of the power of utterance. This was Johanna Anders. The suspense was growing momentarily more unendurable, and Gottlieb Anders shouted for help in the vain hope that he would be heard, and that all that was dear to him in the world would even yet be succored. But at intervals, above his voice and above the yells of the exultant Shawanese and the crackling of burning timbers, were heard the agonizing cries of the innocent child. Now it was that three of the eight chose the desperate alternative of risking their lives in an attempt to escape from the beleaguered house in preference to that of certain death by the horrors of fire. Watching his chance, at a moment when the sentinel, who was guarding the dormer-window below, had left his post, young Sturgis boldly leapt out, ran for his life, and won it. Susan Partsch followed him, and reached the meeting-house unobserved. Behind this she secreted herself, leaving her covert on the approach of the Indians later in the evening and retreating down the valley toward the river. George Fabricius was the third to take the desperate leap, and evidently with hesitation, as the fire had already passed over him. He had reached the ground, had sprung to his feet, and was safe as he thought from his relentless persecutors, when they discovered him. In an instant he was pierced simultaneously by two balls and fell. Rushing upon him, the infuriated savages buried their tomahawks in his body and scalped him down to the eyes. Next day his mangled corpse was found in a pool of blood on the spot where he had been butchered, and by its side, guarding the lifeless remains of its master, was couched his faithful dog. Five of the inmates of the house on the Mahoning, therefore, met death in the fire.

Having finished their bloody work, the Indians (so we are told by Susan Partsch, who watched their movements from her hiding-place) proceeded to pillage and burn the other houses of the settlement. First the barn and stable, and next the kitchen, the bake-house, the Single Brethren's house, the store, the mill, and finally the meeting-house, until the whole valley was light as day with the glare of the conflagration, athwart which could be seen, in bold relief, the dusky figures of the fiendish Shawanese as they hastened to and fro in the closing scene of the tragedy they had that night so perfectly enacted. And when this was done, they collected around the spring-house, where, having divided their plunder, they feasted with blood-stained hands.

Then loading up their spoils on stolen horses, they filed off leisurely in the warrior's path that led to Wyoming.*

---

* The following are the names, with brief notices, of the victims of the massacre:

Anna Catharine Sensemann, m. n. Ludwig, born 1717, in Lichtewarn, Upper Silesia. Immigrated to Pennsylvania with her husband in June of 1742. They had been residents on the Mahoning since the 5th of August, and were acting as steward and stewardess.

Gottlieb Anders, gardener, born 1719, in Neumarck, Silesia. Immigrated to Pennsylvania in November of 1743. Was Chaplain to the Family on the Mahoning since November of 1754.

Johanna Christina Anders, m. n. Vollmer, born 1720, in Homburg an der Höh', his wife, and

Johanna, born 1754, at Friedensthal, on the Nazareth tract, their infant daughter.

Martin Nitschmann, cutler, born 1714, in Zauchtenthal, Moravia. Immigrated to Pennsylvania in 1749. Since August, a resident on the Mahoning.

John Leonhard Gattermeyer, blacksmith, born 1721, in Ratisbon. Immigrated to Pennsylvania in 1749. Joined the Family on the Mahoning in October.

George Christian Fabricius, scholar, born 1716, in Nyburg, Fünen. Entered the Theological Seminary on the opening of that Church-institution in the village of Barby, in May of 1754. In September immigrated to Pennsylvania, and was assigned to the Family on the Mahoning, there to acquire the Delaware, preparatory to entering the mission. The facility with which Fabricius learned the language had already qualified him to make translations of portions of the New Testament. He was Lector, and also taught the Indian children at Gnadenhütten East.

George Schweigert, farmer, born 1724, in Heidenheim, in Wirtemberg. Immigrated to Pennsylvania in 1750. In 1754 was sent to Gnadenhütten.

Martin Presser, carpenter, born 1709, in Weimar. Immigrated to Pennsylvania in 1750. Worked at his trade at Gnadenhütten.

John Frederic Lesley, shoemaker, born 1732, in Conestoga, Lancaster

Intelligence of this terrible blow was brought to Bethlehem by David Zeisberger at three o'clock in the morning of the next day, and it was broken to the Brethren and Sisters, who had been summoned to meet in the chapel at five o'clock (an hour earlier than the customary time for

---

County. In 1747 came to Bethlehem. Had been a resident on the Mahoning only a few weeks.

In 1788 a memorial-stone was placed over the spot in the graveyard where the body of Fabricius and the bones of the others had been interred. The burial-place is on the summit of the rising ground, west of Lehighton. The stone covers the entire grave. Upon it are inscribed the names of the eleven, and of them it is touchingly said, "*They had lived at Gnadenhütten unto the Lord, and ended their lives by a surprise of Indian warriors.*" Below is the Scriptural assurance that "Precious in the sight of the Lord is the death of his Saints!"

The following are the names, with brief notices, of those who escaped the massacre:

Peter Worbas, carpenter, born in 1722, in Colding, Jutland. In 1753 immigrated to Pennsylvania, and was assigned to Gnadenhütten. Resided successively at Bethlehem, New Gnadenhütten, Hope (Warren County, New Jersey), and on the erection of Nazareth, in 1771, settled in that place, and built the first house there. It was removed in 1865. Worbas deceased at Nazareth in 1806.

George Partsch, born 1719, in Langendorf, Upper Silesia. Immigrated to Pennsylvania in 1743. After his escape from the Mahoning, he removed to Bethlehem, where, excepting the interval between May of 1762 and July of 1763, spent on St. Thomas, he resided until his decease in July of 1765.

Susan Louisa, m. n. Eller, his wife, was born 1722 in Büdingen, in the Wetterau. She deceased at Bethlehem in 1795. The late Mr. Matthew Krause, of Bethlehem, was a great-grandson.

Joachim Sensemann, deceased in Jamaica.

Joseph Sturgis (Sturgeous), from Philadelphia, attached himself to the Brethren at Bethlehem, in May of 1757. At the time of his escape he was in the seventeenth year of his age. He deceased at Litiz, Lancaster County, Pennsylvania, in June of 1817, and left numerous descendants.

daily devotions), by Bishop Spangenberg. Only a few were informed of what had happened, and although there were vague rumors among the rest of some great calamity, these failed to lessen the painful suspense which harassed them as they sat in silence awaiting the entrance of their respected father. The organ gave forth mournful notes as the worthy man came in, and took his accustomed seat. Surveying his Brethren and Sisters to the right and to the left with a countenance which bore evidence of some recent contest which had taken place in his inmost soul, he spoke most feelingly and said: "My dear Brethren and Sisters, it may appear to some as if the Saviour had dealt severely with us;" and then, having recited the tragic occurrence of the previous evening, he rallied and proceeded to say, "But, no! He has been pleased for a wise purpose to lead some of our number as victims to the slaughter. We are short-sighted, and perhaps too much stricken to be able to interpret this mysterious providence. But are we not triumphantly vindicated in the eyes of our neighbors who clamor for our lives and for the destruction of dear Bethlehem, publishing to the world that we are in league with the French, because, when all men around us hastened to arms in utter consternation, we alone were undismayed, and waited for the Lord?"*

---

* It is well known that the Moravians were averse to bearing arms, and that they regarded offensive warfare as incompatible with the gentle teachings of the religion of Jesus Christ. The attitude they assumed in the Indian war was altogether defensive. They stockaded their settlements on the Nazareth tract, the exposed portions of Bethlehem, built watch-towers, and exercised constant vigilance by day and by night, so as to avoid the necessity of repelling an attack which precaution on their part might have prevented. And after all they looked chiefly to the Lord, remembering that except He keep the city the watchman waketh in vain. Hence when, soon after the outbreak

It is to this distressing period in the history of Provincial Pennsylvania that the records thus introduced belong.

---

of hostilities, warm friends in New York dispatched a supply of arms and ammunition to Bethlehem, bidding the Brethren to take them, go forth, and fight the Indians, Bro. Spangenberg felt called to make the following exposition. The gentleness of the rebuke it administers, the feeling of tender compassion for the slayers of his Brethren, and the spirit of forgiveness and of calm trust in the wisdom and mercy of the Saviour it expresses, will furnish the reader with prominent points in the character of the man who at that time was set to watch over the Brethren's Church in America. He here speaks, not like some pompous prelate ex cathedra, but in lowly speech, and yet with Christian majesty; his words falling impressively upon the ear and reaching the heart, as do those of the fatherly Ambrose, or even as those of the Apostle of the Gentiles, when speaking, not in his own dignity, but with the solemn earnestness inspired by his Master.

"MY DEAR BRETHREN AND SISTERS,—

"I think it necessary to be plain with you, for I observe that some of you do not know what to make of the Brethren. I have received letters in one day, all written in love, and out of a tender concern for us, but in substance opposite to one another. Some of them advised us to make no resistance to the barbarous enemy, but rather to come away from our settlements. Others write us to stand upon our defense, and to oppose such wicked and abominable creatures who are doing the work of their father, who was a murderer from the beginning.

"We know, God be thanked, what we are doing, and are not in doubt about the course we should pursue. Our Saviour is with us and we feel both in private and in public his Gracious Presence. His Spirit is not less to us than a tender mother guiding us into all truth according to our Saviour's gracious promise. We have his Word, which certainly is truth, and we can depend upon it that we shall not be misled if acting according to his dictates, and we need not now first inquire what his designs are in regard to us, but He made us sensible of his purposes before these troubles broke in upon us.

"We are of opinion that governments ought to protect their subjects. Rulers are servants of God, and the sword is given them by a Superior Power, who is King of Kings and Lord of Lords. This sword given

They relate to the posture of the Brethren in the times immediately succeeding the massacre on the Mahoning, and

---

them they hold not in vain, but they are to protect the weaker ones and save the innocent. It is not only permitted unto them to oppose and punish all such as will hurt, kill, steal, &c., but it is their duty to do so, and if they neglect this their office they will be answerable for it to their Master.

"A minister of the Gospel is a sheep sent among wolves, who is to be prudent like a serpent and harmless like a dove. His arms are not carnal but spiritual, and he conquers by no other weapons than by the blood of the Lamb, by the sword of the Gospel, by faith in Christ, by prayers and by tears. If one smites him on the right cheek he is to turn him the other also. If one takes away his coat he is to give him also his cloak. Confer *Matthew*, v. 38, 39. Such an one if he would handle weapons becoming a soldier, would show his ignorance of his commission.

"A common man such as they call a layman, if he hath wife and children, is to provide for his family and to protect them against mischief. It would not be right in him to see his wife ravished by a wicked fellow and to sit still at it. It would be very wrong in him if wicked wretches should fall upon his children and he be indolent and patient at the murdering of them. If it is right in a pastor to kill rather a wolf than to see the lambs killed, it is certainly right for a father to stand up for the life of his children.

"Now I will tell you what we have been doing hitherto since our Brethren were killed and burned at the Mahoning. We have received those that escaped the cruel hands of the savages with great thankfulness to the Lord. We have praised the Lord for taking so many of our Brethren and Sisters all at once like a sacrifice to himself. We have mourned for those poor creatures who were Satan's instruments in doing evil; and oh how we wish they may once repent and be pardoned!

"When we were told how the enemy had boasted that they certainly would have done with all the Forks, especially with Bethlehem and Nazareth, before the *Great Day* (they mean Christmas), we committed our life and all into the hands of our good Saviour believing that there is no one to save us from the wicked one but He alone. Then we agreed to be on our guard and to keep good watch, thinking

to a part of their experiences during the continuance of the war.

---

that to be a means of deterring the enemy. And we hope that the Lord hath blessed our endeavors, poor as they are, for that purpose.

"The watchmen then proposed whether it would not be good to have some guns, partly to give a signal to the rest of the guard, partly to hinder the cruel enemy from falling upon the Sisters and children, and using them after his abominable manner. They said, 'What shall we do? If the savages would be satisfied with taking our lives it might be so; but shall we leave our Sisters and our children a prey to their devilish designs?' I could not say, 'Let the savages do what they please with our Sisters and our children.' No indeed! For how could a father or a husband do so and not think himself guilty of neglecting his duty? But this I have told my Brethren, 'Pray rather to God that he may send fear and trembling upon the enemy and thereby keep him a great way from us, for I should neither like to see an Indian, nor one of my Brethren nor their wives and children, killed at Bethlehem, at Nazareth, or at any of our places.'

"We do not trust in weapons nor in arms. For we know for certain that if the Lord will have us suffer, no arms will keep us free. If He will have us safe, not all the devils will be able to hurt us in the least. What could Satan do to Job, to his children, and to his cattle and his horses, before he was permitted by God? But after he was told that they had been given into his hands he soon made away with all that Job had in the world.

"We cannot remove from Bethlehem and Nazareth with such a body of men, women, and children. Where should we go to be safer? Here we know Providence has placed us. Should we think ourselves more secure in the towns, and should we expose our children to the temptations and the wicked practices so common there, and finally should we throw ourselves into the hands of men to live dependent upon their goodness and their mercy? No! *We would rather fall into the hands of the Lord.* Who knows but He will preserve us alive for the good of this whole Province, and how many thanks will be given to Him if He does!

"Now, my dear Brethren and Sisters, as I have told you my heart and the heart of my Brethren and Sisters, I thank you for sympathizing so much with us in our present situation. The tokens of your compas-

Gnadenhütten East, the seat of the mission since June of 1754, was deserted in the fatal night, and the missionaries and their converts, upward of seventy men, women, and children, fled to Bethlehem. The presence of these refugees at that place, at a critical juncture, when men's voices were being raised in bitter imprecations indiscriminately against a race that was perpetrating daily atrocities around them, perplexed the Brethren even more than concern for providing for the fugitives in the future, should their sojourn be prolonged by the chances of war. They nevertheless welcomed them with open arms, for they loved their "*brown brethren and sisters*," or "*the brown hearts*," as they affectionately called them, as dearly as the apple of their eye. And hence when the former came fleeing to them before the dreaded vengeance of their kinsmen, who had threatened to cleanse their ears with a red-hot iron, the latter opened the gates of the city of refuge and took them in.

Always disposed to act in conformity with the requirements, and in matters of moment with the sanction, of Government, the Brethren notified the magistrates of the sudden transfer of their mission. At the same time they approved of a desire their Indians expressed of throwing themselves on the protection of Government as loyal subjects, and as such,

---

sion were welcome and I wish you many blessings for them. Continue in your love, and let your prayers and our prayers be offered for one common object, viz.: that the Lord may rebuke the wicked Prince of Darkness who is the great leader of these idolaters that are now crying against Christ's people; and that He may fill these poor ignorant wicked creatures with fear and trembling, and thus cause them to return to their hills and mountains as the proper companions of wolves and bears, and other wild beasts, till the Lord please to open their eyes and to call them from the power of Satan into his glorious kingdom.

"SPANGENBERG.

"*Bethlehem*, Dec. 23, 1755."

of claiming assistance in time of need. These accordingly addressed Governor Morris.* In his reply, the Governor not

---

* The following is the correspondence that passed between the Moravian Indians and Governor Morris. It is prefaced by a letter addressed by Bishop Spangenberg to the Justices of the County of Northampton, and dated Bethlehem, November 29, 1755, as follows:

"Inclosed is an address of the Indians who came down from Gnadenhütten, to the Governor and the Assembly, which I think should first be shown to the Magistrates of this County and then go down with their opinion, for it is a matter of great importance, they being the only men at present who can do the Government the greatest service.

"I cannot help letting you know that Gnadenhütten is of as great importance to our Government as Shamokin; for if that place be not secured, not only all the settlers who live behind the Blue Mountain must be going from their houses and farms, but the Indians can run down with freshes in a few hours into any part of the Forks, yea, quite down to Philadelphia.

"If the Government should think well to build there a fort, we will give of the land we have there, ten acres, for that purpose, in a place which can command the Lehigh and a great way on all sides.

"If they choose our offer, they must needs keep a guard there before the houses and mill are burned down, which can be of great service to them at first while they are building a fort. The Indians, our friends, have all their corn there, for they fled for their lives, naked, in the night. If the said corn is fetched for them, they will not be a burden to the County, which they never yet have been. If this corn be left there, they must needs be provided for, and it will not be good to leave the corn to the enemy. Twelve wagons, may be, would fetch it, and it will be too much to let this be the Brethren's charge.

"I am, Sirs,

"Your humble servant,

"SPANGENBERG."

"Upon perusing the foregoing letter, we are clearly of opinion that the several matters therein contained are of very great weight, and if

only assured the petitioners of his sympathy, but at the same time expressed his conviction that they were deserv-

---

carried into execution, would be of the greatest service to all this part of the country.

"WM PARSONS,
"TIMY HORSFIELD,
"THOS. CRAIG,
"HUGH WILSON.

"November 30, 1755."

The humble Address of the Indians, late residing at Gnadenhütten, at their instance, taken from their own mouths as followeth, to wit:

"First, we present our love, respect, and duty to the Honble Robert Hunter Morris, the Governor of Pennsylvania, and because we are not able to express ourselves as it should be, we beg that the best construction may be put upon what we have to lay before him.

"We have hitherto been poor heathen, who knew nothing of God, but lived in blindness and abominable sins.

"The Brethren have told us words from Jesus Christ our God and Lord, who became a man for us and purchased salvation for us with his blood.

"We have heard these words, taken them to heart, received them in faith, and are baptized in the name of Jesus Christ.

"The Brethren since that time have faithfully cared for us, and not only further instructed us in God's word, but have also permitted us to live upon their land and plant our corn, at the same time instructing our children.

"It is now a great many years that we have lived in quiet and peace under the protection of the Government of this Province, so that we have not been burdensome to any, nor has anybody molested us. But now it has come to pass that wicked people who serve the Devil have committed horrible murders and inhumanly butchered even our own Brethren.

"We well knew that we had nothing better to expect at their hands as long as we continued with the Brethren under this Government. For which cause we sought to save our lives by flight, leaving everything behind which we had in Gnadenhütten, to wit: not only our

ing subjects of charity. Thus assured, the Brethren drew upon the Provincial Commissioners for reimbursement in

habitations but also our clothing and provisions, fleeing in the dark night, naked and empty, away with our wives and our children.

"Now we are here in Bethlehem with our Brethren, willing rather to suffer and live with them as heretofore. We cannot but declare to our Honor^ble^ Governor,

"1. That we are thankful from the bottom of our hearts for the protection and peace that we have hitherto enjoyed in this Province.

"2. That none of us have any hand in the abominable murders lately committed by the Indians, but we abhor and detest them.

"3. It is our desire, seeing that we are persuaded that our lives will be principally sought after, to put ourselves as children under the protection of this Government. We cannot say otherwise but that we are entirely devoted to the English Government and wish success and prosperity to their arms against their and our enemies.

"We hope that our Honble Governor will give us a gracious answer to this our humble petition, and provide for our future welfare and security.

"JOSHUA, *Mohican*,
"AUGUSTUS, *Delaware*,
"JACOB, *Mohican*,
"ANTON, *Delaware*,
"JOHN PETER, *Wampanoag*,
"JOSHUA, *Delaware*,
"ANDREW, *Wampanoag*,
"MICHAEL, *Monsey*,
"JONATHAN, *Delaware*,
"PHILIP, *Wampanoag*,
"JOHN, *Mohican*,
"JOHN, *Delaware*,
"DANIEL, *Mohican*,
"MARK, *Mohican*.

"BETHLEHEM, November 29, 1755."

THE GOVERNOR'S REPLY.

"*To the Indians lately residing at Gnadenhütten and now at Bethlehem, greeting:*

"BRETHREN,—

"You may always depend on the most favorable construction being put on whatever you lay before me.

part of expenses they were incurring in providing for loyal Indians and for Christians who had fled to fellow-Christians for protection.

"It gives me a true pleasure to find you are under the force of religious impressions, and speak in so affectionate a manner of the Author of the Christian Salvation, our Lord Jesus Christ.

"As you have made it your own choice to become members of our civil society, and subjects of the same Government, and determine to share the same fate with us, I shall make it my care to extend the same protection to you as to the other subjects of his Majesty, and as a testimony of the regard paid by the Government to the distressed state of that Province where you have suffered so much, I have determined to build a fort at Gnadenhütten, from which you will receive equal security with the white people under my care.

"I have not the least suspicion of your having been concerned in the late mischief. Your precaution and flight are an evidence of your innocence, and I take in good part your professions of truth and fidelity to your Brethren, and thank you for them.

"I heartily commiserate your losses, and think you entitled to relief, and as I intend to send for all our friendly Indians to come and confer with me in this time of danger, I shall let you know the time when I shall meet them, and desire you to be present, that I may speak to you at the same time.

"In the mean time I desire you will be of good behaviour, and remain where you are.

"Given under my hand and the Lesser Seal of the Province, at Philadelphia, the fourth day of December, A.D. 1755.

"ROBERT HUNTER MORRIS."

Answer of the Moravian Indians to Gov. Morris's Reply, "which was taken from their own mouths, and being literally translated, was read and communicated to them in their own tongue, before signing."

"HON[BLE] GOVERNOR,—

"We received thy letter, and thy words being interpreted to us, we have heard with our ears and well understood. Our women and our children have also heard them. It has rejoiced us much, and we are heartily thankful that thou wilt be pleased to provide for and take us

The accounts of the "above seventy Indians who escaped from Gnadenhütten," in the following transcript are incomplete, in as far as they are preceded by two statements, one amounting to £51 9*s*. 5½*d*. from November 28, 1755, to February 20, 1756, and another to £13 18*s*. 3*d*. from February 28 to April 1, of the last named year. Furthermore, they were continued as late as April of 1758. On several occasions the Province demurred honoring these drafts on her exchequer, it having been seriously impoverished by outlays incurred in prosecuting the war, and in conducting tedious overtures for the restoration of a permanent peace. The representations made by the Brethren, however, in which they reminded Government of its pledge, of the comparatively trifling cost it incurred for every Moravian Indian (it amounting only to 1¾ pence per day); which cost, they argued, was almost outweighed by the services

---

under thy protection against our enemies, in these troublesome times; that we may abide with our Brethren in peace, and daily hear sweet words of our God and Saviour to the refreshment and comfort of our poor hearts.

"We assure and promise thee herewith that we will be obedient to thy order, and with our wives and children behave ourselves still and orderly among our Brethren, and be governed peaceably and quietly toward every man.

"We are heartily willing to come and hear more words from thee, whenever thou shalt please to call us.

"In the mean time we poor Indians recommend ourselves to thy kind remembrance, hoping we shall not be forgotten by thee.

"We offer our kind salutations to thee, wishing thee health and prosperity, and remain

"Thy obedient and faithful Brethren,

"AUGUSTUS, *Delaware* (*his mark a Turtle*).

"JOSHUA, *Mohican* (*his mark a Turkey*).

"Signed by the Order and in behalf of all the rest, 9th December, 1755."

that some of their number had rendered the Province, in the capacity of runners or of interpreters, and on dangerous embassies, finally prevailed.* The accounts were ac-

---

* "MAY IT PLEASE YOUR HONOR,—

"The inclosed is the humble request of the Brethren in Bethlehem to your Honor, occasioned by the Honorable Commissioners refusing to pay the accounts of their expenses toward maintaining the friendly Indians, who nevertheless have done the Government many great services, and never demanded anything from this Province, as long as they were quietly left in their settlements upon the Mahoning on the Brethren's lands.

"Now, as I hope, your Honor will be pleased to consider, that at another time many other Indians may think, 'It is better for Indians to join the enemies of the English, for then they will get presents and rewards; but if the Indians join the English and behave friendly, they will not only afterwards be left destitute, but will also be left a prey to their enemies, after it comes to a peace;' which probably will be the case with those Indians who were ever faithful to this Government, and are now at Bethlehem—hated by all the Indians of their tribe because they were not with them against the English in the last war. And such thoughts will not turn out for the good of the Province. However, I hope of your goodness better things.

"Your Honor's most humble servant,

"SPANGENBERG.

"BETHM., Apr. 20, 1757."

The Brethren's Address to Governor Denny.

"MAY IT PLEASE YOUR HONOR,—

"*Whereas*, some time since when the late Indian troubles took their beginning, the Brethren's valuable settlement on the Mahoning, together with eleven human lives, were destroyed, and our people were thereby losers of at least £2000, a loss which we shall feel while we live;

"*And whereas*, at the same time a number of Indians who were then living on our land at Gnadenhütten, and in a fair way of getting a competent and comfortable livelihood, without being burdensome for it either to the Province or to their neighbors thereabouts, having

cordingly recognized as just obligations and liquidated in full; not, however, without hesitancy, in overcoming which

---

been preserved by means of the Brethren in their friendship and alliance with this Government, were even therefore at the same time forced to fly for their lives, lose their all, and take their refuge to the Brethren at Bethlehem, destitute of everything to support life;

"*And whereas*, your Honor's predecessor, considering their circumstances, has told and given it them in writing that they should be treated friendly and supported in their necessitous circumstances by the Province; upon the good faith of which the Brethren in Bethlehem have furnished them with necessaries of life, and charged the expenses to the Province account;

"*And whereas*, at sundry times the Brethren have produced their accounts before the honorable the Commissioners, and had them punctually paid till now, when Mr. Schmalling, one of the Brethren, delivered our account, amounting to a mere trifle each day per head, was refused payment. I am, therefore, to represent our hard case to your Honor in behalf of our much aggrieved community, and to beg your Honor's favorable interposition with the honorable the Commissioners; for although the Indians residing here in Bethlehem on one hand are not inclined to settle again in the Indian country for fear of their lives, and on the other cannot resolve to live below Philadelphia for want of hunting opportunity, which makes a great part of their livelihood; and although on that account the Brethren at Bethlehem have consented to let them settle on a piece of ground belonging to us not far from here, we humbly conceive that this is not a sufficient ground to cut them off from the hitherto usual allowance they have had from this Government as long as they are not yet settled upon that intended spot, nor as long as the Government maintains so many other Indians who have murdered many of the inhabitants, enslaved others, and destroyed their possessions. We therefore hope your Honor will in good reason think those who have faithfully adhered to this Government entitled to the same beneficial allowance which such Indians as were enemies still enjoy.

"We have that confidence in your Honor that you in equity and justice will support our request, and not suffer that these poor, friendly, but at present necessitous Indians, shall either be thrown entirely upon

Mr. William Edmonds was largely instrumental. This was in June of 1758.

The specified accounts that constitute the bulk of the transcript in this paper were rendered to the Commissioners, pursuant to an order given to the Brethren by Governor Morris,* that they provide for such of the enemy as should come into the settlements, after his proclamation for a suspension of hostilities. Some of these came with a desire to return to their allegiance, others to throw themselves on the protection of the Province, and others to treat for peace. War had been formally declared against the Delawares in April of 1756. In May, and again in July, hostilities were suspended; in the last month they were remitted preparatory to the first of a series of treaties. This lull was followed by an influx of Delawares and allied Indians to Bethlehem, which lay in the route from their country to Easton, the place that had been selected for negotiations. Government was imposing an additional burden upon the Brethren when it committed

---

the Brethren at Bethlehem already so very great losers in this Province, or be left to the mercy of their embittered Indian brethren.

"Not doubting of your Honor's equitable resolution,

"We rest your Honor's most obedient humble servants,

"Signed in behalf of the Brethren,

"MATTHEW SCHROPP, *Steward.*

"BETHM., Apr. 22, 1757."

* "I do hereby empower the Brethren and request them to receive into their houses at Bethlehem all such friendly Indians as shall come to them and desire to be taken in, and to support and maintain them till they have my further orders; always taking care to advise me from time to time of the arrival of any Indians, mentioning their place of abode, their tribe, and such other circumstances as shall be necessary to give me a just and proper account of them, and any expenses attending this service will be paid by the Government."—*Gov. Morris to Tim'y Horsfield, Esq.* Philadelphia, June 23, 1756.

this lawless crowd to their keeping; and although aware of this, its assurance that their knowledge of Indian character rendered them desirable custodians, and that at Bethlehem the hated Indians would be safe, outweighed all other considerations. In vain did the Brethren deprecate this measure as one that was likely to cause them serious inconvenience, to prove hurtful to the welfare of the Christian Indians, and to involve themselves in difficulties with their neighbors. Their repeated appeals to the Governor, to the Assembly, and to the Commissioners for relief were ineffectual. "We are at a loss how to act," Bishop Spangenberg writes to Governor Denny, "with those Indians that come out of the woods and want to stay at Bethlehem. They are very troublesome guests and we should be glad to have your Honor's orders about them. Our houses are already full and we must be at the expense of building winter-houses for them if more should come; which likely will be the case if we are to believe the accounts of those who are here. Furthermore, we are told that some of our neighbors are growing uneasy at our receiving such murdering Indians, as they style them. I fear we shall be obliged to set watches to keep such of them off as are disposed to quarrel with, or may attempt to hurt any of them. Now we are willing to do anything that lays in our power for the service of that Province in which we have enjoyed peace for many years. But we desire your Honor's orders for every step we take, and we humbly beg not to be left without them; the more so as we have reason to fear that an Indian may be somehow hurt or killed, which certainly would breed new troubles of war. There was a case last week to the point, one of the Indians having been fired at, when out in the woods a little way from Bethlehem." And thus for almost two years (from April of 1756 to April of 1758) they were annoyed by the presence of these troublesome pensioners on the Province. Some of them were savages, some were half civilized, and some were renegades from the mission. The latter were objects of their special commiseration, and it pained them to see such as had once publicly renounced the ways of wickedness, in the company of those who had taken the lives of their fellow-beings in a barbarous warfare. Conspicuous among these was the man who led the Delawares and their allies in war against the English. This was Teedyuscung. Of him we know the following:

According to his own statement, he was born about the year 1700, in New Jersey, east of Trenton, in which neighborhood his ancestors of the Lenape* had been seated from time immemorial. Old Captain Harris, a noted Delaware, was his father. The same was the father also of Captain John, of Nazareth, of young Captain Harris, of Tom, of Jo, and of Sam Evans,—a family of high-spirited sons who were not in good repute with their white neighbors. The latter named them, it is true, for men of their own people, and Teedyuscung they named "Honest John;" yet they disliked, and then feared them; for the Harrises were known to grow moody and resentful, and were heard to speak threatening words as they saw their paternal acres passing out of their hands, and their hunting-grounds converted into pasture and plowed fields. These they left with reluctance, and migrated westward, in company with others of the Turtles or Delawares of the Lowlands, some from

* The Delawares styled themselves *Lenni Lenape*, *original people*, that is, an *unchanged people*. The eastern division of this nation was divided into three tribes,—the *Turtles*, or Delawares of the sea-shore (*lowlanders*), the *Turkeys*, or Delawares of the woods (*uplanders*), and the *Wolves*, or Delawares of the mountains (*highlanders*); named in their language respectively the *Unamies*, the *Unalachtgos*, and the *Monseys*.

the Raritan, some from below Cranberry and Devil's Brook, some from the Neshannock, and some from the mouth of Squan and the meadows on Little and Great Egg Harbor. Crossing the great river of their nation,* they entered the Province of Pennsylvania in its Forks. This was about 1730. Finding no white men here, they gypsied unmolested along the Lehietan, Martin's and Cobus Creeks, the Manakasy,† the Gattoshacki,‡ and the Hockendocque,§ all south, and along the Aquanshicola‖ and Pocopoco¶ north of the Blue Mountain. On crossing this barrier they reached the land of their kinsmen, the Wolf Delawares, or Monseys. By these hardy mountaineers they were kindly received, and with them they would often speak of their compulsory exodus from the east, to which the Monseys made no reply, but only smiled.

Scotch-Irish immigrants began to crowd the Delawares in the Forks south of the mountain as early as 1735. Two years prior whites had surveyed and located unpurchased lands in the Upper Valley of the Delaware,** thereby exasperating the Monseys, and engendering in their hearts

---

* The Delaware, called the *Lenapewihittuck*, i.e. the *River of the Lenape*.

† Written variously *Menagassi*, *Monocasy*, *Monakessi*, *Manokasy*, *Monockisy*, *Manakasy*, Delaware, signifying *a stream with several large bends*.

‡ Written also *Catosacque*, corrupted into *Catasauqua*, Delaware, signifying *the earth is thirsty*.

§ Written originally *Hackiundachque*, but now *Hockendaqua*, Delaware, signifying *searching for land*.

‖ *Achquoanschicola*, Delaware, signifying *the place of fishing with bush-nets*.

¶ Corrupted from *Pockhapocka*. Written also *Pohopoka* and *Buchcabuchka*, Delaware, signifying *two mountains butting toward one another and separated by a stream of water—a water-gap*.

** The *Minnisinks*, i.e. *the habitation of the Monseys or Minsis*.

an implacable resentment, which they cherished long after the Turtle Delawares had buried the hatchet and were willing to treat for redress. These highlanders were the warriors who, moody and sullen, hung back at Trout Creek, in July of 1756, when Teedyuscung and his company were already in Easton, and engaged in negotiations for peace. In September of 1737 the one and a half days' walk was performed. Captain John and other Fork Indians south of the mountain were expelled from their corn-lands and peach-orchards in 1742.* Even Moses Tatemy was threatened exile. Thus wrong was being heaped on wrong against a day of retribution.

Zinzendorf's reconnoissance in July of that year introduced the Brethren's missionaries into the homes of the Eastern Delawares; and from that time they preached the Gospel to them on both sides of the mountain. Teedyuscung too heard them, first on the Aquanshicola and then on the Mahoning. Impressed by the words of the plainly-clad preachers from Bethlehem, his religious feelings were moved, and a time came when he was convicted of sin, and then sought for admission into Christian fellowship with the Mohicans and Delawares of Gnadenhütten by baptism.

The Brethren hesitated long before they acceded to his request; for they tell us that the man was unstable as water and like a reed shaken before the wind. Hence they granted him a time of probation, and as he reiterated his request at its close, they consented to admit him into their communion. On the 12th of March, accordingly, he was

---

* See minutes of a council held with heads of the Six Nations in the Great Meeting House at Philadelphia, July 12, 1742 (*Colonial Records*, also *Büdingische Sammlung*, vol. ii.), for papers relating to the negotiations of the Brethren with Captain John for an amicable release to them of his claims on lands at Nazareth.

baptized in the little turreted chapel on the Mahoning, Bishop Cammerhoff administering the rite.* The ceremony was performed in accordance with the solemn ritual observed among the Brethren at that time in the baptism of adults; and when the straight-limbed Delaware, robed in white, rose from bended knee, he rose as Gideon, the namesake of "the son of Joash, the Abiezrite, who threshed wheat in the wine-press to hide it from the Midianites."

Thus Teedyuscung became a member of the Christian Church, and yet failed, as so many do, to become a Christian. The lessons of the Divine Master whom he had promised to follow proved distasteful to him, as he found they demanded renunciation of self, the practice of humility, the forgiveness of injuries, and the return of good for evil. They were different from the doctrines taught in the school of Nature in which he had long been educated. Hence he ill brooked the restraints imposed upon him in the "Huts of Grace," and resisted the influence of the Good Spirit that sought to dispossess him of the resentment that burned within his soul when he remembered how his countrymen were being injured by the whites, and how they had been traduced and were being oppressed by the imperious Iroquois. And once when his untamed Brethren came down from the Minnisinks to Gnadenhütten, bringing their unshod ponies and their broken flint-locks to the smithy, they opened their hearts to him wide, and took him into their councils. These intended war. Telling him that the hour was come to prepare to rise against their oppressors, they asked him to lead them and be their king. That

* In the record of Indian baptisms for the year 1750, Bishop Cammerhoff makes the following entry: "*March* 12. To-day I baptized *Tatiuskundt*, the chief among sinners." His words are "*ein κατ' ἐξοχην grosser Sünder.*"

was the evil moment in which he was dazzled by the prospect of a crown, and trafficked his peace of mind for the unrest of ambition. This was in the spring of 1754. Mohican Abraham also turned renegade, and the two chieftains together prevailed with seventy of the congregation to remove to Wyoming, there to live neutral or to array themselves under their standard.

Braddock was repulsed on the Monongahela in July of 1755. Hereupon assembling his Delawares and allied Mohicans and Shawanese at Nescopeck, Teedyuscung marked out a plan of the campaign for the coming autumn and winter. Its operations were restricted to the walking purchase, within which it was resolved to chastise the English first by waging against them a war of extermination. And so it came to pass. From their lurking-places in the fastnesses of the Great Swamp, the savage warriors, led by their King in person, would sally forth on their marauds, striking consternation into the hearts of the defenseless settlers, ruthlessly destroying with torch and tomahawk, and then retreating, with what booty and prisoners they had taken, into its protecting glades. It threatened to be a repetition of the war of Philip and his Pequods. Plantation after plantation was pillaged, and before the close of December the enemy had overrun the greater part of Northampton, and Nazareth was literally on the frontiers. On the 1st of January, 1756, the Brethren met with a second loss, for on that day Gnadenhütten East was totally destroyed,* the company of Provincials stationed there having been surprised and cut to pieces.

Such was the warfare that scourged the Province into the

* The following is a statement of the pecuniary loss sustained by the Brethren in the destruction of the farm on the Mahoning and the Mission at Gnadenhütten East:

early months of 1756, when in March, Government sought

Appraisement of the United Brethren's Loss, suffered at the hands of the Indians, on the Mahoning and at Gnadenhütten.

I. ON THE MAHONING.

	£	s.	d.	£	s.	d.
One mare, 7 years old........................	15					
One do. 10 do.	12					
One horse, 10 do.	8					
One do. 4 do.	15					
Three colts, 1 year do........................	9					
				59		
Seven cows, past 4 years old..............	24	10				
Seven do. 4 years old......................	21					
Seven heifers, 2 do.	17	10				
Seven calves, 1 year do....................	5	5				
Two oxen, 2 years old.......................	5					
Three do. 3 do.	10	10				
Four do. 4 do.	18					
Eight do. 5 and 6 do........................	40					
				141	15	
65 Bu. of oats, bo't the same day @ 2*s*.	6	10				
11 loads of hay, @ 40*s*....................	22					
10 do. rowing do., @ 30*s*..............	15					
5 do. oats, @ 60*s*........................	15					
2 do. steeped flax, @ 50*s*..............	5					
1 do. hemp..............................	1	10				
5 do. wheat, @ £5....................	25					
4 do. rye, @ £4........................	16					
1 do. barley..............................	3					
500 lbs. butter..................................	12	10				
10 bu. of meal, @ 5*s*..................	2	10				
12 do. buckwheat, @ 1*s*. 8*d*..........	1					
3 do. Indian corn, @ 3*s*.............		9				
1½ do. flaxseed, @ 3*s*. 6*d*..............		5	3			
4 do. of beans, @ 4*s*.................		16				
6 do. of salt, @ 3*s*.....................		18				
24 lbs. beeswax, @ 1*s*. 6*d*................	1	16				
				129	4	3
Carr^d forw^d....................................				229	19	3

to propitiate the man who was its chief abettor and most

	£	s.	d.
Bro[t] forw[d]	229	19	3
Horse gears, saddles, &c.	10		
House and kitchen furniture	98		
Clothes, bedding, &c., for 17 persons	294		
Two silver watches and 1 house-clock	17		
Smith's tools, burnt or stolen	11		
A meeting-house (*Gemeinhaus*) with dwelling rooms	200		
A dwelling-house and smith-shop	100		
A bake-house	10		
A kitchen and watch-house	10		
A dwelling-house	30		
A stable and barn	100		
A spring-house	5		
A store-house	50		
Goods in the store	150		
A grist and saw-mill	200		
8,000 or more feet of pine boards	24		
	1638	19	3

2. AT GNADENHUTTEN EAST.

	£	s.	d.			
Eighteen log-houses, most of them of squared logs, @ £6	108					
Twelve Indian cabins, @ 30*s*	18					
A large meeting-house with dwelling rooms	150					
	276			1914	19	3

Personally appeared before me, Timothy Horsfield, Esq., one of the Justices in and for the County of Northampton, George Klein, Joseph Powell, Henry Frey, all of Bethlehem in the said county, yeomen, and upon their solemn affirmation according to law did respectively declare and depose,—That they these affirmants had exact knowledge of all the articles and particulars contained in the above account, and to the best of their skill and understanding do believe the same are noted therein at the lowest and most reasonable prices possible; and

active in its prosecution. Messengers were now dispatched to Teedyuscung with an invitation to meet his friends, the children of William Penn, and to tell them the causes of an alienation which was as unexpected as it was calamitous. An appeal was also made to the Six Nations to lift up their authoritative hand and stay the destroyer. These measures proved effectual. Pursuant to them, Teedyuscung met Governor Morris in treaty at Easton, for the first time, in July of 1756, and Governor Denny in November of that year and again in November of 1757.

These conferences resulted in the pacification of the Delaware King, on assurances being given him that his grievances should be fully redressed. On these occasions, we are told, Teedyuscung stood up as the champion of his people, fearlessly demanding restitution of their lands, or an equivalent for their irreparable loss, and in addition the free exercise of the right to select, within the territory in dispute, a permanent home. The chieftain's imposing presence, his earnestness of appeal, and his impassioned oratory, as he plead the cause of the long-injured Lenape, evoked the admiration of his enemies themselves. He always spoke in the euphonious Delaware, employing this Castilian of the New World to utter the simple and expressive figures and tropes of the native rhetoric with which his harangues were replete, although he was conversant with the white man's speech.

---

that the above contains a true and just account of the said sufferers' losses. And further these affirmants say not.

GEORGE KLEIN.
JOSEPH POWELL.
HENRY FREY.

Taken and affirmed to at Bethlehem ye 4 Febr^y^ 1756, before me

[L.S.] TIM^Y^. HORSFIELD.

It would almost appear from the minutes of these Conferences, that the English artfully attempted to evade the point at issue, and to conciliate the indignant chieftain by fair speeches and uncertain promises. The hollowness of the former he boldly exposed, and the latter he scornfully rejected; so that it was soon perceived that the Indian King was as astute and sagacious, as he was unmovable in the justice of his righteous demands. This conviction forced itself upon his hearers, and then they yielded to the terms he laid down.

In forming an estimate of his position and of his endeavors to maintain it, it should not be forgotten that Teedyuscung was contending with a twofold enemy, with the English and with the Iroquois. The insulting words of Canassatego, spoken to the Fork Delawares in July of 1742,* had stung him to the quick. Since then he looked forward to the time when he should be enabled, after having won redress from the English, gained their confidence and then their alliance, to wipe out the blot which tarnished the escutcheon of the immemorial Lenape, ever since the Five Nations had insidiously made women of them. This he failed to do, according to the stern demands of an unjust law, by which the rights of the weaker party are made to succumb to the superior power of those who are strong in coalition.

---

* "Let this Belt serve to chastise you," he said, turning to the Delawares. "You ought to be taken by the hair of the head and shaken severely till you recover your senses, and become sober. You don't know what ground you stand on, nor what you are doing. This land that you claim is gone through your guts long ago. We conquered you, we made women of you. You know you are women and can no more sell land than women. We charge you to remove instantly. We don't give you the liberty to think about it, for you are women."

In the spring of 1758 Teedyuscung removed to Wyoming, where, agreeably to his request and the conditions of treaty, a town had been built for him and his followers by the English, in the historic valley on the east side of the Susquehanna. Here he now lived not unmindful of his long-cherished object, and here he was burned to death in the night of the 19th of April, 1763, while asleep in his lodge. The Iroquois, it is said, were the instigators of this cowardly act, for they hated the man who testified against their arrogant assumption and who opposed their lust of power. As long as he lived, therefore, he was a standing rebuke to their designing oppression, and although they no longer dreaded his arms, they feared his words, which left their guilty consciences no peace. Hence it was resolved in council that he ought not to live; and when news was brought back to Onondaga that the lodge of the Delaware King and the lodges of his men of war had disappeared in flames, the perfidious Six Nations triumphed in having destroyed an enemy whose spirit they had failed to subdue.

In the historical records following this introduction, the reader will find additional notices of the Delaware King who was the hero of the war of 1755. The concurrent testimony of his time agrees in representing him as a man of marked ability, a brave warrior, a sagacious counselor and a patriot among his people. Although he was governed by strong passions, and a slave of that degrading vice which was the bane of his race, he was not devoid of feeling, being susceptible of the gentler influences of our nature. Numerous are the anecdotes extant, illustrating his love of humor, his ready wit, his quickness of apprehension and of reply, his keen penetration, and his sarcastic delight in exposing low cunning or artifice.

After the suspension of hostilities, and during negotiations for peace, he was much at Bethlehem, and at one time fixed his residence there. His attachment to the Brethren he openly avowed, expressing his determination to keep by them in preference to others of the whites. Elsewhere he exulted in being called a Moravian. Although he had broken his vows and had been unfaithful to his profession, he would frequently, when in conversation with the Brethren, revert to his baptism, and feelingly deplore the loss of the peace of mind he had once enjoyed. And hence we doubt not that there were times when, marshaling his savage warriors for deeds of blood in the wild highlands of the Delawares, there would come over him a vision of the "Huts of Grace" in the peaceful valley of the Mahoning, and of the turreted chapel, in which he had knelt in baptism, and which he had entered so often on holy days at the sound of the church-going bell.

The preparation of this piece of history in Pounds, Shillings, and Pence was much facilitated by consulting the Colonial Records and the Pennsylvania Archives in conjunction with the Diaries of Bethlehem and her Indian Congregation. By these means the editor has been enabled to illuminate what otherwise might have remained obscure, to brighten fading colors, to recall forgotten things, and to furnish the reader with a history in short-hand of the times to which these records relate. The antiquary will find in them occasional genre-pieces, not unlike those painted by Teniers, the elder, and his associates of the Flemish school; or here and there meet with a choice morsel, trifling perhaps, and yet such as the true antiquary can relish and digest far more effectually than what is served up for him in state on the great historian's table.

Nevertheless a hero makes his appearance even though he be a barbaric king.

Finally, should the editor appear to have at times taken too much pains in raising up a dead Indian or Provincial private, he has erred, he thinks, not in his calling (for the historian is a resurrectionist), but in the zeal with which he has followed the pursuit.

PROVINCE OF PENNSYLVANIA

IN ACCOUNT WITH THE UNITED BRETHREN, AT BETHLEHEM, PA.

For Supplies and Entertainment furnished to the Christian Indians who had fled thither after the massacre on the Mahoning, and to Indians who sojourned there with the knowledge of Government, pending negotiations for Peace between it and Teedyuscung, King of the Delawares, 1756 *and* 1757.

I. ACCOUNT SENT TO YE COMMISSIONERS IN PHILA. JULY 21, 1756.*

1756.

July 21. Province of Pennsil[a] to the Stewards† of Bethlehem, DR.
For sundries deliv[d] to above 70 Indians‡ who escaped from Gnadenhütten, from April 1 to July 17, 1756, viz.:

---

* Two accounts had been presented to the Commissioners prior to this one; the first amounting to £51 9*s.* 5½*d.*, from November 28, 1755, to February 28, 1756, and the second amounting to £13 18*s.* 3*d.*, from February 28 to April 1, of the last-mentioned year.

Provincial Commissioners at this time were John Mifflin, Benjamin Franklin, Joseph Fox, Evan Morgan, and John Hughes. Appointed by the Governor "to audit, liquidate, adjust, and settle all accounts, claims, and demands held against or made on the Province."

† Stewards for "the Family," at Bethlehem, were Matthew Schropp, John Bechtel, and George Klein.

‡ Their names and nationalities were:

MOHICANS (35).

Men.	*Women.*	*Boys.*	*Girls.*
Jacob,	Rachel,	Joshua,	Anna Johanna,
Joshua,	Bathsheba,	Elias,	Rachel,
John,	Lorel,	Abraham,	Rosina,

1756.		£	s.	d.
July 21.	For 5692 lbs. bread, @ 1½d....................	35	11	6
	" 85½ bushs Indian corn beside their own	14	19	3
	" 540 lbs. beef, @ 4d.........................	9		
	Carrd forwd..............................	59	10	9

Men.	*Women.*	*Boys.*	*Girls.*
Philip,	Lydia,	Gabriel,	Judith,
Daniel,	Elisabeth,	Michael.	Martha,
Andrew,	Catharine,		Agnes,
Michael,	Eve,		Christiana,
John Peter,	Esther,		Sophia,
Marcus,	Judith.		Anna Johanna.
Amos,			
Renatus,			
Philip.			

DELAWARES (38).

Men.	*Women.*	*Boys.*	*Girls.*
Augustus,	Augustina,	Levi,	Julianna,
Anton,	Johanna,	John,	Esther,
Joshua,	Agnes,	Ezra,	Maria Elisabeth,
Jonathan,	Verona,	Michael,	Christiana,
Joachim,	Benigna,	Abraham,	Beata,
Aquila,	Mary,	Nett,	and three girls
Gottlieb,	Anna Justina,	Petitti,	more.
Namaan.	Naomi,	Achgonema,	
	Thamar,	Quisch,	
	Erdmuth,	Quichkschal.	
	Amelia,		
	Rebecca.		

These refugees were quartered in the "*Indian House*" that had been built in October of 1752, on the west bank of the Manakasy, for the entertainment of visitors from Gnadenhütten and elsewhere, just above the stone bridge that crosses the creek in Water Street. It was 52 by 40 feet, of one story, and of stone; and yet within these narrow limits the "*above seventy who escaped*" were domiciled. In the summer of 1756 a log-house, 63 by 15 feet, containing a chapel, beside

		£	s.	d.
1756.	Bro[t] forw[d]	59	10	9
July 21.	For 16 lbs. dried pork, @ 5*d*		6	8
	" 157 lbs. butter, @ 6*d*	3	18	6
	" 1 bush[l] salt		4	
	" 2 gall[s] linseed oil,* @ 4*s*		8	
	Carr[d] forw[d]	64	7	11

apartments, was built due south of the other. There are old residents of Bethlehem who remember the "stone-house." It was removed in the early part of the present century. Portions of the tile-pavement or floor are remaining. The spring that empties into the creek immediately above the bridge rose in the cellar of the "*Indian House.*" The chapel was transferred to Nain in the autumn of 1758, and was the place of worship until the erection of a more commodious one in May of 1763.

The missionaries Bernhard A. Grubé and John Jacob Schmick, ministered to the Christian Indians, and kept school for their children during their temporary sojourn at Bethlehem. Occasionally they would repair to the Brethren's Chapel to attend divine service. So as to lighten the burden they imposed on their benefactors by their presence, the men assisted in the labors of the farm, or watched in times of danger, and the women plaited baskets and made brooms and wooden ware. In the autumn and winter months the former followed the chase; and although they were restricted in this to a small range, confining themselves exclusively to Bethlehem lands (for there was a strong feeling against Indians in the neighborhood), "it was no uncommon occurrence," says the diarist, "for the hunters to bring in two or three deer in a day." They also conducted the shad-fishery in the Lehigh, which yielded plentifully. "May 10, 1756, our Indians took upward of 2000 shad." Between fifteen and twenty thousand was the annual yield. Quantities of these were salted down. In March of 1758 there was a pigeon-roost, seven miles above Bethlehem, on the Lehigh, whither for fourteen days the wild pigeons moved in countless numbers, affording a temporal source of supply for the poor Indians.

* The Brethren at Bethlehem erected a mill for pressing linseed-oil early in 1745. It burned down in November of 1763. In 1765, Christensen, an ingenious millwright, constructed the works of a

		£	s.	d.
1756.	Bro^t forw^d.	64	7	11
July 21.	For 13 galls soft sope, @ 1s.		13	
	For sundries deliv^d to ye Indian messengers, Newcastle and others, by their going to Wayomik. (See *Voucher* 1)	6	5	
	For sundries deliv^d to ye 4 Indian messengers and other Indians, per order of Newcastle. (See *Voucher* 2)	3	13	7
	For sundries deliv^d to Jo Peepy, Nicodemus, and others, who came from Diahoga to Bethlehem. (See *Voucher* 3)	27	6	7½
	For sundries deliv^d to ye 4 Indians, viz., Samuel, Pachshenoscha's son, his son-in-law and one other, as pr. order of Mr. Horsfield. (See *Voucher* 4)	14	3	9
	For sundries deliv^d 31 Indians, viz., Tattewaskundt and company who came to Bethlehem ye 17 July. (See *Voucher* 5)	5	9	
		121	18	10½

Vouchers belongg to the foregoing Account.

1.

Province of Pennsil^a Dr. to Bethlehem.

		£	s.	d.
1756.	For sundries deliv^d to the Indian messengers, Newcastle and others, by their going to Wayomik,* viz.:			
June 27.	For breakfast, @ 4*d*. each		1	4
	" 30 lbs. dried beef, @ 5*d*.		12	6
	Carr^d forw^d		13	10

second, one of a set of mills in the building long known as the "Bethlehem Oil and Buckwheat Mill."

* *Cashiowaya*, or *Kanuksusy*, a Six Nation Indian, rendered eminent service to the English, in capacity of messenger to the disaffected Indians, on the opening of the war of 1755. When a child he had been formally presented by his parents to William Penn, at New Castle. In August of 1755, Governor Morris publicly conferred on him the

		£	s.	d.
1756.	Bro[t] forw[d]		13	10
June 27.	For 7 quarts rum, @ 1*s.* 3*d.*		8	9
	" 7 lbs. English chease, @ 8*d.*		4	8
	" 1½ bush[s] oats, @ 2*s.* 6*d.*		3	9
	" 1½ deer skins		18	
	" keeping 4 horses from y[e] 23 June, to y[e] 15 July	3	4	
July 15.	" Hire of a man to bring up their horses to Gnadenhütten.*		12	
		6	5	

name of *Newcastle*, in remembrance of that event, addressing him, on the occasion, in these words: "In token of our affection for your parents and in expectation of your being a useful man in these perilous times, I do, in the most solemn manner, adopt you by the name of Newcastle, and order you hereafter to be called by that name." He confirmed his words with a belt of eight rows. A few weeks after the declaration of war against the Delawares (April 14, 1756), Newcastle, accompanied by Jagrea, a Mohawk, William Laquis, a Delaware, and the Moravian Indian, Augustus, alias *George Rex*, undertook an embassy to Wyoming, bearing these words from the Governor to the Indians there: "If you lay down the hatchet and come to terms, we, the English, will no further prosecute the war." He was now on his way to Diahoga, with an invitation from the Governor to the Delawares, Shawanese, Monseys, and Mohicans, to meet him in conference at Conrad Weisser's. His traveling companions were John Pompshire, Thomas Stores, and Joseph Michty, Delawares, from New Jersey. The four had arrived at Bethlehem on the 12th of June. Here they were detained until the 27th by the intelligence that "one hundred men were gone from the Jerseys on a scalping-party," the Governor of that Province having not been advised of the proclamation for a suspension of hostilities for twenty days, lately issued by Gov. Morris.

This hazardous mission to Diahoga, undertaken by Newcastle, was

* On his return from Diahoga, and when at Fort Allen, he notified the Brethren, in approved Indian style, of his arrival, and his horses were accordingly taken up to the fort. The Brethren still applied the name of Gnadenhütten to its site.

2.

Province of Pennsil[a] Dr. to Bethlehem Store.*

		£	s.	d.
	For sundries deliv[d] to y[e] 4 Indian messengers and other Indians, per order of Newcastle,			
1756.	viz.:	£	s.	d.
June 26.	For 4½ lbs. of tobacco taken with the 4......		1	6
	" leather and awls for mending their mackisens		2	4
	Carr[d] forw[d]...............................		3	10

effectual in bringing about a conference between the Governor and Teedyuscung, at Easton, in July following. This opened negotiations for a peace.

* In July of 1753 a store was opened by the Brethren, for the benefit of the "Family," or "Economy," in the west end of the old stone-house still standing on Market Street, opposite the Moravian grave-yard. It was probably the first store in the Forks of Delaware, and one of the few at the time conducted in the rural districts of the Province. Most of the wares exposed for sale were of home manufacture. The following is an inventory of domestic staples the Brethren proposed to contribute toward the stock. It serves to show the variety of industrial pursuits in which their community engaged, and their independence of others, in consequence, in providing themselves with the necessaries and comforts of life:

"Apron-skins, powder-horns, glue, shoes, slippers, shoe-lasts, wooden and horn heel-pieces, saddle-trees, saddles, horse-collars, bridles, halters, saddle-bags, girths, pocket-books, martingales, straps, stockings, caps, gloves, socks, hats, felt caps and felt slippers, spinning-wheels, reels, boxes, guns, tea-caddies, writing-desks, deer and calf-skins dressed for breeches, buckwheat-groats, oat-groats, barley-groats, malt, millet, dried peaches, dried apples, dried cherries, rusks, ginger-bread, cakes, iron bands for chests, nails, plows, axes, hatchets, grubbing hoes, hoes, corn-hoes, grind-stones, whet-stones, punk, flint and steel, pipe-stems, pipe-heads, shirt studs, pewter plates, tea-pots, lanterns, tallow candles, soap, starch, hair-powder, sealing-wax, wafers, tobacco boxes, buckles, buttons, spoons, bowls, shovels, brooms, baskets, wheat, flour, butter, cheese, handkerchiefs, neckcloths, garters,

		£	s.	d.
1756.	Bro^{t} forw^{d}..................................		3	10
June 26.	For 2 y^{ds} Osnaburgs, for bags....................		2	8
	" 1 ivory comb....................................		1	2
	" Cash p^{d} for oats..............................		1	3
	" do. p^{d} for powder horns and shot bags		4	
July 18.	To Cash p^{d} for tobacco..........................		3	
	" 1 lb. coffee....................................		1	2
	" 1 doz. pipes....................................			8
	" 1 p^{r} of knee-buckles deliv^{d} to Newcastle			8
	" 2 lbs. sugar, @ 7*d*..........................		1	2
	" 1 lb. butter....................................			6
	" 3 pipe heads deliv^{d} to ye Indians, @ 1*s*..		3	
	" Cash p^{d} for shoeing a horse................		2	3
	" " p^{d} for a coat for Joseph*.............	1	14	
	Carr^{d} forw^{d}..............................	2	19	4

knee-straps, linen, white, blue and check woolens, currant-wine, beer, whisky, tar, potash, turpentine, pitch, lamp-black, sulphur-matches, vinegar, flaxseed, linseed oil, rape seed and oil, nut oil, oil of sassafras, ammonia, rasped deer's-horn, 'bush-tea,' medicine chests, brushes, shovels and tongs, chafing-dishes, combs, currycombs, glove-leather, leather-breeches, ropes, blank-books, soft-soap, rakes, knives, drawing-knives, guitars, violins, tobacco and tobacco-pouches, snuff, oil of turpentine, hemp, flax, buckets, milk-pails, tubs, pottery, cotton yarn, cord, hatchels, oven-forks, linen nets, augers, hammers, pincers, candlesticks, tin ware, chisels, mill-saws, homespun, boots, whips, harness, wheelbarrows, wagons, coffee-pots, chains, canoes, boards, bricks, roofing-tiles, lime, preserves and pickles, quills and slate pencils." In addition the Bethlehem Store was furnished with "tea, chocolate, coffee, brown sugar, loaf sugar, salt, rum, steel, blankets, powder, lead, shot, broadcloth, wine, silk neckhandkerchiefs, camlet, silk, iron pots, spices, copper and brass kettles, and paper and ink." Joseph Powell was the first storekeeper. William Edmonds succeeded him in 1754. The stock at this time was valued at £277 3*s*. 6*d*.

* Joseph Michty was a *Crosswicks* Indian. His companions, *Pompshire* and *Stores*, were respectively from *Crosswicks* and *Cranberry*. They had all been with the Brainerd brothers, and were associated with Newcastle in the late embassy, "*being they were among the best and the discreetest of the Jersey Delawares.*"

		£	s.	d.
1756.	Bro^t forw^d..............................	2	19	4
July 18.	For 1 p^r shoe buckles for Tattewaskundt*....		1	3
	" 1 p^r stockings deliv^d to Jo Peepy..........		5	6
	" 1 p^r shoes " " "		7	6
		3	13	7

3.

Province of Pennsil^a Dr. to Bethlehem.

For sundries deliv^d to Jo Peepy, Nicodemus, and others who came from Diahoga to Bethlehem ye 23d† of June, 1756, and other charges, viz.:

---

* Captain Newcastle returned to Bethlehem in the evening of the 17th. With him came Teedyuscung and upward of thirty other Indians, men, women, and children, pursuant to the Governor's invitation. This was the first appearance of the chief within the settlements since he had taken up the hatchet. On the 18th he met Major Parsons in conference in Justice Horsfield's office. It was a memorable interview, in as far as on that occasion Teedyuscung for the first time proclaimed his kingship. His private counselor, *Tapescawen*, or *Tapescohung*, Newcastle, Captain Insley, from Fort Allen, and a few others were present. John Pompshire interpreted. Producing a string of wampum whereby to confirm what he designed to say, he dictated this message to the Governor in reply to the invitation he had received to meet him in Tulpehocken. "Brother, the Governor of Pennsylvania: I have received the word by your messenger kindly. Upon it I have come, as you have given me good words, which are called council-fire. At the Forks of Delaware we will sit down, and wait there, and shall be ready. I am exceeding glad that there are such thoughts and methods taken in respect to our women and children. I shall I hope be ready to let you know a little further when we shall meet. This what I have now in short spoken is not only from me, but also from my uncle, the Mohawk (*the Six Nations*), and from four other nations (the *Delawares*, *Shawanese*, *Monseys*, and *Mohicans*), which in all makes ten, and these ten have but *two heads of kings* between them."

† These two had come to claim protection of government, declaring themselves friends of the English, although it was well known that

1756.	£	s.	d.
To some expresses to Easton* on their acct. per order of Mr. Horsfield.................		15	
"Acct. an express to his Honor ye Governor†	1	10	
Carrd forwd..............................	2	5	

they had taken active part in councils and treaties at the commencement of the war. Not knowing how they would be received, they had prudently left their familes a day's journey beyond Fort Allen. Newcastle brought these down under an escort of Provincials, a few days later. Both the Governor and Major Parsons were informed by express concerning this arrival, and in a letter to the former, Spangenberg writes in the following terms:

"Now to tell your Honor the truth, I do not believe that either Jo Peepy or Nicodemus and their families can stay at Bethlehem. We have been obliged to put people out of the house to make room for them. But this is not all; there is such a rage in the neighborhood against the said poor creatures, that I fear they will mob us and them together. For Jo Peepy having lived among the Presbyterians, and treacherously being gone from them, hath exasperated them in the highest degree. We have put two men with them to be their safeguard, but your Honor knows very well that this will not hinder the stream when it is coming upon them and us at the same time. I, therefore, humbly beg of your Honor to remove the said Jo Peepy and Nicodemus, and their families, the sooner the better to Philadelphia; for

* Easton was laid out in 1750, at the Forks of Delaware, in Bucks County, pursuant to an order of Thomas Penn, written to Dr. Graeme and Secretary Peters:

"I desire," writes the Proprietor, "that the new town be called Easton, from my Lord Pomfret's house, and whenever there is a new county that shall be called Northampton."

Northampton was erected in 1752.

† Robert Hunter Morris. Commissioned by the Proprietaries, John, Thomas, and Richard Penn, with approbation of the king, their "Lieutenant-Governor and Commander-in-Chief of the Province of Pennsylvania, and Counties of New Castle, Kent and Sussex, on Delaware," in London, May 14, 1754. Entered upon office October 3, 1754. Retired from office August 20, 1756.

	£	s.	d.
1756. Bro[t] forw[d]	2	5	
To Acct. of victuals deliv[d] them from y[e] 23 June to y[e] 11 July, viz.:			
517 lbs. bread, @ 1½*d*.	3	4	7½
61½ lbs. beef, @ 4*d*.	1		6
33 lbs. butter, @ 6*d*.		16	6
17 lbs. gammons, @ 6*d*.		8	6
3 quarts of salt			8
7 bushl[s] Indian corn, @ 3*s*. 6*d*.	1	4	6
24½ gall[s] beer, @ 1*s*.	1	4	6
17 quarts of rum, @ 1*s*. 3*d*.	1	1	3
4 quarts molassis		3	
108 lbs. white meal, @ 1½*d*.		13	6
" victuals deliv[d] to 4 men who accompanied them from Fort Allen p[r] order of Mr. Horsfield		2	4
" keeping 5 horses* from y[e] 23[d] June to y[e] 17 July, no pasture being to be had near Bethlehem where people would answer for y[e] horses	4	6	3
Carr[d] forw[d]	16	11	1½

there they are in the heart of the country, and mischief may be prevented which could breed evil consequences."

Jo Peepy, alias *Weholelahund*, was originally from Cranberry, and had been one of Brainerd's Indians. Thence he removed to the Aquanshicola. Several members of his family were baptized by the Brethren. Immediately before the war he resided among the Scotch-Irish of the Craig settlement, near the Lehigh Water Gap. His family consisted of Sarah, his wife, and their children, James, Isaac, Sarah, Isaiah, and Mettshish.

Nicodemus, alias *Weshichagechive*, alias *Jo Evans*, half-brother of Teedyuscung and *Capt. John*, of Nazareth, was baptized by Bishop Cammerhoff, at Bethlehem, June 15, 1749. Withdrew from the mission at Gnadenhütten in 1754, returning to the Indian country. Nicodemus's family comprised Zacharias, Christian, Nathan, Thomas, Gashatis, and Dorothea, most of them baptized at Gnadenhütten.

Lodgings were given this company in a house near "The Crown."

* The horses belonging to Newcastle's company.

		£	s.	d.
1756.	Bro[t] forw[d].......	16	11	1½
	To 3 bush[s] oats for y[e] horses sent to Gnadenhütten for some Indians who was a coming.......		7	6
	" 1 lb. candles.......			7
	" 1 gall. soft sope		1	
	" 2 men's watching to be their safeguard and therefore obliged to stay with them day and night, from y[e] 23 June to y[e] 17 July, being 24 days, @ 2*s.* 6*d.* each per day.	6		
	" 3 shirts per order of y[e] Governor.......	1	7	11
	" 3 blankets " "	1	16	
	" 3 p[r] Indian stockings "	1	2	6
		27	6	7½

4.

Province of Pennsil[a] Dr. to Bethlehem.

For sundries deliv[d] to y[e] 4 Indians,* viz.: Samuel, Pachshinoscha's son, his son-in-law, and two others, as p[r] order of Mr. Horsfield,† viz.:

---

* A party of Shawanese who had met Newcastle on his way to Diahoga, and who were come on a friendly visit, and with a letter of recommendation from him. *Kolapeka*, alias Samuel, was *Paxanosa's* youngest son. His companions were *Shekaschcno*, *Mekitshachpe*, and *Wenimah*, all Shawanese, formerly of Wyoming. They arrived at Bethlehem in the evening of the 5th of July, and during their sojourn attended divine worship devoutly. The Brethren were inclined to believe, nevertheless, that they had participated in the attack on the Mahoning. In course of conversation with Justice Horsfield, they stated that nine Indian nations they knew were attached to the English. On being asked how the Delawares were disposed, the speaker replied, "About them I can say nothing." Their arrival, and the intelligence they gave, were duly reported by express to the Governor. They set out for Fort Allen, under escort, en route for their homes, on the 11th, taking with them a string and a message from the Governor to King Paxanosa, inviting him to come to Philadelphia. While at Bethlehem they were lodged in the store-building.

† Timothy Horsfield, whose name appears repeatedly on these re-

1756.	£	s.	d.
For 4 shirts......................................	1	17	6
" 6 yds. linnen for bags, and making.......		9	
" 8 lbs. tobacco, @ 4*d*........................		2	8
" 4 blanketts, @ 12*s*.........................	2	8	
" 3 yds. of strowds, @ 10*s*.....................	1	10	
" 4 quarts salt......................................			7
" 2 expresses to his Honor, ye Governor, pr. order of Mr. Horsfield.................	3	2	4
" 2 expresses to Easton.........................		5	
" victuals deliv^d^ them from ye 5 to ye 11 July, being 6 days, @ 1*s*. each per day	1	4	
Carr^d^ forw^d^................................	10	19	1

cords, was born in Liverpool, O. E., in April of 1708. He immigrated to America in 1725, and settled on Long Island. Here he married Mary Doughty in 1731. His first religious impressions were received, he tells us, under Whitefield's preaching; and his connection with the Brethren dates from his acquaintance with Bishop Nitschmann and Peter Böhler, in the winter of 1741. He placed his children at the Brethren's schools prior to his removal to Bethlehem in 1749. Here he built the east end of the old stone-house on Market Street, opposite the Moravian grave-yard. His residence on Long Island was now rented by the Brethren, and became the seat of a "Family," or "Economy for Pilgrims." In May of 1752 he was appointed a Justice of the Peace for the newly-erected County of Northampton, along with Thomas Craig, Daniel Brodhead, Hugh Wilson, James Martin, John Van Etten, Aaron Depui, William Craig, and William Parsons, by Governor Hamilton. This office, as well as a lieut.-colonel's commission that he had received early in the Pontiac war, he resigned in December of 1764. A number of letters written by him to the Governor and other officials during the disturbed times of the Indian wars are preserved in the Archives of the State, and have been published in the Colonial Records. Mr. Horsfield's position enabled him to render the Brethren's interests material service. He deceased at Bethlehem, March 9, 1773. The late Dr. Thomas Horsfield, Librarian of the East India House, London, and author of *Plantæ Javanicæ rariores*, was a grandson. Other descendants are living at Bethlehem.

1756.		£	s.	d.
	Bro[t] forw[d]	10	19	1
	For 4 quarts beer		1	
	" keeping 2 men with them as a safe-guard, 6 days,* @ 2*s.* 6*d.* per day	1	10	
	" 160 lbs. meal deliv[d] them at their departure, @ 1¼*d.* pr. lb		16	8
	" victuals given to 6 men who went with them to Gnadenhütten		5	
	" 6 quarts beer		2	
	" their horse			6
	" victuals deliv[d] to do. by their return		5	
	" 6 quarts beer		2	
	" hay and oats		1	
	" the entertaining of an express from Gnadenhütten		1	6
		14	3	9

5.

Province of Pennsil[a] Dr. to Bethlehem.

		£	s.	d.
1756.	For sundries deliv[d] to 31 Indians,† viz., to Tattewaskundt and company, who came to Bethlehem y[e] 17 July, viz.:			
	To an express to Easton		5	
	Carr[d] forw[d]		5	

* This precaution was rendered necessary by the hostile state of feeling prevalent in the neighborhood in reference to the Indians.

† This company had been joined on its way from the Indian country by Joachim and his wife and Anton's mother-in-law—all formerly of Gnadenhütten. Joachim, who, since the dispersion in the night of the 24th of November last, had been living along the Susquehanna, confirmed the truth of a report that had reached the Brethren in reference to the fate of Susanna Nitschmann, supposed by them to have lost her life with the other inmates of "the Family" on the Mahoning. He stated as follows: That she had been taken prisoner to Wyoming; that there, on meeting with the Sisters Sarah and Abigail, she had piteously implored their aid; that thence she had been conveyed, in midwinter, to Diahoga, where, after having been subjected to the horrors of In-

1756.	£	s.	d.
Brot forwd		5	
To earthenware		3	
" 2½ doz. spoons, @ 5s		12	6
" victuals deliv[d] them and 4 soldiers who came wth them, viz.:			
24 lbs. butter, @ 6d		12	
40 do. beef, pease, &c		18	10
8¾ gall[s] beer		8	9
17½ do. milk, @ 8d		11	8
Indian corn meal		2	
170 lbs. bread, @ 1½d	1	1	3
" 1 bridle		4	
" the hire of 2 men to be with them 2 days, @ 2s. 6d. each		10	
	5	9	

dian captivity in its most revolting form, she had sunk into deep melancholy, death releasing her from suffering on the 9th of May last. Joachim furthermore stated that he had conversed much with her, and could testify to her fate and end.

Teedyuscung and his companions were escorted to Easton on the 19th, pursuant to the Governor's order, issued to Major Parsons. "The Council approved the Governor's letter to that officer, in which he ordered him to remove such friendly Indians as were or should come to Bethlehem, to Easton, as there was no room at the former place, as the Moravian Brethren were uneasy, and as there were no troops stationed there."—*Minutes Prov. Council, July* 11, 1756.

Nicodemus, Jo Peepy, and families were suffered to remain at Bethlehem, they having expressed themselves desirous of living near their former friends.

II. Account sent to ye Commissioners in Phila. ye 16 August, 1756.

Province of Pennsil^{a} to the Stewards of Bethlehem, Dr.

1756.		£	*s.*	*d.*
Aug. 16.	For sundries delivered about 80* Indians from ye 17 July to ye 14 August, 1756, viz.:			
	For 1491 lbs. bread, @ 1½*d*....................	9	6	4
	" 332 lbs. beef, @ 4*d*..........................	5	10	8
	" 310 gall^{s} milk, @ 8*d*.......................	10	6	8
	" 4 do. sope, @ 1*s*..........................		4	
	" 1 do. linseed oil..........................		4	
		25	11	8
	For the sum of the account deliv^{d} ye 17 July last......£121 18 10½			
	Off, cash p^{d} per Wm Edmonds, for Joseph's coat 1 14			
		120	4	10½
	For sundries deliv^{d} to Tattewaskundt and company, &c. (See *Voucher* 1)............	10	14	2½
	For sundries deliv^{d} Jo Peepy, Nicodemus, &c. from ye 18 July to ye 3^{d} August. (See *Voucher* 2)....................................	15		8½
	For sundries deliv^{d} Capt. Newcastle and company. (See *Voucher* 3)..................	4	14	7
	For sundries deliv^{d} on acct. of ye treaty with ye Indians at Easton in July last. (See *Voucher* 4)..	13	5	6
July 21.	For an express to his Honor ye Governor, p^{r} order of Mr. Horsfield..................	1	5	
	Carr^{d} forw^{d}...........................	165	4	10½

* The refugees from Gnadenhütten, and returned converts.

1756.		£	s.	d.
	Brot forwd...........................	165	4	10½
July 21.	For cash laid out for to bear Indians* to Philadelphia, per Mr. Edmonds†......	2	5	
	" a shirt for Indian Benjamin,‡ per order of Maj. Parsons.§........................		12	6
	Carrd forwd...........................	168	2	4½

* Newcastle and some of Teedyuscung's companions from Diahoga, whom William Edmonds escorted to Philadelphia. The former was the bearer of the King's invitation to Governor Morris to meet him in conference in the Forks.

† William Edmonds was born October 24, 1708, at Colford, Gloucestershire, O. E. His father was a merchant, and the family were attached to the Established Church. William learned skin-dressing in Monmouth. In 1736 he immigrated to America, established himself in business in New York, and in 1739 married Rebecca de Beauvoise, a French Huguenot. She bore him four children. He became attached to the Brethren in 1741, and joined their Society in New York. After the decease of his wife, in 1749, he made a voyage on the "Irene," to Holland and England, serving on board in capacity of cook. In 1749 he removed to Bethlehem. In March of 1755 he married Margaret Anthony, of New York. In October of that year he was elected to the Assembly from Northampton. Until the close of the "Economy," he resided at Bethlehem, serving "the Family" as tradesman, shopkeeper, and in various ways in his public capacity. In 1763 he removed into the neighborhood of Nazareth, and commenced a store in Bushkill Township, at "the Rose." Thence he was called to Nazareth, in 1772, to conduct the Society's store opened in that village. Here he deceased September 15, 1786. Descendants of his are residing in Bushkill, Northampton County. Seven of his great-grandsons, sons of Squire Edmonds, of Bushkill Township, above Filetown, entered the service of the United States in the war of the Rebellion.

‡ One of Teedyuscung's company, "an impudent, forward youth, who had enlisted in the Jersey Companies, and afterwards deserted,

§ William Parsons became a resident of Easton in 1752. In December of that year, he tells us, the incipient capital of the new county of Northampton numbered eleven families, who proposed staying there during the winter, and then ventures the hope, that when the Prison is

		£	s.	d.
1756.	Brot forwd	168	2	4½
July 25.	For mending 8 gun locks for Capt. Arndt's company		16	6
	" mending 2 do. for Capt. Wetherhold's compy		7	
	" medicines for Capt. Arndt, and curing on one of his soldier's hand	1	1	
	" an express to his honor ye Governor in New York	3		
	Carrd forwd	173	6	10½

going over to the enemy Indians at Diahoga." Three members of the Council, having been sent to notify the King (Easton, July 24, 1756) that the Governor was come, on attempting to use John Pompshire, "one of the best and discreetest of the Jersey Indians," as interpreter, he, the King, produced the aforesaid Benjamin as his choice,—whereupon Pompshire declared he would not be concerned in interpreting if Benjamin were allowed to speak. Pompshire subsequently became the King's favorite interpreter.

finished (it was under roof) there would be an increase in the population! Parsons had been a shoemaker in early life. During his residence in Philadelphia, between 1734 and 1746, he was Librarian of the City Library. In 1743 he was appointed Surveyor-General. Ill health compelled him to resign this office in June of 1748. In 1749 he was a Justice of the Peace in Lancaster County. December 29, 1755, he was appointed Major of all troops to be raised in Northampton County, with Easton as his head-quarters. "As I think," writes James Hamilton to Captains Martin and Craig, from Easton, December 29, 1755, "it will be for the good of the service in general that the troops raised in Northampton County should be under the care and superintendence of a field-officer, I have, with that view, in virtue of the power granted me, appointed William Parsons, Esq., to be Major of the said troops." His immediate command, however, was a Town Guard of twenty-four men, stationed at Easton. Held the office of Prothonotary, Clerk of the Courts, Recorder, Clerk of the Commissioners, and Justice of the Peace. Deceased at Easton in December of 1757. Much of Parson's correspondence is in the Archives of the State, and valuable for its historical information.

		£	s.	d.
1756.	Brot forwd	173	6	10½
Aug. 2.	To the tavern, for victuals delivd 2 soldiers of Capt. Wetherhold's compy		1	8
11.	For mending 5 guns for Capt. Reinhold's compy*	1		6
	" medicines delivd to do		11	6
	To the tavern, for victuals delivd to a sergeant from Fort Allen,† and oats for his horse		2	2
		175	2	8½

* These were detachments of the Provincial forces on their way to or on their return from the Treaty held at Easton, July 28 to July 31.

† Fort Allen, the first of a cordon of stockades or block-houses erected in the Indian wars for the protection of the frontier along the line of the Blue Mountain, from the Susquehanna to the Delaware. The most important of these rude defenses were Forts Hunter, Henry William, Allen, Norris, Hamilton, and Hyndshaw, following from southwest to northeast in the order given. Fort Allen was built in January of 1756 by Franklin, and stood on the right bank of the Lehigh, nearly opposite the mouth of Mahoning Creek, where Weissport was commenced by Colonel Jacob Weiss in 1785. The well of the fort, sixteen feet deep and four in diameter, walled with cobbles from the river, is on the premises of the Fort Allen House, and well preserved. How the great philosopher came to enlist in the service of Mars, and with what composure he exchanged the pen for the sword, he tells us as follows:

"The Governor prevailed upon me to take charge of our Northern frontier and to provide for the defense of the inhabitants by raising troops and building a line of forts. I undertook this military business, although I did not consider myself well qualified for it. He gave me a commission with full powers. I had but little difficulty in raising men, having soon 560 under my command. My son, who had, in the preceding war, been an officer in the army raised against Canada, was my aid-de-camp, and of great use to me." Preparatory to moving on the frontier, Franklin, in company with his colleagues, Fox and Hamilton, with a detachment of fifty men, visited Bethlehem for the first time, on the 18th of December, 1755. He made this place his headquarters from January 7 to January 15, 1756, and then marched for the Lehigh Gap. The diarist tells us that the Colonel dined with the heads of the Brethren on the 10th, and was entertained with music. On the 11th he attended the Sunday's sermon which Bro. Abraham Reincke preached from I. John, iii. 8. He gives the following account of his visits and sojourn at Bethlehem. "In order to march to Gnadenhütten, which place was thought a good situation for one of the forts, I assembled the companies at Bethlehem, the chief settlement of the Moravians. I was surprised to find it in so good a posture of defense; the destruction of Gnadenhütten had made them apprehend danger. The principal buildings were defended by a stockade; they had procured a quantity of arms and ammunition from New York, and had even placed a quantity of paving stones between the windows of their high stone houses, for their women to throw down upon the heads of any Indians that should attempt to force into them. The armed brethren too kept watch, and relieved each other as methodically as in any garrisoned town. In conversation with the bishop, Spangenberg, I mentioned this my surprise; for knowing they had obtained an Act of Parliament exempting them from military duties in the Colonies, I had supposed they were conscientiously scrupulous of bearing arms. He answered that it was not one of their established principles, but that, at the time of obtaining that Act, it was thought to be a principle with many of their people. On this occasion, however, they, to their surprise, found it adopted by but a few. So it seems they had either deceived themselves or deceived Parliament; but common sense, induced by present danger, will sometimes be too strong for whimsical opinions. On my return I was at their Church, where I was entertained with good music, the organ being accompanied with violins, hautboys, flutes, clarionets, &c. The sermon I heard was to the children, who came in and were placed in rows on benches; the boys under the conduct of a young man, their tutor, and the girls conducted by a young woman. The discourse seemed well adapted to their capacities, and was delivered in a pleasing, familiar manner, coaxing them, as it were, to be good. They behaved very orderly, but looked pale and unhealthy, which made me suspect they were kept too much within doors, or not allowed sufficient exercise. The Moravians furnished me five wagons for the conveyance of our tools, stores, baggage, &c. to Gnadenhütten."—*Autobiography of Ben. Franklin, edited from his MS. by John Bigelow.* Philadelphia, 1868.

"To day we hoisted your flag," writes Franklin to Governor Morris, January 26, 1756, "made a general discharge of our pieces, which had been long loaded, and of our two swivels, and named the place For Allen, in honor of our old friend. It is 125 feet long, 50 feet wide, and the stockades, most of them, a foot thick. They are three feet in the ground, and twelve feet out, pointed at the top." The fort stood near "New Gnadenhütten," which had been recommended by Spangenberg as an eligible site for a defensive work. The following is the correspondence that passed between him and the Secretary of the Province on the subject:

BETHLEHEM, *Nov.* — 1755.

REV. RICHARD PETERS:

DEAR SIR,—I write to you at this time about a subject which is not so very proper for me. You will excuse it, however, considering that at this time every one who is concerned for the public welfare should be at liberty to speak his thoughts, though it is not his place or office. You will have heard of the mischief done at the Mahony by the Indians, whereby not only our houses, barns, stables, stores, &c. were laid into ashes, but eleven of our people cruelly killed, scalped, and burnt. You will also have heard that all the Indians and white people who lived in Gnadenhütten fled for their life to Bethlehem (where they are still), leaving behind them all they had in the world. Since that time I have considered that if Gnadenhütten is emptied and left to the enemy it may prove the ruin not only of all the settlements lying along the Lecha and Delaware, but also of Philadelphia. For troops may be marched from Wyomik to Gnadenhütten in one day, and if they take possession thereof, they can run down with freshes in six hours to Bethlehem, and from thence to Philadelphia in one night. I therefore have mentioned this matter to the Magistrates of this County, and have represented unto them the great calamity which could be brought upon the whole country by the loss of that part of the Province. For the situation of the hill which joins Gnadenhütten is so extraordinary for a fort, that gentlemen of judgment who have seen it are of opinion there could be no better.

It lies in the road (Indian path) which comes from Wyomik, and commands not only the Lecha a great way, but all sides, up and down, before and behind.

If the French once come and build there a fort, it will cost as much, if I am not mistaken, as the taking of Crown Point to get it out of their hands. For if they put a garrison in the Gaps of the mountain, and make there also a fortification, you cannot come at them at all with any great guns. But they can at pleasure come down both by land and water and overrun all plantations, not only on the other side of the Blue Mountain, but on this side also. I therefore think that place should needs be kept and well secured for our Government by a fort, as well as a good garrison. If the Government will accept of ten acres of land so favorably situated for such a fort from the Brethren at Bethlehem, poor as they are, having sustained such a loss, they are willing to give them freely. But we do think that as there are at least fifteen little habitable block-houses, it will be good to send up men before the enemy either burns or takes them.

I am, dear sir,
Your humble servant,
A. G. SPANGENBERG.

To this letter the Secretary replied as follows:

PHILA., *Dec.* 5, 1755.

DEAR SIR:

I think myself favored by your letter, and have done my utmost to represent the situation of Gnadenhütten to be a very important one, and accordingly the Governor and Commissioners have agreed to build a wooden Fort there, and would be glad if the Brethren would undertake the superintending of it. Many marks of Divine displeasure manifest themselves every day and presage a heavy blow. May God, through his Blessed Son and Holy Spirit, sanctify this afflicted state of things to our reformation and sanctification. My prayers will never cease for all orders, that however they may differ in speculation or in rites and ceremonies, we may all agree to love Christ and one another, and look up to Heaven in the decent use of means for protection and deliverance.

I am, dear sir, your
affectionate humble servant,
RICHARD PETERS.

Vouchers belongg to the foregoing Account.

I.

Province of Pennsil^{a} to Bethlehem, Dr.

1756.		£	s.	d.	£	s.	d.
July 18.	For sundries deliv^{d} to Tattewaskundt and company, &c., viz.:						
	138 lbs. bread, @ 1½*d.*		17	3			
	50 lbs. beef, @ 4*d.*......		16	8			
	29 lbs. gamnions, @ 5½*d*....................		13	3½			
	10 lbs. butter, @ 6*d.*....		5				
	16 gall^{s} milk, @ 8*d.*....		10	8			
	1 bridle		4				
					3	6	10½
	For mending 4 guns.........		10				
" 18.	To the tavern for 18½ gall^{s} beer		18	6			
	For victuals deliv^{d} to Tattewaskundt, &c.........		1	6			
	" 8 quarts beer.............		2				
	" 2 boles punch*...........		3				
					1	15	
" 19.	For eating and drinking deliv^{d} to 2 soldiers from Easton................................					1	4
	" hay and oats for their horses, pr. order of Mr. Horsfield.........................					1	2
	" eating and drinking deliv^{d} to 12 soldiers, 5 meals, who came from Easton to fetch Tattewaskundt and company....				1	9	
	Carr^{d} forw^{d}...........................				6	13	4½

* On the evening before setting out for the Treaty.

	£	s.	d.	£	s.	d.
1756. Bro^t^ forw^d^...........				6	13	4½
July 30. For an express to Easton....		5				
Aug. 1. *To the tavern for 14 quarts beer........................		4	8			
" 10. For an express to Easton.....		5				
" 11. To the tavern for victuals deliv^d^ to 5 soldiers from Easton, who went with some Indians to Gnadenhütten........................		6	8			
For provisions for ye Indians........................		6	10			
				1	8	2
Carr^d^ forw^d^...........................				8	1	6½

* On the evening of the 31st of July the Indians began to pass through Bethlehem on their return from the Treaty. This had formally opened on Saturday the 28th.

Besides the Governor, and William Logan, Richard Peters, Benjamin Chew, and Jno. Mifflin, of his Council, and the Commissioners, Josh. Fox, Jno. Hughes, and William Edmonds, there were present officers of the Royal American Regiment, a detachment of the Provincial forces, magistrates of the Province, and a deputation of Friends from Philadelphia. The Indians were represented by Teedyuscung and fourteen other chiefs, principally Delawares. Conrad Weisser was interpreter for the Six Nations, and Ben "ye Indian who speaks English," interpreter for the Delawares. Pompshire and Peepy were also in attendance. The results of the conference, which closed on the 31st, were not definitive, although Teedyuscung gave the assurance "that he would exert himself faithfully and to the utmost of his power in the service of the Province, hoping," he added, "that matters would be brought to a happy issue, that there might be a firm friendship and a lasting union between the Six Nations and the people of Pennsylvania, and that they might be one man." Captain Newcastle, furthermore, was formally appointed agent for the Province in negotiations with the hostile Indians, and, in conjunction with the King, "invested with the authority to do the public business."

It was designed to hold this Treaty at Bethlehem. The messenger

		£	s.	d.	£	s.	d.
1756.	Bro^t forw^d				8	1	6½
Aug. 11.	For 2 men's watching 3 days, @ 2*s.* each per day..............					15	
" 13.	For sundries deliv^d to Tattewaskundt's son,* &c., per order of Mr. Edmonds, viz.:						
	Shoeing 2 horses		3				
	Bread and meat at their departure..............		5	3			
	Mending a gun lock and knife.....................		6				
	To the tavern for eating and drinking......................		16	8			
	For a p^s. of leather for mending shoes..................		3				
	" 1 man's watching, 1½ days, @ 2*s.* 6*d*		3	9			
					1	17	8
					10	14	2½

(Daniel Kunkler), who, on the 21st July, had been dispatched to Philadelphia, with an account of the interview held with the King in Mr. Horsfield's office, returned on the 23d with a letter from Governor Morris to Spangenberg, in which the Governor writes: "On communicating to the Council my purpose of treating with the Indians at Easton, many reasons were offered, which convinced me that that will by no means be a proper place, I therefore find myself laid under the necessity of countermanding my orders to Mr. Parsons, and of appointing the Treaty to be held at Bethlehem, and therefore request the favor

* Teedyuscung had three sons, Amos, the oldest, *Kesmitas*, and John Jacob. The first, *Tachgokanhelle*, was baptized at Gnadenhütten by Bishop Cammerhoff, December 14, 1750. He was then twenty-two years of age. His wife, *Pingtis*, a sister of Agnes Post, was baptized on the same day, and received the name of Justina. She was a Jersey Delaware. Amos was fitting out for an embassy in behalf of his father to the Alleghanies.

2.

Province of Pennsil^{a} to Bethlehem, Dr.

1756.	£	s.	d.	£	s.	d.
For sundries deliv^{d} Jo Peepy, Nicodemus, &c., from ye 18 July to ye 3d August, 1756, viz.:						
423 lbs. bread, @ 1½*d.*	2	12	10½			
59 lbs. beef, @ 4*d.*...		19	8			
32 lbs. butter, @ 6*d.*.		16				
1 bush^{l} Indian corn...		3	6			
3 " white meal, @ 5*s.*		15				
115 gall^{s} milk, @ 8*d.*...	1		2			
				6	7	2½
For 2 quarts salt			5			
" 19 gall^{s} beer...............		19				
" 14 quarts rum, @ 1*s.* 3*d.*		17	6			
" 15 " beer, @ 3*d.*...		5				
" 8 " " @ 4*d.*...		2	8			
July 18. To the tavern for victuals deliv^{d} 4 men, evening and morning, who came from Easton with Maj. Parsons on acct. of Jo Peepy,* &c.		4				
				2	8	7
Carr^{d} forw^{d}............................				8	15	9½

of you and the Brethren to afford me and my attendance what accommodations are in your power, which I do not mean shall be attended with any expense to you." Preparations were being made by the former for the reception of the promised visitors, when the Indians reiterated the wish they had first expressed to meet the Governor "*at* the Forks;" and to this he finally assented. Anthony Benezet, and others of "the deputation from the inhabitants of the City of Philadelphia of the people called Quakers," visited at Bethlehem and at the "Upper Places" after the Treaty. They were much interested in the Nursery, or Institute for Children, into which the children from all the settlements of the Brethren had been gathered in this time of alarm.

* Pursuant to an order from the Governor to escort him and the other Indians who had arrived from Diahoga to Easton.

		£	s.	d.	£	s.	d.
1756.	Brot forwd...........				8	15	9½
July 18.	For hay and oats for 5 horses..................		4	7			
	" hay for 3 horses for 5 days......		10				
	" hay for 4 horses for 8 days, @ 8*d.* each a day.....................	1	1	4			
	" hay for 5 horses, for 3 days....................		8	6			
					2	4	5
	For 6 qts. rum, @ 1*s.* 3*d*...		7	6			
	" medicines.................		15	6			
	" 2 men's watching 7 days, @ 2*s.* 6*d.* each pr. day.................	1	15				
	" 1 man's watching for 9 days to inst............	1	2	6			
					4		6
					15		8½

3.

Province of Pennsila to Bethlehem, Dr.

		£	s.	d.	£	s.	d.
1756.	For sundries delivd Capt. Newcastle* and company.						
July 17.	To the tavern for 4 galls beer		4				
" 31.	" " " 2 "		2				
						6	
	Carrd forwd............................					6	

* Newcastle returned to Bethlehem at the close of the Treaty, and, "on the 3d of Aug.," says the diarist, "the faithful old chief, who had ventured his life for the restoration of peace, set out for his home. He took with him the Indians who had been here occasionally during the past two weeks, and was accompanied to Gnadenhütten by Nicholas Garrison, Jr."

					£	s.	d.
1756.	Brot forwd.					6	
July 31.	For hire of 3 horses to Phila. and back, @ 7*s.* 6*d.* each				1	2	6
Aug. 2.	For 1 quart good milk						3
	" 1 saddle	£1					
" 3.	" hay and oats for their horses 3 days		9	4			
	" 18 quarts beer		6				
	" mending 4 guns	1	5	6			
					3		10
	" 1 man's watching, 2 days, @ 2*s.* 6*d.*					5	
					4	14	7

4.

Province of Pennsila to Bethlehem, Dr.

		£	s.	d.
1756.	For sundries delivd on acct. of ye Treaty with ye Indians at Easton in July last.			
July 25.	For hire of a man to go with ye Governor's soldiers* to Easton		5	
	" 4200 white wampums, old and new, of ye best sort, @ 3*s.* pr. ct.†	6	6	
	Carrd forwd	6	11	

* A detachment of the First Battalion of the Pennsylvania Regiment.

† The Brethren were generally well provided with this species of currency, for use in their intercourse with the Indians. "*New York, March* 26, 1749," writes Bro. Kingston, "Bro. Boemper will bring the wampum you wrote for, along. I have procured of the wampum-maker 1000 white, @ £1 10*s.*, and 1000 black, @ £2 5*s.*" The Jersey Indians were skillful artificers in wampum.

Newcastle, in the course of the Treaty, advised the Governor to accept the belt that Teedyuscung had offered him, without hesitation, stating that it had been sent by the Six Nations to the Delawares, and that it ought to be preserved among the Council Wampum. At the

		£	s.	d.
1756.	Bro^{t} forw^{d}	6	11	
July 27.	To ye tavern for sundries deliv^{d} Mr. Conrad Weisser's comp^{y} as pr. bill	4	18	6
	To ye doctor for curing Capt. Newcastle.*	1	10	
	For hire of 3 horses to Easton, @ 2*s.* each		6	
		13	5	6

same time, he urged the propriety of returning another by way of response. "The King," he proceeded, "will want abundance of wampum, and if he has it not, the cause will suffer. I hope the Council-bag is full, and desire it may be emptied in the lap of Teedyuscung." Hereupon the Secretary was ordered to bring all the wampum he had into Council, and there were found to be 15 strings and 7 belts, and a parcel of new black wampum, amounting to 7000 pieces. There being no new white wampum, nor any proper belt to give in return for Teedyuscung's Peace Belt, a messenger was sent to Bethlehem, and he returned with 5000. Upon which the Indian women were employed to make a belt of a fathom long and sixteen beads wide, in the center of which was to be the figure of a man, meaning the Governor of Pennsylvania, and five figures to his right, and five to his left, meaning the ten nations mentioned by Teedyuscung.—*Colonial Records.*

* "The day before the opening of the Treaty, Newcastle came to the Governor and stated that the Delawares had bewitched him, and he should soon die. Teedyuscung he declared had warned him, in a friendly manner, that he would not live long, having overheard two Delawares say they would put an end to his life by witchcraft. The Governor endeavored to show him that he was in no danger, but he made no impression, Newcastle insisting that this information be committed to writing and inserted in the Minutes of Council and communicated in a special message to the Six Nations. *Easton, July* 28. 'To the surprise of everybody, Captain Newcastle was seized this morning with a violent pleurisy and thought to be in great danger, but on losing some blood and taking proper physic, the violence of the distemper abated, and he recovered.' "—*Pennsylvania Archives.*

Late in October, Newcastle returned to Philadelphia from an embassy to the Six Nations, to whom he had been dispatched to inquire into the character and credentials of Teedyuscung. He reported these words from one of their principal counselors, "The Delaware chief

Copy of Conrad Weisser's Bill.*

The Commissioners of Pennsil[a] to the Innkeeper at Bethlehem Ferry, Dr. July 27, 1756.

	£	s	d
For supper and breakfast for 48 men, Conrad Weisser and comp[y], including hay for y[e] horses	3	1	
On their return from Easton for dinner to the same comp[y]	1	17	6
	4	18	6

1 Aug[t] 1756. Nicholas Schaefer.†

The above acct. left unpaid by me, amounting to four pounds eighteen shilling and sixpence.

CONRAD WEISSER.

---

did not speak truth when he told the Governor he had authority from the Six Nations to treat with Onas." Soon after, he was taken ill of smallpox, and died during the Governor's absence at the second Treaty, held in Easton. Here his decease was publicly announced, and a string of wampum and eleven black strouds given the Indians in behalf of the Province to remind them of the "good man who had been very instrumental in promoting the good work of peace, and to wipe away their tears, and take grief from their hearts."—*Colonial Records.*

* Conrad Weisser was commissioned Lieutenant-Colonel 1st Battalion Pennsylvania Regiment on May 5, 1756. "Upon the present exigency of affairs, as Mr. Weisser is known to be well attached to his Majesty's government, and to have distinguished himself by raising a large body of men to oppose the incursions of the enemy and to defend the several parts of the county where he resides that lie most exposed to their depredations, it was judged proper to give him the command of the companies that should be raised in that county (Berks), and accordingly the Governor executed a commission, appointing him Colonel of the forces that were raised and should be raised in said county."—*Minutes Provincial Council, October* 31, 1755.

† A son of Michael Schaefer, of Tulpehocken. Succeeded J. God-

III. ACCOUNT SENT TO Y^E COMMISSIONERS IN PHILA., SEPTEMBER 14, 1756. DATED SEPTEMBER 11, 1756.

Province of Pennsil^a to the Stewards of Bethlehem, Dr.

1756.		£	s.	d.
Aug. 14.	For the sum of the account deliv^d.............	200	14	5
Sept. 11.	For sundries deliv^d 82 Indians* from ye 14 August to 11 Sept^r, viz.:			
	1840 lbs. bread, @ 1¼*d*.........................	9	11	8
	304 lbs. beef, @ 2½*d*............................	3	3	4
	45½ bush^s Indian corn deliv^d since ye 17 July, their own being consumed, @ 3*s*. 6*d*.	7	19	3
	159 galls^s milk, @ 8*d*............................	5	6	
	3 quarts linseed oil @ 1*s*.........................		3	
	2 galls^s soft sope, @ 1*s*...........................		2	
	2 lbs. candles, @ 7*d*..............................		1	2
	2 bushl^s pease, @ 6*s*............................		12	
		26	18	5
	To the Bethlehem Tavern, for sundries. (See *Voucher* 1)................................	12	5	2
	To the Bethlehem store, for sundries. (See *Voucher* 1).......................................		18	6
Aug. 15.	For an express to bring ye Indians Christian and Samuel† to Phila...........................	2	2	6
" 17.	For 3 bushl^s meal deliv^d Tadyuscund and company, @ 5*s*................................		15	
	Carr^d forw^d............................	42	19	7

frey Grabs, at "the Crown," in April of 1756. Schaefer's wife was Jeannette, the oldest daughter of Isaac Ysselstein. Frederic Schaefer, who deceased at Nazareth in 1830, was a son.

* The refugees from Gnadenhütten.

† Two Moravian Indians, formerly of Gnadenhütten, who had come from Diahoga, and who, at their request, were escorted to Philadelphia.

		£	s.	d.
1756.	Bro^t forw^d.............................	42	19	7
Aug. 23.	For an express to his Honor ye Governor with letters, being obliged to wait several days for ye Governor's* answer..............	2	5	10
	Carr^d forw^d.............................	45	5	5

* This express was the bearer of the following congratulatory letter and memorial from Spangenberg to Lieutenant-Governor William Denny, who had recently arrived from England, with his commission from Thomas and Richard Penn:

MAY IT PLEASE YOUR HONOUR,

We, his Majesties most dutiful and Loyal Subjects, Members of the Unitas Fratrum, residing in Northampton County and Province of Pensylvania, and our United Brethren in said Province, having with pleasure heard of Y^r Hon^rs safe Arrival in Philadelphia, cannot but return Almighty God Thanks for his gracious Preservation of Y^r Hon^r on your Voyage at this Time of Danger.

We beg Leave to congratulate Your Honour at your Entrance on this important Station, which so immediately concerns the Welfare of so many Thousand People, and especially at this critical Juncture, and we thankfully receive You as a Minister of God, appointed from above, to the Deterring and Obstructing of Evil, and to the Encouraging and Promoting of that which is good.

We also thank his Majesty, our most gracious Sovereign King, George the Sec^d, for his paternal care towards this Province, as also towards all other the Territories (which the Lord of Lords and King of Kings has entrusted to him), demonstrated in sending Wise and Prudent Governors, in his Name faithfully to promote the Welfare of this Country. May his Majesty enjoy a long and happy Reign over us! and let all the Enemies of his Royal Family be as Chaff before the Wind, and as Stubble before the Fire.

We gratefully acknowledge that we have hitherto lived under this Government with Contentment, and esteem ourselves happy that we reside in a Country furnish'd with such good Laws, govern'd by so wise a Sovereign, and which, by the Regulation of the late Hono^ble Proprietor, W^m. Penn, Esqre, of happy Memory, has a Pre-eminence, and if the Proprietor^s Governor and Country harmonize together, (which is our earnest wish) might become the Flower of America.

The English Nation, as it is in general of generous Principles, not

		£	s.	d.
1756.	Bro[t] forw[d]	45	5	5
Aug. 23.	For an express to Easton		5	
" 27.	To the tavern for sundries deliv[d] to Pennsil[a] Regiment, as pr. receipt of Mr. Conrad Weisser*	5	3	11
	Carr[d] forw[d]	50	14	4

forcing any one's Conscience or restraining his Liberty, but leaving the Hearts to God, has also been so favourable to our Brethren, as by an Act of Parliament to exempt such of them as conscientiously scruple the Taking of an Oath, and the Bearing of Arms. And to the Praise of this Govern[t], we must declare that they have hitherto dealt with us agreeable to the Same, having forced none of us either to take an Oath or go to the War.

Our principal Endeavour has been to delight the Heart of our dear Lord Jesus Christ, and to live to his Honour, whom we adore as our Creator, and who also was manifested in the Flesh, became a Sacrifice for us, and redeemed us from the Dominion of Sin and Satan by his own Blood. And we hope that our Labour has not been in vain, although we must confess that we are infinitely indebted to Him still.

Our next Concern has been to make the Offices of Govern[t] (which are in themselves heavy enough) as easy and light as possible to the Magistrates, and under them to lead a quiet and peaceable Life in all Godliness and Honesty. And to order our Matters with such Decorum and Industry, that our Fellow Subjects, instead of Complaint against us, might be rather induced to thank God for sending hither the Offspring of those Confessors, of whom many Hundreds boldly seal'd with their Blood that Truth which they knew to be the Word of God. With regard to this Point, all those who know us right, will, we hope, have a favourable opinion of us.

Thirdly, ever since we came into the Country, our hearty desire has been for the Furtherance of the Gospel among the poor Heathen, who are the most miserable Slaves of the Devil, and worship him still as their God. In order to bring them effectually acquainted with the

* "*August* 26. Col. Weisser, with a detachment, passed through to the frontiers."—*Bethlehem Diarist.*

		£	s.	d.
1756.	Bro^t forw^d........	50	14	4
Sept. 3.	For an express to bring Shikellimy* and his wife to Phila., expenses, horse hire, &c ...	3	15	
		54	9	4

Way of Life, which is Jesus Christ, that is, to believe on Him, to love Him, and to be obedient to Him. Our blessed Saviour has also given some success to this our undertaking, by rendering through the Gospel many a Monster (for such they are till they come to Him), not only humanized, but also Lovers of their Creator. And a little Flock of such Indians there are living with us in Bethlehem, and ever since the commencement of the War, having from the Beginning desired and enjoy'd as Children the Protection of this Government. We beg leave herewith heartily to recommend them to Y^r Honour's Protection and Favour.

As to the Recompense we have had from the Savages for all the Faithfulness shewn to them, for all our dangerous Journeys to them, and Perils among them, it need not now be related, it being already notoriously known. Yet this shall not discourage us from proceeding to use our best Endeavours to bring those poor Creatures, possess'd by more than One Demon, to Faith in Christ.

We conclude with recommending this and all other Our Congrega-

* John Shikellimy, alias *Tachnachdoarus*, son of old Shikellimy, and his wife, reached Bethlehem on the 1st of September, from Diahoga, en route for Philadelphia, whither he had been summoned by the Governor. While at the former place, he was examined by "David Zeisberger, a Moravian Brother, who speaks the Indian language well," in the presence of Justice Horsfield. He reported the condition of affairs in the Indian country, stated that "in the previous winter the Six Nations had sent many belts to the Delawares and Shawanese desiring them to leave off doing mischief, that at last they were obedient, that Teedyuscung was the only person who had incited the Indians against the English, that the Six Nations were highly displeased with him, but that now he had altered his mind and spoke very much to the English interest to the Indians." Shikellimy was at this time an agent for the Province in its business with his countrymen.

Vouchers belongg to the foregoing Account.

I.

Province of Pennsil[a] to Bethlehem Tavern,* Dr.

1756.					£	s.	d.
Aug. 15.	For victuals deliv[d] 2 Indians and 2 soldiers, evening and morning, who came from Easton.......... £		6				
	" 5 q[ts] beer..........................		1	8			
	" 1½ q[ts] rum..................		1	10			
						9	6
	Carr[d] forw[d]...............................					9	6

tions in this Province to Y[r] Honour's kind Favour and Protection, at the same time sincerely beseeching God to give Y[r] Honour Wisdom, Courage, and Success in all your Undertakings, for the good of the Country during your Administration in Government.

We are, with all Respect, Y[r] Honour's

most obedient and humble Serv[ts].

BETHLEHEM, August 21, 1756.

Sign'd in behalf of the above mentioned Members of the Unitas Fratrum and their United Brethren. Joseph, alias Augustus Gottlieb Spangenberg, *Ordinarii Unitatis Fratrum Vicarius Generalis in America.* *m. p. p.*

The Governor in his reply thanked the Brethren for their good wishes, and assured them of his purpose to protect their interests and their persons in this time of danger, as far as lay in his power. The bearer of the above address was also intrusted with a letter from Spangenberg to the late Governor Morris, in which he returned thanks to him for the regard that he had had for himself and the Brethren during his term of office.

* "The Crown" (die Krone), originally the cabin of a Swiss squatter, Ritsche by name, who settled on the south bank of the river in 1742. In February, 1743, the tract of 274 acres, on which he was seated, was purchased by the Brethren of Wm. Allen. They bought the squatter off and out, leased the premises to one Anton Gilbert, from Germantown, then to one Adam Schaues, and in 1745, after having enlarged

			£	s.	d.
1756.	Bro[t] forw[d]			9	6
Aug. 18.	For eating evening and morning, deliv[d] to King Tadyuskund,* 6 Indians, and 2 soldiers, who escorted them from Gnadenhütten £	4			
	" rum and punch	4			
	" 15 q[ts] beer	5			
	" hay and oats for 3 horses	5			
				18	
	Carr[d] forw[d]		1	7	6

the building, opened it for public entertainment. It was stocked in May of that year with gill and half-gill pewter wine-measures, with 2 dram-glasses, 2 hogsheads of cider, 1 cask of metheglin, 1 cask of rum, 6 pewter plates, iron candlesticks, and whatever else could minister to the creature comforts of the tired traveler. Here he was served with a breakfast of tea or coffee at four pence, a dinner at six pence, a pint of beer at three pence, a supper at four pence, or if hot at six pence; with lodgings at two pence, and night's hay and oats for his horse at twelve pence. Jost Vollert was the first landlord for the Brethren. The succession of publicans to the close of this piece of history was as follows: Hartmann Verdries, J. Godfrey Grabs, Nicholas Schaeffer, and Ephraim Culver. In 1794 the sign-board, emblazoned with the British Crown, that had often served as a mark for the arrows of the wild Indian boys of "Teedyuscung's company" was taken down and the old hostelry converted into a farm-house. It stood near the site of the Union Depot of the Lehigh Valley and North Pennsylvania Railroads until about 1860. At an early day the Brethren had built several houses near the Crown, and thus a small settlement sprung up on the south side of the river. A school for girls, and subsequently one for boys, "*auf der Geduld*," was temporarily conducted here in 1747.

* "In the evening of August 17, Teedyuscung, who since the Treaty, had been loitering by Fort Allen, returned to Bethlehem with a few of

		£	s.	d.	£	s.	d.
1756.	Bro^{t} forw^{d}................................				1	7	6
Aug. 18.	For victuals deliv^{d} 1 soldier from Gleissen's* who escorted Nathaniel and company to Bethlehem, and hay and oats for his horse £		1	10			
Sept. 11.	" victuals deliv^{d} to Nathaniel,† his wife, and 2 children, and 1 other Indian, from ye 13 August to ye 11 Sept^{r}, being 29½ days, @ 4*s.* p^{r} day.........	5	13				
	" keeping his horse from ye 13 Augt to ye 11 Sept^{r}, @ 8*d.* per day..............		19	4			
					6	14	2
	" victuals and drink, hay and oats for ye soldiers that escorted ye King Tadyuscund's wife and family from Fort Allen to Beth^{m}		2	6			
	Carr^{d} forw^{d}...........................				8	4	2

his associates, for the twofold purpose of enticing his niece Theodora away, and of prevailing with our Indians to accompany him to Diahoga. He set out for the Fort next day, without having accomplished his object. On the 21st his wife and children arrived. The King they stated was gone to the Minnisinks to arrest his Indians there in their depredations."—*Bethlehem Diarist.*

* Quære—Where was Gleissen's?

† These were Moravian Indians who had withdrawn or been enticed from the mission at Gnadenhütten, in the summer of 1755, and had gone up the Susquehanna. Nathaniel, a Delaware from Tenkhanneck, twenty miles above Wyoming, had been baptized by Bishop Cammerhoff, May 17, 1749. His wife was Priscilla. The third Indian was Thamar, Anton's mother. They were quartered at "the Crown."

		£	*s.*	*d.*	£	*s.*	*d.*
1756.	Bro^{t} forw^{d}..........		2	6	8	4	2
	For victualing ye king's wife* and 3 children from ye 21 Augs^{t} to ye 11 Sept^{r}, being 21 days, @ 2*s.* 6*d.* per day......................	2	12	6			
					2	15	
	" eating, beer and rum deliv^{d} Shikellimy his wife, and 2 soldiers from Fort Allen					14	
	" eating evening and morning, deliv^{d} to 7 soldiers from Fort Allen, who brought 2 prisoners† to Easton.....................					5	10
	" beer do...............	£	2	4			
	" hay and oats for do...		1	4		3	8
					12	5	2

2.

Province of Pennsil^{a} to Bethlehem Store, Dr.

		£	*s.*	*d.*
1756.	For sundries, viz.:			
July 5.	" ½ lb. cotton wick deliv^{d} for Fort Norris.‡..................................		2	
	Carr^{d} forw^{d}		2	

* Her Christian name was Elisabeth. Baptized March 19, 1750, by Martin Mack, at Gnadenhütten, on the Mahoning. In the evening of August 21 she had been escorted from Fort Allen, in accordance with her wish to reside at Bethlehem while in the settlements. She and her children were quartered at "the Crown."

† Quære—Corporal Weyrick and Lieutenant Müller for insubordination? See *Penn. Archives*, vol. i. pp. 749 and 754.

‡ Fort Norris, named for Isaac Norris, Speaker of the Assembly, was built in the spring of 1756, on Head's Creek (Höth's), in Chestnut Hill Township, Monroe County, not far from the site of the Wequetanc Mission. "It stands in a valley, midway between the North mountain and the Tuscarory, 6 miles from Each on the high Road towards the Minnisink, it is a Square about 80 f^{t} Each way with four

			£	s.	d.	£	s.	d.
1756.		Brot forwd....................................					2	
July 5.	For	3 quires paper delivd to Capt. Insley,* per order of Mr. Horsfield.............					3	
	"	1 half gallon measure..		2	6			
	"	1 funnel, delivd per order of Mr. Horsfield for to measure rum for ye Forts......		2				
							4	6
" 21.	"	2 quires paper delivd for Fort Norris.....					2	
Aug. 14.	"	5 qts linseed oil...........		5				
	"	¼ lb. cotton wick........		1				
							6	
		Delivd per order of Maj. Parsons for ye men posted at Easton.						
Sept. 7.	"	1 quire paper delivd for Capt. Arndt's† compy..					1	
							18	6

---

half Bastions, all very Compleately Staccaded, and finished, and very Defenceable, the Woods are Clear 400 yds. Round it, on the Bastions, are two Sweevle Guns mount'd, within is a good Barrack, a Guard Room, Store Room, and Kitchen, also a Good Well. Provincial Stores, 13 gd Muskets, 3 burst Do., 16 very bad Do., 32 Cartooch boxes, 100 lbs. Powder, 300 lbs. Lead, 112 Blankets, 39 Axes, 3 Broad Do., 80 Tamhacks, 6 Shovels, 2 Grub Hoes, 5 Spades, 5 Drawing knives, 9 chisels, 3 adses, 3 Hand Saws, 2 Augers, 2 Spliting knives. July 2nd, 1756.

"JAS. YOUNG,

"Comissy Genl of ye Musters."

The well of the old fort may yet be traced on the property of William Serfass.

* Joseph Insley, Sr., Captain of one of the Associated Companies in Bucks County.—*Pennsylvania Archives*, vol. ii. p. 20. His son, Joseph Insley, Jr., was the ensign in his father's company.

† Jacob Arndt, of Bucks County, acting commandant of Fort Allen, commissioned Captain of 1st Battalion Pennsylvania Regiment, April

Copy of Conrad Weisser's Receipt belongg to the foregoing Account.

The Account of the Expenses of the officers of Pennsila Regt to Lieut.-Col. Weisser, Maj. Parsons, and Capt. Insley, with 18 private men, including the disserters from the French-Indian, and hay and pasturing to 14 horses at the In of Bethlehem, amtg in the whole to five pound three shilling and eleven pence. Augst 27, 1756.

The above is a true account.

CONRAD WEISSER.

£5 3*s.* 11*d.*

IV. ACCOUNT SENT TO YE COMMISSIONERS IN PHILA. YE 24 NOVR, DATED YE 23 NOVR.

Province of Pennsila to the Steward of Bethlehem, Dr.

1756.		£	*s.*	*d.*
Nov. 22.	For ye ballance of accts delivd..................	118	1	1
	" sundries delivd Tadyuskund's family from ye 11 Sepr last. (See *Voucher* 1)	5	7	7½
	" sundries delivd Nathanael and family since 11 Sepr last. (See *Voucher* 2).	5	3	6
	" sundries delivd Sam Evans and company. (See *Voucher* 3)..................		18	2
	Carrd forwd..............................	129	10	4½

18, 1756. Assigned to the command of Fort Allen, October 9, 1756. Major of troops at Fort Augusta (Sunbury) in 1758. In 1760, Mr. Arndt purchased a mill-seat, three miles above Easton, on the Bushkill. Christensen, the millwright at Bethlehem, and projector of the first water-works at that place, built Arndt's mill. In October of 1764, Mr. Arndt was elected captain of an independent company, raised in his neighborhood for home defense against the Indians. In 1774 he was appointed one of a Committee of Northampton, to co-operate with the Committees of other counties of the Province, for the purpose of convoking a General Congress of Committees, which should devise means for resisting the Boston Port Bill. In 1776, a member of the Executive Council of Pennsylvania. Deceased at Easton, Pennsylvania, in 1805.

		£	s.	d.
1756.	Brot forwd	129	10	4½
Nov. 22.	For sundries delivd Nicodemus and family since they came up from Phila. (See *Voucher* 4)	2	12	5½
	To the tavern at Bethlehem for sundry entertainment. (See *Voucher* 5)	5	12	1¼
	" the smith at Bethlehem. (See *Voucher* 6)	1	9	
	" the doctor at Bethlehem. (See *Voucher* 7)	1	1	6
	" Bethlehem store for sundries. (See *Voucher* 8)	4	15	
		145		5¼
	Off 5*s*., being paid by Capt. Reynolds for repairing a gun which ye Province was charged 14 Augt last		5	
		144	15	5¼

Vouchers belongg to the foregoing Account.

1.

Province of Pennsila Dr. to Bethlehem.
For sundries delivd Tadyuskund's family from ye 11 Septr last, viz.:

		£	s.	d.
1756.	To the tavern for victuals, &c., to ye 1 Octr, being 20 days, @ 3*s*. 4*d*. per day	3	6	8
	And then since Oct. 1.			
	126 lbs bread, @ 1¼*d*		13	1½
	15 lbs. beef, @ 2½*d*		3	1½
	6 lbs. pork, @ 3*d*		1	6
	6¼ lbs. butter, @ 6*d*		3	1½
	54 qts milk, @ 1½*d*		6	9
	1¼ bush. Indian corn, @ 2*s*		2	6
	1 quart beer			4
	1 pint cydar			2
	½ lb. candles			4
	Carrd forwd	4	17	7½

		£	s.	d.
1756.	Bro[t] forw[d]	4	17	7½
Oct. 30.	To hire of a waggon to bring them to Easton*		10	
		5	7	7½

2.

		£	s.	d.
	Province of Pennsil[a] Dr. to Bethlehem.			
	For sundries deliv[d] Nathanael and family since Sept. 11 last, viz.:			
	To the tavern for victuals &c. to y[e] 1 Oct., being 20 days, @ 2*s*. 8*d*. per day	2	13	4
	And then since y[e] 1 Oct.			
	174 lbs. bread, @ 1¼*d*.		18	1½
	38 lbs. beef, @ 2½*d*.		7	11
	6 lbs. pork, @ 3*d*		1	6
	7 lbs. butter, @ 6*d*.		3	6
	78 q[ts] milk, @ 1½*d*.		9	9
	1⅛ bush. Indian corn, @ 2*s*.		2	3
	1 pint beer			2
	1 gall. cydar		1	
	1 pint rum			7½
	½ lb. candles			4
Nov. 11.	To hire of a man and horse for bring[g] Ruth† and her children to Easton		5	
		5	3	6

* On request of Teedyuscung, who had arrived there for the impending Treaty. "Last night (October 29), in pursuance to your orders," writes Weisser to Gov. Denny, "I arrived here (Easton); about a quarter of an hour after my arrival came in Teedyuscung. The old man appeared extremely glad to see me, and so was the rest, especially three of the Six Nation Indians. They told me that several of their cousins, the Delawares, stood back at Gnadenhütten, and some further off, till they should understand whether or no it would be safe for them to come."—*Colonial Records.*

† Ruth, formerly of Gnadenhütten, who had for some time been quartered with her family at "the Crown." She was accompanied thither by most of the other Indians, all desirous of being present at the Treaty.

3.

1756. Province of Pennsil[a] Dr. to Bethlehem.

		£	s.	d.
Nov. 22.	For sundries deliv[d] Samuel Evans* and company, viz.:			
	76 lbs. bread, @ 1¼d.		7	11
	9 lbs. beef, @ 2½d.		1	10½
	2¼ lbs. butter, @ 6d.		1	1½
	37 quarts milk, @ 1½d.		4	7½
	1½ lbs. pork, @ 3d.			4½
	⅛ bush. Indian corn, @ 2s.			3
	1 pint beer			2
	4½ quarts cydar		1	6
	½ lb. candles			4
			18	2

4.

Province of Pennsil[a] Dr. to Bethlehem.
For sundries deliv[d] Nicodemus and family since they came up from Phil[a].† viz.:

---

* *Sam Evans*, a Delaware, a half-brother of Teedyuscung, who had come with the King to Easton, arrived at Bethlehem on the 31st of October. He and his family were quartered at "the Crown" during their stay. Father and mother came to see their daughter Theodora, who was an inmate of the "Single Sisters' House." They had an affecting interview at the Indian quarters at the Manakasy in the presence of missionary Schmick. "I rejoice to see you, my daughter," said her mother; "you have many blessings which are denied me; you have meat and drink, and I suffer privation." "Dear mother," responded the maiden, "while I lived at Gnadenhütten wicked Indians came and killed the white Brethren and Sisters, and I then wished to go to Bethlehem and be happy there. And my wish has been granted. And the Saviour too has been merciful to me. He has filled my heart with love toward him and the congregation, and I thank him from the bottom of my heart."

† Nicodemus and family had left for Philadelphia early in August. Fear of small-pox, prevalent among the Indians there, was the cause of their return.

1756.	£	s.	d.
74 lbs. bread, @ 1¼d.		7	8½
32 lbs. beef, @ 2½d.		6	8
2½ lbs. butter, @ 6d.		1	3
23 quart milk, @ 1½d.		2	10½
2 bush[l] Indian corn, @ 2s.		4	
½ lb. candles			4
1 gall. cydar. 1 pint rum		1	7½
9 lbs. white meal. 1 q[t] salt		1	6
For attending y[e] above families each day since y[e] 1 Oct., being 53 days, @ 6d. per day	1	6	6
	2	12	5½

5.

Province of Pennsil[a] to the tavern at Bethlehem, Dr.

	For sundries deliv[d] sundry other Indians and soldiers, viz.:	£	s.	d.
Oct. 13.	" victuals &c. deliv[d] 2 soldiers and some Indians from Easton, per order of Mr. Horsfield		3	
14.	" victuals deliv[d] some soldiers and Indians from Easton		6	6
	" hay and oats for their horses, pr. order of Maj. Parsons		4	3
15.	" 115 lbs. bread deliv[d] sundry Indians who came from Easton, @ 1¼d.		11	11¾
27.	" y[e] Indian Peter* and family, eating and drinking, evening and morning, pr. order of Mr. Horsfield		3	4
	Carr[d] forw[d]	1	9	¾

* Alias *Young Capt. Harris*, half-brother of Teedyuscung, formerly of Gnadenhütten. Baptized at that place January 31, 1750, by Bishop Cammerhoff. Peter, Sam Evans, Christian (son of Nicodemus or Jo Evans), and Tom Evans were, according to Henry Hess's deposition (taken during the sessions of the second Treaty at Easton), of the party headed by Teedyuscung that surprised his father's planta-

		£	s.	d.
1756.	Bro[t] forw[d]	1	9	¾
Oct. 29.	For eating and drinking for Jeremiah Trexler, and hay and oats for his horse, per order of Maj. Parsons		2	
30.	" entertainment deliv[d] 4 Indians from Easton, with their horses, pr. order of Mr. Horsfield		5	4
Nov. 17.	" sundries deliv[d] Capt. Reynolds,* Lieut. Wetherhold,† 1 ensign, 1 soldier, &c., which came with y[e] Indians from y[e] Treaty‡ at Easton, viz.:			
	Carr[d] forw[d]	1	16	4¾

tion in Lower Smithfield, on January 1, 1756.—*Pennsylvania Archives*, vol. iii. p. 56.

* George Reynolds, commissioned Captain 1st Battalion Pennsylvania Regiment, May 17, 1756. In command of a company of Provincials raised in Lebanon Township, Lancaster County. An ancestor of the late Major-General John Fulton Reynolds, who fell at the battle of Gettysburg?

† Jacob Wetterhold, commissioned Lieutenant in Major Parson's Town Guard, December 20, 1755. A captain in the Pontiac war. Surprised with a detachment of his men in the night of October 7, at John Stinton's public house (now Simon Laubach's, a mile and a quarter northwest of Howertown, in East Allen), mortally wounded, and died at Bethlehem, October 9, 1762. Was buried in the graveyard south of the Lehigh.

The following is an account of the attack on Stinton's tavern from Gordon's History of Pennsylvania. "The captain designing to proceed to Fort Allen early next morning, ordered a servant to get his horse ready. On leaving the house he was immediately shot down by the

‡ On Monday the 8th of November, the second Treaty with Teedyuscung was opened at Easton. Besides the Governor, and Wm. Logan and Rich'd Peters of his Council, there were present of the Commissioners, Benjamin Franklin, Joseph Fox, Wm. Masters, and John Hughes; of the officers of the Provincial Forces, Lieut.-Col. Weisser,

		£	s.	d.
1756.	Bro^{t} forw^{d}	1	16	4¾
Nov. 17.	Supper and 1 pint wine		3	6
	7 q^{ts} beer and 1 gill rum		2	8
	Lodging for them		1	3
	Hay and oats for 5 horses		4	7
	Carr^{d} forw^{d}	2	8	4¾

---

enemy; upon which the captain on going to the door was also mortally, and a sergeant, who attempted to draw him in, dangerously wounded. The lieutenant then advanced; whereupon an Indian jumping on the bodies of the two others, presented a loaded pistol to his breast, which the lieutenant putting aside, it was discharged over his shoulder, and in this way he succeeded in getting the Indian out of the house. The savage then went round to a window and shot Stinton, as he was in the act of getting out of bed. The wounded man rushed from the house, ran a mile, and dropped down dead. His wife and two children meanwhile secreted themselves in the cellar, and although they were fired upon three times, they were uninjured. The captain, notwithstanding his wound, crawled to a window and shot one of the Indians who was in the act of firing the house. The others took up the dead body of their comrade and left." Next day the dead and wounded Provincials were taken to Bethlehem. The dead were buried on the "Burnside plantation," on the Manakasy.

Maj. Parsons, Capt. Wetterhold, Capt. John Van Etten, and Capt. Reynolds; also Lieut. McAlpin and Ensign Jeffreys, Recruiting Officers of the Royal Americans, and a number of gentlemen and freeholders from the several counties, and from the city of Philadelphia. Teedyuscung, the Delaware King, was attended by sixteen of his nation, four Six Nation Indians, two Shawanese, and six Mohicans. John Pompshire interpreted for the King. Teedyuscung opened the Conference by stating that he had kept the promise made by him at the last Treaty, having since then informed all the Indian nations of the disposition of the English for peace. On being asked by the Governor whether he the Governor or the Province had ever wronged him, and why he and his Indians had struck the English, the Delaware proceeded to state that the false-hearted French King had tam-

		£	s.	d.
1756.	Brot forwd	2	8	4¾
Nov. 17.	Hot supper of meat &c. for 41 Indians	1		6
	46 qts beer		15	4
	2 qts wine for ye King		4	
	Hay for 14 Indian horses and 2 qts oats for ye King's horse		7	3
	Carrd forwd	4	15	5¾

pered with the foolish young men of his people; but chiefly they had taken up the hatchet because the English had defrauded them of their land. "*I have not far to go for an instance,*" continued the speaker: "*this very ground that is under me*" (striking it with his foot) "*was my land and my inheritance, and is taken from me by fraud. I mean all the land lying between Tohicon Creek* [a stream heading near Quakertown and emptying into the Delaware, fifteen miles east of that place] *and Wyoming.*" The Governor, hereupon offering him redress, Teedyuscung closed the Conference by stating that he was not empowered to accept of it, that he would meet the Governor at some future time, that then he would lay before him the extent of his grievances, and they could treat for a settlement of all disagreement and for a lasting peace.

"Late in the afternoon of the 17th, after the close of the Treaty, Governor Denny and his suite arrived at Bethlehem. Having been shown the objects of interest in the town, they visited the Indian quarters at the Manakasy. Here they were formally received by our Indians who had been drawn out in line before their dwellings. The Governor manifested gratification at the reception given him, addressed the Indians with marked friendliness, and stated his satisfaction at the arrangements in their quarters. At nine o'clock he sat down to supper, during which he was entertained with music. On the morning of the 18th, the visitors set out on their return. Bro. Spangenberg conducted them as far as the ferry, passing between two lines of children and Brethren and Sisters, who had been drawn out in front of his lodgings on the Square. The trombonists performed from the terrace of the Single Brethren's House until the Governor and his retinue had crossed the river. In the evening of the previous day, a few Indians

		£	s.	d.
1756.	Bro^t^ forw^d^	4	15	5¾
Nov. 17.	To ye baker for 110 lbs. bread at their departure		11	5½
	For eating and drinking deliv^d^ 1 soldier, with an express to Readingtown,* from his Honor ye Governor, with hay and oats for his horse		5	2
		5	12	1¼

---

under escort of Lieut.-Col. Weisser and a detachment of troops arrived from the Treaty on their return to Diahoga, and passed the night."—*Bethlehem Diarist.* "I left Easton about four o'clock," reports Weisser in the Journal of his proceedings, kept by order of the Governor, "accompanied by the officers of the Escort and Deedjoskon, Pompshire, Moses Deedamy, and two more Indians on horseback; we reached Bethlehem after Dark, and after the Soldiers and Indians were quartered at the Publick Inn this side of the Creek, I gave Deedjoskon the slip in the Dark, and he went along with the Rest to the said Inn, and I stayed at Mr. Horsfield's, having acquainted the officers with my Design, and gave the necessary Order before hand. On the 19th the Soldiers and Indians rose early and got ready to march, Deedjoskon could not get his Wife away, she wanted to stay in Bethlehem, because for his debauched way of Living, he took all the Children but one from her; at the Brethren's Request I interceded, and prevailed upon her to go with her husband. We left Bethlehem by Ten of the Clock."

"*Nov.* 18th. Toward evening a number of Indians arrived from Easton and were lodged in part in the town and in part on the other side of the river. We enjoined it on our Indians to remain at their quarters. *Nov.* 19th. Teedyuscung signified his wish to Bro. Schmick that Elisabeth and the children accompany him to Diahoga. To this she consented with reluctance. Sam Evans's wife bade adieu to her daughter Theodora."—*Bethlehem Diarist.*

* The town of Reading was laid out in the autumn of 1748 on a tract of 450 acres of land, for which warrants had been taken out by John and Samuel Finney in 1733.

6.

Province of Pennsil[a] to the smith* at Bethlehem, Dr.

1756.	£	s.	d.
For shoeing 1 Indian horse......................		1	
" mending a gun for Capt. Arndt's comp[y]		1	6
" " for Capt. Wetherhold's† comp[y]		6	6
" making a spring for a trap for y[e] Indian Smallman,‡ per order of Mr. Horsfield		5	
" making 3 screws for an Indian, per order of do..		2	
" stocking Sam Evans his gun, &c., pr. order Maj. Parsons........................		13	
	1	9	

7.

Province of Pennsil[a] to the Doctor§ at Bethlehem, Dr.

	£	s.	d.
Nov. 22. For curing a soldier's shoulder belonging to Capt. Arndt's comp[y], per his order......		10	
Carr[d] forw[d]................................		10	

* Daniel Kliest, smith, from Frankfort-on-the-Oder. Came to Bethlehem in May of 1749, with a large colony of Brethren, known as "John Nitschmann's Colony," on the Irene, on her first return voyage from Europe. Master locksmith to the Family. On its abrogation in 1762, Daniel Kliest bought the locksmithy, stock on hand and tools being appraised at £64 7*s.* Deceased at Bethlehem in March of 1792.

† John Nicholas Wetterhold, commissioned Captain 1st Battalion Pennsylvania Regiment, December 21, 1755.

‡ Quære—Johnny Smalling, or Swalling, a grandson of the King, present at the first Treaty?

§ John Matthew Otto, born 1714, in Meinungen. Studied medicine and surgery at Augsburg. Came to Bethlehem on the Irene, with "Henry Jorde's Colony," in June of 1750. For thirty years physician and surgeon of the Brethren's settlements. A skillful operator. Deceased at Bethlehem in August of 1786.

		£	s.	d.
1756.	Bro^t^ forw^d^..............................		10	
	For medicines deliv^d^ Capt. Wetherhold......		5	6
	" " " Capt. Reynolds.........		4	6
	" " " Capt. Arndt.............		1	6
		1	1	6

8.

Province of Pennsil^a^ to the Bethlehem Store, Dr.

		£	s.	d.
Oct. 14.	For sundries deliv^d^ ye Indian messengers, Zaccheus and George,* per order of Maj. Parsons, viz.:			
	2 pair of buckles, @ 1*s*. 8*d*.................		3	4
	1 " "		1	
	3 large blankets, @ 13*s*....................	1	19	
	2 pr. men's shoes............................		5	6
	2 y^ds^ of blue strouds for stockings.........	1	1	
	1 knife, pipes, &c...........................		3	2
	2 lbs. powder, @ 3*s*. 6*d*....................		7	
		4	15	

* Zaccheus and George, Delawares. The first, formerly of Gnadenhütten. They were messengers sent by the King to Maj. Parsons, and had arrived at Easton on the 11th of October. Their errand was to ascertain the state of feeling on the part of the Government in reference to Teedyuscung, he reporting by them that since his return to the Indian country he had received three words and three belts, purporting to come from Sir William Johnson, by all of which he had been warned against the English; that he and four other chiefs and a large number of Indians were arrived at Wyoming, desirous of coming down to a Treaty, and that as a token of the sincerity of his purpose he had sent with the messengers the prisoners taken in Smithfield, Henry Hess, William Weeser, and George Fox, and also Samuel Clifford. Furthermore, he desired that Elisabeth, his wife, should be permitted to accompany the messengers from Bethlehem, on their return. At the King's request, Augustus, and Joshua (the same who had accompanied Count Zinzendorf to the Susquehanna) were invited by Maj. Parsons to be present at the delivery of his message. Bro.

V. ACCOUNT SENT TO YE COMMISSIONERS* IN PHILA. YE 21 JANY, 1757.

Province of Pennsila to the Steward of Bethlehem, Dr.

Date	Item	£	s.	d.
1757.				
Jan. 21.	For sundries delivd 82 Indians since ye 11 Sept. last, who reside at Bethlehem, viz.:			
	7511 lbs. bread, @ 1¼d.	39	2	4¾
	770 lbs. beef, @ 2½d.	8		5
	86 lbs. mutton, @ 2d.		14	4
	61¾ lbs. butter, @ 6d.	1	10	10½
	297½ galls milk, @ 6d.	7	8	9
	140 " " @ 8d., delivd this month	4	13	4
	⅛ bush. white meal			6
	¾ " salt		4	1½
	14½ galls linseed oil, @ 4s.	2	18	
	19¾ " soft sope, @ 1s.		19	9
	¾ bush. Indian corn, @ 2s.		1	6
	1 quart rum		1	3
		65	15	2¾
1756.				
Nov. 18.	For victuals delivd Tattama,† ye Indian who came from Easton, and hay and oats for his horse, pr. order of Mr. Horsfield		2	4
22.	" 2 galls cydar, delivd ye Indians that came from ye Treaty		2	
	Carrd forwd		4	4

Grubé accompanied them to Easton. On the 14th the company came to Bethlehem. Here Parsons delivered the messengers his reply in behalf of the Governor for Teedyuscung, extending him a hearty invitation to come down with his people to a Treaty. On the 15th, Zaccheus and George set out on their return. Elisabeth was disinclined to go with them.

* Benjamin Franklin, John Mifflin, Joseph Fox, William Masters, John Baynton, and Joseph Galloway.

† Moses Tatemy. Written variously *Tattama*, *Totami*, *Titamy*, &c. Sometimes called *Old Moses*, also *Tundy*. Registered as a *Mountain Indian* at the Conference held in the Great Meeting-House at Crosswicks, in February of 1758. A convert of, and some time interpreter

		£	s.	d.
1756.	Brot forwd.		4	4
Nov. 29.	For 15 lbs. bread and 3 qts milk, delivd Anthony,* and his wife, and 2 old men, who came from Fort Allen, pr. order of Mr. Horsfield.		1	11¼
30.	" 1 pint of wine, delivd Akoan,† ye Indian who brought some intelligence of ye Indians, pr. order of Mr. Horsfield.		1	
	" visits, medicines, bleeding, &c., delivd ye Indian Capt. Harris, at Easton, pr. order of ye Governor.		17	6
Dec. 3.	" expences on bringing ye Indians Abraham, Luquas.‡ and Emas Shaw, to Phila.		16	6
8.	" an express with letters to his Honor ye Governor, concerning the murdering in Allemängel§ and ye aforesaid intelligence.	1	5	
	Carrd forwd.	3	6	3

---

to David Brainerd, in the Forks of Delaware. Attended most of the Treaties held with Teedyuscung, in the capacity of assistant interpreter. His name does not occur in the Colonial Records subsequent to 1760.

* A Delaware of *Tenkhanneck*, formerly of Gnadenhütten, baptized February 8, 1750, by Bishop Cammerhoff. A brother of Nathaniel.

† A Mohican, a son of Catharine, had arrived from the Susquehanna with the intelligence that three Cayugas, who had been present at the late Treaty, "were gone toward Allemängel to kill the white people," and that "a Shawanese whom he had met sixteen miles above Fort Allen had opened his bundle and given him a piece of tallow, and on being asked where he had got it, the Shawanese had told him he and others had killed a cow near the Fort, and also a horse, because they could not catch it, and he showed him the bell the horse had on."

‡ Mohicans, formerly of Gnadenhütten.

§ See *Pennsylvania Archives*, vol. iii. p. 77, for Horsfield's letter of November 30, 1756, to Governor Denny, for information brought by

		£	s.	d.	£	s.	d.
1756.	Bro^{t} forw^{d}...........................				3	6	3
Dec. 10.	For cash paid Ludwig Joung for going express with ye Governor's letters to Fort Allen, Fort Hamilton,* &c. &c., pr. order of Mr. Horsfield...............					18	
1757. Jany. 3.	" mending 1 gun and 3 gun locks, for Capt. Arndt, pr. his order........................					19	
	" sundries deliv^{d} to ye Indian messengers, Jo Peepy and Lewis Montour, pr. order of Mr. Horsfield, viz.:						
	1 pr. shoes, for Lewis Montour................		7	6			
	1 pr. shoes for Jo Peepy		7	6			
	Leather for mend^{g} shoes		2				
	Cash deliv^{d} them for ye journey................	3					
	Hire of a man and a horse to go with them to Fort Allen..........		12				
	A red Union Flag.......		6	6			
					4	15	6
	Carr^{d} forw^{d}...........................				9	18	9

Bro. John Holder, concerning an attack made by three Cayugas on one Schlosser's house in Allemängel.

* Fort Hamilton, named for James Hamilton, of the Governor's Council, and built 1756, near the junction of McMichael's and Brodhead's Creeks, in Lower Smithfield, Northampton County, "stands in a Corn field by a Farm house in a Plain and Clear Country, it is a Square with 4 half Bastions, all Very ill Contriv'd and finish'd, the Staccades open 6 inches in many places, and not firm in the ground, and may be easily pull'd down, before the gate are some Staccades drove in the Ground to cover it which I think might be a great Shelter to an enemy, I therefore order'd to pull them down, I also order'd to fill up the other Staccades where open.—Provincial Stores. 1 Wall Piece, 14 G^{d} Muskets, 4 Wants Repair, 16 Cartootch Boxes, filled with Powder and Lead, 28 lbs. Powder, 30 lbs. Lead. 10 Axes, 1 Broad

		£	s.	d.
1757.	Bro^t forw^d	9	18	9
	To Bethlehem Tavern for sundries deliv^d ye Indian messengers, Jo Peepy and Lewis Montour. (See *Voucher* 1)	1	2	5
	For sundries deliv^d John Smalling and his wife, and George Hays and his wife. (See *Voucher* 2)	8	2	5¼
	" sundries deliv^d Nicodemus and family, Nathanael and family, Joel and family, Ruth and 2 children, &c. (See *Voucher* 3)	9	19	1½
	To Bethlehem Store for sundries. (See *Voucher* 4)	1	17	5
		96	15	4¾

Vouchers belongg to the foregoing Account.

I.

COPY OF JO PEEPY'S* RECEIPT, JANY 14, 1757.

The expenses of Jo Peepy and Lewis Montour† at Bethlehem Tavern, when they

---

Axe, 26 Tomhawks, 28 Blankets, 3 Drawing Knives, 3 Spliting Knives, 2 Adses, 2 Saws, 1 Brass Kettle.

"JAS. YOUNG,

"Comissy. Genl. of ye Musters.

"July 2nd, 1756."

The old fort stood on the property of the daughters of the late Dr. Samuel Stokes, in the borough of Stroudsburg.

* Jo Peepy, having duly repented of his secession from the English, espouses their cause, is appointed envoy extraordinary in the Provincial service, next assistant interpreter, and leaves the stage of history under the more dignified appellation of Mr. Joseph Peepy.

† Lewis Montour, a Mohawk, younger brother of Andrew, was occasionally employed by Government in the capacity of a messenger. In 1754 he resided near Aucquick Old Town, where Weisser complained of his disturbing the Indians by bringing liquor to them. "They cannot help buying and drinking it," reports the interpreter,

1757.

were sent by ye Governor to ye Indians, delivd to us by Ephraim Colver,* as witness his hand.	£	s.	d.
To a pint wine....................................		1	
" a pint wine....................................		1	
" a supper....................................		1	
" a quart cydar....................................			4
" a pint wine....................................		1	
" 3 drams to give ye Indians for stringing wampoms....................................		1	
" a breakfast....................................		1	
" a pint of mum†....................................		1	
" a dinner....................................		1	
" a half pint of wine....................................			6
" a supper....................................		1	
" a half pint of wine....................................			6
Carrd forwd....................................		10	4

"when they see it, and Lewis sells it very dear to them, and pretends that his wife, which is a ugly squaw, does it."

On the 12th of January these worthies arrived at Bethlehem from Philadelphia. They were on their way to the Mohawk country, whither they had been dispatched by George Croghan, Deputy Agent to Sir Wm. Johnson (His Majesty's sole Agent and Superintendent of the affairs of the Six Nations, their allies, and dependents), with an invitation to the Susquehanna Indians, at Otsaningo, and to Teedyuscung, at Diahoga, to meet him in Conference at Harris' Ferry, in the spring. Nathaniel accompanied them. This embassy led to the Treaty held at Lancaster in May of 1757, at which the Mohawks, Onondagas, Oneidas, Cayugas, and Tuscaroras were represented, and which a few Senecas, Nanticokes, and Delawares attended. As Teedyuscung failed to appear, and as the representation of the Senecas was incomplete, no business of importance was transacted.

* Ephraim Colver, born July, 1717, in *Quittopehilla*, deceased at Bethlehem, March, 1775.

† A sort of strong beer, so named for one Christian Mumme, who first brewed it in 1492. Originally introduced from Brunswick, in Germany, and hence often called *Brunswick mum*.

		£	s.	d.
1757.	Brot forwd		10	4
	To a hot dram			6
	" 2 drams in ye morning			8
	" a breakfast		1	
	" a pint of wine		1	
	" a breakfast for Nathanael who went with them			6
	" breakfast for Nicodemus and his son, on their account		1	
	" 2 nights' lodgings			8
	" keeping 2 horses 2 days on hay and oats		4	6
	" a quart rum and ye bottle		1	11
	" one dram			4
		1	2	5

His
Jo X PEEPY.
mark.

2.

Province of Pennsila to the Stewards of Bethlehem, Dr.

		£	s.	d.
1757.	For sundries delivd John Smalling* who had ye small Pox and his wife, and George Hays and his wife, from ye 27 Nov., 1756, to ye 18 Jany, 1757, per order of Mr. Horsfield, viz.:			
	181 lbs. bread, @ 1¼d.		18	10¼
	38 lbs. beef, @ 2½d.		7	11
	1 lb. butter			6
	1 bush. Indian corn		2	
	⅞ do. white meal, @ 4s.		3	6
	Carrd forwd	1	12	9¼

* Quære—*John Swalling*, a grandson of Teedyuscung, who had been in attendance at Easton during the first treaty? George Hays, one of Teedyuscung's Delawares.

		£	s.	d.
1757.	Brot forwd.	1	12	9¼
	2 fouls for Jno. Smalling, @ 6d.		1	
	2½ bushs turnops, @ 8d.		1	8
	1 qt. linseed oil		1	
	1¼ gall. cydar, @ 1s.		1	3
	¼ lb. of sope			2
	1 earthen pot.			4
	Cash advancd George Hays		1	6
	Mendg a gun for do.		4	
	do. a saddle for do.		14	
	Medicines delivd to do. and bleeding		3	6
	Visits and medicines delivd Jno. Smalling and for incisions and dressing of above 10 impostunes	2	10	9
	A coffin for John Smalling		10	
	Burying of him*		10	
	For attending ye above Indians each day from ye 18 Novr to inst., being 61 days, @ 6d. per day	1	10	6
		8	2	5¼

3.

Province of Pennsila to the Stewards at Bethlehem, Dr.

		£	s.	d.
1757. Jan. 21.	For sundries delivd Nicodemus and family, Joel† and family, Ruth and 2 children, &c., 22 in number, since ye 22d Novr. last, viz.:			
	802 lbs. bread, @ 1¼d.	4	3	6½
	150 lbs. beef, @ 2½d.	1	11	3
	10½ bushs Indian corn, @ 2s.	1	11	
	Carrd forwd.	7	5	9½

* In the grave-yard that had been laid out on the south side of the Lehigh, on the hill west of "The Crown" (in 1747), for the interment of persons attached to the Brethren residing in Saucon Township.

† Joel, a Delaware, formerly of Gnadenhütten.

		£	s.	d.
1757.	Bro^t forw^d	7	5	9½
Jan. 21.	For 6 lbs. white meal, @ 1¼d.			7½
	35 galls. milk, @ 6d.		17	6
	19 do. @ 8d (*being new and very scarce*)		12	8
	9 quarts salt		1	6½
	1 pint beer			2
	1¼ bush^s turnops, @ 8d.			10
	" attend^g ye above families, each day since ye 22^d Nov. last, being 60 days, @ 6d. per day	1	10	
		9	19	1½

4.

Province of Pennsil^a to Bethlehem Store, Dr.

		£	s.	d.
1757.				
	For sundries, viz.:			
	3 yds. linnen and thread for ye Indian George Hays for a shirt		9	2
	" 4 quires cartridge paper for Capt. Arndt		1	8
	" 2 yds. Osnaburgs for Jo Peepy to make a bagg		3	4
	" 1 knife, 7 flints, and mak^g a handkerchief for do.		2	6
	" 2½ yds. linnen and thread for a shroud to bury ye deceased Indian, John Smalling		9	6
	" gunsmith's work for Capt. Arndt's company		11	3
		1	17	5

VI. Account deliv^d ye Commissioners in Phila. by Wm. Christopher Schmaling,* dated ye 11 April, 1757.

Province of Pennsil^a to the Stewards of Bethlehem, Dr.

1757.		£	s.	d.
April 11.	For sundries deliv^d 82 Indians in Bethlehem, since ye 21 Jany last, viz.:			
	4725 lbs. bread, @ 1¼*d*.	24	12	2¼
	426½ lbs. beef, @ 3½*d*.	6	4	4½
	109 lbs. bacon, @ 5*d*.	2	5	5
	232 galls. milk, @ 6*d*.	5	16	
	1 bush^l salt.		5	
	12½ gall^s of sope, @ 1*s*.		12	6
	4 do. linseed oil for lamps, @ 4*s*.		16	
	25 bush^ls Indian corn, @ 2*s*. 6*d*.	3	2	6
	A coffin for Jno. Peter,† who died of ye small pox.		10	
	Do. for his child.		5	
		44	8	11¾
	For storage‡ of the Province provisions for use of ye Provincial troops in the years 1755 and 1756.	5		
Jany. 26.	" sundries deliv^d ye Indians opposite Bethlehem, viz.:			
	" medicine and attendance on Capt. Harris and another Indian§ when going			
	Carr^d forw^d	49	8	11¾

* William C. Schmaling was on board the Brethren's snow "Irene" when she was taken by a French privateer in November of 1757. On his arrival at Dinan, Bretagne, in March of 1758, he wrote a narrative of her capture.

† Served as hospital steward to the Indians at Bethlehem. Buried in the old Moravian grave-yard.

‡ Principally during the time of Franklin's halt, preparatory to his moving on the frontier.

§ "*Tokayiendisery* was very sick when we left Easton. We brought him along in the wagon. I desired Mr. Otto, the Doctor in Bethle-

		£	s.	d.
1757.	Brot forwd.................................	49	8	11¾
Jany. 26.	through Bethlehem to Fort Allen, from ye last Treaty................................		2	6
	N. B.—This charge was entered in ye last acct. (included in the 17*s.* 6*d.*) but not allowed, because it was by a mistake said to be delivd at Easton, whereas it was delivd at Bethlehem.			
	For sundries delivd to 59 Indians, viz., 16 men, 21 women, and 22 children, since ye 21 Jany last, of which 23 returned to ye Indian country* at sundry times, viz.:			
	Carrd forwd.............................	49	11	5¾

hem, to come and see him. The Doctor believed he would get the Small Pox, and advised him to remain, but we could not prevail on him. When we came to the Fort he was most gone, but would not stay. His companions begged of me to get a horse for him to ride on, and they would return it in the spring. I could not refuse them any longer, they having requested three or four times. I bought a horse, saddle, and bridle for him, for Five Pounds. After all the sick man could not ride on horseback, so the Indians made a litter, but I believe he will never see his own country again."—*Weisser's Journey from Easton to Fort Allen, November,* 1756.

* All from Diahoga. Solomon and Zaccheus, formerly of Gnadenhütten. "February 26, 1757. There arrived Zaccheus and wife, Solomon, wife and child, 3 women and 5 children. One woman and child came some days before. Part of them returned to the Indian country the 1st of March, and the rest the 4th, excepting 2 women and 4 children, which Zaccheus desired might stay in Bethlehem till the King comes. These women and children I sent over the water to the other Indians."—*Horsfield to Governor Denny. Bethlehem, March* 14, 1757.

March 22, 1757. "Ten Indians," writes the Diarist, "arrived from Diahoga. They were lodged over the water, where there are at present upward of 30. They brought the intelligence that 100 of the Six Nations were come down to Shamokin in company with Peepy and Mon-

			£	s.	d.
1757.		Bro^{t} forw^{d}	49	11	5¾
Jany. 26.	For	1 Indian corn hoe for Solomon		3	
		Steeling a tomehacke for Zaccheus		1	6
		Shoeing Zaccheus' horse		1	6
		Leather for mend^{g} shoes, deliv^{d} Solomon, Zaccheus, &c., who went to ye Indian country ye 4 March last		3	6
		1550 lbs. bread, @ 1¼*d.*	8	1	5½
		479 lbs. beef, @ 3½*d.* (*being scarce and dear*)	6	19	8½
		36½ gall^{s} milk, @ 6*d.*		18	3
		¼ hundred fine flower		3	
		2½ bush^{s} of beans, @ 3*s.* 6*d.*		8	9
	"	building a wigwam for 10 Indians that came ye 22^{d} March last, pr. order of Mr. Horsfield	1	10	
	"	sundries deliv^{d} these 10, viz., 3 men, 6 women, and 1 child, pr. order of Mr. Horsfield:			
Mar. 22.	"	4 gills rum		1	4
		supper for ye 10		3	4
		2 quarts beer			8
23.	"	breakfast for ye 10		3	4
		2 quarts beer and 2 gills rum		1	4
		2 " cydar and 1 gill "		1	
28.	"	sundries deliv^{d} to Mr. George Schanzenbach, who came with them to Bethlehem		1	10
31.	"	sundries deliv^{d} 8 Indians,* viz., 3 men, 2 women, and 3 children, that			
		Carr^{d} forw^{d}	68	14	11¾

tour, on their way to Harris' Ferry." At this time 30 acres of land were allowed the Indians at "The Crown," to put to corn and beans toward their support.

* Amos and John Jacob, sons of the King, Jo Evans and wife, and Christiana and three children, returned from Diahoga.

			£	s.	d.
1757.		Bro[t] forw[d]	68	14	11¾
Mar. 31.		came y[e] 31st March, per order of Mr. Horsfield, viz.:			
		For ½ gill rum and 1 pint cydar			4
		2 gills rum			8
		supper for 7 Indians		2	4
		2 q[ts] of beer			8
April 1.	"	breakfast for 2 Indians		1	2
	"	supper and pint of beer for y[e] soldier that came with them			8
2.	"	½ gill of rum for do.			2
	"	breakfast for do.			4
	"	dinner and pint of cydar, deliv[d] Nathanael, who went with Jo Peepy to y[e] Indians in Diahoga when he came came back			8
6.	"	supper for 4 Indians who came y[e] 6 April			2
	"	breakfast, &c., supper and 1 gill rum for y[e] soldier that came with them		1	4
	"	attend[g] y[e] Indians each day from y[e] 21 Jan[y] to y[e] 11 April, being 80 days, @ 6*d*. per day	2		
9.	"	an express* to his Honor y[e] Governor, at the desire of Maj. Parsons	1	5	5
	"	fire wood, since November last	2	10	
Feb. 18.	"	cash p[d] y[e] Indian man Elias, for his gun lent y[e] Irish settlement people in November, 1755, which is lost, pr. order of Mr. Horsfield	2	5	
	"	cash p[d] an Indian that brought a prisoner† to Easton, per order of do.	1	10	
		Carr[d] forw[d]	78	13	10¾

* With a letter informing the Governor of the restoration of a captive.

† "This is to acquaint your Worship that the day before yesterday, arrived here four Indians from Susquehanna, above Diahoga, and have

		£	s.	d.
1757.	Brot forwd.	78	13	10¾
Feb. 18.	To Bethlehem Tavern for sundries. (See *Voucher* 1)	4	14	2
	" Apothecary and Surgeon of Bethlehem (See *Voucher* 2)		12	6
	" ye Locksmith of Bethlehem. (See *Voucher* 3)		16	4
	" Bethlehem Store, for sundries. (See *Voucher* 4)	4	9	4
		89	6	2¾

Vouchers belongg to the foregoing Account.

I.

Province of Pennsila to Bethlehem Tavern, Dr.

		£	s.	d.
1757.				
Jan. 28.	For keeping Jo Peepy's* horse from ye 13 to ye 28 Jany, being 15 days		11	8
	" expences sendg ye horse to Phila		5	
	" sundries delivd to 15 Indians, viz.: 2			
	Carrd forwd.		16	8

brought one white prisoner, whose name is Nicholas Ramston; he was taken at the same time that Christian Pember was killed."—*Maj. Arndt to Maj. Parsons, Fort Allen, April 5th*, 1757. Christian Boemper was a son of Abraham Boemper, of Bethlehem. Was married to one of Frederic Hoeth's daughters, living on Head's Creek, and was killed in a running fight with the Indians at that place in January of 1756.

"I imagined it would not be disagreeable to your Honour, to hear that the Indians had restored another of their captives. The person now returned is a young German, and was taken prisoner about 15 months ago by some of Teedyuscung's party. He states that the Indians used him pretty roughly at first."—*Parsons to Governor Denny, April* 8, 1757.

* During his absence with Montour in the Indian country.

Date		Item	£	s.	d.
		Bro^t^ forw^d^		16	8
		men, 7 women, and 6 children that came from ye Indian country ye 25 and 26 Febr^y^ last, per order of Mr. Horsfield, viz.:			
1757.					
Feb. 23.	For	1 supper and 2 qts. beer and 1 gill rum		2	
26.	"	1 breakfast for 3, 1 qt beer and 1 gill rum		1	8
		Keeping a horse on hay and oats		1	
		3 gills of rum, a supper and 2 qts. beer for 2 men, 5 women, and 6 children		5	6
27.	"	1 do. do. to ye 2 men			4
		1 dinner and 2 gills of rum for them all		5	11
		1 supper for them all		4	6
28.	"	2 gills of rum in ye morning for do.			8
		1 breakfast and dinner for them all		9	9
		1 qt. beer and 2 gills rum		1	
		1 supper for 2 men, 7 women, and 3 children		3	9
March 1.	"	2 gills of rum in ye morning			8
		Breakfast for 12 and dinner for them all		9	3
		Supper for 1 man, 5 women, and 2 children		2	6
2.	"	Breakfast for 7 and supper for 6 women and 2 children		4	10
3.	"	1 gill of rum, and 1 quart of beer			8
		Breakfast for 1 man, 6 women, and 2 children		2	10
		Dinner and supper for do.		6	3
4.	"	Breakfast for 9		3	
		3 gills of rum and 1 qt. beer for those that went away		1	4
			4	14	2

2.

Province of Pennsil[a] to Apothecary and Surgeon of Bethlehem, Dr.

1757.		£	s.	d.
Feb. 28.	For sundries, viz.:			
	" Bleeding Zaccheus and his wife..........		2	
	" do. an Indian woman................		1	
Mar. 1.	" Medicines and bleeding Nicodemus and his wife....................................		2	6
23.	" do. and do. the Indian woman *Sisinhahs*		2	
24.	" drawing a tooth of Nicodemus' son......		1	
	" curing Mr. George Schanzenbach's arm, one of Capt. Arndt's comp[y], per his order charg[d] to ye Province............		4	
			12	6

3.

Province of Pennsil[a] to the Locksmith of Bethlehem, Dr.

1757.		£	s.	d.
Feb. 18.	For sundries, viz.:			
	" gun flints deliv[d] to Capt. Arndt..........		1	4
	" mending 5 provincial gun locks for do..		15	
			16	4

4.

Province of Pennsil[a] to Bethlehem Store, Dr.

1757.		£	s.	d.
March 1.	For sundries deliv[d] Solomon *Mashelamakee* and others, per order of Mr. Horsfield, viz.:			
	1 blanket, @ 15*s.* and 2 do., @ 12*s*......	1	19	
	5 yd[s] Osnaburgs, @ 1*s.* 7*d*..................		7	11
	2 lbs. sope, 1 qt. salt, and 1 lb. powder..		5	2
	3 lbs. lead, 3 lbs. shot and tobacco........		4	10
	1 snuff box, 10*d.* 1 oz. snuff, 4*d.* butter and pipes..................................		2	9
	Carr[d] forw[d].........................	2	19	8

		£	s.	d.
1757.	Brot forwd	2	19	8
March 1.	For 1 3 galln cagg, 3s. and 1 quart molassis for Zaccheus, 9d		3	9
	2 yds. Osnaburgs, @ 1s. 7d. 2 lbs tobacco and pipes		4	10
25.	Pipe heads for ye Indian Thomas		1	8
April 1.	Gun flints delivd Capt. Arndt and butter for Amos ye Indian		18	11
9.	1 lb. butter for *Tomechy* returning to Fort Allen			6
		4	9	4

VII. ACCOUNT DELIVD TO YE COMMISSIONERS PR. WM. EDMONDS, DATD 28 MAY, 1757.

Province of Pennsila to the Stewards of Bethlehem, Dr.

		£	s.	d.	£	s.	d.
1757.							
April 11.	To an acct. delivd				91	1	11¾
16.	For an express to Easton to carry a packett which came from Col. Weisser for Maj. Parsons on his Majesty's service					5	
	" sundry provisions sent to Fort Allen, pr. order of Maj. Parsons,* viz.:						
	8 loaves of bread, wt. 131 lbs. @ 1¼		13	7¾			
	200 lbs. of gammons, @ 5½d.	4	11	8			
	8 bushls Indian corn meal, @ 3s. 6d	1	8				
	Carrd forwd				91	6	11¾

* To feed the Indians who were coming in to the treaty appointed for Lancaster.

		£	s.	d.	£	s.	d.
1757.	Bro^t forw^d...........				91	6	11¾
April 16.	For 12 cwt. 4 qr. 1 lb. meal, @ 10s. pr. cwt.........	6	2	7			
	As per receipt of Antonius Müller. (See *Voucher* 1.)						
	" 2 large sacks for ye bread and gammons..		7				
	" carriage of the above to Fort Allen..............	1	16				
18.	" an express from Mr. Horsfield to Maj. Parsons.....................		5				
					15	3	10¾
22.	" do. to Philadelphia, with letters to his Honor ye Governor, concerning ye murdering by ye enemy Indians*				1	5	
	Carr^d forw^d...............................				107	15	10½

* Captain John Van Etten's letter to Major Parsons, dated Fort Hamilton, April 21, 1757. "I am sorry to inform you," he writes, "of what hapened sins I sa you last on the 20 day of this instant, after I came to Fort Hammelton, about two a'clock, and as I made all the hast I could to Fort Hyndshaw, about one a'clock at night an express came to me that a man was ciled and scalped at Fort Hammelton, which I found to be tru, and had the man burried the 21 of this instant. Pray, sir, consider my afairs, as I am but weake now, and all the neighbors about the Fort is mounted in the Fort, which I compel'd to stan santriey next the soldiers tel forther orders; pray, sir, excuse haste." John Van Etten was commissioned a captain in the 1st Batt. 1st Pennsylvania Regiment, April 19, 1756.

See deposition of John Williamson, *Penna. Archives*, vol. iii. p. 139, concerning "Andreas Gundryman whom the Indians pursued with their Tomhocks and murdered him very barbarously, scalping him quite to the eyes." Also deposition of one Michael Roup, "a man well known and worthy of credit," who reported Peter Soan and Christian Klein, "killed by a bullet and Tamehacks," near Philip

		£	s.	d.	£	s.	d.
1757.	Bro^{t} forw^{d}				107	15	10½
April 28.	For medicine sent Capt. Arndt, pr. his order. (See *Voucher* 2)				1	7	8
	" sundries paid for, & deliv^{d} to ye Indian messengers, Nathanael & Zacharias,* per order of Mr. Horsfield, viz.:						
	" an express to Easton to Maj. Parsons for a guard for them with the Governor's message to Tattiwaskund		5				
	" making a hatchet for them		2				
	" shoeing a horse for Jeremiah Trexler, who went with them at the request of Maj. Parsons		1	6			
	" a gun for Nathanael	1	15				
	" hire of 2 men & 1 horse for accompanying them to Hays†		6				
					2	9	6
	Carr^{d} forw^{d}				111	13	½

Bozart's house, seven miles from Fort Hamilton.—*Col. Records*, vol. viii. p. 492.

* Zacharias, a son of Nicodemus, formerly of Gnadenhütten, and Nathaniel had been dispatched by Deputy Croghan to acquaint Teedyuscung with the impatience of the Indian deputies met at Harris's Ferry, at his prolonged absence. They set out from Bethlehem May 4.

† John Hays kept a public house on the road from Bethlehem to Gnadenhütten on the Mahoning, which road had been laid out in 1747, it being urged by the petitioners "that many inhabitants of this and the neighboring Provinces have frequent occasion of going beyond the

		£	s.	d.
1757.	Bro^t forw^d	111	13	½
April 28.	For Jno. Hays' acct. at the desire of Tim^y Horsfield	1	1	
May 5.	" mending a gun left by an Indian at ye first treaty. (See *Voucher* 3)	2		
23.	" an express to Easton with letters to Maj. Parsons		5	
27.	To ye Store, for sundries. (See *Voucher* 4).	8	4	5½
	" the Tavern for sundries deliv^d to sundry Indians since ye 11 April. (See *Voucher* 5)	5	1	3

For sundries deliv^d ye Indians opposite Bethlehem since 11 April, viz.:

	£	s.	d.
1705 lbs. of bread, @ 1¼*d*	8	17	7¼
49½ lbs. of beef, @ 3½*d*	7	3	4¼
27 bush^s Indian corn, @ 2*s*. 6*d*.	3	7	6
20 lbs. veal, @ 2*d*.		3	4
20 lbs. of gammons, @ 5½		9	2
160 galls. of milk, @ 6*d*.	4		

	£	s.	d.
Carr^d forw^d	128	4	9

Blue Mountain to Mahoning Creek and to the 'Healing Waters' lying not far from thence." Hays' tavern-stand was Mr. Jacob Fatzinger's place, in Weaversville, East Allen Township, seven miles northwest of Bethlehem. Weisser tells us that on his return from the second conference at Easton he "dined at one Hays', the Indians and soldiers upon cold beef and sider, Deedjoskon and four or five more with me. The Indian account came to fifteen shillings and threepence. The landlord has other accounts of the same nature against the Province."

				£	s.	d.
1757.	Brot forwd............			128	4	9
May 27.	For 1⅝ bushs white meal, @ 4s....................	6	6			
	⅝ bushls salt, @ 5s.. ...	3	1½			
	⅛ do. beans, @ 4s ..		6			
	1¾ lbs. butter, @ 6d...		10½			
	Steeling an ax...........	2				
				24	13	11½
	" attending the Indians each day from ye 11 April to ye 27 May, being 46 days @ 6d. per day..............................			1	3	
	" building another wigwam for ye Indians over ye water..................................			2		
	" mending a gun for ye Indian Hendrick *Quomon*,* pr. order of Mr. Horsfield				5	6
	" repairing a gun for ye Indn Samy Evans, pr. order of Maj. Parsons...............			1	13	8
				158		10½

Vouchers belongg to the foregoing Account.

I.

BETHLEHEM, ye 16 April, 1757.

A list of sundry provisions sent up from Bethlehem to Fort Allen for the use of the Indians coming down to the Treaty, by order of William Parsons, Esq., viz.:

---

* Captain *Henry Quamash*, a Delaware of Teedyuscung's company who lay sick at Bethlehem from the second treaty at Easton to October of 1760. Before setting out for the Indian country, in that month, he addressed a letter to Governor Hamilton, expressive of his gratitude for the kind attention and care he had experienced from the Government, and also from the Brethren at Bethlehem. "In particular," he writes, "I am thankful to Mr. Horsfield for his great love toward me, for the horse, the blankets, stockings and hat, and meal and medicines he has given me to take with me."

Two hundred pound of gammons.

Eight bushels of Indian corn meal.

Ten loafes of bread.

Thirteen hundred seventy-three pound of flower.

15 new Osnabrigs bags.

2 large sacks, with the bread and bacon.

Rec[d] the above particulars by Bethlehem wagon, by the hands of Paal Christian Stouber,* by me,

ANTONIUS MÜLLER.

2.

Province of Pensilvania to Apothecary of Bethlehem, Dr.

1757.		£	s.	d.
April 28.	For medicines deliv[d] Capt. Arndt, per his order:			
	To 10 oz. empl. ad rupt.		5	
	" 6 " " de minio		4	
	" 14 " ungt. basilic		1	8
	" 3½ " spirit. rectific.		2	
	" 3 " " terebinth		1	
	" 2 " balsam vulne.		4	
	" 1 " camphor		3	6
	" 1 " pulv. antispasm		2	6
	" 1 " " lax., 4 dos		4	
		1	7	8

FRED[K] OTTO.†

---

* Paul Christian Stauber, from Frankfort-on-the-Main. Came to Bethlehem with Henry Jorde's colony of young men, on the Irene, in June of 1750. Removed to North Carolina in 1767. Descendants are living there.

† John Frederic and his wife, Maria Otto, came to Bethlehem in November of 1743, with the second "Sea Congregation," on the "Little Strength." He was apothecary and druggist for "The Family."

3.

Province of Pensilvania, Dr.

1757.		£	s.	d.
April.	To new stocking a rifle gun....................		12	
	" new brass mounting for rifle gun..........		12	
	" a bullet mold for "		3	
	" a screw and drawer for "		2	
	" new boreing the barrell (rifle fashion)...		6	
	" cleaning " " outside..........		1	6
	" a new trigger..................................		1	6
	" cleaning the lock and 2 screws, &c........		2	
		2		

N.B.—The gun was ordered to be mended the first Treaty held at Easton, and left by an Indian under the care of Wm. Edmonds, who had the late Governor Morris' order for that amongst other things to send them well satysfy'd away, and since mended, but not charged till now by me,

Witness, DANL KLIEST,
WM. EDMONDS. Locksmith at
Bethlehem.

4.

Province of Pensilvania, to Bethlehem Store, Dr.

		£	s.	d.
1757.	For sundries delivd, viz.:			
April 13.	For butter and mending a gun for ye Indian, *Tapescawen** and his companion messengers from Tadiuskund...................		1	4
	Carrd forwd............................		1	4

* *Tapescawen* or *Tapeuscung*, alias *Samuel*, Teedyuscung's counselor, had arrived from Diahoga with two messages from the King to Maj. Parsons. The communications were forwarded to him and delivered in presence of the Moravian Indian Paul. The King, they stated, was preparing to come down, and with him were coming chiefs of the Six Nations. He had been far back in their country, and so had been detained.—*See page* 366.

			£	s.	d.
1757.		Bro^t^ forw^d^		1	4
April 18.	For	29 y^ds^ Osnabrigs for bags, to carry provisions, @ 1s. 6d.	2	3	6
	"	thread, and cash pd. for making do......		4	6
25.	"	1 lb. butter, deliv^d^ do........................			6
26.	"	butter and bread, del^d^ Tadiuskund's and Nutimus's sons*........................		1	
28.	"	100 oil flints deliv^d^ Cap^n^ Arndt for his comp^y^....................................		8	
May 1.	"	pipes and tobacco for ye Indian messenger from Lancaster†....................			10
4.	"	sundries deliv^d^ Nathanael and Zacharias, messengers, for their journey to Wayomick and Diaogu,‡ pr. order of Mr. Horsfield, viz.:			
		Carr^d^ forw^d^...............................	2	19	8

* *Old Nutimus* was a well-known chief of the Fork Delawares, and their representative at the Treaty in Philadelphia in July of 1742, at which Canassatego rib-roasted them well, and then bade them be off and out of the Forks, subject to a heavy penalty if they were recusant. *Isaac*, his son, reported to Justice Horsfield that ten days previously he had left a place 30 miles above Diahoga, and had met French and Indians coming down on the frontiers with intent to murder. "On asking him and Amos, Teedyuscung's son, why they did not catch the rogues," writes Horsfield to Parsons, "they made no answer, only smiled."

† A Mohawk, who had come to Bethlehem, escorted by Capt. Wm. Trent, at the request of the Indians at Lancaster, to bring Teedyuscung and the rest of the Delawares, should they have arrived, to that city. The Sachem delivered his message in the presence of Mr. Horsfield to the Indians at "The Crown," who agreed to send a number of their chiefs and some of the women. They set out on the 2d, having left wampum with word for the King to follow with the rest, on his arrival.

‡ See *note to April 28, in the early part of this Account*. "On the 5th of May the messengers set out; Bro. Schmick, at his request, having furnished Nathaniel with a Delaware translation of the Gov-

		£	s.	d.
1757.	Bro^t forw^d	2	19	8
May 4.	1 oz. blew thread, @ 6*d.*, and 2½ y^ds blew strowds, @ 11*s*	1	8	
	2 tin kettles, @ 2*s.* 6*d.*, and 500 white wampums, @ 2*s.* 3*d.* per cent		16	3
	2 ivory combs, do. horn combs		4	4
	6 gun flints and 2 lbs. gun powder, @ 3*s.* 6*d.*		7	6
	2 lbs. small shot, @ 8*d.*, and 2 knives, @ 1*s*		3	4
	4 lbs. lead, @ 8*d.*		2	8
	8 yds. ribbon, @ 1*s.* 5*d.*, for their stockings		11	4
	2 fine pockett books		8	
	2 lbs. butter, @ 6*d.*		1	
	2 fine pipe heads, lin'd and cover'd with brass, @ 1*s.* 3*d.*		2	6
	1 silk handkerchief, @ 6*s.* 6*d.*, and needles, 2*d.*		6	8
5.	For 1 p^r sissars and ⅛ y^d strowds		2	½
	" 2 pockett bottles, butter and bread		3	
	" cash paid for mending Nathanael his buckles			4
16.	" 1 lb. butter, do. sugar, del^d Nathanael his wife, who being with child, desired care might be taken of her in his absence, pr. order of Mr. Horsfield		1	
20.	" mending a gun lock for Captn Arndt his comp^y		4	6
	" mending a gun for do		1	6
	To 1 doz. eggs and 1 lb. sugar, deliv^d Nathanael his wife, pr. order of Mr. Horsfield			10
		8	4	5½

Errors excepted by

WM. EDMONDS,

Store Keeper.

---

ernor's message, for committal to memory on the journey."—*Bethlehem Diarist.*

5.

Province of Pensilvania to Bethlehem Tavern, Dr.

For sundries deliv[d] to sundry Indians, &c., per order of Mr. Horsfield:

Date		£	s.	d.
1757. April 12.	" breakfast, dinner, and supper deliv[d] 1 Indian man, 1 Indian woman, with a soldier of Capt. Arndt's Comp[y]........		4	
	" 3½ quarts of cydar for do..................		1	2
	" dinner, supper, and breakfast deliv[d] y[e] Indian Gabriel*..........................		1	4
	" 1½ quart cydar for do......................			6
	" keeping his horse 1 night, with hay and oats....................................		1	
13.	" supper and breakfast for 2 Ind. men and 1 boy....................................		2	6
	" 2 gills of rum..............................			8
16.	" dinner 2 times, and supper deliv[d] 2 Indians....................................		3	
	" 1 qt. cydar..................................			4
			14	6
	" supper and 1 quart of beer for 2 Indians		1	4
18.	" breakfast and dinner for 4 do.....		3	4
	" supper and 1 quart cydar for 3 do.....		1	10
19.	" breakfast and 2 quarts cydar deliv[d] 2 Indians who returned to y[e] Indian country..................................		1	4
	" 2 quarts beer for 2 Ind. women and 2 children............................			8
23.	" dinner, supper, and breakfast for 3 Indians....................................		4	
	" 3 gills of rum and 2 quarts of cydar for do..		1	8
			14	2
	Carr[d] forw[d]............................	1	8	8

* Formerly of Gnadenhütten.

		£	s.	d.
1757.	Bro^t forw^d	1	8	8
April 23.	For supper 2 times, breakfast and dinner for 2 Indians		3	8
	" 1 quart of beer and 1 gill of rum			8
24.	" supper and 3 quarts cydar deliv^d to do		2	
25.	" breakfast and 2 quarts cydar for do		1	4
	" supper and 1 pint cydar for 2 do		1	2
26.	" breakfast and 1 quart cydar for 1 do			8
	" supper and 1 quart cydar for Zaccheus and his wife		1	4
27.	" breakfast and 1 gill of rum for do		1	
	" 1 quart cydar for Nicodemus.			4
			12	2
	" supper and 2 gills of rum deliv^d Joel, Tom Evans, and their mother		2	2
28.	" 2 gills of rum for do. and Zaccheus, &c.			8
	" breakfast and supper for 4 Indians		3	4
	" 1 quart beer for do			4
	" dinner and supper and 1 quart cydar, for Zaccheus and his wife		2	4
30.	" 2 gills rum for do			8
	" keeping Zaccheus' horse 4 days		2	8
	" supper, 1 gill of rum, and 1 quart cydar for Tom Evans and his son with the soldier		2	2
May 1.	" breakfast for 2 of do. and 1 gill of rum		1	
	" dinner and supper for Tom Evans		1	
2.	" breakfast and 1 gill of rum for do			8
			17	
	" keeping Zaccheus' horse 2 days		1	4
	" ½ pint rum for do. going to Lancaster			6
	" 1 gill rum for his wife, being not well			4
4.	" 3 gills of do. and 2 quarts beer for sundry Indians		1	8
	Carr^d forw^d		3	10

		£	s.	d.
1757.	Bro[t] forw[d].........................		3	10
May 4.	For supper and breakfast for 2 men, who went with y[e] Indians to Fort Allen....		2	
	" 3 quarts of beer for do......................		1	
	" keeping their horses on hay and oats 2 nights.......................................		2	
	" breakfast and 2 gills of rum deliv[d] Nathanael and Zacharias going with a message from y[e] Governor to Tattiuskund.......................................		1	8
9.	" dinner, supper, and 2 quarts beer deliv[d] Moses Tattamy............................		1	8
	" supper, 1 quart beer, and 1 gill rum for Sam Evans, his wife and 2 children, with a soldier of Capt. Arndt..........		2	4
10.	" breakfast and 1 gill of rum for y[e] soldier			10
			15	4
	" breakfast, dinner, and 1 gill of rum for Sam Evans................................		1	2
	" do. and do. and 1 do. of do. and 1 quart of beer for Tattamy...........		1	6
	" supper and 1 quart of beer for do.........			9
11.	" breakfast, dinner, supper, 1 gill of rum, and 1 quart of beer for do...............		2	
12.	" breakfast and 1 gill of rum for do........			8
	" keeping his horse 3 days on hay and oats.......................................		3	6
17.	" dinner, supper, and breakfast deliv[d] a soldier of Capt. Arndt's company......		1	4
	" 1 gill of rum and 1 quart of beer.........			8
18.	" supper for Tattamy's son....................			6
19.	" breakfast, supper, and 1 gill of rum for do...		1	2
			13	3

1757.		£	s.	d.
May 19.	For supper and 1 quart beer deliv[d] Tattamy, Gabriel's wife and 2 children, with a soldier		2	6
20.	" breakfast for Tattamy and the soldier....			8
	" 1 quart of beer for do			4
	" breakfast for Tattamy's son			4
	" dinner and supper for Tattamy and his son		2	
21.	" breakfast and 1 gill of rum for do		1	4
	" dinner and 1 quart of beer for do		1	4
	" keeping Tattamy's horse on hay 2 days..		1	4
26.	" dinner and 1 gill of rum for Tattamy....			10
			10	8
	" supper and 1 pint beer for do			10
	" dinner and 1 pint beer for a soldier			8
27.	" 1 gill of rum, breakfast, dinner, and 1 pint of beer for Tattamy		1	4
	" dinner and 1 qt. of cydar for 2 Indians* that came from Lancaster		1	4
			4	2
	Sum total	5	1	3

* On their way to the Susquehanna with a message from Governor Denny to Teedyuscung, containing an account of the proceedings of the treaty held at Lancaster between the 12th and 20th of May, a promise to redress all grievances, and an invitation for him to come down with his uncles, the Senecas, when it suited his convenience.

VIII. ACCOUNT DELIVD YE COMMISSIONERS IN PHILADELPHIA, PR. WM. EDMONDS, DATED YE 28 MAY, 1757.

Province of Pensilvania to the Stewards of Bethlehem, Dr.

1757.		£	s.	d.
May 27.	For sundries deliv^d 82 Indians in Bethlehem since 11th April last, viz.:			
	2893 lbs. of bread, @ 1¼d	15	1	4¼
	484 lbs. of beef, @ 3½d..................	7	1	2
	20 lbs. of gammons, @ 5½d............		9	2
	93 galls. of milk, @ 6d....................	2	6	6
	73 bush^ls of Indian corn, @ 2s. 6d.......	9	2	6
	½ do. beans, @ 4s........................		2	
	½ do. salt, @ 5s..........................		2	6
	10 galls. of soft sope, @ 1s................		10	
	3⅜ gall^s linseed oil for lamps, @ 4s.....		13	6
		35	8	8¼

IX. AN ACCOUNT SENT TO YE COMMISSIONERS, DATED YE 6 AUGUST, 1757.

1757.	Province of Pensilvania to the Stewards of Bethlehem, Dr.	£	s.	d.
June 4.	For hire of a waggon to Easton with 3 men to guard. do. for carrying powder and lead to do. for the use of ye Province, pr. order of Mr. Horsfield...		18	
22.	To the tavern for sundries deliv^d 11 soldiers. (See *Voucher* 1)...............................		19	10
24.	For sundries deliv^d on acct. of ye Ind^n messenger, pr. order of Mr. Horsfield. (See *Voucher* 2).....................................	6	12	7¼
July 12.	To Bethlehem Store for 20 lbs. gun powder for the use of Captn Wetherhold's company, @ 3s. 6., pr. order of Capt. Arndt. (See *Voucher* 3).	3	10	
	Carr^d forw^d..............................	12		5¼

		£	s.	d.
1757.	Bro[t] forw[d].	12		5¼
July 12.	To 1 cask for do.		2	
	For sundries deliv[d] Jo Peepy and Hugh Crawfford. (See *Voucher* 4)	4	17	2
	For medicines, &c. &c., for Capt[n] Harris, &c. (See *Voucher* 5)	1	18	
29.	To Bethlehem Store for sundries. (See *Voucher* 6)		9	7
Aug. 1.	For sundries deliv[d] on acct. of y[e] Indians coming and going to and from Fort Allen, pr. order of Mr. Horsfield. (See *Voucher* 7)	6		
	" stocking and repairing, &c., sundry guns, &c. (See *Voucher* 8)	9	4	6
5.	To the Tavern for sundries deliv[d] y[e] Indians coming from and going to Fort Allen, pr. order of Mr. Horsfield. (See *Voucher* 9)	29	17	6
	For sundries deliv[d] y[e] Indians opposite Bethlehem, since y[e] 27 last May. (See *Voucher* 10)	26	14	
		91	3	2¼

Vouchers belongg to the foregoing Account.

1.

		£	s.	d.
1757.	Bill of fare for eleven soldiers at Bethlehem Tavern, June 21 and 22, 1757:			
June 21.	For supper for do. @ 6*d*		5	6
	" 5 quarts beer		1	8
22.	" breakfast for do., @ 6*d*		5	6
	" dinner for do., and 5 quarts beer		7	2
			19	10

N.B.—The Insign is included, and came with the soldiers to have their arms repaired at Bethlehem.

Received the above for myself and 10 men at s[d] tavern, pr.

JACOB SCHNEIDER,* Insign.

* Jacob Schneider, commissioned Ensign in Capt. Arndt's company, 1st Battalion Pennsylvania Regiment, May 19, 1756.

2.

Province of Pensilvania to the Stewards of Bethlehem, Dr.

		£	s.	d.
	For sundries deliv[d] y[e] Indians messengers, Nathanael, Zacharias, and Paul,* pr.			
1757.	order of Mr. Horsfield:			
May 28.	For 15½ lbs. of bacon, deliv[d] them for their journey to Diaogu (*omitted in last account*), @ 3½*d*..............................		7	1¼
June 4.	" soling and mending Zaccheus' shoes.....		2	6
16.	" an express to Easton with letters to Maj. Parsons on the Province service.......		5	
24.	" hire of 2 men 6 days for going with them to Phila[a], and staying for them there, @ 3*s*. per day each.........................	1	16	
	" cash paid for hire of 5 horses.............	1	11	
	" cash paid for expenses on the road........	2	11	
		6	12	7¼

---

* On the 18th of June the first two reached Bethlehem on their return, with the intelligence that the King would be in the settlements within eight days. They set out on the 21st for Philadelphia to report to the Governor. In a letter to Deputy Croghan, under date of June 23, the Governor writes: "The messengers, Nathaniel and Zacharias, are returned with an answer that Teedyuscung was one hundred miles above Diahoga, that he had been very diligent in performing the several matters he undertook at Easton, that he was exceedingly glad to receive my message, and would set out about eight days after the messengers. He may be expected here about the first week in July, or perhaps he may come sooner. I give you this notice by the express, desiring you will order your matters so as to have time enough to attend the treaty, which I will not open unless you be present. Teedyuscung desires I should be ready, and not detain him longer than is absolutely necessary."

Paul had accompanied *Tapeuscung*, June 1st, on his return to the King, with a reply from Government.

3.

JACOB ARNDT'S ORDER, &c., DRAWN ON TIMOTHY HORSFIELD, &c., ON ACCT. OF Y^E PROVINCE.

July 11, 1757.

MR. HORSFIELD:

SIR,—Lieut. Wetherhold hath desired me to write an order that you might be pleased to send with the Bearer hereof, Peter Reg, Twenty Pounds of Powder and Sixty Pounds of Lead, for the use of Lieut. Wetherhold's men. I hope you will oblige your Friend.

I am your hble. servant,

JACOB ARNDT.

MR. EDMONDS:

Please let the Bearer, Peter Reg, have 20 lbs. powder, and charge it to the Province account.

I am yours,

TIMY. HORSFIELD.

BETHM., July 11, 1757.

Recd of Wm. Edmonds of Bethm Store, the above ordered 20 lbs. of Powder, on acct. of the Province. I say, recd for the use of Capt. Wetherhold's men at Allemängel, pr.

PETER REEG.

N.B.—The above order was drawn in order to be delivered here, by reason they would not get the Powder at Easton, Maj. Parsons being absent.

BETHLEHEM, July 11, 1757.

Recd of ye Province of Pensilvania by the hands of Timy Horsfield, 60 lbs. of Lead for the use of Captn Wetherhold's men Posted at Allemängel, pr.

PETER REEG.

N.B.—I have delivd the above 60 lbs. of Lead out of a Parsell that was in my Hands belonging to ye Province.

TIMY. HORSFIELD.

BETHM., July 11, 1757.

4.

Province of Pensilvania, Dr.

	For sundries deliv^d to Jo Peepy and Hugh			
1757.	Crawfford,* viz.:	£	*s.*	*d.*
May 21.	500 blue wampons, @ 2*s*..................		10	
	2 y^ds Osnabrigs, @ 1*s*. 8*d*..................		3	4
	thread and needles..........................			5
	1 lb. sope....................................			6
	1 y^d blue strowds............................		11	
	5 lbs. powder, @ 3*s*. 6*d*....................		17	6
	8 lbs. lead, @ 8*d*...........................		5	4
	1 large hunting knife.......................		1	8
	1 tin quart..................................		1	4
	2 wooden pipes lined with brass..........		3	2
	1 quire writing paper.......................		1	4
	1 brass inkhorn..............................		2	
	4 lbs. tobacco, @ 4*d*.......................		1	4
	2 combs......................................			8
	1 knife		1	8
	1 bottle......................................			7
	leather for a p^r of shoes....................		1	4
	3½ yds linnen, @ 3*s*. 2*d*., and thread, 4*d*.		11	5
	1 p^r shoes for Crawfford (pumps).........		12	
June 1.	For mending a gun for Capt. Arndt's soldiers		3	8
	" sundries deliv^d ye Indian Zaccheus.......		1	
	" salt deliv^d ye Indians over the water.....		1	3
	" cash paid for shoeing ye Indian Petrus his horse....................................		1	2
	" pipes and tobacco sent† for Teedyuscung			6
	Carr^d forw^d..............................	4	14	2

* Hugh Crawford, an Indian trader, from "*Aughwick* (now Shirleytown, in Huntingdon County), on the great Path to the Ohio," and Jo Peepy, were bearers of dispatches to Sir William Johnson, from Deputy Croghan, at Lancaster, and were fitting out for the journey.

† By Paul and Tapescawen.

		£	s.	d.
1757.	Brot forwd..............................	4	14	2
June 11.	To cash paid Jos. Brown as pr. receipt signed by Crawfford..........................		3	
		4	17	2

The above has been delivd out of Bethlehem Store.

WM. EDMONDS.

5.

Province of Pensilvania to Surgeon at Bethlehem, Dr.

		£	s.	d.
1757.				
June 18.	For medicine and attendance on Captn Harris, the Indian, from ye 18 May to ye 18 June, he having a very dangerous hurt in his arm, attended with a caries or rotteness in the bone.................	1	16	
July 11.	" bleeding the Indian Jo Peepy's wife.....		1	
	" do. the Indian Nathanael's wife....		1	
		1	18	

JOHN MATTHW. OTTO.

Bethm., the 11 July, 1757.

6.

Province of Pensilvania Dr. to Bethlehem for sundries out of the Store.

		£	s.	d.
1757.				
July 29.	For tobacco, pipes, &c., to the Nanticocks* during their stay here, in going to Easton		2	10
	Carrd forwd		2	10

* The Nanticokes ("*tide-water people*"), a small member of the Algonquin family, had their seats, when the Europeans first met them, on the Eastern Shore of Maryland. Thence they migrated northward about 1748, following the course of the Susquehanna, and planting in part at Wyoming and in part higher up the river, at Chenango and Chemung. Five of these Indians halted at Bethlehem on the 29th of

		£	s.	d.
1757.	Bro[t] forw[d].............................		2	10
July 29.	For do. at their departure from Easton.......		2	-
	" 2 sweet cakes for Bill Tattamy*..........			3
	Carr[d] forw[d].............................		5	1

July, on their way to the treaty at Easton. Bro. Spangenberg had a formal interview with them, at which there was the customary exchange of compliments and of wampum. They stated that they had come to condole with their old friends, the Brethren, in their recent losses, expressed regret that intercourse with them had for so long a time been suspended, brought greeting from old Paxanosa, and a message that he and Mohican Abraham intended to pay them a visit. Of these proceedings Bro. Spangenberg prudently advised Weisser, at Easton, in the following letter:

"BETHLEHEM, July 30, 1757.

"SIR,—

"Last night, being in Nazareth, I heard that three Nanticoke chiefs, *John Curtis*, *Tom*, and *Abraham*, were come to Bethlehem, and that they had some words to speak to the Brethren. Their captain intended to go to Easton, and therefore I made haste to return home again. Enclosed is the compliment they made on their way, and the answer we gave them. The reason of their complacence is this, viz.: they were in great want of provisions about four years ago, when they yet lived at Wayomik. They applied to the Brethren who then lived at Gnadenhütten, and wanted to be relieved in their great hunger. The Brethren upon that gave them 60 bushels of flour, which they fetched from our mill at Gnadenhütten. They then came and gave us thanks and told us they would remove from Wayomik and go higher up the Susquehanna, but they would pay us a visit in two years' time again; and this made a particular acquaintance between the Nanticokes and the Brethren. I let you know this because I hope you will acquaint the Governor and Mr. Peters with it if you find it well and think it needful. I will add no more, for I suppose your time is much taken up. But be sure I think often of you and wish you good success in your Treaty.

"Farewell sir, your humble servant

"SPANGENBERG."

* Son of Moses Tatemy.

		£	s.	d.
1757.	Bro[t] forw[d].		5	1
July 29.	For cash paid for mending a gun in Capt[n]. Arndt's comp[y].		2	
	" tobacco and leather for mend[g] shoes.		2	6
			9	7

Paid and deliv[d] as above,

pr. W[M]. EDMONDS, Storekeeper.

7.

Province of Pensilvania to the Stewards of Bethlehem, Dr.

		£	s.	d.
	For sundries deliv[d] on acct. of the Indians coming from and going to Fort Allen,			
1757.	pr. order of Mr. Horsfield:			
June 15.	" hire of 2 men to guard Indian Gabriel, his wife and 2 children, and sundry others to John Hays'.		6	
16.	To John Hays, for conducting said Indians to Uplinger's* as per his acct.		5	
	For stocking a gun pr. order of Col. Weisser, given about y[e] 1st treaty.		17	
29.	" mending a gun lock per order of Capt[n] Arndt.		2	
	Carr[d] forw[d].	1	10	

* Nicholas Opplinger kept public-house on the road to Fort Allen, where said road, on leaving the river just above the Gap, skirts the "Fire-Line Hill" along the Aquanshicola, a mile from its mouth. The house and mill-seat are now owned by Mr. Peter Snyder. "We arrived that night at one Nicholas Opplinger. After I had settled with the landlord next day the Indian account, which amounted to £1. 10*s.* 11*d.*, chiefly for sider, this being the last place where they could get it, we sott off and arrived at Fort Allen by 10 of the clock."—*Weisser's Journal*, Nov. 19, 1756.

		£	s.	d.
1757.	Bro[t] forw[d].	1	10	
July 11.	For an express to y[e] Governor, with letters of Col. Weisser* and expences in the town for his and his horse waiting 3 days	2		
	" an express to y[e] Governor with letters of Mr. Horsfield concerning Teedyuscung's arrival in Fort Allen†	1	5	
	" expences in y[e] town.		3	
23.	" hire of a man to go with Teedyuscung's mother-in-law‡ to Easton at the request of y[e] Governor		5	
	Carr[d] forw[d].	5	3	

---

* Weisser passed through Bethlehem for Easton on July 14. He sent a letter to the Governor by express, in which he informed him of his arrival, and, at the same time, of the friendly disposition of the Delawares. "The Indians," he writes, "are altogether good-natured, and Teedyuscung, considering how much he loves strong drink, behaves very well, and I have not seen him quite drunk since I came, to this time. I find they are all desirous to come to a lasting peace."

† "Last night" (July 5), writes Horsfield to the Governor, "an express came from Capt. Arndt, of Fort Allen, advising me of the King's arrival. The captain writes as follows: 'These are to inform you that Detiuscung is arriv'd here yesterday evening, and there be at present about 200 Indians with him, with young and old. Detiuscung is intended to stay here about five or six days, and in this time he expects 100 Senecas here, and then he is intended to go to Easton in hopes to meet with his Honor the Governor.'"

‡ Erdmuth, mother-in-law of Teedyuscung, formerly of Gnadenhütten, so named for Erdmuth Dorothea, Countess of Zinzendorf. She left for Easton at the request of Governor Denny, to whom Bro. Peter Böhler wrote as follows:

"MAY IT PLEASE YOUR HONOUR,—

"When Capt. Arndt delivered your Honour's Letter to me, Teedyuscung's Wife's Mother was not found at home, she being gone out a couple of miles to seek Huckleberries, and is not expected home be-

		£	s.	d.
1757.	Brot forwd.	5	3	
July 28.	For hire of a man for accompanying 2 Ind. men, 4 women, and 7 children to Easton, and 3 Inds. from do. to Bethlehem.		7	6
	" 1½ bush. Indian corn delivd some Indians returning to Fort Allen..		4	6
Aug. 1.	" hire of a man for going with 10 Indn men, 2 women, and 4 children to Easton		5	
		6		

8.

Province of Pensilvania to the Gunsmith in Bethlehem, Dr.

1757.		£	s.	d.
June 13.	To mending 3 guns for Captn Wetherhold's compy		10	
14.	" mending 1 gun lock for Captn Arndt's compy		1	
29.	" mending 1 do. for do.		4	
July 9.	" " 1 do. for do.		1	6
24.	" stocking, repairing, &c., 15 guns and 1 pistol, pr. order of Jacob Schneider, Insign, viz.:			
	" stocking 8 guns, @ 9s	3	12	
	Carrd forwd.	4	8	6

fore night. Our Brethren will not be wanting on their part to forward her to Easton.

"I am sorry though that yr. Honour has had such a groundless information as if we had refused her going to Easton. None of us did ever hear that Teedyuscung or his wife had desired her mother should come to them, and therefore it could not be that we refused her to go. Hoping that yr. Honour will clear us from such an aspersion, at least in your own mind, I am

"Your Honour's most obedient and
"most obliged humble servant,
"PETER BÖHLER."

		£	s.	d.
1757.	Bro[t] forw[d]	4	8	6
July 24.	To putting a piece on a gunstock		4	
	" repairing 2 old gunstocks and making 2 rammers		2	
	" cleaning and straightening 11 gun barrells	1	2	6
	" making 2 new breech pins, and mend[g] several others		10	
	" mending and sodering a gun barrell		2	
	" boring a touch hole		1	
	" making 6 new loops to several barrels		2	
	" making 2 new brass loops to the gun stocks		1	
	" making 7 cross screws through the breech pins and 4 plates to the triggers		5	6
	" making a sight and band on a barrell		1	6
	" cleaning 10 gun locks		5	
	" repairing 2 plates for gun locks		3	6
	" mending 3 cocks and hardening 6 hammers		6	
	" hardening, &c., 6 hammers and making 2 screws		5	
	" making 7 screws, &c. &c		7	
	" " 2 screws for tumblers, and a plate on a cock		2	6
	" making 15 screws for gun locks		7	6
	" " 1 brass guard for a pistol		2	6
July 30.	" " 1 screw for a tumbler, and hardening a steel hammer for a soldier from Fort Allen		1	6
Aug. 1.	" making a wiper for a rival, stealing a hammer, mending a screw for the gun lock for the Indian *Tonnis*, pr. order of Mr. Croghan		4	
		9	4	6

DANIEL KLIEST,
Locksmith.

BETHLEHEM, 1 Augs[t], 1757.

9.

Province of Pensilvania to Bethlehem Tavern, Dr.

Date	Particulars	£	s.	d.	£	s.	d.
	For sundries deliv[d] y[e] Indians coming from and returning to Fort Allen, &c. &c., pr. order of Mr.						
1757.	Horsfield:						
May 27.	To supper and 1 quart of beer for Tatamy.......... £			10			
28.	" 3 meals and 1 do. of do. for do....................		1	10			
29.	" 3 meals and 1 gill of rum for do....................		1	10			
30.	" 2 meals and 1 q[t] beer for do....................		1	4			
	" 1 q[t] wine and 2 quarts beer for 8 Indians with Hugh Crawford*.......		2	8			
31.	" 1 meal and 1 gill of rum for Tatamy..............			10			
	" 1 quart and ½ pint of rum for Jo Peepy to take on the road to Fort Allen.............		1	11			
						11	3
	Sundries deliv[d] 8 Indians and 1 soldier coming from Lancaster, as per acct., signed by Mr. Hugh Crawford:						
June 5.	To supper for 3 Indians and 1 soldier............ £		2				
	Carr[d] forw[d]					11	3

* While at Bethlehem, and fitting out for his journey to Sir Wm. Johnson.

Date	Item	s.	d.	£	s.	d.
1757.	Bro^t forw^d................................				11	
June 5.	To 2 gills of rum and 2 quarts of cydar for do. £	1	4			
6.	" 1 meal and 1½ gill of rum for do...............	2	6			
	" keeping their horses on hay and oats...........	1				
	" 1 supper for 4 Indians...	2				
7.	" 1 meal for 6 Indians and 1 soldier.................	3	6			
12.	" 3 gills of rum and 3 q^{ts} cydar for 5 Indians and 1 soldier...........	2				
	" 1 supper for do...........	3				
					17	4
13.	" 2 meals for do........... £	6				
	" 3 gills of rum and 6 q^{ts} cydar for do............	3				
15.	" 2 meals for 5 Indians...	5				
	" 2 quarts of cydar for do.		8			
	" 1 pint and 1 gill of rum deliv^d at their return to Fort Allen...........	1	1			
	" 2 meals for Moses Tatamy coming from Easton....................	1				
	" ½ gill of rum and ½ gill of rum for do...........		4			
	" keeping his horse.........		8			
					17	9
17.	" 2 meals for 1 Indian and 1 soldier.................. £	2				
	" ½ gill of rum and 1 q^t cydar for do...........		6			
18.	" 1½ gill of rum for 2 Indians and 1 soldier....		6			
					9	6
	Carr^d forw^d......................			2	6	4

				£	s.	d.
1757.	Bro^{t} forw^{d}..................................			2	6	4
June 18.	To supper for 5 Indians and 1 soldier.................. £	3				
19.	" 2 meals for 2 Indians and 2 soldiers..	4				
	" 2 gills of rum and 2 quarts of cydar for do.	1	4			
22.	" 1 meal and 4 gills of rum for 6 Indians and 1 soldier.................	9	8			
	" 10 quarts of beer for do.	3	4			
26.	" 1 meal and 4½ gill of rum for do...............	5				
	" 3 quarts of beer for do...	1				
				1	10	4
	" 1 meal for 4 Indians and 1 soldier.................. £	2	6			
	" 3 gills of rum and 4 quarts of beer...........	2	4			
27.	" 3 meals, 4 gills of rum, 6 q^{ts} of beer for do.....	10	10			
28.	" 1 meal, 3 gills of rum, 2½ do. for do..........	4	4			
29.	" 1 meal, 1½ gill of rum, 1½ q^{t} of beer for 2 Indians and 1 soldier..	2	6			
				1	2	6
July 3.	" supper and breakfast and 1 gill of rum deliv^{d} to an express from Fort Allen..................... £	1	4			
	" 1 peck of oats for his horse.....................	1				
4.*	" supper for 1, 5 pint beer,					
	Carr^{d} forw^{d}...............................			4	19	2

* Amid the excitement prevalent in view of the impending Treaty, and the passing and repassing of Indians and soldiers, the Brethren

		s.	d.	£	s.	d.
	Bro^{t} forw^{d}...............................			4	19	2
1757.	and 5 half gill rum, deliv^{d} *Tom Evans** and 2 other Indians coming from Easton... £	1	8			
July 5.	To supper and breakfast deliv^{d} an express from Fort Allen...............	1				
	" 1 gill of rum and 1 q^{t} of beer to do...............		8			
	" 1 peck of oats and pasture for his horse.......	1	6			
					7	2
10.	" 2 meals for 9 Indians, viz., *Solomon*, *Emmas*,† &c. &c., coming from Philadelphia..... £	9				
	" 5½ q^{ts} beer and 4½ gill of rum for do..........	3	4			
11.	" meals for do...............	9				
	" 5½ q^{ts} of beer and 4½ gill of rum for do......	3	4			
	" 2 meals for *Sam Evans* and 1 soldier coming from Easton............	2				
	" 2 q^{ts} of beer for do.......		8			
	Carr^{d} forw^{d}...............................			5	6	4

commenced their annual harvest on "*July* 4," without intermitting the festivities with which they were wont to mark the ingathering of the fruits of the earth. The women with sickles, and under an escort of Indians, in one company, and the men in another, moved in procession, amid the notes of flutes and horns, to the fields that lay to the east and west of the town.

* One of the Harris family.

† Quære—Amos Teedyuscung?

				£	s.	d.
	Bro^{t} forw^{d}................................			5	6	4
1757. July 12.	To 1 meal and 1 q^{t} beer for do	1	4			
	" keeping their horses on hay and oats...........	2	3			
				1	10	11
16.	" 2 meals and 1 q^{t} beer for *Abraham*,* who came from Philadelphia......	1	4			
	" 4 q^{ts} beer and ½ gill rum for 3 Indians and 1 soldier.................	1	6			
	" 1 peck of oats for their horses.....................		6			
17.	" breakfast and ½ gill of rum for *Abraham*......		8			
25.	" 1 meal, 1 gill of rum, and 1 q^{t} beer deliv^{d} to an express from Easton..	1	2			
	" ½ peck of oats for his horse		6			
					5	8
27.	" dinner, 9 q^{ts} cydar, and 9 gills of rum deliv^{d} to 17 Indians and 1 soldier from Fort Allen £	15				
	" supper, 9 q^{ts} cydar, 9 gills rum for do.........	15				
28.	" breakfast, do. do. for do.	15				
	" dinner and 10 q^{ts} cydar for 17 Indians..........	11	10			
	" supper, 9 q^{ts} cydar, 9 gills rum for do.........	14	6			
	" keeping 6 horses 2 days and 2 nights for do....	12				
				4	3	4
	Carr^{d} forw^{d}..........................			11	6	3

* Quære—Mohican Abraham?

					£	s.	d.
1757.	Bro[t] forw[d]................................				11	6	3
July 28.	To 2 meals, 6 q[ts] cydar, and 1½ gill of rum for 3 Indians..................	£	5	6			
29.	" dinner, 4 q[ts] cydar, and 4 gills of rum deliv[d] 7 Indians and 1 soldier from Fort Allen........		6	8			
	" supper, 2 q[ts] cydar, and 4 gills of rum for do..		7	4			
	" 2 meals, 3 q[ts] beer, 3 gills rum, 3 pint cydar for Nathanael and 2 other Indians from Easton....................		5	6			
30.	" breakfast, 8½ gills rum, 8½ q[ts] cydar, for 17 Indians..................		14	2			
					1	19	2
	" breakfast, 5 pint beer, and 2½ gill rum for 5 Indians..................	£	4	2			
	" dinner, 5 gills rum, and 5 q[ts] beer for 9 Indians and 1 soldier from Fort Allen........		8	4			
	" dinner and 4 pints cydar for 3 Indians and 1 soldier from Easton...		2	8			
	" supper and 10 q[ts] cydar for 20 Indians...........		13	4			
31.	" breakfast, 12½ q[t] cydar, and 12½ gill rum deliv[d] 25 Indians.........	1		10			
	Carr[d] forw[d]...............................				13	5	5

					£	s.	d
1757.	Bro^{t} forw^{d}..................................				13	5	5
July 31.	To dinner and supper and 26 q^{ts} cydar deliv^{d} 26 Indians..................	£ 1	14	8			
Aug. 1.	" breakfast, 14 q^{ts} cydar, and 10½ gill of rum deliv^{d} 28 Indians......	1	2	2			
	" entertaining 9 horses 2 days and 2 nights......	1	2	6			
	" dinner and supper and 12 q^{ts} cydar for 12 Inds.....................		16				
	" entertaining 9 horses 1 day and 1 night.........		8				
					7	12	8
2.	" breakfast, 3 gills rum, and 7 q^{ts} cydar, deliv^{d} to 14 Indians......	£	10	4			
	" dinner and supper and 14 q^{ts} cydar for do.....		18	8			
	" entertaining 8 horses 1 day and 1 night........		8				
3.	" breakfast, 1 q^{ts} cydar, and 6 gills of rum, deliv^{d} 12 indians		8	8			
	" dinner and supper, 14 q^{ts} cydar and 7 gills rum deliv^{d} 14 Indians	1	1				
	" entertaining 8 horses 1 day and 1 night........		8				
					3	14	8
4.	" breakfast, 3 q^{ts} cydar, and 7 gills rum for 14 Indians..............		10	4			
	Carr^{d} forw^{d}..............................				24	12	9

				£	s.	d.
1757.	Bro^t forw^d...			24	12	9
Aug. 4.	To dinner and supper, 9 q^ts cydar, and 7 gills rum for do.................... £	19	4			
5.	" breakfast, 3 quarts cydar, and 7 gills rum for do.	10	4			
	" dinner and supper, 6 q^ts cydar, and 7 gills rum for do....................	18	4			
				2	18	4
				27	11	1

BETHLEHEM, 6 August, 1757. GEORGE KLEIN.*

10.

Province of Pensilvania to the Stewards of Bethlehem, Dr.

	For sundries deliv^d the Indians opposite Bethlehem, since the 27 last May, viz.:	£	s.	d.
1757. Aug. 5.	To 2377 lbs. bread, @ 1¼d......................	12	7	7¼
	" 293 lbs. beef, @ 3½d......................	4	5	7¼
	" 51 lbs. do. dry, 4½d......................		19	1½
	" 77 lbs. dry venison, @ 3d..................		19	3
	" 5 lbs. bacon, @ 5½d......................		2	3½
	" 24 lbs. veal, @ 2d........................		4	
	" 20⅛ bush. Indian corn, @ 3s..............	3		4½
	" 90½ galls. milk, @ 6d......................	2	5	3
	Carr^d forw^d..............................	24	3	6

* George Klein. Born March, 1705, in Rückstadt. Immigrated to Pennsylvania prior to 1742, and settled in Lancaster County. In 1747 he donated a piece of ground to the Brethren, on which a church and parsonage were erected by them in 1748. In 1749 the worshipers there were organized into a congregation, known as the "Warwick Congregation." In 1755, Klein and his family removed to Bethlehem. He deceased there in July of 1783.

		£	s.	d.
1757.	Bro[t] forw[d]	24	3	6
Aug. 5.	To 3¼ bush. white meal, @ 4*s*		13	
	" ⅝ bush[s] beans, @ 4*s*		2	6
	" attending y[e] above Indians each day from the 27 May to 5 August, 1757. Beeing 70 days, @ 6*d*	1	15	
		26	14	

Bethlehem, 6 August, 1757.

C. F. Örter.*

II.

Ephraim Colver, Tavern Keeper, deliv[d] to Hugh Crawford for the use of the Province, being sent with the Indians that came from Lancaster, and in number 8:

		£	s.	d.
1757.				
May 29.	To dinner (4*s*.), 1 pint wine (1*s*.), 13 qts. cydar (4*s*. 4*d*.)		9	4
	" supper for 6 Indians		2	
30.	" 3 qts. cydar (1*s*.), 1 pint wine (1*s*.)		2	
	" breakfast for 9 Indians and 1 white man		5	
	" dinner for 8 do. and 1 do		4	
	" 8 qts. cydar for 8 do		2	4
	" supper (3*s*.), 4 gills of rum (1*s*. 4*d*.) to do.		4	4
	" breakfast for 10 Indians and 1 white man		5	6
	" keeping 3 horses 2 days on grass, hay and oats		4	9
	" 3 qts. cydar		1	
		2		3

These recv[d] by me,

Hugh Crawford.

Bethlehem Tavern, the 31 May, 1757.

* Christian Frederic Örter, *studios. jur.*, from Schleiz, in Voigtland, came to Bethlehem with the second "Sea Congregation," in November, 1743. In 1744, organist, and in February, 1746, appointed bookkeeper to "The Family." Deceased at Bethlehem, April, 1793.

X. An Account sent to the Commissioners in Philadelphia, dated the 30th August, 1757.

Province of Pensilvania to the Stewards of Bethlehem, Dr.

1757.		£	s.	d.
Aug. 6.	To an account deliv[d]	91	3	2¼
10.	" 20 galls. rum deliv[d] French Margareth, per order of Col. Weisser and George Croghan. (See *Voucher* 1)	6		
	" saddles, &c. &c., mending. (See *Voucher* 2)	9	18	6
	" Bethlehem Store, for sundries. (See *Voucher* 3)	2	2	9
16.	" smith work. (See *Voucher* 4)	1	1	6
25.	" John Matthew Otto's bill. (See *Voucher* 5)	21	12	3
	" stocking, mending, &c. guns. (See *Voucher* 6)	27		
26.	" Bethlehem Tavern, for sundries deliv[d] the Indians from Fort Allen. (See *Voucher* 7)	13	4	10
28.	" sundries deliv[d] Teedyuscung and comp[y] and Capt[n] Arndt. (See *Voucher* 8)	10	18	9½
29.	" sundries deliv[d] the Indians coming from the Treaty. (See *Voucher* 9)	110	3	8¾
	" sundries deliv[d] the Indians opposite Bethlehem. (See *Voucher* 10)	9	15	9
		303	1	10½
	Teedyuscung's wife desired Mr. Horsfield to have a cabbin to live by herself, which he ordered to be built, for which we charge	1		
		304	1	10½

Gentlemen—

The Indians that came from the Treaty* and many others that since that Time Come and Go have ransack't and plundered Our Orchard,

---

* In the afternoon of the 8th of August the Indians began to pass through Bethlehem on their return from the Treaty. Upwards of one hundred came, among them Paxanosa, the Shawanese King of Wyoming, and French Margaret. Colonel Weisser, with a detachment of Provincials under Captain Arndt, was their escort. On the next day the King and his family, Mohican Abraham, and Isaac Nutimus arrived. Some of these unwelcome visitors halted for a few days, and some proceeded as far as Fort Allen and then returned, undecided as to where to go and what to do. During the month full two hundred were counted, men women, and children, among them lawless crowds who annoyed the Brethren by depredations, molested the Indians at the Manakasy, and wrangled with each other over their cups at "The Crown."

Toward evening, on Sunday the 7th of August, Governor Denny and his retinue arrived unexpectedly at Bethlehem, crossed the ferry, and spent the night at "The Crown." He declined accepting the hospitalities of the Brethren on this side, although he was waited on in their behalf by Bro. Böhler. The young men accordingly entertained him with the music of wind and stringed instruments, from boats on the Lehigh in front of his lodgings. He set out for Philadelphia next morning.

The third Treaty at Easton, held between Teedyuscung for the Indians and George Croghan for the English, opened formally on July 27th and closed on August 7th. Governor Denny and members of his Council, and a number of gentlemen from Philadelphia, among whom the Friends were largely represented, were in attendance. There were present of the Indians 159 of Teedyuscung's counselors and warriors, and 119 Senecas; among these, representatives of the "Ten Nations who had only two heads of Kings between them." Pompshire interpreted for the Delaware, Captain Thomas McKee for the Crown, and Conrad Weisser for the Province. Teedyuscung having demanded a secretary to take down the minutes for his revision, it was reluctantly granted him, and he chose Charles Thomson, "Master of the Public Quaker School in the City of Philadelphia"—the same Thomson who in the "Enquiry" pleads the cause of the Delawares with the calm

going into our Gardens &c. shaking the Fruit from the Trees (we did not think proper to forbid them at this critical time with the Indians)

---

composure of an advocate who is conscious of the innocence of his client, and of the certain triumph of truth and justice. After an exchange of the compliments usually preliminary to business on such occasions, and the utterance of mutual assurances of regret for the past and of good hopes for the future, the King stated that the *purchase of lands by the Proprietaries from Indians who had no right to sell, and their fraudulent measurement subsequently, whether by miles or by hours' walks, had provoked the war.* This charge he demanded should be closely investigated, and on evidence appearing that injury had been done to the Indians they should have redress. "In that case," he said, "*I will speak with a loud voice and the nations shall hear me.*" Hereupon he stated his purpose to settle with his countrymen in Wyoming, adding that he would build a town there such as the white men build, and provide for the introduction of the Christian religion among his countrymen and for the education of their children. In conclusion, he demanded that the deeds by which the lands in dispute were held should be produced, that they be publicly read, and that copies be laid before King George and published to all the Provinces under his government. "What is fairly bought and paid for," he went on to say, "I make no further demands about; but if any lands have been bought of Indians to whom these lands did not belong, and who had no right to sell them, I expect satisfaction for these lands. And if the Proprietaries have taken in more lands than they bought of true owners, I expect likewise to be paid for that. But as the persons to whom the Proprietaries may have sold these lands which of right belonged to me have made some settlements, I do not want to disturb them or to force them to leave them, but I expect full satisfaction shall be made to the true owners for these lands, though the Proprietaries, as I said before, might have bought them from persons who had no right to sell them." After some hesitation on the part of the Province, in consequence of difference of opinion as to the propriety of complying with the Delaware's request, in as far as Sir William Johnson had been commissioned by royal appointment to hear the particulars of the charge brought against the Proprietaries, and the Proprietaries' defense, and in consequence of Teedyuscung's reluctance to treat with the Baronet and his Indians, some of whom, he alleged, were parties to the unauthorized sale of lands, the deeds relating to the purchases north of the Tohickon were

and Carrying what they pleased away, but as this is a very great Damage to us especially as our Family is very Large, we hope the Hon-

---

produced and read. Agreeably to his request furthermore, copies of them were promised him for dispatch to Sir William Johnson, to be transmitted by the latter to King George for his determination. Upon this the Delaware rose to his feet, and, taking up two Belts tied together, spoke as follows: "I desire you would with attention hear me. By these two Belts I will let you know what was the ancient method of confirming a lasting peace. This you ought to have considered and to have done; but I will put you in mind. You may remember when you took hold of my hand and led me down, and invited my uncles (several of whom are present), with some from each of the Ten Nations, when we had agreed, we came down to take hold of one of your hands, and my uncles came to take hold of your other hand. Now, as this day and this time are appointed to meet and confirm a lasting peace, we, that is, I and my uncles, as we stand, and you, as you stand, in the name of the great King, three of us standing, we will all look up, and by continuing to observe the agreements by which we shall oblige ourselves one to another, we shall see the clear light, and friendship shall last to us, and to our posterity after us forever. Now, as I have two Belts, and witnesses are present who will speak the same by these Belts, Brothers, in the presence of the Ten Nations who are witnesses, I lay hold of your hand (taking the Governor by the hand), and brighten the chain of friendship that shall be lasting, and whatever conditions shall be proper for us to agree to may be mentioned afterwards. This is the time to declare our mutual friendship. Now Brother the Governor, to confirm what I have said I have given you my hand, which you were pleased to rise and take hold of. I leave it with you. When you please, I am ready Brother, if you have anything to say as a token of confirming the peace, I shall be ready to hear, and as you rose I will rise up, and lay hold of your hand. To confirm what I have said I give you these Belts."

"We now rise and take you into our arms," replied the Governor, "and embrace you with the greatest pleasure as our friends and Brethren, and heartily desire we may ever hereafter look on one another as Brethren and children of the same parents. As a confirmation of this we give you this Belt." Gave a very large white Belt, with the figures of three men upon it, representing his Majesty, King George, taking

orable the Commissioners will Generously consider this Affair, and make us an equitable Allowance for the Damage.

I am in behalf of
the Brethren, Gentlemen
Your Humble Servant,

BETHLEHEM, Aug 30th, 1757. C. F. ÖRTER.

Vouchers belongg to the foregoing Account.

I.

1757. Province of Pensilvania, Dr.
Received on acct. of the Province three men's saddles, @ 35*s*. each. They being fifteen shillings dearer than the order, but they being good, I chose them instead of 2 lbs. vermilion, rather than to stay longer. Also
2 snaffle bridles, @ 4*s*. each.
20 galls. rum, in four caggs, @ 6*s*. per gall £6

Her mark
X
FRENCH MARGARET.*

BETHM., 10 August, 1757.

---

hold of the Five Nation King with one hand, and Teedyuscung, the Delaware King, with the other, and marked with the following letters and figures: G.R., 5N., D.K., for King George, Five Nations, Delaware King.

* French Margaret, a Canadian, and niece of Madame Montour, was living, prior to 1745, with her Mohawk husband, on the Alleghany. In that year Martin Mack met her at the lodge of her cousin, *Andrew Sattelihu*, on an island in the Susquehanna, near Shamokin. In 1753 she was residing in a village of her own at the mouth of Lycoming Creek (quære—Newbury?) a few miles west of Montoursville. Scull's map of 1759 notes it as "*French Margaret's Town.*" Here Mack called upon her in the summer of 1753. "At 9 A.M. August 28," he writes in his Journal, "Bro. Grubé and I arrived at French Margaret's. She received us heartily, conducted us to her lodge, and set milk and watermelons before us. 'Do you remember me, mother?' I asked. 'I do,' she said, 'but I have forgotten where and when I met you.' 'On the island below, at Sha-

2.

Province of Pensilvania to the Sadler in Bethlehem, Dr.

1757.		£	s.	d.
Aug. 10.	To 3 new hunting saddles, @ 35s.	5	5	
	" 2 snaffle bridles..................		8	
	deliv^d French Margaret, pr. order of Col. Weisser and Mr. George Croghan.			
	Carr^d forw^d........................	5	13	

mokin,' I replied; 'eight years ago when my wife and I were spending some time among the Indians there.' She at once recalled the occasion of our first meeting, and signified her satisfaction at our having traveled so far to visit her. In course of conversation, for she was very communicative, she stated that her son and son-in-law had been killed in the winter while on a maraud against the Creeks. On asking permission to deposit our packs with her, until our return from the Delaware town of *Quenischachschachky* (Linden), 'Oh!' said she, 'the Indians there have been drinking hard the past weeks, and you will likely find them all drunk.' On our return she gave us a refreshing draught of milk, and entertained us with family news, speaking of *Andrew*, and of her husband *Peter Quebec*, who she said had not drunk rum within six years. She has prohibited its use in her town, and yet although she has initiated other reformatory measures within her little realm, she enjoys the respect and confidence of her subjects. Margaret's children understand French, but are averse to speaking it."

This lesser Indian queen frequently attended treaties, at Easton, Philadelphia, and at Albany. Sometimes she interpreted. Government, desirous of retaining the Montour influence for the English, always met her with marked deference; and yet she was an uncertain ally, as appears from Weisser's statement to Peters in a letter written to the Secretary in May of 1755. "French Margaret with some of her Family is gone to the English Camp in Virginia, and her son Nicklaus is gone to Ohio to the French Fort. I suppose they want to join the stronger Party, and are gone to get information."

In July of 1754, French Margaret and her Mohawk husband and two grandchildren, traveling in semi-barbaric state, with an Irish groom and six relay and pack-horses, halted a few days at Bethlehem on their way to New York. During her stay she attended divine

		£	s.	d.
1757.	Bro^t forw^d	5	13	
Aug. 10.	To repairing 2 saddles for Patshenosh*	2		
	" Leather for mending shoes, &c. &c		3	6
	" 1 new saddle and bridle for Teedyuscung	2		
	" repairing 1 bridle		2	
		9	18	6

GOTTLIEB LANGE.†

3.

Province of Pensilvania, for sundries deliv^d at Bethlehem Store, Dr.

		£	s.	d.
1757.				
Aug. 8.	To pipes, &c		2	
9.	" 6¼ yds. linnen, @ 3*s.* 2*d.*, to make a shrowd, cap, &c., for Bill Tattamy		19	9½
	Carr^d forw^d	1	1	9½

---

worship, expressed much gratification at the music and singing, and was also pleased to find Sisters who were conversant with French. (One of these was Sister Judith Otto, relict of David Bruce, and daughter of John Stephen Benezet.)

* *Paxanosa*, or *Paxnous*, "in April of 1754 the chief man in Wyoming," affected loyalty toward the English on the alienation of the Delawares and his countrymen, although he maintained but a doubtful neutrality. The chief was always well inclined to the Brethren, and had befriended them signally at the time of the outbreak of hostilities along the Susquehanna. He had not visited Bethlehem since the occasion of his wife's baptism in February of 1755. From her he now brought greeting, and regrets that lameness prevented her from coming to visit her Brethren and Sisters. Paxanosa set out on his return on the 13th, in company of Mohican Abraham. In May of 1758 he removed with his family to the Ohio country. Paxanosa was the last Shawanese King, west of the Alleghanies.

† John Gottlieb Lange, master saddler for "the Family," came to Bethlehem with Henry Jorde's Colony in June of 1750. On the abrogation of the Economy in 1762, he bought the saddlery stock on hand and tools, at a valuation of £144. Deceased in July of 1764.

1757.		£	s.	d.
	Bro^{t} forw^{d}	1	1	9½
Aug. 10.	To cash p^{d} for 4 caggs to put French Margaret her rum in		8	
	" a p^{r} of spectacles for Paxinosa		1	
	" fishing hooks for Abraham and him			6
	" a comb, snuff, gingerbread, and sope for Teediuscung		1	10
	" a p^{r} of buckles (1*s.* 8*d.*), pipes and tobacco for Paxinosa		3	
	" salt deliv^{d} for Nicodemus and Abraham, &c., over ye water			7½
	" cash p^{d} for mending Jo Davis* his sadle.		6	
		2	2	9

Errors excepted, pr.
Wm. Edmonds,
Bethlehem Storekeeper.

4.

Province of Pensilvania to the Smith in Bethlehem, Dr.

1757.		£	s.	d.
Aug. 12.	To 2 new tomehakes		6	
	" steeling 6 do.		6	
	" shoeing horses with 6 new shoes		6	
	" mending a pan		2	
16.	" mending and steeling 2 tomehakes, deliv^{d} the Indians that came from ye Treaty, pr. order of Col. Weisser		1	6
		1	1	6

5.

Province of Pensilvania to John Matthew Otto, Dr.

1757.		£	s.	d.
July 28.	To visits, dressing, and curing an impostume in the thigh of Christoph Pock, a soldier of Captn Arndt's Comp^{y}, from ye 9 to 28 July, pr. order of Captn Arndt	2	1	
	Carr^{d} forw^{d}	2	1	

* A Delaware.

		£	s.	d.
1757.	Bro^t forw^d..	2	1	
Aug. 9.	To medicines, visits, attendance, &c. &c., for the Indian Wm. Tattamy,* from ye 8 July to ye 9 August, who was shot through his thigh in the Irish settlement, and having lodged at Mr. John Jones	16	18	9
	Carr^d forw^d	18	19	9

* A son of Moses Tattamy. In the forenoon of July 8, this young Delaware was recklessly shot by a Scotch-Irish lad, a few miles to the northwest of Bethlehem, as he was straying from the main body of Indians who were on their way to Easton, under escort of Capt. Arndt. This unprovoked act excited much remark among the Delawares, and it was feared might serve to embarrass the negotiations at the impending Treaty. Dr. Otto, of Bethlehem, was called in the afternoon to visit the wounded man, and had him conveyed that evenng to the house of Mr. John Jones, a farmer living a mile east of the Bethlehem tract. Here he attended him. Of this occurrence, Capt. Arndt makes the following statement in a letter to the Governor, dated

"EASTON, July 8, 1757.

"MAY IT PLEASE YOUR HONOR:

"SIR,—According as Titiuskong arrifed att fort Allin the 4th of these Instend July, with aboud 150 Indins, with young and old, and aboud fivety was there allredey with young and old, and according as Titiuskong hath Informed me that above one houndered of the Sinekers Indins would Come after him, that he was Intented to waid fore them att fort Allin six or seven Days, but as I fal wery shord with Provisions I was obligd to march with the Indins yesterday from fort Allin, there number was 150 that went with me to Easton, and the Remainder Stayd att fort Allin * * * sum went back with a litle Provision fore there famly Down, and yeasterday I Came so fare with them as to John Haysis, and there Wee Stayd all night and these Day, wee set off from there and arrifed Safe at Easton, with all the Indins except one, William Dattame, an Indin, went withoud my Knowledge, and against my orders to Bathloham, and it hapened on his Road Wen he had Turned off that a foolish wite boy, aboud 15

		£	s.	d.
1757.	Bro[t] forw[d]...............................	18	19	9
Aug. 20.	To ointment deliv[d] Lieut. Engel* for a wound in his leg...........................		4	
	" medicine del[d] Jo Peepy's wife for a rheumatism on the arm.....................		6	
	" medicines deliv[d] and dressing Ind[n] Nicodemus's son, having a sore leg..........		10	
	" medicines for 6 Indians, and bleeding...		7	6
	Carr[d] forw[d]............................	20	7	3

years of eage, folowed him, and Shot him in the Right Thigh of the out sid bone, but not morterly, and Just when I Came with the Indins and Ten men of my Company to escord the Indins to Easton, William Hays Came after me excepress with these Information, that William Dattamy was Shot, and according as mayor Parsons is absand from Easton, I considered that it was wery necessecery to stay with my men att Easton, fore to Protackt the Indins and to hinder all Scrobel and * * * which might fall out between Wite People and the Indins, until I shall Receve your houners fourter orders.

"I am Sir, with all due Respect,

"Your humble Servind att Command,

"JACOB ARNDT."

Dr. Otto reported on the case to Justice Horsfield as follows:

"BETHLEHEM, 27th July, 1757.

"MR. HORSFIELD:

"SIR,—I yesterday attended Wm. Tatamy twice; His Wound looks well, is without inflammation, and discharges its Pus regularly. The swelling is also gone. To Day he turned himself alone, which he has not been able to do before, so that I believe, with good nursing and attendance, if nothing unforeseen happen, he may, by God's Help, recover. The violent Pain he complains of, at times, I apprehend, proceeds from some of the bones in his Groin being shot thro', or at least

* Andrew Engel, commissioned Lieutenant in Capt Arndt's Company of 1st Battalion of 1st Pennsylvania Regiment, January 5, 1756.

		£	s.	d.
1757.	Brot forwd.	20	7	3
Aug. 25.	To visits, medicines, and attendance delivd Conrad Haffner, a soldier of Lieut. Engel's compy, from ye 10 July to 25 August, having a gored eye.	1	5	
		21	12	3

JOHN MATTHEW OTTO.

BETH., 25 August, 1757.

---

the tendinous parts being much lacerated. You may depend upon it, I shall do all in my power to perfect a Cure.

"I am Sir,

"Your most humble Servt,

"JOHN MATTHEW OTTO."

And to Governor Denny in these words:

"BETHM., July 31st, 1757.

"MAY IT PLEASE YOUR HONOR:

"By the letter I sent last Thursday, the 28th July, I gave your Honor an Account how it was with Wm. Tatamy, and the Circumstances of his Wound that Morning. The same Evening I found him in great Pains, the Wound did not look so well as before, and discharged very little of its Pus, and that mixt with Blood, and he had a very bad Night.

"*Jul. 29th.* In the Morning came nothing from the Wound but a little Blood, mix'd with Water. In the Evening he felt some Ease from his great Pains, but was Weaker than ever before, and his Pulse was very low, in which Circumstances Dr. Moore has seen him, who promis'd me to acquaint your Honor therewith. In the Night thereupon he slept pretty much, but mostly out of Weakness. Yesterday he continued to sleep now and then, and his Pulse was something better; he slept also last night better than before.

"This Morning, it being Sunday, Jul. 31st, I open'd his Thigh on the lower part, where for several Days I had observed a gathering, and the opening discharg'd half a Pint of extravasated Blood, with some offensive Matter. As soon as I had made the Incision, the Indian said he did feel himself much eased, and I hope it will have a

6.

Province of Pensilvania to the Gun Smith in Bethlehem, Dr.

For sundry work for the Indians that came from the Treaty at Easton, pr. order of Conrad Weisser and Georg Croghan, Esq., and by the direction of the Indian chiefs Pachenosa and Abraham,* viz.:

1757.		£	s.	d.
Aug. 5.	To making a cock and cleaning and mending a gun lock....................................		4	6
	Carr^d^ forw^d^..............................		4	6

good Effect. His Hands and Feet which have been almost continually cold, I have found to-day in a natural Warmth.

"I shall further acquaint your Honor how I find him from day to day.

"I am your Honor's

"Most obedient Humble Servant,

"JOHN MATTHEW OTTO."

Teedyuscung, in the second session of the Conference, on July 26, called the Governor's attention to the outrage perpetrated on William Tattamy. "One of the messengers," he said, "who was employed in conveying your messages to us, sent to promote this good work of peace, is now in a dangerous condition, having been shot by one of your young men. As I desire to be used with justice according to your laws, I insist that if this young man die, the man who shot him may be tried by your laws, and die also, in the presence of some of our people, who may witness it to all the nations that the English have done them justice."

The Governor, in reply to this injunction, after reminding the King of the uncertainty of life in times of war, told him that the man who had committed the act was held in confinement, and promised that in case the Indian died of the wound, the former should be tried by the laws of the country which required blood for blood, and in the

* Mohican Abraham, or Captain Abraham, or *Abraham Shabasch*, one of the first converts from the Indians; first of Shecomeco, and then of Gnadenhütten. Withdrew from that mission in 1754. Deceased in Wyoming in December of 1762.

		£	s.	d.
1757.	Bro^{t} forw^{d}..........		4	6
Aug. 9.	To do. a foresight for a soldier from Fort Allen..			6
	" do. a breech screw and steel for a gun...		5	6
	" drawing out ye barrel and making 2 sights to it..		3	6
	" stocking a long gun, a new lock, cleaning, filing, and straightening the barrel, and making a loop in it....................	1	6	10
	" stocking, cutting over, cleaning, mending, &c., a rifle..................................	1	16	10
Aug. 10.	" mending sundry gun locks..................		17	
	" stocking a gun, making a brass attire, sodaring the barrel, mending the lock, &c..	1	9	6
	" stocking a riffle, making sundry screws, a breach pin, a screw plate, a wiper, &c.	1	8	8
	" mending and repairing a gun...............		5	
	" stocking a gun, making a sight, &c........		10	6
11.	" cutting over a riffle, making a breach pin, mending the stock and the lock, &c. &c................................	1	3	4
	" mending a gun lock..........................		5	
	" " " and cleaning the barrel..		4	6
	" stocking a gun, making a breach plate, &c.		18	8
	" repairing a rifle with 2 barrells and mending the locks................................		7	10
	Carr^{d} forw^{d}................................	11	7	8

presence of such of his countrymen as he the King should depute to attend the trial. This promise he confirmed by a string; and turning to the afflicted father, "Brother Moses Tattamy," he said, "you are the father of the young man who has been unfortunately wounded. It gives us great concern that anything of this kind should happen. We have employed the most skillful doctor that is amongst us to take care of him, and we pray that the Almighty would bless the medicines that are administered for his cure. We, by this string of wampum, remove the grief from your heart, and desire no uneasiness may remain there."

		£	s	d.
1757.	Brot forwd.	11	7	8
Aug. 11.	To mending a gun lock			6
15.	" mending a gun stock, making a breach pin, and cleaning the barrell		5	9
	" drawing a gun barrell and mending the lock		5	
		11	18	11
16.	" mending a gun stock, repairing the lock, &c.		12	6
	" mending a gun		2	
	" making a main spring, &c.		4	6
	" repairing a gun, &c.		2	6
	" mending a gun lock, making a steel, &c.		6	6
	" " " and a barrell.		6	
	" repairing a rifle and a lock		7	6
	" " " "		11	6
	" mending a rifle and a lock		9	
	" cutting over a rifle, mending the lock and the stock		12	6
	" mending a gun lock, making a breech pin, &c.		6	6
	" mending a gun lock			6
	" " " making brass loops to the stock		5	6
	" do. and do.		4	6
	" cutting over a rifle, mending the gun lock, making 2 loops and a wiper, &c.		16	8
	" setting a piece on a gun stock		4	
18.	" mending a gun lock		5	
	" stocking a rifle, &c.		15	6
	" " cutting over the barrell, and mending the lock	1	4	
	" mending a gun and a lock		18	
	" cutting over a rifle, and mending the lock		11	6
	" " and making a wiper, a brass guard, &c.		13	
	Carrd forwd.	21	18	1

		£	s.	d.
1757.	Bro[t] forw[d].	21	18	1
Aug. 20.	To stocking 2 rifles (£1 8s.), cutting over and cleaning (15s)........................	2	3	
22.	" mending 2 gun locks, and other repairs to sundry guns, with some brass work.	1	14	4
24.	" mending 2 gun stocks for Capt[n] Arndt's comp[y]....................................		2	6
25.	" do for Lieut. Engel's comp[y].....		14	8
	" mending the locks for do..............		8	
		27		7

7.

Province of Pensilvania to Bethlehem Tavern, Dr.

	For sundries deliv[d] the Indians coming from and going to Fort Allen, &c. &c., viz.:	£	s.	d.
1757. Aug. 6.	To breakfast and cyder for 14 Indians........		9	4
	" dinner and 19 pints cyder for 19 "		12	8
	" supper and 19 " for 19 "		12	8
7.	" breakfast and 19 " for 19 "		12	8
	" dinner and 20 " for 20 "		13	4
	" supper and 29 " for 29 "		19	4
8.	" breakfast and 29 " for 29 "		19	4
	" dinner and 20 " for 20 "		13	4
10.	" supper, 15 half gills rum, and 15 pints beer, deliv[d] 15 soldiers from Easton...		12	6
11.	" breakfast, 15 half gills rum, and 15 pints beer, for do..................................		12	6
15.	" 5 half gills of rum for 5 Indians from Fort Allen.................................			10
	" supper and 5 pints cyder for do...........		3	4
16.	" breakfast, 5 gills rum, and 5 pints cyder for do.................		4	2
	" dinner and 5 pints cyder for do...........		3	4
	" supper and 5 " for do............		3	4
	" " ½ gill rum, and 1 pint cyder for 1 Indian.................................			10
	Carr[d] forw[d]............................	7	13	6

		£	s.	d.
1757.	Brot forwd..............................	7	13	6
Aug. 17.	To breakfast, 6 half gills rum, and 6 pints cyder, for 6 Indians..........................		5	
	" dinner and 6 pints cyder for do...........		4	
	" supper, 6 half gills rum, and 6 pint cyder for do...............................		5	
		8	7	6
	" supper, 8 half gills rum, 8 pint cyder for 8 Indians................................		6	8
18.	" breakfast, 13 half gills rum, and 13 pint cyder, for 13 Indians......................		10	10
	" dinner and 14 pint cyder for 14 Indians..		9	4
	" " ½ gill rum for 1 Indian from Fort Allen.................................			8
	" supper and 8 pint cyder for 8 Indians....		5	4
19.	" breakfast, 18 half gills rum, and 18 pint cyder for 18 Indians.......		15	
	" dinner and 12 pint cyder for 12 Indians..		8	
	" supper and 18 pint " for 18 " ...		12	
20.	" 18 half gills rum delivd 18 Indians returnd to Fort Allen........................		3	
23.	" dinner and supper and 3 half gills rum deliverd 3 Indians coming from Lancaster.*......................................		3	6
	Carrd forwd.............................	12	1	10

* These were the three Nanticokes who had passed through Bethlehem in July, on their way to Easton. On arriving there they desired of Major Parsons that the Governor would grant them an escort to Lancaster, stating that they had come to remove the bones of their friends that had deceased there during the Treaty, to their own town for burial. "The presents were delivered to the Indians in their camp, after which Mr. Croghan condoled with them on account of some of their people who died of Small Pox since they came, and gave them a piece of strowd to cover the graves of the deceased, agreeable to the ancient custom of the Six Nations."—*Minutes of Treaty at Lancaster, May*, 1757.

On the 23d of August, the three reached Bethlehem with the re-

		£	s.	d.
1757.	Brot forwd...............................	12	1	10
Aug. 23	To supper and 2 pint cyder for 2 Indians from Fort Allen...........................		1	4
24.	" breakfast and 2 qts cyder, 2 half gills rum for do..		3	
	" breakfast and dinner and 3 pint cyder for 3 Indians....................................		3	6
	" supper and 3 pint cyder for do............		2	
25.	" breakfast and 12 pint cyder for 14 Indians		9	
26.	" supper and 4 pint cyder for 4 Indians....		2	8
	" 2 gills of rum for do........................			8
	" supper, 1 pint cyder, and ½ gill rum for 1 Indian			10
		13	4	10

GEORGE KLEIN.

8.

Province of Pensilvania to Bethlehem Tavern, Dr.
For sundries delivd Tattitiskund, 13 soldiers,
Captn Arndt, with 2 waggons, pr. order of
Collonel Weisser, viz.:

		£	s.	d.
1757. Aug. 9.	To supper, 16 half gills rum, and 16 pints beer for 16.................................		13	4
	" supper for Captn Arndt and 1 pint wine..		2	
10.	" breakfast, 16 half gills of rum, and 16 pints cyder for 16 do......................		13	4
	" dinner, and 15 pints beer for 15 do.......		10	
	Carrd forwd.............................	1	18	8

mains of their chief, and after a halt of two days, set out for the Indian country. Heckewelder states that "the Nanticokes were known to go from Wyoming and Chemung to fetch the bones of their dead from the Eastern Shore of Maryland, even when the bodies were putrescent, so that they were compelled to take off the flesh and scrape the bones before they could carry them along. I well remember having seen them between 1760 and 1780, loaded with such bones, which being fresh, were highly offensive, as they passed through Bethlehem."

		£	s.	d.
1757.	Bro[t] forw[d]...	1	18	8
Aug. 10.	To supper, 15 half gills rum, and 15 pints cyder for 15..................................		12	6
	" 2 meals for Capt[n] Arndt, and 1½ pint wine..		3	3
11.	" breakfast, 15 half gills rum, and 15 pints cyder for 15..................................		12	6
	" dinner, 14 pints beer for 14.		9	4
	" supper, 14 half gills rum, and 14 pints cyder for 14..		11	8
	" 2 meals for Capt[n] Arndt and 1½ pint of wine...		3	3
12.	" breakfast, 14 half gills rum, and 14 pints cyder for 14..................................		11	8
	" dinner, 14 pints beer for 14....................		9	4
	" 2 meals, and ½ pint wine for Capt[n] Arndt		3	3
	" pasture for 9 horses, 3 days and nights, @ 6*d*. per day for each....................		13	6
	" 40½ peck of oats for do., @ 9*d*. per peck	1	10	4½
	" hire of a horse 2 days.........................		5	
		8	4	3½
26.	" sundries deliv[d] Taduskund* and comp[y], with wife and children, after his return from the Indian country, viz.:			
	" breakfast for him, his wife, and 2 children		1	8
	Carr[d] forw[d]...	8	5	11½

---

* Immediately after the Treaty, Teedyuscung passed through Bethlehem on his way to the Indian country. Thence he returned on the 25th of August, bringing with him a Peace Belt which he had received from four Alleghanies above Wyoming. Bro. Edmonds escorted him to Philadelphia, whither he took the token, for delivery to the Governor. In an interview with him, he stated that the Alleghanies had told him that they had struck their brethren the English, at the instance of the French. "This belt," he proceeded to say, "they gave me to confirm these words, 'We have heard, O Teedyuscung, of the good work of peace you have made with our Brethren the English,

		£	s.	d.
1757.	Bro^t forw^d	8	5	11½
Aug. 26.	To 10 q^ts beer, 3 half gills rum, 1¼ pint wine		5	4
	" dinner for him, his wife, and 3 children.		2	
	Carr^d forw^d	8	13	3½

and that you intend to hold it fast. We will not lift up our hatchet to break that good work you have been transacting.'"—*Colonial Records*, vii. p. 725.

In the afternoon of the 27th, the Brethren Spangenberg, Böhler, and Mack had a conference with the Delaware King, Augustus George Rex acting as interpreter. The interview was sought by the Brethren, and the following is the substance of what transpired on the occasion: "In response to an invitation, Teedyuscung and his family met us this afternoon at a cup of coffee. It was plainly perceptible that the King was gratified at the opportunity given him in this way of expressing his views on the war, on which the conversation soon turned. He told us that he was solicitous for peace, that the Six Nations had empowered him to effect one, and that the other Indians looked to him for its speedy consummation. He then produced a fourfold string of wampum that had been given him by four Alleghany Indians at Tenkhanneck, and also a Belt, both of which he had deposited with Bro. Horsfield on his arrival. They signified, he told us, the intention of the senders to comply with the decisions of the Treaty lately held at Easton, and added that he would carry these tokens to the Governor in person, and that he had dispatched his son and the four abovementioned Indians with the large Belt given him at Easton, to Alleghany. We encouraged him to persevere in his purpose of bringing about peace, even if he were to imperil or lose his life in the attempt; observing at the same time, that peace was an unspeakable blessing, and almost above price. We went on to say that we the Brethren oftentimes ventured our lives in bringing the Gospel to the Heathen who were ignorant of a Saviour, that we had come to the country for this purpose, and not to purchase land of the Indians; that what land we had, we bought of the whites, and finally that we had never purchased nor ever desired to purchase as much as a handsbreadth of land from his countrymen.

"Bro. Spangenberg next asked him for an explanation in reference

		£	s.	d.
1757.	Bro[t] forw[d]................................	8	13	3½
Aug. 26.	To 7 pints wine, 10 q[ts] beer......................		10	4
27.	" breakfast for him, his wife, and 2 Indians		2	
	" 7 pints wine, 5 q[ts] beer, and 2 gills rum..		9	4
	Carr[d] forw[d]...........................	9	14	11½

---

to a string that had been carried by Jo Peepy to Lancaster, accompanied by the words 'I am grieved to see my countrymen at Bethlehem and in the Jerseys held as captives, and forbidden to hunt where they please. I desire that they be set free, that they hunt where they please, and that they remove to Susquehanna'—which string and words were reported to have come from him the King." (See *Minutes of a Conference held with the Indians at John Harris', April 2, 1757, Colonial Records*, vol. vii.)

"Teedyuscung in reply acknowledged that he had sent the message, alleging, however, that the string and words had been dispatched to him for delivery by the Alleghanies.

"Bro. Spangenberg hereupon made the following statement. 'The Brethren are not censurable for the stay of the Indians in the settlements. Twelve years ago (*May 24th to July 12th*, 1745), I journeyed to Onondaga in company with David Zeisberger (*Anousseracheri*), purposely to treat with the Six Nations about the removal of our Indian Brethren and Sisters to the Susquehanna. On my return we made a proposition to the Mohicans at Shecomeco to remove there. They expressed a disinclination to do so. On their arrival at Bethlehem (1746) we laid the proposition before them a second time, telling them it would be well for them to entertain it, and that Bro. Mack, accompanied by *Abraham Shabasch and Gideon Mauweesemen*, were gone to Wyoming to perfect preliminaries. When the time was come for them to give a decisive answer, they told us that they had concluded not to go. We accordingly permitted them to plant at Bethlehem, and then at Gnadenhütten on the Mahoning, where we had purchased lands for them as you the King well know. Augustus can also testify that we had recommended our Indian Brethren at Meniolagomeka to remove to the Susquehanna; and he well remembers that the Brethren Mack and Grubé and myself had proposed the measure in his lodge in the village. We made this proposal to the Indians of Meniolagomeka a second time at Bethlehem. Both offers were re-

		£	s.	d.
1757.	Bro^t forwd................................	9	14	11½
Aug. 27.	To dinner for him and 3 Indians...............		2	
	" 2½ pint wine, 10 q^ts beer....................		5	10
28.	" breakfast for him, his wife, and 3 Indians		2	6
	Carr^d forw^d..............................	10	5	3½

jected. When some time afterward they were compelled to vacate their settlement on the Aquanshicola, we permitted them to remove to Gnadenhütten, as the season was already far advanced and the time for planting corn would be past on their reaching the Susquehanna. A few years ago some Nanticokes came down from the River and asked us to open our arms and permit the Indians to remove to their neighborhood. We told them that while we would not compel our Indian Brethren to remain at Gnadenhütten, we would reluctantly have them go and live among savages who loved wickedness and not the Saviour, adding, that were they to remove there unattended by one of the Brethren who could care for them and their children, the removal would be ruinous to their souls.

"In the next place we informed Teedyuscung that we had purchased a tract of land near Bethlehem, on which we proposed to establish our Indian Brethren and Sisters, and then asked him whether he objected; remarking that the whites were at liberty to settle where they chose and that the Indians we thought were entitled to the same privilege. He made answer that probably the white man was under no restriction in the choice of a home, but that if he settled in the white man's country he was subject to the white man's law.

"Bro. Spangenberg remarked in reply that his observations were just, and the inference to be drawn from them was incontrovertible.

"Teedyuscung resumed by asking the following question: 'Why cannot the Indians who love the Saviour remove to the Indian country and plant along the Susquehanna?' and then added, 'the Brethren surely can visit them, preach to the men and women, and instruct the children.'

"Bro. Spangenberg rejoined by saying that in case our Indian Brethren and Sisters were to remove there, they would require a town of their own, and in it a school and a church where the Gospel could be freely preached. For this he would stipulate in advance. And furthermore he would make it a condition, that all Indians who

		£	s.	d.
1757.	Bro^{t} forw^{d}	10	5	3½
Aug. 28.	To 3 pints wine, 2 q^{ts} beer, and 2 gills rum..		4	4
	" dinner for him, his wife, and 4 Indians..		3	
	" 2 q^{ts} cyder and 1 pint wine		1	8
	Carr^{d} forw^{d}	10	14	3½

should be desirous of hearing of the Saviour, should be at liberty to come to the town; and on the other hand all that were disinclined to his service, or did wickedness, or were seducers, should be excluded. There would in fact be no occasion for the latter class to resort to, or to take up their abode in the town under consideration, as the Indians had ample lands and room for settlement elsewhere along the River.

" Teedyuscung took no exception to these conditions, assented to all that had been said, and then expressed a wish that the Indians who loved the Saviour might live together.

" 'If there be any likelihood of this coming to pass,' resumed Bro. Spangenberg, 'I desire that the settlement be made in the valley where the Shawanese had their seats fifteen years ago; and if the owners of the land make us a proposal to buy, Bro. Mack and myself will gladly go up to Wyoming and view the place and select a spot. Even in that event, however, our Indian Brethren must be permitted to exercise the right of preference, so that those who choose to remain at Bethlehem can remain, and those who choose to remove to the Susquehanna can do so. I insist on this demand, as it involves a principle which must remain inviolate.'

"At this stage of the interview Bro. Spangenberg informed Teedyuscung of the intention he had had, soon after the opening of hostilities, to repair to the Indian country, in order to treat with the Indians for a peace. This cherished project, he added, he had been obliged to abandon, as it failed to meet with the approval of Governor Morris.

" In course of conversation, Teedyuscung stated that during hostilities the wildest reports prejudicial to the Brethren had been in circulation among the Indians. It was currently believed by them, among other things, that the Brethren had decapitated the Indians that had fallen into their hands, had thrown their heads into sacks and sent them to Philadelphia. This charge and others equally extravagant had so exasperated the Indians that a number of them had conspired to attack the Brethren's settlements and cut off the inhabit-

		£	s.	d.
1757.	Bro^t forw^d	10	14	3½
Aug. 28.	To shoeing his horse		1	6
	" hay and oats for do		3	
		10	18	9½

GEORG KLEIN.

---

ants without regard to age or sex. That Paxanosa, and he the King, had on one occasion persuaded 200 warriors who had banded together for this purpose to desist from their intention until they had certain assurance of the truth of the charge. He also stated that the Shawanese brave whom he had killed near Easton on the way to the Treaty, had led the attack on the Mahoning.

"In conclusion, we brought to his consideration the case of the strange Indians who since the suspension of hostilities had resorted to Bethlehem, telling him that while we were disposed to feed the hungry and to clothe the naked and to entertain our friends, our means would not long permit us to provide for these visitors in large numbers. To this he replied that as soon as his countrymen were again settled, and consequently in a condition to make a livelihood, they would refund the cost of their present support. Meanwhile it was the duty of the Governor and of the Commissioners to make proper provision for them and to reimburse the Brethren; that he would call their attention to this thing, and lest he should forget to do so, we should be pleased to address them a letter, and give it in the care of Mr. Edmonds, who was to be his escort to Philadelphia.

"Throughout the interview the King was animated and strictly attentive. He is naturally quick of apprehension and ready in reply. In the course of the conversation he frequently alluded to his baptism, and to his former membership in the mission, observing in this connection with apparent regret that he had lost the peace of mind he once enjoyed, that he hoped, however, it would return, and that it was his sincere desire to remain in connection with us in preference to any other people among the whites."

9.

Province of Pensilvania to the Stewards at Bethlehem, Dr.

			£	s.	d.
1757.		For sundries deliv[d] y[e] Indians coming from y[e] Treaty, &c., per order of Col[l] Weisser.			
Aug.	8.	To supper for 75 Indians, and each ½ gill rum and 1 p[t] cydar	3	2	6
	9.	" breakfast for 75 do. do. do. do	3	2	6
		" dinner for 170 do. and pint cydar each	5	13	4
		" supper for 215 do. ½ gill rum and 1 pint cydar each	8	19	2
	10.	" breakfast for 215 do. do. do. do	8	19	2
		" dinner for 215, and each 1 pint cydar	7	3	4
		" supper for 215, and do. ½ gill rum and 1 pt. cydar	8	19	2
		" 2 expresses to y[e] Justices Craig and Wilson, and W[m] Parson, Esq[r], to acquaint them of Bill Tattemy's death, Mr. Horsfield being absent		7	
		" a coffin, diging the grave, and burying him*	2	2	
	11.	" breakfast for 215, and each ½ gill rum and 1 pint cydar	8	19	2
		" dinner for 215, and each 1 pint cydar	7	3	4
		" supper for 215 and each ½ gill rum and 1 pint cydar	8	19	2
	15.	" breakfast for 215, and do. and do	8	19	2
		" dinner for 215, and each 1 pint cydar	7	3	4
		Carr[d] forw[d]	89	12	4

* After lingering for a month, young Tattamy died, in the house of John Jones, on the 9th of August. Meanwhile he had been visited by Brethren from Bethlehem, and ministered to spiritually by Bro. Jacob Rogers, as he had been under John Brainerd's teaching at Cranberry, and professed Christianity. Intelligence of his decease was immediately expressed to Justices Thomas Craig and Hugh Wilson, of the Irish Settlement. On the 11th the remains were interred in the old grave-yard, near the Crown, in the presence of upwards of two hundred Indians, Bro. Rogers reading the burial service.

		£	s.	d.
1757.	Brot forwd.	89	12	4
Aug. 15.	To supper for 70, and each ½ gill rum and 1 pt beer	2	18	4
13.	" 70 half gills rum for do.		11	8
	" pasturing 42 horses 4 days and nights, at 6*d.* per day and night for each	4	4	
	" 2 coffins for 2 Indians that came sick from Easton and died here*	1		
	" 119 lbs. bread, @ 1¼*d.*, and 1 bushl Indian corn, @ 3*s.*, delivd some Indians returning to Fort Allen		15	4¾
	" hire of a man and horse as a guard for the Indians to John Hays		5	
	" a horse delivd to French Margareth, she having lost 2 horses, as she said, unless helpt with one must be detained on the Province expence	5		
20.	" pasturing 20 horses 7 days and nights, @ 6*d.* each per day	3	10	
29.	" do. 6 horses 9 days and nights, @ 6*d.* per day and night	1	7	
	" sundry men watching in the night when the large company of Indians was here, some of them coming over in the night, and made much disturbance by breaking the windows, and other mischief	1		
		110	3	8¾

C. F. Örter.

* Immediately after Bill Tattamy's interment, Bro. Schmick, at her urgent request, baptized a Delaware woman from *Lechawachnec*, as she was lying under a tree near "The Crown" in the last stage of consumption. She received the name of *Johanna*. The next night she passed away, and on the 13th received Christian burial. On the same day the remains of an Indian boy were buried by the savages with heathen rites, in one corner of the consecrated ground.

10.

Province of Pensilvania to the Stewards at Bethlehem, Dr.

		£	s.	d.
1757.	For sundries deliv[d] the Indians opposite Bethlehem, since the 6 August last.			
Aug. 29.	To 1044 lbs. of bread, @ 1¼*d*................	5	8	9
	" 176 lbs. of beef, mutton, &c., @ 3*d*......	2	4	
	" ¼ bush[l] white meal		1	
	" 7 bush[s] Indian corn, @ 3*d*.................	1	1	
	" 18 galls. milk, @ 6*d*.........................		9	
	" attending the above Indians 24 days, from the 5 to 29 August, 6*d*. per day..		12	
		9	15	9

C. F. Örter.

XI. An Account sent to ye Commissioners in Philadelphia, dated 31 October, 1757.

Province of Pensilvania to the Stewards at Bethlehem, Dr.

		£	s.	d.
1757.	For sundries deliv[d] accord[g] to instruction.			
Sept. 15.	To an express to the Governor with a letter of Capt[n] Arndt,* advising of the enemy's coming on the frontiers, and expences and loss of time in the town, waiting 3 days for an answer, @ 5*s*. pr. day..	2		
	Carr[d] forw[d]	2		

* This letter brought the intelligence that a body of French and Indians had been met above Diahoga, on the way to the Minnisinks, their mission being to examine the strength of the defenses along the line of the northern frontier. Justice Horsfield informed the Governor, by this same express, of Teedyuscung's request that he, the Governor, without delay, fix the rewards on scalps and prisoners, and send him a belt of black wampum with an account of it. The measure, the King added, was unavoidable.

		£	s.	d.
1757.	Bro[t] forw[d].	2		
Sept. 20.	To cash p[d] Lewis Young and Jacob Folk going with 3 Indians to Joseph Keller's place,* 2 days, at request of Teedyuscung, @ 2*s*. 6*d*. each per day		10	
	" sundries deliv[d] in Nazareth Tavern to do. (See *Voucher* 1)		10	9
	" hire of a man and horse to go with Teedyuscung to Easton		5	
	" a messenger going to John Hays to conduct some Indians on their journey to Fort Allen		3	6
Oct. 13.	" making a coat and jacket for Teedyuscung, and sundries deliv[d] for do. (See *Voucher* 2)	1	13	3
22.	" Bethlehem Store, for sundries. (See *Voucher* 3)	1	17	2½
23.	" an express to the Governor, with a letter advising the enemy having tacken Joseph Keller's wife and 3 children captives, and expenses and loss of time in the town, waiting 2¼ days, @ 5*s*. per day	1	16	3
	" medicines, bleeding, &c., Indians, &c. (See *Voucher* 4)	1	6	9
27.	" sundry gun-smith work. (See *Voucher* 5)	5	5	7
	" leather deliv[d] Teedyuscung, for mending shoes		2	
	Carr[d] forw[d]	15	10	3½

* Joseph Keller was a German farmer, and lived on this side of the Wind Gap, about five miles north of Nazareth. In an affidavit transmitted to the Governor he deposed " that on the 16th of September, while assisting his neighbors at plowing, three Indians had carried off his wife and three of his sons, aged respectively fourteen, five, and three years. They left a child of six months lying in the cradle without doing any damage to it, or to anything in the house."

		£	s.	d.
1757.	Bro^t forw^d..................................	15	10	3½
Oct. 27.	To sundries deliv^d the Indians out of the Tavern, coming and going to and from Fort Allen, &c. (See *Voucher* 6)	3	19	
	" sundries deliv^d out of the Tavern to Teedyuscung and family. (See *Voucher* 7)	19	3	2
	" sundry provisions, &c. deliv^d to the Indians opposite Bethlehem. (See *Voucher* 8).	36	19	
		75	11	5½

BETHLEHEM, 31 October, 1757.

C. F. ÖRTER.

Vouchers belonging to ye foregoing Account.

I.

Province of Pensilvania, Dr.

To sundries deliv^d at Nazareth Tavern to Jacob Folk, Lewis Young, and 3 Indians who was sent by Teedyuscung to Joseph Keller's place, to satisfy him of the truth of Keller's wife and children being taken captive.

		£	s.	d.
1757. Sept. 18.	To victuals and drink (4*s.* 10*d.*), ½ peck oats (6*d.*).......................................		5	4
19.	" do. do. (4*s.* 4*d.*), ½ do. do. (6*d.*).........		5	5
			10	9

HARTMAN VERTRIES.

NAZARETH TAVERN,* 20 Sept., 1757.

* "The Rose," built in 1752, one mile north of the Whitefield House, on the Nazareth tract, and so called from the red rose painted on its sign-board, in remembrance of the condition on which the Penns had sold the manor, which condition required the payment, if demanded, of "a red rose in June of each year forever."

2.

Province of Pensilvania to the Stewards of Bethlehem, Dr.

		£	s.	d.
1757.	For sundries delivd Teedyuscung:			
Oct. 13.	To 1¾ yds brown linnen for his coat and jacket, given him by the Friends in Philadelphia,* @ 2s. 4d.		4	1
	" 1¼ yd buckram, @ 2s.		2	6
	" 2 doz. coat buttons, @ 1s. 4d.		2	8
	" 1½ doz. west do., @ 8d.		1	
	" 3 sticks mohair, best sort, @ 1s.		3	
	" silk		2	
	" making the coat and jacket..		18	
		1	13	3

3.

Province of Pensilvania, Dr.

		£	s.	d.
1757.	To sundries delivd out of Bethlehem Store:			
Sept. 1.	" 1 lb. powder and 3 lbs. shot.................		5	6
4.	" 2 quires paper delivd Captn Arndt, @ 1s. for making cartridges......................		2	
	Carrd forwd..............................		7	6

* During his two weeks' stay in Philadelphia, whither he had gone under escort of Mr. Edmonds, on the 6th of October. In that interval he was present at a conference with deputies of the Cherokees, Senecas, and Mohawks, who were being interested by the Governor in gaining over other Indian tribes to the English cause. Teedyuscung also conferred with the Governor on the present posture of the war, and stated that on reconsideration he thought it advisable to postpone sending the Black Belt until spring, adding that meanwhile the Peace Belt might be instrumental in bringing about the desired result. In conclusion, the Governor informed him of the appointment of commissioners to superintend the building of a town for him and his Indians at Wyoming, agreeably to the stipulations of the last Treaty. "The Secretary acquainted the Governor that yesterday the King applied to him for wampum and some money to pay his reckoning, and that he had given him three belts, ten strings, and two pieces of eight." —*Prov. Records*, vol. vii. p. 756.

		£	s.	d.
1757.	Bro[t] forw[d].		7	6
Sept. 16.	To ¼ bush[l] salt for the Indian over the water		1	3
	" 1 lb. powder deliv[d] the white men and Indians sent to Keller's		3	6
	" 1½ lbs. of shot, @ 8*d.*, 6 pipes, @ 1*d.* to do.		1	6
	" ⅛ bush[l] salt deliv[d] Paxino's son*.			7½
20.	" check for a pair trowsers for Teedyuscung		7	1
	" pipes and tobacco for do.			6
	" ¼ lb. of powder for do.			11
	" shot, sugar, and couckeys for do.		3	10
Oct. 11.	" cash gave to bring home the horse at our return from Philadelphia			6
22.	" cash gave for expences to the messenger sent to Pumpshire and Tatemy, pr. order Mr. Hughes†		10	
		1	17	2½

W[M] Edmonds, Storekeeper.

* He had arrived at Bethlehem on September 15th, with the intelligence that the French Indians had been compelled to halt at Diahoga, the Delawares refusing to permit them to pass that point. The Shawanese set out on his return on the 19th, taking with him two belts from Teedyuscung for the Ten Nations who had taken hold of the Peace Belt at Easton. The first was sent to testify to his command that they discover the perpetrators of the late assaults on the settlers south of the mountain, and that they restore all captives; and the second to notify them of his residence at Bethlehem, where, should their chiefs come from Alleghany, they would be referred to him, and he would give them safe escort to Philadelphia.

† John Hughes, one of the commissioners appointed by the Governor, on October 5th, to build "Teedyuscung's Town" and erect a fort at Wyoming. (See *Col. Records*, vol. vii. p. 754, for the Commission.) At the King's request, he was come to escort him to Wyoming to consult with the commissioners about the settlement. On the 27th the two, accompanied by a number of Indians from "The Crown," set out on the journey, and the Brethren entertained the hope that this exodus

4.

Province of Pensilvania to John Matthew Otto, Dr.

1757.		£	s.	d.
Oct. 8.	To medicines for Henry Arndt, Captn Arndt's brother, being in his company..........		4	6
22.	" medicines for Teedyuscung's wife and children, and bleeding at sundry times		7	3
	" curing an impostume on his son's thigh..		6	
	" bleeding 7 Indians opposite Bethlehem, and medicines for do. at sundry times.		9	
		1	6	9

BETHLEHEM, 23 Octr, 1757.

JOHN MATTHEW OTTO.

5.

Province of Pensilvania to the Gunsmith in Bethlehem, Dr.

	For sundry work done for Captn Arndt's			
1757.	Compy on the Province arms, viz.:	£	s.	d.
Sept. 3.	To putting a piece on a gun-stock............		4	
	" making 3 loops on ye barrell		1	
	" mending 2 do. to the stock			6
	" making a screw to the strap ring..........			6
	" cutting of the barrell and mending the sight....................................			6
9.	" boring and drawing out a gun barrell.....		5	
	" putting a piece on the stock................		3	6
	Carrd forwd............................		15	

---

would be followed by others, and ere long by a full release from the presence of their troublesome Indian neighbors. Teedyuscung returned December 1, hastened to Philadelphia, and there acquainted Governor Denny of his wish that the work of building the town be postponed to the following spring. Stating that he intended to go to Burlington on some business, he desired his passport and an order on the commissioners "to allow him ten pounds for his journey, and something proper for Pompshire and Moses Tatamy."

			£	s.	d.
1757.		Brot forwd.		15	
Sept. 9.	To	boring the touch hole		1	
	"	mending the lock and making a screw to it		1	
	"	making a main spring			6
	"	making a dog and a screw		1	6
	"	do. a loop to the stock			9
	"	hardening the steel			6
	"	mending the briddle.		1	
	"	do. the lock and tumblers		1	
16.	"	putting a piece on a gun-stock		3	
	"	making 3 loops to the barrell		1	
	"	do. 2 do. for the ram-rod		1	4
	"	do. 1 lock screw			6
19.	"	do. 3 screws for a gun		1	6
23.	"	mending a gun-lock plate		1	
	"	making 4 screws to the lock		2	
	"	do. a new cock on a gun-lock		3	
	"	mending the tumbler and making a screw to it		1	
29.	"	making 2 screws on a gun-lock		1	
Oct. 7.	"	boring a touch hole and making a worm on the ram-rod		1	6
26.	"	stocking 4 guns, @ 9*s*.	1	16	
	"	cleaning 2 gun barrells		2	
	"	boring 2 touch holes		2	
	"	making 4 lock screws		2	
	"	do. a new breech pin		3	
	"	cleaning 2 locks		1	6
	"	making a cock-screw		1	
	"	do. a cross screw and trigger plate		1	
	"	do. 2 new breech plates of brass		8	
	"	do. 3 loops for the ram-rod		2	
	"	repairing 2 guns for 2 Indians, pr. Tadyuscung's desire, on their parting for Wayomik, viz.:			
	"	a new tumbler and dog for a riffle lock		4	
		Carrd forwd.	5	3	7

		£	s.	d.
1757.	Bro^t^ forw^d^	5	3	7
Oct. 26.	To boring a touch hole		1	
	" making 2 lock screws		1	
		5	5	7

Bethlehem, 27 October, 1757.

Daniel Kliest.

6.

Province of Pensilvania to the Stewards of Bethlehem, Dr.

		£	s.	d.
1757.	For sundries deliv[d] out of the Tavern to the Indians coming and going to and from Fort Allen, not included in the other account for Teedyuscung.			
Aug. 30.	To supper for 3 Indians		1	6
	" 3 half-gills of rum and 3 pints beer		1	
31.	" breakfast for do		1	6
	" 3 half-gills of rum and 3 pints beer		1	
	" dinner and supper and 6 pints beer for do		4	
Sept. 1.	" breakfast, 3 pints beer, and 3 half-gills rum for do		2	6
	" pasture for 2 horses for 2 days and nights for do		2	
10.	" do. for 1 do. for 8 days and nights		4	
15.	" dinner, 2 half-gills rum, and 5 pints cydar for 5 Indians		3	8
	" supper and 5 pints cydar for do		3	4
19.	" keeping 2 horses 7 days and nights, @ 10*d*. each		11	8
24.	" keeping 1 do. 11 days for an Indian from Diaogu*		9	2
	" 1 gill rum for do			4
	Carr[d] forw[d]	2	5	8

* "*September* 24. Fourteen strange Indians arrived from Diahoga."
—*Bethlehem Diarist.*

		£	s.	d.
1757.	Bro^t^ forw^d^...............................	2	5	8
Sept. 24.	To dinner and 1 gill rum for 9 Indians and 5 children came from the Pensbury....		6	6
	" breakfast for do..............................		6	2
Oct. 2.	" supper, 2 half-gills rum for 2 Indians.....		1	4
4.	" breakfast and 1 qt. cydar for 2 do.........		1	4
	" keeping 2 horses 2 days and nights.......		3	4
20.	" dinner, 4 qts. cydar, and 2 gills rum deliv^d^ to 10 Indians and 3 boys y^t^ came from Pensbury*...........................		8	
	" supper for 8 Indians and 2 boys...........		4	8
	" do. and 1 qt. beer for 2 Indians and 2 children y^t^ came from Pensbury......		2	
		3	19	

N.B.—The Indians being Delawares, Teedyuscung said at the Treaty he had liberty to call them into this Province; accordingly, some of them came from the Jersey to Pensbury, and afterwards here.

ANDREAS HORN.

BETHM, 31 Oct., 1757.

7.

Province of Pensilvania to the Stewards of Bethlehem, Dr.

	For sundries deliv^d^ out of the Tavern to			
1757.	Teedyscung and family, &c., viz.:	£	s.	d.
Aug. 30.	To 1 pint wine......................................		1	6
Sept. 6.†	" 1 quart beer..			4
	Carr^d^ forw^d^..............................		1	10

* "*October* 20. Young Captain Harris (*Peter*) arrived with twenty Indians from Pennsbury."—*Ibid.*

Pennsbury, a Proprietary Manor in the southeast corner of Bucks County, on the Delaware, was laid out pursuant to William Penn's directions, written to William Markham, in a letter dated "ye 13 2^d^ mo., 1689," as follows: "I send to seat my children's Plantation that I gave them, near Pennsbury, by Edward Blackfan."

† On this day Teedyuscung returned from Philadelphia, after the delivery of the Peace Belt, sent him by the Alleghanies, to the Gov-

			£.	s.	d.
1757.		Bro[t] forw[d]......		1	10
Sept.	7.	To breakfast and supper for him and his wife		2	
		" 2 half-gills rum and 1 qt. beer for do.....			8
	8.	" breakfast, dinner, and supper for do.......		3	
		" 2 gills rum......			8
	9.	" breakfast, dinner, and supper, 2 half-gills rum for do......		3	4
		" 3 pints wine, 2 half-gills rum, and 2 quarts beer for do. and other Ind[s]......		5	6
	10.	" breakfast and dinner and 2 qts. beer for him and his wife......		2	8
	12.	" do. and do. and supper, and 3 qts. beer for him, his wife, and 2 children, the grown people @ 6*d*. and the children @ 4*d*......		6	
	13.	" breakfast and dinner, and 3 q[ts] beer for do......		4	4
	14.	" breakfast and dinner, 1 p[t] wine, 4 q[ts] beer for do......		6	2
	15.	" 1 pt. wine for him, having eat nothing that day......		1	6
	16.	" breakfast for him, his wife, and 2 children, and 1 pt. wine instead of rum...		3	2
		" supper and 1 q[t] cydar for do......		2	
	17.	" breakfast and 3½ gills of rum for do.....		2	10
		" dinner and supper, 3 qts. beer for do.....		4	4
		" 4 qts. beer, and 2 p[t] wine for do. and other Indians......		4	4
	18.	" breakfast, dinner, and supper, and 1 gill of rum for him, his wife, and 2 children......		5	4
		" 3½ qts. beer and 2½ pints wine for do. and other Indians whom he sent to Keller's place to inquire about a mischief done there......		4	2
		Carr[d] forw[d]......	3	12	4

ernor. He signified a wish that the Brethren would permit him to pass the winter at Bethlehem.

		£	s.	d.
1757.	Bro[t] forw[d]	3	12	4
Sept. 19.	To breakfast, dinner, and supper, for him, his wife, and 2 children		5	
	" 4 gills rum, 4 q[ts] beer, 2 q[ts] cydar, and 2½ pints wine for do. and other Indians		6	4
20.	" breakfast, dinner, and supper for do		5	
	" 4 gills rum, 5 qts. cydar, and 1 bowl of punch for do. and other Indians		4	6
	" dinner, 3 qts. beer, 1½ gill rum, and 1 p[t] wine deliv[d] 3 Indians who returned from Jos. Keller's		4	6
21.	" breakfast, dinner, and supper for him, his wife, and 2 children		5	
	" 2 q[ts] beer and 2 gills rum for do		1	4
22.	" breakfast, dinner, and supper for do		5	
	" 2½ q[ts] beer and 1½ gill rum for do		1	4
23.	" breakfast and supper, and 1½ gill rum for do		3	10
	" 2 p[ts] wine for do. and other Indians		3	
	" 12 q[ts] beer, 11 gills rum, and 1 q[t] wine, when he dispatsch[d] Indians (1 Paxanos' son) to Diaogu with a belt of wompum to the chiefs, to inquire about the murder and prisoners made at Keller's		10	8
24.	" breakfast, dinner, and supper for him and his family		5	
	" 1 qt. beer, 1 gill rum for do			8
25.	" breakfast, dinner, and supper for do		5	
	" 2 q[ts] beer, 1 gill rum, and 1 p[t] wine for do		2	6
26.	" breakfast, dinner, and supper for him, his wife, daughter, and 2 sons, @ 4*d.*		6	6
	" 1 gill of rum and 1 qt. beer for do			8
	Carr[d] forw[d]	7	8	2

24

		£	s.	d.
1757.	Bro[t] forw[d]	7	8	2
Sept. 27.	To breakfast for him, his wife, and the 2 sons		2	2
	" dinner for his 2 children			8
	" ½ pint wine			9
	" 2 bowls of punch for him and his guests		2	
	" 9½ q[ts] of beer for do		3	2
28.	" breakfast, dinner, and supper, and 2 q[ts] beer for himself, his wife and daughter, @ 6*d*., and 2 sons, @ 4*d*		7	2
29.	" breakfast, dinner, and supper, and 1 q[t] beer for him, his wife, and 2 children		5	4
30.	" breakfast, supper, and 1½ qt. beer for do.		3	10
	" dinner for Teedyuscung's 2 children			8
Oct. 1.	" dinner and supper for him, his wife, and 2 children		3	4
	" 3 p[ts] beer and 1 gill rum for do			10
2.	" breakfast, dinner, and supper, and 5 p[ts] beer for do		5	10
	" 1 p[t] of wine, 4½ gills rum, and 3½ q[ts] beer deliv[d] for him and others on his sending 2 belts to *Epulalohend* to Diaogu		4	2
3.	" breakfast, dinner, and supper for him, his wife, and 2 children		5	
	" 2½ q[ts] beer, 1 gill rum for do		1	2
4.	" breakfast, dinner, and supper, 3 qts. beer and 2 gills rum for do		4	
5.	" breakfast, supper, 1½ qt. beer, ½ gill rum for do		4	
6.	" breakfast, dinner, and supper, and 1 gill rum for do		5	4
7.	" breakfast, dinner, and supper for his wife, daughter, and 2 child[rn]		5	
8.	" breakfast and supper for do		3	4
9.	" do. and do. for his wife and 2 child[rn]		2	4
	Carr[d] forw[d]	10	18	3

		£	s.	d.
1757.	Bro^t forw^d.	10	18	3
Oct. 10.	To breakfast, dinner, and supper for do.		3	6
	" supper for Teedyuscung, and 1 other Indian		1	
	" 2 p^{ts} wine and 2 q^{ts} beer for do., on his return from Phila.		3	8
11.	" breakfast, dinner, and supper for him, his wife, and 2 children		5	
12.	" do. do. do. and 1 gill rum for do., 1 p^t beer		5	6
13.	" do. do. do. and 1 gill rum for do., hay for his horse 10 days and nights, from the 27th Sept. to the 7 October, @ 10*d*. p^r day and night		8	4
	" 2 bush^{ls} and 28 q^{ts} of oats for do., being deliv^d in small measure by the hostler		11	6
14.	" breakfast, dinner, and supper for him, his wife, and 2 children		5	
15.	" do. do. do. for do.		5	
16.	" do. do. do. for do.		5	
	" 5 gills rum, 2 pints wine, and 4 qts. beer for do. and guests		6	
17.	" breakfast for him, his wife and 2 children		1	8
	" dinner and supper for his wife and 2 children		2	4
18.	" supper for, him and his wife, and 2 children, ½ p^t wine, 2 q^{ts} beer		2	9
	" breakfast and dinner for his wife and 2 children		2	4
19.	" breakfast, dinner, and supper, and 1 gill of rum for him and do.		5	4
20.	" breakfast, dinner, and supper, and 2 q^{ts} beer and 1 gill rum for do.		6	
21.	" breakfast, dinner, and supper, and 1 gill rum for do.		5	4
22.	" breakfast, dinner, and supper, for do.		5	
	" 9 gills of rum and 1 q^t beer for him and 14 Indians, on rec^t of Mr. Hughes' letter.		3	4
	Carr^d forw^d.	15	11	10

		£	s.	d.
1757.	Bro[t] forw[d]	15	11	10
Oct. 22.	To a meal and 1 gill of rum for an Indian, to his order, whom he sent to Pumpshire and Tatemy			10
23.	" breakfast and dinner for him, his wife, and 2 children		3	4
	" 23 gills rum and 3 q[ts] beer for him and his Indians, at their conclusion of going to Wayomig		8	8
24.	" breakfast, dinner, and supper, for him, his wife, and 2 children		5	
	" 2 q[ts] beer and 1 gill rum for do		1	
25.	" breakfast and dinner for do		3	4
	" 2½ q[ts] beer and 6 gills of rum for do., and other Indians		2	10
26.	" breakfast, dinner, and supper for do		5	
	" 4½ q[ts] beer and 3 gills rum for do		2	6
27.	" breakfast for do		1	8
	" 21 gills of rum for him and the other Indians that went with him to Wayomig		7	8
	" hay for horse 13 days and nights, @ 10*d.* (10*s.* 10*d.*), and 3 bushl[s] of oats delivered in small measure by y[e] hostler	1	2	10
	" dinner and supper for his wife and 2 children		2	4
	" supper, ½ gill rum, 1 p[t] beer for the Ind. that was sent by Teedyuscung for Bumshire			10
28.	" supper for Teedyuscung's wife and 2 children		1	2
31.	" dinner and supper for do		2	4
		19	3	2

8.

Province of Pensilvania to the Stewards of Bethlehem, Dr.

	For sundries del[d] the Indians* opposite			
1757.	Bethlehem since the 30 August last, viz.:	£	*s.*	*d.*
Aug. 30.	To 2 coffins	1		
Oct. 31.	" 3792 lbs. bread, @ 1¼*d.*	19	15	
	" 590½ lbs. meal, @ 3*d.*	7	7	7½
	" 18 bushl's Indian corn, @ 3*s.*, being of the old stock	2	14	
	Carr[d] forw[d]	30	16	7½

* The wish that had been expressed by the Delaware King on the 8th of September, to fix his residence at Bethlehem, during the winter, was granted, although reluctantly. He accordingly had a lodge built him near "The Crown." Here he held court and here he gave audience to the wild embassies that would come from the Indian country, from the land of the implacable Monsey, from the gates of Diahoga, and from the ultimate dim Thule of Alleghany or the Ohio country. Occasionally he would repair to Philadelphia or to the fort to confer with the Governor or with the commandant on the progress of the work of peace he was apparently solicitous of consummating without delay. Thus the dark winter months passed; and when the swelling of maple buds and the whitening of the shad-bush on the river's bank foretokened the advent of spring, there were busy preparations going on in "Teedyuscung's company over the water," for their long-expected removal to the Indian Eldorado on the flats of the Winding River. Thus April passed; and it was the sixteenth of corn-planting month, the month called TAUWINIPEN, when the Delaware King, his queen, his counselors and his warriors, led by the Commissioners, and under escort of fifty Provincials, took up the line of march for Fort Allen, beyond there to strike the Indian trail that led over the mountains, by way of Nescopeck, to Wyoming Valley. Nicodemus and his family were permitted by the Brethren to plant at Nazareth, Nathaniel at Gnadenthal, and Jonathan at the Friedensthal mill.

And on the going out of these spirits "The Crown" was swept and garnished, and Ephraim Colver, the publican, had rest.

		£	s.	d.
1757.	Bro^t forw^d.	30	16	7½
Oct. 31.	To 2 q^ts linseed oil for lamps		2	
	" 1¼ bush^l white meal, @ 4s.		5	
	" ½ bush^l salt, @ 5s.		2	6
	" ½ bush^l beans, @ 4s.		2	
	" 35¾ gall. milk, @ 6d.		17	10½
	" attending the above Indians each day since 30 last August, being 62 days, @ 6d. per day	1	11	
	" fire wood since the 11 last April, being 25 weeks for 10 fire places.	2	10	
	" boards, &c., railing, &c., to build a cabbin for Sam Evans		12	
		36	19	

BETHLEHEM, 31 October, 1757.

NOTE.—*Tapescawen*, noticed in foot-note on p. 299, was a brother of *George Rex*. The following is his account, copied from the day-book of the store kept at Gnadenhütten, on the Mahoning, by Joseph Powell:

1749.	Tapescawen, Dr.	£	s.	d.
Jany 11.	To 2 yd^s blew strouds		16	
	" 3½ yd^s checks, @ 1s. 9d		6	1½
	" 4 do. red strouds, @ 8s.	1	12	
	" 2¼ do. blew do.		18	
	" 3½ do. check, @ 1s. 9d.		16	1½
	" cash	1	5	2
		5	13	4½

1749.	Tapescawen, Cr.	£	s.	d.
Jany 6.	By a beaver skin, weigh^g 2 lbs, @ 6s.		12	
	" 6 drest deer skins	2	19	
	" 2 fox skins, @ 1s. 6d.		3	
	" 1 beaver skin, 5 oz.		1	10½
	" 1 wild-cat do.		2	3
	" 2 drest deer skins	1	15	3
		5	13	4½

ERRATA.

Page 96. In 4th line from bottom, read *Catawbas* for *Catawabas*.

Page 197. In 14th line from top, read *aun* for *dim*.

Page 258. In 6th line from bottom, read *Voucher* 2 for *Voucher* 1.

Page 359. Add to note.—The Mansion House at Pennsbury had been erected in 1683.

An Index for vols. I. and II. will be furnished in the second volume of the series.

www.ingramcontent.com/pod-product-compliance
Lightning Source LLC
Chambersburg PA
CBHW032043220426
43664CB00008B/832

* 9 7 8 3 7 4 1 1 1 7 9 6 1 *